CW01370123

# SOVIET COLD WAR FIGHTERS

# SOVIET COLD WAR FIGHTERS

ALEXANDER MLADENOV

FONTHILL

Fonthill Media Language Policy

Fonthill Media publishes in the international English language market. One language edition is published worldwide. As there are minor differences in spelling and presentation, especially with regard to American English and British English, a policy is necessary to define which form of English to use. The Fonthill Policy is to use the form of English native to the author or usual to them by way of education. Alexander Mladenov was born and educated in Bulgaria and now lives in Bulgaria; therefore British English has been adopted in this publication.

Fonthill Media Limited
Fonthill Media LLC
www.fonthillmedia.com
office@fonthillmedia.com

First published in the United Kingdom and the United States of America 2016

British Library Cataloguing in Publication Data:
A catalogue record for this book is available from the British Library

Copyright © Alexander Mladenov 2016

ISBN 978-1-78155-496-8

The right of Alexander Mladenov to be identified as the author of this work has been asserted by him in accordance with the Copyright, Designs and Patents Act 1988.

All rights reserved. No part of this publication may be reproduced, stored in a retrieval system or transmitted in any form or by any means, electronic, mechanical, photocopying, recording or otherwise, without prior permission in writing from Fonthill Media Limited

Typeset in 10.5pt on 13pt Sabon
Printed and bound in England

# Contents

*Introduction*   7

1   First Generation   11

2   Second Generation   88

3   Third Generation   186

4   Fourth Generation   249

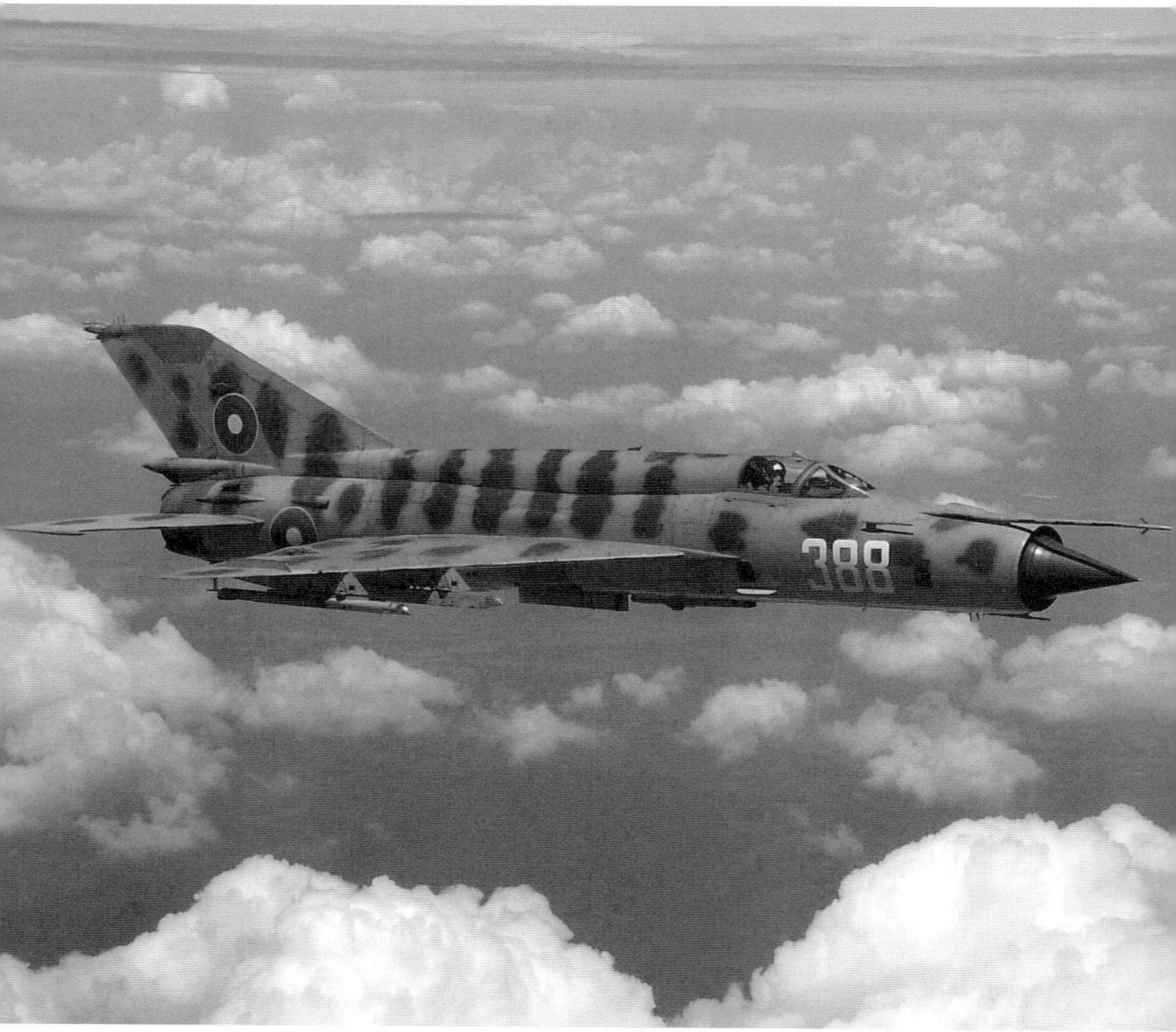
388

# Introduction

## The Cold War Era

The Cold War was a protracted running conflict between the superpowers of the USA and the Soviet Union between 1945 and 1991. Another suitable and precise definition refers to the Cold War as a state of political hostility that existed between a group of countries led by the former Soviet Union and a group led by the United States. Likewise, The Merriam-Webster Dictionary refers to the Cold War as a conflict over ideological differences carried on by methods short of sustained, overt military action, and usually without breaking off diplomatic relations. For many historians, however, the Cold War began soon after the US atomic bombs were detonated over the Japanese cities of Hiroshima and Nagasaki on 6 and 9 August 1945 respectively, and the subsequent surrender of Japan. In fact, the winning wartime alliance between the Soviet Union and its Western allies proved to be too fragile, dissolving already during late 1945 and early 1946 as the Western world gained a monopoly on nuclear weapons. In addition, a wide ideological gulf was claimed by the Soviet leader, Generalissimos Iosif Vissarionovich Stalin, to exist between Soviet communism and Western democracy, prompting him to impose a new hard-line policy that rapidly provoked a symmetric answer from the Western world.

The term 'Iron Curtain' that comes hand-in-hand with the Cold War was pioneered by Winston Churchill on 5 March 1946 in Fulton, Missouri (USA)—it referred to the Soviet Union's initiative to set up loyal, communist-dominated governments in its sphere of influence in Eastern Europe—including Poland, Hungary, Romania and Bulgaria. In 1948, Czechoslovakia was also forced to enter into this fold of client countries.

US President Harry Thurman's doctrine of 'two rival worlds', dating from March 1947, proclaimed the beginning of a general war against communism. From a historical point of view, this announcement could be viewed as the formal declaration of the Cold War.

Two years later, in 1949, Stalin saw the formation of the US-led North Atlantic Treaty Organisation (NATO) as a formal act of hostility committed by the Western world, clearly directed against the Soviet Union. The confrontation between the superpowers the USA and the Soviet Union deepened even further in the following

The Soviet leader Generalissimos Iosif Vissarionovich Stalin (1878–1953), was one of the keenest proponents of the Cold War, and put intense pressure on the aviation industry to compensate for the Soviet jet-technology lag as soon as possible after the end of the Second World War. He also encouraged the adoption of nuclear bomb technology in order to neutralise the USA's advances in this strategically important area. (*Author's collection*)

years as the Cold War entered into its fully-fledged state, with an unceasing arms race and a rapid build-up of nuclear arsenals on both sides of the Iron Curtain. Luckily, this Cold War never progressed into the next level—the so-called 'Hot War', planned by both sides to be fought ruthlessly and with a mass deployment of nuclear weapons.

The Warsaw Pact Treaty Organisation, regarded as one of the Cold War's most emblematic by-products behind the Iron Curtain, was formed in 1955. It was, in fact, a mere formalisation of existing military co-operation agreements (dating from the late 1940s) between the Soviet Union and its satellite countries in Eastern Europe. The pact was firmly dominated by the Soviet Union throughout its entire life, as all other member states were expected simply to follow the general policy set by the leading power in the procurement of new military equipment, training and doctrine.

In the 1950s, the superpowers more or less reached parity in the number of nuclear weapons in their arsenals. This moment has marked the beginning of the Mutually Assured Destruction era, wherein both the superpowers maintained vast arsenals of warheads, missiles and bombers to do the job in a guaranteed way. During the peak years of the Cold War the opposing alliances are reported to have stored enough nuclear weapons to destroy eight to ten times the area of the planet Earth.

The Cold War featured occasional hot moments of encounters in the air; these were more frequent in the early years of the conflict, in the 1950s and 1960s. These encounters involved mainly Western reconnaissance and transport aircraft falling under attacks by Soviet or allied fighters while entering—intentionally or unintentionally—hostile airspace.

The fall of the Berlin Wall on 9 November 1989 was the first firm sign that the Soviet Union was losing the Cold War. Its formal end, however, was marked by the dissolution of the Warsaw Pact Treaty Organisation on 31 March 1991, after thirty-six years of existence. On 26 December 1991 the Soviet Union evaporated for good, dissolving into fifteen independent states—the largest of which were Russia, Ukraine, Byelorussia and Kazakhstan.

The MiG-29 is emblematic of air superiority fighters in the last decade of the Cold War. It was regarded as pretty advanced for the mid-late 1980s. Highly agile and well-armed, it was, however, handicapped by a very notable shortcoming—its short range. (*Author's collection*)

The prevailing explanation for the Soviet defeat in the Cold War is that the communist superpower empire had a dysfunctional ideology; it also simply proved weaker in the economic and arms race during the last two decades of head-to-head competition with the Western world. At the onset of the dissolution in the late 1980s, the last and fairly liberal Communist Party Secretary General, Mikhail Gorbachev, reportedly failed to keep the liberalisation processes of the socialist system under control, leading to the Soviet Union's inglorious break-up and the dissolution of the Warsaw Pact.

## Cold War Fighter Generations

The mass introduction of jet fighters by the Soviet air arms began in 1948–1950, initially with straight-wing designs such as the MiG-9 and Yak-15/17/23, followed by the real game-changer—the swept-wing MiG-15, which had a great debut in the war in Korea.

According to the official Soviet/Russian jet fighter classification, the list of the Gen. 1 fighters also includes the MiG-17, a further-refined MiG-15 derivative with better speed performance and controllability characteristics, as well as the supersonic MiG-19 and the Yak-25 long-range/all-weather subsonic interceptor. All of these three types fielded dedicated radar-equipped interceptor versions armed with guided air-to-air missiles capable of destroying large, non-manoeuvring targets but entirely unsuitable for turning air-to-air combats with other fighters.

Gen. 2, which followed in the mid-1950s, comprised Mach 2-capable fighter types with swept-wing or delta-wing design layout, equipped with sophisticated radars and armed with a variety of a short- and medium-range air-to-air missiles such as the MiG-21, Su-9, Su-11, Su-15, Yak-28P and Tu-128.

Gen. 3, whose first representatives took to the air in the second half of the 1960s, marked a drastic increase in combat effectiveness due to the use of novel aerodynamic layouts, more powerful engines, long-range fire-control radars and new-generation air-to-air missiles. Its most iconic representative was the swing-wing MiG-23, introduced *en masse* in the second half of the 1970s. The Mach 2.83 MiG-25 was another remarkable design—a capable fighter interceptor, purposely-built to counter high-altitude and high-speed threats such as the USAF's Lockheed SR-71 Blackbird reconnaissance aircraft. It was equipped with powerful radar and armed with long-range missiles.

All the three Gen. 4 fighters—MiG-29, MiG-31 and Su-27—took to the air in the second half of the 1970s, and after protracted test and evaluation efforts they were inducted in squadron service in the first half of the 1980s. The trio featured the use of a plethora of novel technologies intended to boost up their overall combat effectiveness and counter the mass fielding in service of its US counterparts such as the F-15, F-16 and F/A-18. The MiG-29 and Su-27 were the most popular representatives of this generation—both were designed from the outset as highly-agile air-superiority fighters employing the so-called integral aerodynamic layout, while the heavyweight/limited manoeuvrability MiG-31 was a further development of the MiG-25 that combined cruise supersonic speed with capable radar and long-range missiles.

During the 1970s and 1980s the swing-wing MiG-23, an emblematic third-generation fighter, lay at the heart of the frontline air superiority and air defence of the Soviet Union and its allied states in Eastern Europe. (*Author's collection*)

# 1

# First Generation

## The Fighter Technology Catch-Up Effort

As the Cold War started upon Churchill's announcement in Fulton in March 1946, the outdated fighter technologies in the Soviet Union saw a rapid advance. These were represented in the first place by the introduction of the jet engine, dramatically increasing the speed, acceleration and rate-of-climb performance of the fighter models of all design bureaus. In the beginning of the Cold War, however, the Soviet Union suffered from a delay of entering into the jet era compared to the USA and Great Britain. These leading Western nations proved to be already well-suited to field operationally capable jet fighters during the end phase of the Second World War, while the Soviet Union was ill-suited to develop an operational jet engine at that time.

Immediately after the end of the war the Soviet leadership and all aircraft and engine design bureaus initiated an ambitious and wide-ranging programme to compensate for the lag as soon as possible. This feat was eventually achieved by fielding trophy German technologies, which were soon after complemented by the use of modern-day British jet-propulsion technologies purchased in 1947. The same is true for the fielding of the nuclear weapons, as the Soviet Union was able to detonate its first atomic bomb in 1949.

The first fighter generation in the Soviet Union was conceived in the mid-1940s. By that time jet propulsion was a known technology in the Soviet Union, mainly thanks to access to the latest German aero engine technologies—represented by the Jumo 003 and BMW 004 models. Although the trophy German jet-propulsion technologies were considered advanced compared to their counterparts developed at the same time by aero design bureaus in the Soviet Union, by 1946 these technologies were considered obsolete, while all indigenous jet engines were still plagued by poor reliability and short life. The problem was solved in a prompt manner thanks to the ready access to two modern Rolls-Royce turbojet designs—the Nene I/II and Derwent V—which developed thrust two times higher than their German designs used on the Soviet Union's first jet fighters. As many as sixty engines were imported from Great Britain, including thirty Nene I/IIs and thirty Derwent Mk.Vs. The vast majority of these were used to power new fighter designs, while the rest were handed over to the leading Soviet aero engine design bureaus for a detailed examination and non-licence copying.

The Soviet aero engine industry worked very hard to reverse-engineer the British designs and launch these in mass production in a very short time, retaining their original performance unchanged. In the event it coped with the huge challenge; as soon as 1948 the first newly-built jet engines, designated as the RD-500 (a Derwent Mk.V copy) and the RD-45 (a Nene II copy), were made available for installation on the newly-developed high-performance jet fighters, already having been flown in prototype form powered by Rolls-Royce products.

## Yakovlev's First Jet Fighters—Yak-15 and Yak-17

There were one experimental and two first-generation single-engine fighters designed by the Yakovlev OKB (Experimental Design Bureau), then officially known as OKB-115 (Experimental Design Bureau No. 115), which entered service with the VVS (Voenno-Vozhushniye Sily—Soviet Air Force) and the Soviet Union's satellite states in Eastern Europe.

In fact, all first Soviet production-standard jet fighters were designed in a very rushed manner in order for the Soviet Union to compensate as soon as possible for its huge lag compared to the Western world in this very sensitive area. The first Soviet fighter jet engine, the RD-10 (designed by the Klimov OKB, officially known as OKB-117), was a direct copy of the German Jumo 004, which powered the Messerschmitt Me 262.

To speed up their jet fighter development effort, Yakovlev's designers used the fuselage of the war-proven Yak-3 piston-engined fighter as a base for designing

In 1946, Alexander Yakovlev (1906–1989), OKB-115's influential Chief Designer and then Designer General (from 1956), used his huge experience and expertise in designing lightweight and agile fighters during the Second World War to create the first Soviet single-engine jet. It was simple enough for production, maintenance and flight operations. (*Yakovlev OKB*)

their first jet-powered model. The idea—pioneered by Evgeniy Adler, one of the members of the design team—called for the accommodation of the engine in the nose fuselage section, replacing the original VK-107 piston engine. In this design layout, the nozzle protruded under the cockpit and the exhaust gases flow had to pass beneath the fuselage belly. The rear bottom section of the fuselage, situated behind the nozzle, had a steel skin panel scabbed-on in order to provide protection from excessive heating caused by the hot exhaust. This engine installation layout was named as the 'keel scheme'. The wing forward spar passing though the fuselage was given an arched form in order to pass over the engine. The armament comprised two NR-23 23-mm cannons with sixty rounds each.

The development of the jet derivative of the Yak-3 was completed in October 1945. It received the new Yak-15 in-service designation, but its first flight was delayed, taking place at last on 24 April 1946 with the test pilot Mikhail Ivanov behind the controls. Then, on 18 August, the Yak-15 was demonstrated, together with the MiG-9, at the big flypast at Tushino Airfield in Moscow. On 5 October that year the first production-standard Yak-15 (NATO reporting name 'Feather') took to the air for the first time, and the type's accelerated flight-testing effort was completed in May 1947.

The jet version of the Yak-3, powered by the Jumo 004, demonstrated promising performance, with a maximum level speed of 805 km/h (434 kt) and 26 seconds for performing a 360-degree turn. In addition, the Yak-15 retained the good manoeuvrability of its piston-powered predecessor almost unchanged; it was capable of performing all standard aerobatic figures, as demonstrated in mid-1947 by the famous test pilot Pyotr Stefanovskiy.

The Yak-15 was designed by using the fuselage of the proven Yak-3 piston-engine fighter, with the jet engine installed in the nose previously occupied by the VK-107 piston engine. (*Yakovlev OKB*)

The Yak-15 was a tail dragger, with the prototypes powered by German-made Jumo 004 jet engines; the production examples used its Russian carbon copy, designated as the RD-10. (*Yakovlev OKB*)

After successfully passing the testing programme, the Yak-15 was launched in production at GAZ-31 in Tbilisi in the end of 1946, with a total of 280 aircraft rolled out. The first ninety of them were unarmed and without any armour protection, while the following 190 examples received two NS-23 23-mm cannons, installed in the nose, just over the engine. These armed aircraft also had improved equipment.

## Yak-15 Specification

| Dimensions: | |
|---|---|
| Wing span | 9.20 m |
| Length | 8.70 m |
| Height | 2.27 m |
| Wing area: | 14.85 m$^2$ |
| Weights: | |
| Empty | 1,852 kg |
| Normal take-off | 2,742 kg |
| Internal fuel | 590 kg |
| Performance: | |
| Max level speed at sea level | 700 km/h |
| Max level speed at high level | 786 km/h |
| Cruise speed | 689 km/h |
| Time to 5,000 m | 4.5 min |
| Practical ceiling | 13,350 m |
| Take-off distance | 440 m |
| Landing distance | 540 m |
| Range on internal fuel | 510 km |

The first Yakovlev jet fighter suffered from numerous design shortcomings, the main one being the high fuel-consumption rate of the RD-10 turbojet, which reduced the range to 445 km (240 kt) only. The specific design layout, however, also proved to be far from ideal, as the tail undercarriage wheel was adversely affected by the hot exhaust gases from the nozzle under the belly. The Russian copy of the Jumo 004 also had a very short time between overhauls (TBO)—only twenty-five hours, which, in turn, necessitated frequent engine changes.

The Yak-21 was a two-seat training jet fighter based on the Yak-15 design, featuring a bubble-shaped canopy. Its newly-added front cockpit for the student pilot was accommodated in front of the existing cockpit of its predecessor, occupying the area previously housing the cannons and their ammunition magazines. However, this two-seat derivative was built only in a single example because it was considered ill-suited for use in the training role due to the tail-dragger undercarriage design.

The Yak-15U was a single-seat training fighter equipped with a tricycle undercarriage; it was introduced in order to level the nose and provide better visibility for the student pilot in the front cockpit. Exactly the same undercarriage scheme was conceived for the improved Yak-21T two-seater, converted from an existing Yak-15 and equipped with a nose undercarriage unit. It made its maiden flight in April 1947, passed the state testing effort successfully and was subsequently recommended for entering service with the VVS, despite the notably shorter range compared to the specification—only 375 km (202 nm) vs the required 600 km (324 nm). There were no better alternatives though and the short-legged jet trainer was promptly launched in serial production under the new designation Yak-17UTI. It proved suitable in the training role as the levelled fuselage (thanks to the use of tricycle undercarriage) significantly improved the forward visibility of both pilots, making the take-offs and landings much easier. In order to further improve the manoeuvrability, the Yak-17UTI also introduced a reworked empennage.

The Yak-15U was a single-seat trainer version submitted for state testing in August 1947. It was armed with two NS-23K cannons (each with 105 rounds) aimed via an ASP-1 lead-computing gunsight. The Yak-15U also had an S-13 gun camera, installed onto the windshield frame. The strengthened wing structure allowed the Yak-15U to carry two 331-litre external tanks for extending range and endurance. It proved to be heavier and slower than its predecessor, as its maximum take-off weight reached 3,240 kg (7,141 lb) and the maximum level speed was reduced to 748 km/h (403 kt). This version was eventually launched in production under the new designation Yak-17. Both the single- and two-seat Yak-17 derivatives were powered by an improved RD-10A turbojet, with TBO increased to fifty hours.

A scan into the Yak-17's cockpit. (*Author's collection*)

The Yak-17 was an improved derivative of the Yak-15 featuring a tricycle undercarriage and powered by an improved RD-10A turbojet with TBO increased to fifty hours; its two-seat version gained more popularity as it was put in mass production for use in jet-familiarisation of pilots converting to both the Yak-23 and MiG-15. (*Yakovlev OKB*)

## Yak-23—The Best Straight-Wing Jet Fighter

The Yak-23 was the definitive member of Yakovlev's first-generation, lightweight, jet-powered fighter family. It retained the fuselage layout of its predecessors in combination with an increased-thrust engine. The RD-500 was a direct copy of the Rolls-Royce Derwent Mk.V, rated at 15.94 kN (3,582 lb st. or 1,625 kgf). The new fighter featured straight wings—inherited from the piston-engined Yak-3—as it was intended to develop the Yakovlev's 'trademark' concept of a lightweight, fast, well-armed and highly-agile fighter to perfection. In fact, the Yak-23 could be regarded as a somewhat-conservative concept when compared to the more advanced swept-wing fighter jets developed at the same time by the Mikoyan and Lavochkin design bureaus. However, the straight-wing fighter represented a proven solution since the sweptback wings were still little-known in the Soviet Union and contained a good many unpleasant surprises in terms of aerodynamics and strength characteristics.

The Yak-23 had a semi-monocoque fuselage, with the rear bottom section featuring double-skin protection and a cooling air duct in order to provide protection for the fuselage belly from the hot and high-speed engine exhaust. The double-skin protection included inner panels from aluminium alloy and outer panels made from temperature-resistant steel. The cockpit remained unpressurised in order to save weight and avoid adding the complex equipment needed for pressurisation. The pilot was accommodated in an ejection seat also designed by Yakovlev, and featured armour protection from projectiles and high-speed fragments, comprising a 57-mm-thick armoured windshield complemented by an 8-mm-thick steel plate built into the seat's backrest.

The Derwent Mk.V-powered Yak-23 prototype took to the air for the first time in July 1947, and some seventeen months later it was launched in large-scale production at the GAZ-31 plant in Tbilisi, Georgia, with the first production examples taking to the air in early 1949. (*Author's collection*)

The mid-mounted and modestly tapered straight wing had a two-spar design and a laminar aerofoil. The wings featured wingtip mounts for installation of external fuel tanks, each accommodating 190 litres of kerosene. The empennage was of a cruciform type and the horizontal stabilisers had an anhedral of -5°. The fuel system included five fuselage tanks with a total capacity of 975 litres, while with external tanks it reached 1,400 litres.

The tricycle-type landing gear used a forward-retracting nose undercarriage unit with a non-steerable wheel, while the main undercarriage units folded into the fuselage. The armament was represented by two NR-23 23-mm cannons with 90 rounds each, installed in the lower part of the nose.

In order to achieve as high a performance as possible, allowing the type to enter into serial production, the head of OKB-115, the famous Soviet aircraft designer Alexander Yakovlev, decided to take the risk to apply a series of radical weight-saving measures. In addition to the non-pressurised cockpit, these included non-assisted elevator, aileron and rudder controls, while the armour protection of the cockpit and the systems was also minimised. As a result, the Yak-23's empty weight proved to be only 1,902 kg (4,192 lb).

The keel design layout also provided some welcome design advantages that contributed to the Yak-23's high performance at the time of its flight test programme. For example, the shorter engine intake and nozzle assembly, lacking an extension pipe, sharply reduced the pressure losses of the engine, contributing to the retention of the thrust rating originally developed by the engine when tested on a ground test bench. The installation of all major systems near the aircraft's centre of gravity also had a fairly good effect onto its manoeuvrability performance.

The first Yak-23 prototype, powered by an original Rolls-Royce Derwent Mk.V engine, was completed in June 1947. It made its maiden flight in the hands of Yakovlev's test pilot Mikhail Ivanov the following month. During the factory test campaign it demonstrated a promising performance, including a maximum speed of 932 km/h (503 kt) at low altitude, while its landing speed was only 157 km/h (85 kt) and the practical ceiling reached almost 15,000 m (49,200 feet). All test pilots who flew the type reported that there were no stability and controllability issues encountered by them in the air. In November 1947, the second Yak-23 prototype was submitted to the NII VVS (Soviet Air Force's Scientific-research Institute, responsible for the military flight testing activities) for undergoing its state testing effort, which saw a plethora of top-notch Soviet test pilots flying it—including Grigoriy Sedov and Pyotr Stefanovskiy. The concluding flight-test report (approved by the VVS C-in-C, Marshal Konstantin Vershinin) noted that the Yak-23's performance, armament and equipment outfit defined it as a lightweight front-line jet fighter suitable for use against enemy fighters and bombers at up to 10,000 m (32,800 feet); as such, the aircraft could be accepted into service. However, the fairly high performance demonstrated by the straight-wing fighter during the tests was achieved with an imported Derwent Mk.V turbojet. Taking into consideration the fact that the indigenous RD-500 turbojet would have a maximum static thrust rating (developed on a test bench) of 15.60 kN (3,570 lb st. or 1,590 kgf), the design team expected that the serial production Yak-23 would have a lower take-off, rate-of-climb and level speed performance. In fact, the RD-500's maximum thrust rating proved to be about 0.44 kN (99 lb st. or 45 kgf) lower than that of the original Derwent Mk.V.

## Yak-23 Specification

| | |
|---|---|
| Dimensions:<br>Wing span<br>Length<br>Height | 8.73 m<br>8.12 m<br>3.31 m |
| Wing area: | 13.70 m² |
| Weights:<br>Empty<br>Normal take-off<br>Internal fuel | 1,902 kg<br>3,389 kg<br>790 kg |
| Performance:<br>Max level speed at sea level<br>Max level speed at high level<br>Landing speed<br>Max rate of climb<br>Time to 5,000 m<br>Practical ceiling<br>Take-off distance<br>Landing distance<br>Range on internal fuel<br>Range on internal and external fuel | 925 km/h<br>910 km/h<br>157 km/h<br>41.4 m/s<br>2.3 min<br>15,000 m<br>440 m<br>540 m<br>1,080 km<br>1,475 km |

The Yak-23's design team continued working on the weight-saving measures during the state testing phase, but this work led to some potentially dangerous airframe strength issues as it turned out that the wings and the fin skin began to suffer from an insufficient thickness.

The Yak-23 entered into serial production for the VVS in late 1948 as a short-legged, lightweight fighter for front-line use. Its production was organised at the aviation factory in Tbilisi known at the time as the GAZ-31 (State Aviation Plant No. 31). The first production-standard examples were rolled out in early 1949 and the field trials carried out by the VVS were conducted between March and June 1949. These trials confirmed that the Yak-23 boasted excellent aerobatic capabilities and was easy to control at all regimes of flight. Its landing speed was pretty low—only 157 km/h (87 kt)—which was welcomed by the front-line pilots.

The Yak-23 'Flora', powered by the RD-500 engine, was the best straight-wing jet fighter designed by the Yakovlev OKB. It was a lightweight, fast and very agile machine, briefly used in service with the Soviet Air Force before the majority of the 310 aircraft were handed over to client states in Eastern Europe. This is an example operated by the Bulgarian Air Force, which took its first Yak-23s on strength in June 1950. (*Author's collection*)

The rate of climb at sea level was very good too, reaching 41 m/s (8,068 fpm), and proved better than that of the rival De Havilland Meteor and the Lockheed P-80 Shooting Star. The practical ceiling was 15,000 m (49,200 feet) but due to the non-pressurised cockpit, the flights were restricted to 12,000 m (39,360 feet) only. The take-off run was 440 m (1,443 feet), while the landing roll accounted for 650 m (2,132 feet). The fighter had a maximum endurance of one hour and fifty minutes when fitted with external fuel tanks at the wingtips.

There were no Yak-23 two-seat variants conceived in the beginning because it was assumed that the Yak-17UTI would be good enough to be used as a conversion-to-type trainer for the pilots destined to fly the new single-seat lightweight fighter. The Yak-17UTI, however, did not prove to be fully suitable for the task due to the different cockpit arrangement and handling characteristics, including the very different stick forces. As a result, in early 1950 the Yakovlev OKB commenced design of a two-seat derivative of the Yak-23 suitable to be used for conversion-to-type and continuation training. The first Yak-23UTI prototype introduced a twin-seat tandem cockpit with the instructor's seat inserted in the fuselage, just behind the seat position of the single-seater's cockpit. This design solution was adopted in order to have as few fuselage modifications as possible, therefore speeding up the developmental and testing activities. In the event, the two-seat configuration gave the instructor in the rear seat a very poor visibility, and the test pilots who flew the Yak-23UTI recommended that the design should

All early Yakovlev jet fighters featured an engine installation layout known as the 'keel scheme', with nose intake and jet nozzle situated under the fuselage—without requiring use of an extension pipe that would cause loss of thrust. This is the Yak-23UTI two-seater, the only example ever built. (*Author's collection*)

be altered and the pilot in the rear fuselage should be given a better visibility at take-off and landing. To satisfy this requirement, the fuselage was lengthened by 200 mm in a bid to accommodate a stepped tandem cockpit that was moved forward compared to the layout used on the single-seater. The two-seater was armed with a single 12.7-mm machine-gun and was declared ready for launch into serial production in the end of 1950. During the flight tests it was found that the two-seater's performance was more or less the same as that of the single-seater. However, at that time the production run of the Yak-23 was nearing its end, so the VVS leadership decided that it would be not practical to continue with the two-seater's launch into production.

As many as 310 Yak-23s were rolled out at GAZ-31 in Tbilisi, and after a short service stint with the VVS most of the aircraft were transferred to a number of Soviet satellite countries in Eastern Europe such as Bulgaria, Poland, Czechoslovakia and Romania.

## Yak-25—The Long-Range Fighter-Interceptor

The Yakovlev design bureau pioneered the concept of a heavyweight loitering fighter-interceptor in the early 1950s. Such design was required by the Soviet Air Defence Forces (PVO) in 1948 and two proposals were examined in the beginning—the I-320 offered by the Mikoyan OKB and the La-200 by the Lavochkin OKB. The latter was declared the winner and the first La-200 prototype took to the air in July 1952. It was submitted for its state testing effort in early 1953, but in late October the same year the state testing commission concluded that the aircraft was plagued by numerous major shortcomings; as a consequence, the commission recommended the termination of any further development work.

The Soviet Council of Ministers issued a new decree calling for the development of a long-range loitering fighter-interceptor by the OKB-115, led by Alexander Yakovlev. Dating from August 1951, it also foresaw the development of a reconnaissance derivative; in the beginning, both aircraft had the common designation Yak-2AM-5, denoting that it was an aircraft type designed by Yakovlev OKB and powered by two Mikulin AM-5 turbojets. Later on the designation was changed to the Yak-25. The fighter-interceptor derivative as requested in the decree was to be submitted for state testing by October 1952.

The two-seat, all-weather fighter-interceptor received the RP-6 Sokol radar, using a single, large-sized antenna installed in the nose. It was capable of detecting four-engine bombers at up to 25 km (13.4 nm) and twin-engined fighters at up to 16 km (8.6 nm). In order to be able to provide the space needed to accommodate the antenna dish in the nose, the design team decided to install the engines under the wings. The radar development, however, was delayed and the fighter-interceptor prototype initially received a mock-up of the radar for use in the flight tests. Later on, the less advanced RP-1 Izumrud radar used two antennas—one intended for target search and the second for target tracking and providing information for aiming the aircraft's guns on the target. The RP-1 featured a maximum detection

The Yak-25 prototype took to the air for the first time on 19 June 1952 and was launched in mass production in September 1953 at the GAZ-292 in Saratov, but the first production-standard aircraft were not rolled out before September 1954. In total, 406 Yak-25s were rolled out from the Saratov plant until 1957. (*Yakovlev OKB*)

range against a four-engined bomber of 12 km (6.4 nm), while the tracking mode enabled firing against targets at up to 2 km (1.1 nm).

The aircraft crew consisted of a pilot and a radar operator sitting in a pressurised tandem cockpit with extensive armour protection and under a common canopy. The list of the aircrew protection features included a 105-mm-thick windshield, a 10-mm steel armour plate in front of the pilot, armour plates and armour headrests on the back of each crew members' seats, while side-on the pilot and operator were protected by 8-mm aluminium alloy plates; the pyrotechnical cartridges of their ejection seats were also shielded by 8-mm plates.

The armament comprised two NR-37L 37-mm cannons with 50 rounds each. The NR-37L was a very powerful weapon, optimised for use against large-sized aircraft, firing highly-destructive projectiles at a muzzle speed of between 710 and 725 m/s (2,329 and 2,378 fps)—but it had a rate of fire of only 400 rpm.

The Yak-25 featured an all-metal semi-monocoque mid-wing fuselage with maximum width of 1,450 mm, with a circular cross-section changing to an oval one in the tail. The wing had a sweep of 45° at the focus line and used TsAGI S-12s and SP-12 profiles in the root and end sections respectively. The wing mechanisation (high-lift devices) included ailerons and hinged flaps. The wingtips housed the auxiliary undercarriage units, Pitot tubes and static electricity dischargers.

The heavyweight loitering fighter was powered by two Mikulin AM-5A non-afterburning turbojets housed in large nacelles under the wings, rated at 25.5 kN (5,730 lb st. or 2,600 kgf) each. In order to avoid foreign-object damage when operating from non-prepared and semi-prepared runways, the compressors featured protection in the form of intake nets.

The control system used hydraulic boosters in the pitch and roll channels (for moving the elevators and ailerons respectively), while the yaw channel had a mechanical linkage between the pedals and the rudder. The aircraft also introduced a new-style bicycle-type undercarriage with a steering wheel on the front unit and auxiliary units in the wingtips.

The Yak-25 prototype (known with its initial designation, '120') made its maiden flight on 19 June 1952 in the hands of V. Volkov. It was submitted to the NII VVS (Soviet Air Force's Science-Testing Institute) the following spring, and the state testing programme was conducted within the period between March and June 1953. The results obtained during this testing and evaluation campaign proved to be positive in general, although a number of shortcomings were discovered—such as the shorter endurance, which proved to be twenty minutes less than that set out in the customer's technical specification.

The Yak-25 was launched in production in September 1953 by Soviet Council of Ministers decree No. 2359-965. It called for commissioning in service of an interim version, equipped with the Izumrud radar, integrated to the ASP-3NM electro-optical gun-sight and powered by AM-5 turbojets. The aircraft had a maximum speed of 1,090 km/h (588kt) at 5,000 m (16,400 feet), while at 10,000 m (32,800 feet) it was able to hit 1,033 km/h (557 kt). The time to

The Yak-25 'Flashlight' was formally inducted in service with the IA PVO in 1954 as a loitering heavyweight interceptor; it continued to serve in the front-line role until the late 1960s. (*Yakovlev OKB*)

10,000 m (32,800 feet) was 5.5 minutes and the practical ceiling with 50 per cent internal fuel reached 15,000 m (49,200 feet). The practical range at 12,000 m (39,360 feet), with 7 per cent remaining fuel and without external fuel tanks, was 2,300 km (1,240 nm), while the maximum endurance was three hours and ten minutes. When equipped with an external tank, its range reached 2,700 km (1,456 nm) and endurance extended to three hours and forty minutes.

The Yak-25 was launched in serial production at the GAZ-292 in Saratov, which was ordered to roll out thirty aircraft in the third quarter and seventy more in the fourth quarter of 1954. The production setup, however, took longer than initially planned, and the first Yak-25 built in Saratov was not rolled out until September 1954. By 30 December that year the plant managed to hand over to the IA PVO only three aircraft, whereas twenty-one more were stored at its airfield, waiting for their testing and acceptance flights.

In total, the GAZ-292 built fifty Yak-25s equipped with the Izumrud radar, distributed into five production series (batches) before switching to the improved Yak-25M equipped with the much more capable RP-6 Sokol radar. It was launched in production in 1955 and the type continued to be rolled out until 1957; as many as 406 aircraft were built.

The Yak-25 was inducted in service with the IA PVO in 1954, becoming the first long-range loitering fighter-interceptor commissioned with the fighter arm of the mighty Soviet air defence forces. The original Yak-25, equipped with the RP-1 Izumrud radar, was capable of all-weather operations against air targets flying at between 2,500 to 15,000 m (8,200 and 49,200 feet), while the improved Yak-25M had expanded capability against low-altitude targets, flying down to 300 m (984 feet). The type equipped the IA PVO regiments stationed in the remote northern and far eastern corners of the Soviet Union lacking well-developed airfield networks, and it remained in front-line service until the late 1960s.

# Yak-25M Specification

| | |
|---|---|
| Dimensions:<br>Wing span<br>Length | 10.96 m<br>15.66 m |
| Wing area: | 28.94 m² |
| Weights:<br>Empty<br>Normal take-off<br>Maximum take-off<br>Normal fuel<br>Max fuel | 6,210 kg<br>9,220 kg<br>10,045 kg<br>2,660 kg<br>3,390 kg |
| Performance:<br>Max level speed at sea level<br>Max level speed at high level<br>Max rate of climb<br>Time to 10,000 m<br>Practical ceiling<br>Take-off distance<br>Landing distance<br>Range on internal fuel<br>Range on internal and external fuel<br>Loitering time on internal fuel<br>Loitering time on internal and external fuel | 927 km/h<br>1,090 km/h<br>45 m/s<br>6.1 min<br>14,500 m<br>800 m<br>850 m<br>2,201 km<br>2,560 km<br>2 hrs 48 min<br>3 hrs 26 min |

In early 1953 the head of OKB-115, Alexander Yakovlev, offered a new, long-range version of the Yak-25 that was capable of destroying heavy bombers in the air and on the ground. It had to use search-and-destroy single-ship tactics, calling for attacking the bases of the enemy heavy bombers in daylight, using the element of surprise. Its maximum sped was to be 1,200 km/h (647 kt), the range up to 4,000 km (2,157 nm) and the ordinance including two 37-mm cannons and twenty 57-mm rockets or four TRS-190 rockets. The main task of this Yak-25 derivative with enhanced performance and extended range was to be capable of attacking all the major US bases housing heavy bombers at a distance of 1,300 to 1,500 km (701 to 809 nm) from the borders of the Soviet Union. In addition to attacking US bases, it was to be also tasked with operating over enemy territory and destroying the enemy aircraft used in transport missions inside supposedly safe rear areas. This derivative of the Yak-25, referred to as a 'pirate-fighter' class, had to be powered by the AM-5F reheat turbojets rated at 21.77 kN (4,892 lb st. or 2,220 kgf) each, later on replaced by the increased-thrust AM-9 rated at 31.88 kN (7,163 lb st. or 3,250 kgf). This engine was to enable a maximum speed of 1,150 km/h (620 kt) at 5,000 m (16,400 feet) and 1,100 km/h (593 kt) at 10,000 m (32,800 feet), while endurance on internal fuel reached two hours; with an external tank, at

12,000 m (39,360 feet), this was extended to four hours. During the construction of the prototype, the 37-mm cannons were replaced by the lighter 23-mm NR-23s, and two bays for housing rockets were added into the forward fuselage.

This new 'pirate-fighter' received the new designation Yak-120M and had to be submitted for state testing in June 1954. As usual, the plans suffered a delay, and by the time it began flight tests, the Yak-120M had already been considered obsolete because of the advent of the first supersonic fighters. As a consequence, the IA PVO abandoned the project and the sole prototype remained as an experimental aircraft, used in late 1955 as a flying testbed for the new AM-9F (M-9F) afterburning turbojet. Later on, the Yak-120M design was used as a baseline for developing a new family of supersonic twin-engine fighters, bombers and reconnaissance aircraft.

A Yak-25 derivative was also tested with air-to-air missiles; following a trend of integrating first-generation beam-riding air-to-air missiles on all Soviet gunfighters operated by the IA PVO of the mid-1950s, the Yak-25M, equipped with the new Sokol radar, was modified to fire the K-5 missile. The modification works were carried out in 1955, and in the following year a squadron of missile-armed Yak-25Ms was handed over to the service. It was operated by the training centre at Krasnovodsk in the operational evaluation and testing role. However, due to the lack of operational Sokol radars at the time, the initial missile-carrying fighters used the old RP-2U Izumrud-2 radar, modified to guide the K-5 beam-riding missile. The new version received the Yak-25K-5 designation and was produced through a retrofit of existing Yak-25Ms.

There was also a project to integrate the more modern K-7L missiles—in 1956 it was tested on the Yak-25, equipped with the new Almaz radar, for the first time. The works on the integration of the K-75 missile were carried out in 1956, but both projects remained in an experimental phase and never had the chance to be inducted in the IA PVO service.

The K-8 missile, equipped with an infrared seeker, was another guided weapon

The radar-equipped Yak-25M, equipped with the Sokol air-intercept radar, was made capable of firing RS-2US (K-5) radar beam-riding air-to-air missiles. (*Yakovlev OKB*)

tested on the Yak-25 (this time equipped with the Sokol-2K radar). It was a large weapon, weighing 225 kg (496 lb), and when flying with two missiles under the wings the maximum speed was reduced by 70 to 80 km/h (38 to 43 kt). There were extensive carry tests with missile mock-ups, followed by real-world firings. It turned out, however, that by the time of completion of the protracted testing programme, the Yak-25 had been phased out of production and was an obsolete platform for use of the K-8.

The first production-standard Yak-25s were delivered to the 148th Combat Training and Aircrew Conversion Centre at Savastleyka, near Moscow, while the first front-line unit of the IA PVO to take the new type on strength became the 611th IAP (fighter regiment) stationed at Dorokhovo, near Moscow, in late 1954. It achieved an initial combat capability in late 1955, equipped with twelve Yak-25s and six Yak-25Ms. The regiment was also tasked with carrying out the Yak-25's field trials, which were successfully completed in 1956.

Each IA PVO regiment who took the new fighter on strength usually had three component squadrons, and one or two of these were equipped with the Yak-25 or Yak-25M, while the others flew the single-engined, short-legged MiG-17P/PF. In the second half of the 1960s, all the IA PVO regiments operating the type had mixed fleets. For instance, the 611th IAP (in addition to ten Yak-25/Ms) also operated five MiG-17Fs, nineteen Su-15s and one Su-7U two-seater. The 146th IAP, based at Vasilkov, near Kiev (in today's Ukraine), flew two squadrons equipped with the Yak-25 and one with the MiG-17PF; the former type was tasked to intercept targets at a distance of 400 km (216 nm) from Kiev, while the short-legged MiG-17PF was to engage incoming targets at a much closer range.

In total, the Yak-25 and Yak-25M were operated by no less than twenty IA PVO regiments stationed over the entire territory of the Soviet Union—from Kaliningrad, on the Baltic Sea (next to the Polish border) in the west, to Kamchatka Peninsula, in the Soviet Far East region. The first Yak-25/M-equipped squadrons began to phase out their subsonic loitering fighters and took more modern types in 1963, while the last IA PVO front-line units operating the type continued until the end of decade. However, there were a few Yak-25s that continued to be used in the test-bed role until the late 1970s.

There are no documented instances of the use of the Yak-25 and Yak-25M in anger, although the type was employed in numerous occasions to shoot down high-flying reconnaissance balloons (free-floating aerostats) launched in a mass manner from 1954, flying at 20,000 to 30,000 m (65,600 to 98,400 feet) in an eastern direction and crossing over Soviet territory.

## MiG-9—The Soviet Jet Pioneer

The Mikoyan OKB (then also known as the OKB-155) was tasked by the Soviet government to design a jet fighter at the end of the Second World War. In fact, the first decree of the Soviet State Defence Committee ordering all fighter design bureaus to commence the development of jet-powered aircraft dates back to May 1944. Initially the process was very slow due to the lack of suitable engines, as the only indigenous design—the RD-1, made by Arkhip Lul'ka—proved to be have a clearly insufficient thrust rating. This unfavourable situation was not rectified before the acquisition of a large quantity of trophy German turbojet engines following the occupation of Germany in the end of the Second World War.

The all-new jet fighter developed by the Mikoyan OKB was to be powered by trophy BMW 003 turbojets, rated at 7.85 kN (1,763 lb st. or 800 kgf) each. The first work commenced in June 1945, and the initial schedule called for it to be rolled out by 15 October that year. However, the undertaking proved to be more protracted than expected. The formal development of the new aircraft, designated I-300(F), was initiated following the Council of People's Commissars (the predecessors of the Soviet Council of Ministers) decree dated 26 February 1946. It ordered the Mikoyan OKB to develop a fighter with a maximum speed of 900 km/h (486 kt) at sea level and 910 km/h (491 kt) at 5,000 m (16,400 feet). Its practical ceiling was at 13,000 m (42,640 feet) and the range extended to 820 km (442 nm), while time from the ground to 5,000 m (16,400 feet) was to be no longer than four minutes. The armament was to include one 57-mm or 37-mm and two 23-mm cannons. The development phase foresaw the construction and testing of three prototypes.

Initially the design team considered installing the two engines under the wings, replicating the general layout of the Messerschmitt Me 262. At a later stage, however, the design team decided to accommodate the engines side-by-side in the

Artem Mikoyan (1905–1970) was the founder of the famous MiG (Mikoyan & Gurevich) Experimental Design Bureau in 1939, together with Mikhail Gurevich. From 1946 onwards, the fighter design house was actively involved in creating four generations of mass-produced jet fighters for both the Soviet Air Force (VVS) and the Soviet Air Defence Forces (PVO). (*Author's collection*)

fuselage, using a nose air intake. Such a novel design solution allowed the wings to remain clean, reducing the drag, while at the same time avoiding controllability issues in one-engine inoperative conditions inherent to the layouts featuring engines suspended under the wing.

The design concept was approved in late 1945 and construction of the first prototype was initiated immediately afterwards. The mock-up of the new jet fighter got the VVS approval in January 1946 and a government order followed, tasking the Mikoyan OKB with building and testing the aircraft.

Known under the I-300 internal designation, it featured a mid-mounted straight wing with slotted flaps, frise-type ailerons and cruciform tail surfaces. The cockpit was unpressurised and the aircraft had unassisted controls. The rear fuselage's bottom area was protected from the engine's hot exhaust gases by the means of a heat screen. The cruciform tail was well outside the exhaust, and the pitch control used control push-pull rods, while the rudder was actuated by control cables. The I-300F was the first Soviet fighter to use a tricycle undercarriage, with the main units retracting inside the wing panels, while the nose unit retracted to the rear in a well inside the fuselage.

The fuel system consisted of four fuselage and six wing tanks with a total volume of 1,625 litres. The aircraft used kerosene fuel—originally intended for tractor engines—with each engine provided with a starter working on aviation gasoline.

The jet-powered prototype was armed with one N-57 57-mm cannon installed in the nose (its muzzle protruded from the centre vertical intake separator wall) with 40 rounds and two NS-23 23-mm cannons (with 80 rounds each) with mizzles situated beneath the air intake. The N-57 was removed soon after the commencement of the flight test because of the serious problems it created; its place was occupied by a smaller N-37 37-mm cannon with 40 rounds.

The aircraft was rolled out on 6 March 1946 for commencing ground tests and engine runs at Mikoyan's experimental facility in Moscow. With flight safety considerations in mind, the Mikoyan OKB imposed a limit of only ten hours of useful life for the trophy BMW 003 engines. On 19 April that year, the I-300F-1 made its maiden flight at Ramenskoye (later known as Zhukovskiy) Airfield, southeast of Moscow, flown by the Flight Research Institute test pilot Alexey Grinchik. This first flight was only twenty minutes long and had the distinction of being the first performed by a Soviet jet-powered aircraft. The rival Yak-15 took to the air in its maiden flight three hours later on the same day and at the same airfield; this date therefore marks the birth of the jet combat aircraft era in the Soviet Union.

During the eighth flight of the I-300F-1, the test pilot reported serious vibrations in the engine area that continued to appear in the next three sorties. On the twelfth sortie, however, after strengthening the heat protection screen, the vibration disappeared, and the flight tests continued at a fast pace. The new jet fighter demonstrated a time to 5,000 m (16,400 feet) of five minutes and a 690 km/h (372 kt) maximum speed in shallow dive. During most (if not all) of the fest flights, Grinchik reported that the aircraft had suffered from trembling and vibrations of varying magnitude during many flight regimes, mainly caused by the

The Soviet Union's first jet fighter to take to the air, the MiG-9, was powered by two trophy BMW 003 jet engines, captured by the Soviet forces after the defeat of Nazi Germany; the twin-engine machine demonstrated an impressive speed and rate of climb performance. Here, the first prototype—dubbed 'I-300F-1'—is seen with test pilot Alexey Grinchik posing next to it; he made the first flight of the prototype on 19 April 1946. (*Mikoyan & Gurevich OKB*)

insufficient stiffness of the heat shield applied on the bottom rear fuselage, in the area affected by the exhaust gases.

On 11 June, during the twentieth sortie (intended to display the new aircraft in front of VVS leadership gathered at Ramenskoye), I-300F-1 crashed and Grinchik was killed. At this moment, I-300F-1 had logged six hours and twenty-three minutes total test time. The accident was caused by a torn-out wing root fairing, which separated and severed the aileron control linkage during a high-speed/low-level pass in front of the high-ranking audience.

The two follow-on prototypes, designated I-300F-2 and I-300F-3, took to the air in August 1946 and on 28 October respectively, intended to be used in the joint state testing effort undertaken by the NII VVS (Soviet Air Force's Scientific-Research Institute). During this testing phase, the two prototypes performed aerobatic manoeuvre routines over 200 times—including spins, demonstrated on jet aircraft for the first time in the Soviet Union. The prototypes attained a 920 km/h (496 kt) maximum speed at 5,000 m (16,400 feet), and the time to climb to 5,000 m (16,400 feet) was 4.2 minutes.

The jet engines worked flawlessly during the entire testing campaign of I-300F-2 and I-300F-3. The concluding report signed upon the completion of the state test effort noted that its handling characteristics yielded the I-300F a simple, pleasant, untiring and easy to pilot conversion aircraft. Based on these favourable pilot reports, the state test commission recommended the I-300F for launch into serial production.

The new fighter was launched immediately in production at the GAZ-1 in Kuybishev under the in-service designation MiG-9 and the internal factory designation FS (NATO reporting name 'Fargo'). The Ministry of Aviation Industry order dated 28 August 1946 called for the assembly of ten aircraft until the end of the year. Another order, issued on 12 September that year, called for an even more accelerated production schedule, with as many as fifteen aircraft required to be completed by 20 October 1946. The first small-scale production batch of ten aircraft was launched in production in late August, and the last of these aircraft was assembled by 22 October 1946; five more examples remained in the final assembly hall almost complete, lacking engines, armament and some other systems. It was a fast-track initiative taking only fifty-five days, sped up in order for the MiG-9 to be ready to participate in the flypast over Red Square in Moscow on 7 November 1946. All ten MiG-9s were intended to fly in formation at the flypast, but the event was cancelled due to bad weather.

The production-standard MiG-9s were powered by the RD-20 turbojet, a Soviet copy of the BMW 003, built in Kazan and rated at 7.84 kN (1,761 lb st. or 799 kgf). The first aircraft was rolled out at the GAZ-1 plant on 13 October and made its maiden flight on 26 October, with the famous Soviet test pilot Mark Gallay at the controls.

## MiG-9 Specification

| | |
|---|---|
| Dimensions:<br>Wing span<br>Length<br>Height | 10.00 m<br>9.75 m<br>3.225 m |
| Wing area: | 18.20 m$^2$ |
| Weights:<br>Empty<br>Normal take-off<br>Fuel | 3,533 kg<br>4,998 kg<br>1,298 kg |
| Performance:<br>Max level speed at sea level<br>Max level speed at high level<br>Max rate of climb<br>Time to 5,000 m<br>Practical ceiling<br>Take-off distance<br>Landing distance<br>Range on internal fuel | 864 km/h<br>910 km/h<br>22 m/s<br>4.3 min<br>13,500 m<br>950 m<br>1,060 m<br>800 km |

The initial flight operations with the first Soviet jet-powered fighters revealed a series of design shortcomings; among these were the engine flame-outs when firing the cannons above 7,500 m (24,600 feet), due to the ingestion of powder gases. It also became clear that the jet fighters would need air brakes and an ejection seat in order to grant a safe bail out; this was because pilots were no longer able to exit the cockpit at speeds exceeding 500 km/h (270 kt) due to the excessive aerodynamic forces created by the high-speed airflow. The jet fighter also needed a pressurised cockpit for granting the pilot comfortable conditions in high-altitude flight, as well as fire extinguishers in the engine bays for improved safety. The new propulsion technology's weighty advantages were only evident in high-speed flight, as the jet fighters (heavier than their piston-engined counterparts) demonstrated much worse take-off and landing performance. The MiG-9, for example, had a 910 m-long (3,050 feet) take-off run compared to 234 m (768 feet) for the piston-engine-powered MiG-3.

## The MiG-9's Two-Seater Derivative

The I-301T was a two-seater derivative of the I-300F, later re-designated UTI MiG-9 (internal factory designation FT-1). It featured a tandem two-seat cockpit with a newly-added instructor seat to the rear of the existing one in the single-seater. This necessitated the removal of one of the fuselage fuel tanks and the capacity reduction of another one; as a result, the total fuel capacity was 33 per cent less than that of the single-seater. The student's and instructor's cockpits were provided with individual canopies, opened by sliding to the rear. The two-seater was the first Mikoyan fighter to be equipped with ejection seats and a Mach-meter instrument. It retained the armament of the single-seater, consisting of one N-37 and two NS-23 cannons, with barrels protruding well in front of the nose.

The design of the two-seat derivative was defined in October 1946 and the first example was completed in June 1947, making its maiden flight the same month. In August that year it was submitted to the NII VVS for its state testing programme, but it was soon rejected by the military test pilots due to the lack of forward visibility from the rear cockpit, which rendered it useless for use in the conversion-to-type role. The two-seater remained in use at the Mikoyan OKB for testing various MiG-9 system improvements and flights with underwing external tanks.

The second two-seater, designated as the FT-2, had a redesigned fuselage featuring a raised rear cockpit, petal air brakes, gun-camera, plumbing for external fuel tanks and a larger armoured windshield for a better view of the pilot in the front cockpit. The curvature of the canopy side windows was also altered in order to grant a better view for the instructor, while the transparent separation wall between the cockpits was removed. The FT-2 took to the air for the first time on 25 August 1947, and later on it was used for testing the first Soviet-designed ejection seats. During the state tests conducted at the NII VVS in Shtelkovo, near

The UTI MiG-9 was a two-seat derivative intended for conversion training, but its rear cockpit provided the instructor pilot in the rear cockpit with a very restricted view forward during take-off and landing. The two-seat MiG-9 prototype was the first Mikoyan fighter to be equipped with ejection seats. (*Mikoyan & Gurevich OKB*)

Moscow, in September that year, it logged forty-seven sorties with a total duration of fifteen hours and thirty-two minutes. Based on the test results, the UTI MiG-9 was approved for launch into production, while most if not all of the novelties implemented into its design (such as the air brakes and the underwing tanks) were recommended for introduction into the single-seater's design as well.

The ejection seat testing in 1947 saw the FT-2 flying at a maximum level speed of 700 km/h (378 kt). The tested seat was installed in the front cockpit, and a dummy was initially used for ejection in the first three flights. During the next series of three test flights the ejection seat saw the participation of specially-trained parachutists.

The I-308 (FR), also designated as the MiG-9M, was an improved derivative featuring cannon muzzles moved aft in order to avoid ingestion of powder gases into the engine when firing the cannons. It also had uprated RD-21 engines delivering 0.9 kN (2,022 lb st. or 917 kgf) of thrust, air brakes and a pressurised cockpit. It made its maiden flight in July 1947 and demonstrated a maximum speed of Mach 0.8 as the more powerful RD-21 added 55 km/h (30 kt) compared to the RD-2-powered version, while the time to 5,000 m (16,400 feet) was shortened to 2.7 minutes.

The I-302 (FP) was another prototype with an N-37 cannon installed in the port fuselage, with a muzzle protruding forward in order to prevent powder gases ingestion, but this design solution proved ineffective.

The I-305 (FL) was a prototype powered by a single Lul'ka TR-1A turbojet, rated at 1.47 kN (3,310 lb st. or 1,500 kgf), while the empty weight was reduced

The MiG-9M, which took to the air for the first time in July 1947, was an improved derivative with cannon muzzles moved aft in an effort to avoid ingestion of powder gases into the engine when firing the cannons. (*Mikoyan & Gurevich OKB*)

by some 350 kg (771 lb). It had a redesigned rear fuselage and an altered armament installation layout. The three cannons were installed in the same horizontal plane; one N-37 with 45 rounds was placed in the centreline, with the two NS-23s with 80 rounds each accommodated on the sides. The airframe for the I-305 (FL) was completed in late 1947 but the TR-1A proved notoriously unreliable and was never installed. The programme was eventually cancelled because another single-engine fighter project, dubbed 'I-310', was considered to be much more promising.

The I-307 (FF) was a prototype powered by two uprated BMW 003 derivatives, rated at 0.98 kN (2,201 lb st. 999 kgf) each, built at the Factory No. 16 and designated RD-20F (later re-designated as the RD-21). It had new wheels and a canopy with a strengthened armoured windshield and armoured plates; the total armour protection weighed 30 kg (66 lb). The I-307 was completed in September 1947 and took to the air that month. The tests were concluded successfully and the aircraft was launched in production.

The I-307 was a prototype with a deflector plate installed onto the protruding barrel of the centreline 37-mm cannon in order to protect the engines from the powder gases, preventing abnormal operation and flame-outs in this way. It was flight-tested in late 1948, but the novelty was not implemented in production since the manufacture of the type had been already stopped. At the same time, the flight tests showed that the deflector plate was ineffective in deflecting the powder gases away from the intake, at the same time creating additional drag and reducing the stability of flight in the yaw axis; as a consequence, the experiments in this direction were discontinued.

The I-320 (FN) was another single-engine derivative, powered by the Rolls Royce Nene I, turbojet rated at 2.1 kN (4,717 lb st. or 2,140 kgf). This new and much more powerful engine had a centrifugal-flow compressor, nine combustor chambers and a single-stage turbine; in the Soviet Union it was launched in non-licensed production under the local designation RD-45, rated at 2.224 kN (4,952 lb st. or 2,247 kgf) and later on (in a slightly improved form) as the RD-45F, rated at 2.270 kN (5,100 lb st. or 2,314 kgf). It also featured an altered cannon installation scheme, with the muzzle of the N-37 cannon in the nose, just behind the intake leading edge, and the NS-23s on the lower port and starboard side with their muzzles also placed well behind the intake line. The I-320's sole prototype entered assembly in 1948 but remained incomplete due to the advent of the much more promising I-310—thus it was never flown.

The MiG-9 was used as a two-seat testbed for the development of the guidance system of the KS-1 Kometa air-launched cruise missile (ALCM), fired by the Tu-16 bomber. The operator of the missile's guidance system occupied the non-pressurised rear cockpit of the aircraft designated as the MiG-9L (FK), while the nose received two radars as used by the KS-1 missile. The first one had an antenna emitting electromagnetic energy towards the target, with receiver antennas in the wing leading edge left and right of the cockpit. The second radar had an antenna situated at the top of the fin, used for communication with the launch platform. During the development phase of the missile, the carrier aircraft was represented by a specially-modified Tu-4 bomber. The FK was flown for the first time in 1949 and its participation in the KS-1 development programme lasted four years.

The total MiG-9 production run between 1946 and 1948 amounted to 602 aircraft. The last four examples were delivered to the VVS in December 1948.

The MiG-9 was notoriously unreliable and it was never turned into a real combat aircraft in the Soviet Union. From 1950–1951, 372 aircraft were donated to China after a brief service with the VVS, as the type was fully replaced by the much more capable and reliable MiG-15.

## MiG-15—A True Aircraft-Soldier

The MiG-15 (NATO reporting name 'Fagot'), often titled as 'aircraft-soldier', was *de facto* the Soviet Union's first operational swept-wing jet fighter. Affordable and capable, it was fairly advanced for its time; built in a mass manner, in the early 1950s it became the standard fighter of the Soviet Union and its client states. Furthermore, its two-seat derivative became the standard advanced jet trainer, remaining in operation in many countries around the world with the MiG-17 and MiG-19-equipped squadrons until the mid-1980s.

The MiG-15's creation became possible thanks to the purchase of the Rolls-Royce Nene I and Nene II jet engines, copied in a very prompt manner and then further developed in the Soviet Union. The MiG-15 had a very fast and successful test campaign, and soon after its launch in mass production it was sent to war in Korea. The Soviet fighter regiments secretively operating in Korea (masked as Chinese combat units) reported fairly good success in general during the air battles against UN aircraft.

When considering its new jet fighter design, Artem Mikoyan, chief designer of the OKB-155, preferred the heavier Rolls Royce Nene I instead of the lighter and less powerful Rolls-Royce Derwent Mk.V, and the design bureau received three Nene engines needed for the development works.

The development of the new fighter was initiated following a Soviet Council of Ministers decree dated 11 March and the corresponding Ministry of Aviation Industry (Aviaprom) order dated 15 April 1947. In fact, the first design work on the new project was begun well in advance, during January 1947. The Aviaprom specification, coinciding with the VVS requirements, called for a maximum speed of 1,000 km/h (540 kt) at sea level and 1,020 km/h (550 kt) at 5,000 m (16,400 feet). The time to 5,000 m (16,400 feet) was to be 3.2 minutes and the practical ceiling 13,000 m (42,640 feet), and the maximum range at 10,000 m (32,800 feet) altitude was to reach 1,200 km (647 nm). The take-off run was to be 700 m (2,300 feet) long, while the landing roll was to be 800 m (2,625 feet). The armament was to include one 45-mm and two 23-mm cannons; later on the 45-mm cannon was replaced by a 37-mm one upon VVS request. The hardpoints under wings were required to be made capable of carrying two external fuel tanks or up to 200 kg (441 lb) of bombs.

In order to achieve high speed performance, the new fighter was fitted with swept wings, tested for the first time in a wind tunnel at TsAGI (Soviet Union's Central Aerodynamics Institute). The chief shortcomings of this scheme were the low lateral stability (in the roll axis) and the airflow stalls. The optimum swept angle value as calculated at TsAGI was 35°, with 2° anhedral. The upper wing surface featured two fences at each console, needed for stabilisation of the stall vortices. The aircraft also featured a swept T-shaped empennage consisting of a fin and horizontal stabiliser.

The final design of the new jet fighter—dubbed 'I-310'—was rather simple for manufacture, servicing and flying, with its engine located just behind the cockpit and the nozzle positioned at the very end of the fuselage; the trailing-link undercarriage also proved very robust and simple. The new fighter, which later received the official designation MiG-15, proved so successful in terms of flight performance that its aerodynamic configuration became a basis for the development of more capable derivatives such as the MiG-17 and MiG-19, endowed with more swept wings, powered by more powerful engines and boasting better armament and targeting equipment. The pilot was accommodated in a pressurised cockpit, with a canopy providing very good view forward and rearward, and he sat on an ejection seat that granted a reliable bail out in high-speed flight. The canopy was made of two parts—a fixed forward with an armoured windshield and a movable to the rear, opening by sliding aft.

The armament comprised three built-in cannons—one 37-mm N-37D and two 23-mm NS-23s mounted in the lower forward fuselage, with muzzles situated under the starboard (N-37D) and port side of the nose (both NS-23s). All the three cannons were installed onto a common platform, together with the ammunition cases and the spent-cartridge collectors. The gun-carrying platform was made

The first MiG-15 prototype—designated I-310 and powered by a Rolls-Royce Nene I turbojet—made its maiden flight on 30 December 1947, but demonstrated poor performance in terms of maximum speed and acceleration. This was caused by significant thrust losses in the long jet extension pipe running from the turbine to the nozzle in the tail-end. (*Mikoyan & Gurevich OKB*)

detachable and able to be pulled down for servicing of the weapons and loading ammunition, thus shortening the pre-flight between combat sorties. Two airbrake panels were installed onto the rear fuselage.

The new fighter had the distinction of being the first Soviet combat aircraft to introduce a fire extinguishing system inside the engine bay and a fire warning system. It was also the first one boasting the so-called 'blind-landing' instrumentation suite; the OSP-48 suite incorporated an ARK-5 automatic direction finder, an RV-2 radar altimeter and a MRP-48 marker beacon receiver.

The fuselage detached into two sections at frame No. 13 for easy access to the engine, its accessories and the nozzle assembly when servicing or replacement would be needed. The wing panels were attached to the fuselage by bolts, and this fairly clever design solution enabled the rapid installation and removal of the wing panels in field conditions. This design solution also provided versatility of transportation of the fighter in disassembled form, loaded inside a container, accommodated in the cargo compartment of transport aircraft, or when carried on a railway platform.

The first I-310 prototype (dubbed the 'S-1') made its maiden flight on 30 December 1947, with the test pilot N. Yuganov in the cockpit. By late March 1948 the S-1 logged seventeen test sorties, but it showed unsatisfactory performance (in terms of maximum speed and acceleration) due to the significant thrust losses and the tests were stopped in an attempt to fix the problem. The design solution to avoid the thrust loss called for shortening the extension jet pipe connecting the engine and its nozzle at the rear fuselage; this led to reducing the overall length of the fuselage.

The second I-310 prototype (dubbed the 'S-02') was powered by the uprated Nene II turbojet, delivering 2.225 kN (2,200 kgf or 4,928 lb st.) of thrust, and

The detachable armament platform introduced by the MiG-15 contained two 23-mm cannons and one 37-mm cannon, as see here on this ex-North Korean 'Fagot' tested by the USAF in 1953. (*USAF*)

The S-02 was the second MiG-15 prototype with a shortened jet extension pipe and powered by the Rolls Royce Nene II engine. It showed very promising performance from the very beginning in terms of take-off, climb, stability and controllability characteristics as well as airbrake effectiveness, and was used as a basis for the serial production launched in late 1948. (*Mikoyan & Gurevich OKB*)

flew for the first time on 5 April 1948 in the capable hands of the famous LII test pilot Sergey Anokhin. I-310's factory testing took a total of thirty eight flights amassed by the S-1 and thirteen more by the S-2.

Both prototypes underwent their state testing programme in two phases—the first one was held between 27 May and 25 August, and the second one ran from 4 November to 3 December 1948 at Chkalovskaya Airfield in Shtelkovo, east of Moscow. The S-2 was the main aircraft used in the effort while the S-1 was assigned to a secondary role.

The report from the flight tests noted that the I-310 had passed the state tests with a sufficient grade; its performance was meeting the specification, and as a consequence the new design was recommended to be launched in production. The report also recommended that the OKB-155 initiate the development of a two-seat derivative of the I-310 for conversion-to-type training.

The VVS test pilots who flew the I-310 also made very positive comments about the aircraft's take-off, climb, stability and controllability characteristics, as well as praising the airbrake effectiveness. The maximum speed attained during the state testing effort reached 1,028 km/h (554.5 kt) at 5,000 m (16,400 feet). The I-310 demonstrated a climb to 5,000 m (16,400 feet) in 2.3 minutes, which proved much faster than what was required in the specification (3.2 minutes), while the maximum range was 195 km (105 kt) longer and the practical ceiling was 2,200 m (7,216 feet) higher than the requirements contained in the VVS specification. The take-off run and the landing roll lengths were 600 m (1,968 feet) and 765 m (2,509 feet) respectively.

The NII VVS test pilots were especially positive about the I-310's handling characteristics, noting that the aircraft handling was well-suited for pilots with average qualification following the fixture of some minor shortcomings. They recommended that I-310 should undergo an improvement of its controllability and stability characteristics in the roll axis, combined with design measures to improve the undercarriage amortisation ability and the stability during the take-off run.

The ground servicing of the new fighter also proved much easier than that of the twin-engine MiG-9, with a very simple and straightforward engine start-up initiated by pushing just one button situated on the throttle lever.

On 23 August 1948—two days before the completion of the state testing phase—the Council of Ministers of the Soviet Union issued a decree for commissioning the I-310 in VVS service and launching it in production under the new MiG-15 designation. The new fighter was to be built at three plants simultaneously—at the GAZ-1 in Kuybishev, GAZ-153 in Novosibirsk and GAZ-381 in Moscow. Another decree, dated 29 September 1948, obliged the OKB-155 to fix the shortcomings revealed during the MiG-15 state testing effort and submit the improved aircraft for the so-called control testing by the NII VVS in November that year.

The S-3 was the third MiG-15 prototype, built in March 1948 and acting on the lessons learned during the tests of the first two prototypes. It was also powered by the Nene II, and featured new hydraulically actuated and enlarged air brakes; the fin was moved slightly rearwards and the elevator received balancing weights, while the engine bay was equipped with fire extinguishing bottles. The S-3 was also made capable of carrying external fuel tanks under the wings; the same pylons were used to carry two bombs. The cockpit featured an ASP-1N gun-sight and a gun camera. The wing structural design proved to be a serious issue as its strengthening led to a weight increase of some 180 kg (397 lb). It was provided with simple flaps, used on take-off for lift increase, in an effort to shorten the take-off roll, which proved to be 695 m (2,280 feet) compared to S-02's 810 m (2,657 feet). The wing anhedral was increased to -2° in order to reduce the excessively high lateral stability.

The S-03 was completed in March 1948 and took to the air for the first time on 20 June that year, flown by Sergey Anokhin. The factory flight tests, comprising of forty-eight sorties, were completed on 15 October that year; during one of the sorties the aircraft reached a maximum speed equating to Mach 0.934. After the end of the factory test phase the S-3 was submitted for control testing by the NII VVS—a programme that included thirty sorties logged between 4 November and 3 December 1948, with a total flight time of fifteen hours and twenty-one minutes. The maximum speed at 1,600 m (5,248 feet) attained during this testing campaign amounted to 1,047 km/h (565 kt). On 23 December 1948 the VVS Commander-in-Chief, Marshal Konstantin Vershinin, approved the MiG-15's flight test report made by the NII VVS. The report contained a recommendation for commissioning the aircraft in service and launching it in serial production, whilst continuing to improve its design in order to meet the VVS specification over the entire range of its characteristics. Another conclusion in the report referred to the aircraft's ability to operate from dirty, non-paved airstrips. Additionally, the report noted that the flight test programme had not foreseen testing the new aircraft in air-to-air combat, but its performance could allow it to engage in this capacity. The MiG-15 was also tested in inverted flight, and the overall conclusion was that the aircraft had simple handling characteristics and could be flown by pilots with average qualification.

The S-3 was accepted as a pattern aircraft for the serial production, but before that it had to undergo a series of design alterations and refinements in order to be considered fit for production in numbers. The Nene II engine was replaced by its Soviet copy, the RD-45F, built at Motor-Building Factory No. 14 in Moscow. The airframe structure was strengthened and the equipment was improved, while the two NS-23 cannons were replaced by the newer NR-23 and the wing pylons were plumbed for the carriage of 496-litre external fuel tanks. In 1951 newly designed external tanks were introduced, which held 300 litres of kerosene. They sported an improved shape in order to allow the MiG-15's maximum speed with external fuel tanks to be increased to 900 km/h (485 kt)—equating to Mach 0.9 at high altitude—while the manoeuvring limit was set at 5-G with full external tanks and 6.5-G with empty ones.

The MiG-15 was formally commissioned by the Council of Ministers decree dated 20 May 1949; the same decree also called for launching it in mass

A look into the MiG-15 cockpit, belonging to the I-310 prototype. (*Mikoyan & Gurevich OKB*)

The series-production MiG-15 fighter was powered by the Klimov RD-45 turbojet, a non-licensed derivative of the Rolls-Royce Nene II. (*Mikoyan & Gurevich OKB*)

production at four plants simultaneously. They were ordered to immediately stop the production of their existing aircraft (La-15, Yak-17, Yak-23 and Li-2), in a bid to launch the new, promising design as soon as possible.

The first production-standard (the so-called leading aircraft) MiG-15, powered by the RD-45F, was built at the GAZ-1 in Kuybishev. It commenced its state flight testing on 13 June 1949 and completed the effort in January 1950 after amassing fifty-nine sorties with nine in-flight start-ups. The first front-line unit, the 29th Guards IAP, stationed at Kubinka Airfield, near Moscow, received a batch of twenty aircraft in early 1950; they were to be used for conducting the MiG-15's field testing effort. This took as many as 2,067 sorties, with a total flight time of 872 hours and 47 minutes.

## The Two-Seat UTI MiG-15

Development of the two-seat derivative of the MiG-15 began following a Soviet Council of Ministers decree dated 6 April 1949. It obliged the OKB-155 to submit the twin-seater MiG-15 for flight testing by 15 May that year. In fact, the first design work began in November 1948, with the new version receiving the internal designations ST and also I-312. It used the basic airframe and powerplant of the single-seater, with a second cockpit (occupied by the instructor) inserted in the place of the fuel tanks, thus reducing the internal fuel tankage. The new design of the canopy included a sideways-hinging movable part for the front cockpit and an aft-sliding part for the rear one. The ejection seats were the same as those used on the single-seater, and the ejection sequence called for the instructor pilot in the rear cockpit bailing out first and then the student sitting in the front one. The pilots and armament were protected by two 10-mm armoured plates installed in the nose, while both ejection seats were provided with armoured headrests.

The two-seat ST also had a simplified armament selection, initially comprising one NR-23 23-mm cannon with 80 rounds and one YakB-E 12.7-mm machine-gun with 150 rounds. The early production aircraft retained this scheme, but from the sixth production series onwards the cannon was deleted and its place was occupied by the electronic boxes of the OSP-48 blind-landing equipment. The two pylons under the wings were made capable of carrying one 50-kg (110-lb) or 100-kg (220-lb) bomb each on BD2-48 bomb racks. The front cockpit was equipped with the ASP-1N gun-sight, replaced shortly after the commencement of the series production by the improved ASP-3N. The aircraft was also equipped with the S-13 gun camera.

The ST first prototype, dubbed 'ST-1', was modified from a production-standard single-seater at OKB-155's own experimental plant in Moscow between March and May 1949. It took to the air for the first time on 27 June, with test pilot V. Yuganov in the cockpit. The factory flight tests were completed by 20 August and the aircraft was then submitted for its state testing. Conducted between 27 August and 25 September, this effort was completed successfully and the ST was recommended for launch in series production. Then the ST-1 was operated

The UTI MiG-15 two-seater was launched in production in July 1950 and used as a conversion and continuation trainer—not only for MiG-15-equipped units, but also for those flying the more sophisticated MiG-17 and MiG-19. In addition, the 'Midget' used to serve as the Soviet Union's primary advanced and lead-in fighter jet trainer until the early 1970s, continuing to serve in this role in many countries around the world until the late 1980s. (*Mikoyan & Gurevich OKB*)

between October 1949 and April 1950 by the 324th IAD (fighter aviation division) as a trainer, in order to undergo a detailed evaluation of its capabilities.

In April 1950 the ST-1 was returned to the OKB-155 for inspection and fixing the shortcomings revealed during the experimental operation. Upon completion of the works it received the new designation ST-2. During the rework the aircraft was also equipped with the OSP-48 blind-landing equipment, which necessitated the removal of the NR-23 cannon and reducing the capacity of fuel tank No. 1, situated just behind the rear cockpit. The ST-2 was also equipped with a KI-11 back-up magnetic compass and a new spent-cartridge-deflection mechanism to prevent machine-gun stoppages. The ASP-1N gun-sight was replaced by the improved ASP-3N as used on the single-seater. In this new equipment configuration the ST-2 took to the air for the first time on 4 August 1950, and its factory testing effort took a total of nine sorties. The ST-2 was then submitted for its state testing effort, conducted at the NII VVS. After that it was used as a pattern aircraft for the serial production of the version featuring the OSP-48 blind-landing instrumentation suite, the same as installed on the single-seat aircraft.

The two-seat MiG-15 derivative—designated as the UTI MiG-15—was launched in production in July 1950 (in an initial version that lacked the OSP-48

An UTI MiG-15 used by the Soviet DOSAAF auxiliary air training organisation, whose aeroclubs operated the two-seat type for training jet pilots who were later called upon for a service career with the Soviet Air Force. (*Author's collection*)

suite) at the GAZ-1 in Kuybishev, where the type would be in production until 1953. A total of 881 examples were built there in addition to ten more in a kit form and one for use in the ground instruction role. The UTI MiG-15 was then launched at the GAZ-153 in Novosibirsk, where it remained in production until late 1954; as many as 924 aircraft were rolled out. Later, the two-seat MiG-15 was handed over for production at two more plants—the GAZ-135 at Kharkov and the GAZ-99 at Ulan-Ude. The former built 511 examples between 1950 and 1954, while the latter added 1,117 more between 1951 and 1959. The UTI MiG-15 was assigned the NATO reporting name 'Midget'.

## MiG-15bis—The Ultimate 'Fagot'

The MiG-15bis was the ultimate representative of the MiG-15 model family, powered by an increased-thrust engine and sporting a better equipment standard. Its development became possible thanks to the availability of the VK-1 turbojet, rated at 2.6 kN (5,951 lb st. or 2,700 kgf). It had exactly the same size and weight of its predecessor, VK-45F, and its installation onto the MiG-15 necessitated only a few minor design alterations. The development of the new version was launched by a decree of the Soviet Council of Ministers dated 14 May 1949 and the relevant Aviaprom order dated 20 May that year. It called for designing an improved MiG-15 derivative powered by the VK-1 that had to be submitted for state testing by 1 July that year. This was postponed due to the delay in receiving a serial MiG-15 for conversion into the new variant.

Internally known as the SD, the VK-1-powered derivative of the MiG-15 was externally similar to the MiG-15, but the design team used the occasion to introduce a series of additional improvements. The list of these included a stretched fuselage (due to the longer jet pipe of the new engine), a strengthened wing structure, a refined elevator design, and a newly designed wing fence to prevent stalls, while the cannons were moved closer to each other in an effort to reduce projectile dispersion. The airframe also received local strengthening in selected areas in order to comply with new strength requirements for combat

The most capable member of the 'Fagot' family line was the MiG-15bis, powered by an increased-thrust VK-1 turbojet and sporting a better equipment standard combined with a refined flight control system. (*Mikoyan & Gurevich OKB*)

aircraft that were introduced by the VVS in 1947. The pilot had a better protection provided by a 64-mm-thick armoured windshield, and the cockpit pressurisation was also improved.

The pilot wore the PPK-1 anti-G suit for better sustaining G-forces in turning flight, when pulling from 1.085 to 8G; this equipment was copied from a North American F-86 Sabre fighter captured in Korea. In 1952 the MiG-15bis received the first edition of the rear-view TS-23 periscope, mounted on the top of the canopy arc, useful in air combat and while taxiing on the ground. However, this model proved ill-suited during the initial flight test and was immediately replaced by the improved TS-25 featuring a wider field of view, eventually recommended for installation on the production aircraft. The air brake panels were strengthened and the new MiG-15 version received powered ailerons for better controllability in the roll axis. Its top speed was limited to 1,074 km/h (579 kt), equating of Mach 0.92 due to a combination of strength, controllability and flutter considerations.

The modifications were completed in late July, and in August the SD commenced its factory tests, while on 13 September 1949 it was submitted to the NII VVS for commencing its state testing effort. The first sortie at the NII VSS was made on 19 September, but the flights were soon stopped due to engine surges and high-frequency vibrations caused by the engine. The tests were resumed on 21 October but the engine vibrations appeared once again, and the flight tests were stopped. In late January 1950 the SD received a new engine and amassed fifteen sorties until 15 March. The engine vibrations problem was not completely fixed and this made it necessary for the SD to receive yet another new engine—the fourth one since the beginning of the flight testing campaign. The tests were resumed, and despite the presence of high-frequency vibrations, the SD amassed thirty-five more sorties until the completion of the state testing effort. The results from the SD's state testing effort showed that the new aircraft demonstrated considerably better overall performance, and the range only proved shorter by 180 km (97 nm) due to reduced internal capacity and the increased specific fuel consumption of the VK-1 engine compared to that of the RD-45. The maximum speed demonstrated during the state testing was 1,076 km/h (580 kt), and the controllability in the pitch, roll and yaw axis was notably improved. At the same time, the aileron effectiveness was still below the specification, and the aircraft continued to suffer from unintentional banking in high-speed flight (at speeds above 960 km/h [518 kt] at low altitude) and aileron reversal above Mach 0.7, which were even more pronounced than those experienced on the MiG-15 (powered by the RD-45) because of the MiG-15bis' higher maximum speed. To avoid this effect, the initial production MiG-15bis was restricted to 1,040 km/h (561 kt) when flying below 2,500 m (8,200 feet). This restriction was eventually lifted only after the introduction of a strengthened and stiffer wing structure with higher-quality skin, launched in production in October 1950.

The state flight testing report was approved by the Council of Ministers on 1 July 1950, and the aircraft was ordered to be launched in production—replacing the MiG-15 powered by the RD-45. The MiG-15bis was built in two main versions— one equipped with the OSP-48 blind-landing equipment for all-weather operations, day and night, and the other one without this equipment, optimised for day operations only. In 1952, a small number of MiG-15bis received brake parachutes, which were useful for shortening the landing roll when operating from short airstrips. In 1952 the MiG-15bis received a modification for autonomous engine start-up, using a 12-SAM-25 battery capable of providing no less than ten start-ups without recharging, with sortie duration reaching between thirty and forty minutes.

The MiG-15bis was also tested for anti-bomber operations using air-to-air bombs. The OFAB-100 and PROSAB-100 100-kg (220-lb) bombs were dropped by the fighter at 12,000 m (39,360 feet) and 700 km/h (378 kt) while passing overhead bomber formations, and their radio-controlled fuses were activated upon command of the fighter formation leader for mid-air detonation in close proximity to the bombers.

The MiG-15Sbis (SD-UPB) version was built as a long-range escort fighter, equipped with large 600-litre tanks. The long range and endurance necessitated this version receiving an additional oxygen bottle, which was installed in the nose. Flying with such big external tanks, however, imposed serious performance restrictions such as the ban on flying with negative G and with prolonged sideslip that would affect the normal fuel flow in the system; prolonged flights at maximum speed were also banned, in addition to landing with full tanks.

The MiG-15Rbis (SR) was a reconnaissance derivative with a design identical to that of the MiG-15bis, but also equipped with an AFA-40 camera.

In December 1948 the OKB-155 commenced work on an all-weather, radar-equipped version of the MiG-15 (designated as the SP-1) following a

The MiG-15bis featured a strengthened and stiffer wing structure with a higher-quality skin, launched in production in October 1950 in a bid to fix the aileron reversal and unintentional banking issues experienced in high-speed flight. (*Author's collection*)

Council of Ministers decree to develop a derivative capable of attacking air targets without establishing visual contact—i.e. at night, or when the targets flew in clouds. The SP-1 received the Toriy targeting radar, using two antennas—one emitting and one receiving—accommodated in the nose under a common radome. The radar required manual target tracking, which proved too workload-intensive for the pilot during the intercept sequence. The design team working on the SP-1 faced a challenge to retain the MiG-15's performance unchanged despite the installation of the heavy and bulky radar. A production-standard MiG-15, built at GAZ-1, was retrofitted to the new configuration at the OKB-155's experimental facility in Moscow. It was stripped of the two NR-23 cannons and remained armed with the 37-mm N-37D cannon provided with 45 rounds. The ASP-3N gun-sight was also replaced with a new design and the S-13 gun-camera on the top of the intake lip was relocated to the starboard fuselage side. The cockpit received a radar scope, enabling the pilot to track the target, steer the aircraft towards it and measure distance in order to open fire at the appropriate moment. The radar installation necessitated a nose extension by 12 cm, and the airbrake petals were given an altered shape and rotation axis. The fixed part of the canopy was also modified to provide the pilot with a better view and received a 64-mm-thick armoured windshield. The wing anhedral was increased from -2° to -3°, and the nose undercarriage unit was moved forward by 8 centimetres. The aircraft got a powered elevator, driven by a BU-1 hydraulic actuator.

The SP-1 prototype commenced flight tests in December 1949 and underwent its state testing effort between 31 January and 20 March 1950. The aircraft's radar was tested in intercepts against Il-28 and Tu-4 bombers. The flight test report issued after the intercept test sorties noted that the aircraft was found to have serious design deficiencies—such as insufficient stability in the pitch axis on landing and reduced dynamic stability, as it tended to bank to the left while in level flight at speeds from 940 to 950 km/h (507 to 512 kt). The ailerons also had poor effectiveness, limiting the bank angle to just 5°. The conclusion of the test report was that in this form the SP-1 could not be used as a fighter-interceptor in instrument meteorological conditions due to the poor radar performance. Nevertheless, in 1951 the GAZ-1 built five radar-equipped MiG-15bis, and one of them was submitted for the so-called control testing to be conducted by the NII VVS. The results, as could be guessed, were again negative, and the new version was rejected.

The MiG-15 and its follow-on derivatives, MiG-15bis and the two-seat UTI MiG-15, were built in large numbers at as many as nine production plants in the Soviet Union, with the total production run accounting for 13,131 examples. In addition, the MiG-15 was built at Aero in Czechoslovakia (833 single-seat MiG-15s, 2,012 two-seat examples and 620 MiG-15bis), while the single-seater was also launched in production at PZL Mielec in Poland (under the local designation LIM-1 for the first version and LIM-2 for the MiG-15bis). This way, the grand total of the MiG-15/UTI MiG-15 production accounted for no fewer than 18,000 examples.

The ST-7 was a radar-equipped version of the two-seat UTI MiG-15, equipped with the twin-antenna RP-1 Izumrud air-intercept radar. (*Mikoyan & Gurevich OKB*)

# MiG-15 and MiG-15bis Specification

|  | MiG-15 | MiG-15bis |
| --- | --- | --- |
| Dimensions: |  |  |
| Wing span | 10.08 m | 10.08 m |
| Length | 10.10 m | 10.11 m |
| Height | 3.70 m | 3.70 m |
| Wing area: | 20.60 m$^2$ | 20.60 m$^2$ |
| Weights: |  |  |
| Empty | 3,247 kg | 3,582 kg |
| Normal take-off | 4,917 kg | 4,960 kg |
| Fuel | 1,450 kg | 1,470 kg |
| Performance: |  |  |
| Max level speed at sea level | 1,047 km/h | 1,076 km/h |
| Max level speed at high level | 1,031 km/h | 1,045 km/h |
| Landing speed | 170-190 km/h | 170-190 km/h |
| Max rate of climb | 42 m/s | 50 m/s |
| Practical ceiling | 15,200 m | 15,500 m |
| Take-off distance | 940 m | 590 m |
| Landing distance | 850 m | 850 m |
| Range on internal fuel | 1,335 km | 1,200 km |
| Range on internal and external fuel | 1,920 km | 1.976 km |
| Max G-load | 8 | 8 |

# The MiG-15's Combat Career

The MiG-15 saw its baptism of fire in the first half of 1950—it happened in communist China, when the Soviet Air Force's 29th Guards IAP (fighter regiment) was deployed urgently and tasked with providing air defence to the big city of Shanghai. At the time, communist China was at war with the Republic of China (set up at Taiwan Island), but its newly-formed air arm proved too weak to resist the enemy aviation raids; this is why the Soviet Union agreed to provide massive military assistance via a clandestine deployment of two fighter regiments, later complemented by one attack and one mine-torpedo bomber regiment. The first ever MiG-15 kill was reported on 8 April 1950—it was a P-38 Lightning twin-engine fighter downed by the Soviet pilot Capt. Koleynikov.

The second victory was achieved during a night-intercept sortie on 11–12 May 1950—this time the MiG-15's victim was a B-24 Liberator four-engine bomber. In addition, a People's Liberation Air Force (PLAAF) Tu-2 bomber was gunned down by the Soviet MiG-15s after being mistakenly identified as a Republic of China B-25 Mitchell bomber. After the end of the hostilities in Shanghai area, all the 'Fagots' assigned to the 29th Guards IAP were handed over to the People's Liberation Army Air Force (PLAAF), and the Soviet pilots were involved in training their Chinese counterparts.

Then the MiG-15 saw much use in anger in the Korean War, with the first Soviet Air Force regiments—assigned to the 64th IAK (Fighter Air Corps)—clandestinely deployed to the theatre of war in October 1950. These units, equipped with the improved MiG-15bis, were based at airfields in China, some of which were in close proximity to the border with Korea. The Soviet fighter force was tasked to repulse the attacks of the United Nations (UN) aircraft, mostly represented by USAF and USN types.

During the three years of fighting in Korea the Soviet military presence was a closely guarded secret. The MiG-15s flown by the Soviet pilots wore North Korean insignia in an attempt to hide the Soviet participation in the war; the radio chatter in the air, however, was solely in Russian, and this fact alone is said to have exposed the direct Soviet involvement in the war from the very beginning. The Soviet fighters had a ban on operating behind the front line and over the sea, thus being restricted to engaging enemy targets over friendly-held territory only. In addition to the Soviet MiG-15s, the war saw the participation of North Korean and Chinese fighter units equipped with the same type.

The official Soviet/Russian history says that the MiG-15's baptism of fire in this war happened on 1 November 1950, when a 72nd Guards IAP pilot, 1st Lt Chizh, shot down a USAF F-51D Mustang piston-engined fighter, while the first ever air-to-air combat between jet fighters followed suit on 8 November, with four MiG-15s encountering four F-80C Shooting Stars. The Soviet pilots claimed one F-80C, and their USAF counterparts made a claim for a downed MiG-15, but it turned out that the damaged Soviet fighter eventually managed to return to its home base at Mukden Airfield in China and be repaired.

However, the detailed research of two Russian authors, Leonid Krylov and Yuriy Tepsurkaev—who checked almost all available Soviet/Russian military documents from the Korean War era, including the combat reports of each regiment involved in the air battles—shows that the first air combat between MiG-15s and UN aircraft took place on 1 November, but with no results (the Russian F-51D Mustang shoot-down claim proved false). The second combat on the same day, however, could be considered as the first one involving jet fighters from both warring parties. It saw a Soviet claim, as Lt Hominich had claimed one F-80 Shooting Star shot down. The Soviet claim, however, cannot be confirmed by US documents. In regard to the 8 November combat between F-80s and MiG-15s, as Krylov and Tepsurkaev found out, the US claim on one MiG-15 shot down also proved to be a false one. The Soviet MiG-15 which was attacked by the F-80s managed to return home and the documents of the Soviet fighter units involved in combat on these days show that no losses had been reported. A MiG-15 flown by Capt. Haritonov was badly damaged in that combat, but the pilot succeeded in breaking from the attacking F-80s by entering into a steep dive and jettisoning his external tanks (the tanks, containing some jet fuel, exploded upon impact

A USAF F-86 gun-camera sequence showing the shooting down of a MiG-15 during air combat in Korea, with a subsequent bail out of its pilot. (*USAF*)

with the ground). The first confirmed kill in air combat between jet fighters took place on 9 November 1950, when a seven-aircraft MiG-15 group encountered a F9F Panther formation flying off the USS *Philippine Sea*, tasked to escort fighter-bombers and attack aircraft. In this fierce combat the Soviet pilots, who assumed that their enemy was the F-80 instead of the F9F, claimed two kills, but these were not confirmed—they also sustained one own loss. The USN credited this MiG-15 kill to VFA-111's CO, Lt Cdr William T. Amen.

The first air-to-air combat between swept-wing fighters—MiG-15s pitted against the North American F-86s—happened on 17 December 1950, with the Soviet pilots reporting one loss; three days later they a claimed an F-86 kill. In Korea, the Soviet MiG-15 pilots encountered the best USAF fighter, the North American F-86D Sabre; they were flown by skilled pilots, most of them with combat experience dating from the Second World War. As a result there were many air-to-air combats between the two types for gaining air superiority or engaging when the F-86s covered UN bombers and fighter-bombers from MiG-15 attacks.

Compared to the F-86C/D, the MiG-15 had a slight edge in the practical ceiling and the rate of climb above 7,000 m (22,960 feet), and was also equal in the rate-of-climb performance below that level. This performance superiority was achieved thanks to the MiG-15's better thrust-to-weight ratio. The Soviet fighter

This MiG-15bis defected from North Korea on 21 September 1953, a few weeks after the end of the Korean War. It was flown by Lieutenant No Kum-Sok, who flew to Kimpo, South Korea. In the event, he received a $100,000 reward ($890,831 in 2014 dollars) as offered by Operation Moolah for bringing a MiG-15. The trophy MiG-15 was then ferried to Okinawa, where it was test-flown by Capt. H. E. 'Tom' Collins and Maj. Chuck Yeager. (*USAF*)

also had a much more powerful armament compared to the Sabre's six 12.7-mm machine-guns (only at the end of the war did the F-86H version receive four 20-mm cannons), but carried an insufficient ammunition load compared to that of the F-86, and had a much lower rate of fire. On the other hand, the F-86 enjoyed a slightly better turning ability in the horizontal plane due to the better wing mechanisation (thanks to the use of leading-edge slats), and had higher maximum speed and longer range, more effective air brakes and better acceleration in a dive, while the pilot had a considerably better all-round view from the cockpit, wore an anti-G suit and used a much-better gun-sight fed with target range information by a radar range-finder for accurate firing.

The Soviet fighter units were grouped into the 64th IAK, and saw several pilot rotations. The first rotation in the field proved to be the most successful one, staffed by experienced pilots and commanders—all of them Second World War veterans. During the first ten months of the war, one of the 64th IAK component regiments, the 196th IAP, claimed 109 victories against ten own aircraft losses, and four of its pilots were killed in action. There were two distinguished Soviet aces of the Korean War—Nikolay Sutyagin, with twenty-one official kills, and Evegeniy Pepelyaev, with twenty (including twelve F-86s). In fact, Pepelyaev has personally acknowledged only twelve of his kills, noting in informal conversations that the rest could be considered probable kills. Russian researchers Leonid Krylov and Yuriy Tepsurkaev, who analysed all Soviet kill claims, have also arrived at the conclusion that the confirmed kills of Pepelyaev were twelve only. The first Soviet pilot to assume jet ace status was Capt. Stepan Naumenko on 24 December 1950, with one B-29, three F-84s and one F-86 kills under his belt.

The Soviet MiG-15 pilots despatched to the theatre of war in Korea used the proven Second World War air combat tactics formula—'speed-climb-altitude'. This allowed them to successfully engage the enemy in offensive combats. During the war they introduced new, more flexible tactics, calling for the use of six-ship formations instead of despatching in combat entire twelve-ship squadrons. Most of the air combats began with the MiG-15 fighters scrambled to encounter UN aircraft flying towards the North Korean airspace, guided by the 64th IAK's command-and-control (C2) centre situated in Chinese territory. The intent of this air combat phase was to get the MiG-15s into advantageous positions for visual detection and attack on the enemy. Upon reporting visual detection, the ground controllers had only an informative function, with all decisions in combat taken by MiG-15 formation leaders. After the merge, the MiG-15 formations usually split into two- and four-ship elements, dogfighting with the F-86s or attacking the enemy bomber and fighter-bomber groups. In general, 1951 proved to be the most successful year for the Soviet MiG-15 force in Korea thanks to the very skilled pilots of the first rotation, who used suitable tactics. In 1952 and 1953, however, the follow-on rotations saw Soviet pilots despatched in combat with low experience on the MiG-15. As it could be guessed, this rotation manner led to a slightly decreased combat effectiveness and an increased number of losses.

According to the official Soviet/Russian war statistics, during the three years of participation in the war in Korea the Soviet fighter units (comprising regiments provided by the VVS, PVO and the Naval Aviation service) reported 1,872 air combats and claimed 1,106 enemy aircraft shot down, including 650 F-86s. According to the 64th IAK Commander, Lt Gen. Georgiy Lobov, the Soviet air-to-air victories in Korea numbered about 1,300 achieved in Korean and Chinese airspace, while the losses comprised some 345 MiG-15s. There is no data available about the North Korean and Chinese MiG-15 losses sustained during the war. US sources, however, claim that the number of F-86s lost in air combat pitted against the Soviet MiG-15 amounted to 102, while the F-86 pilots reported 345 MiG-15 kills.

In fact, both sides inflated their kill claims during the war, and on many occasions the aircraft claimed as shot down successfully returned to the base. Claims were made mainly on the results of the gun camera, recording hits and damage inflicted by the projectiles fired by the fighter guns (which were not always fully reliable), and also taking into account testimonials of other pilots participating in the same combat and observers on the ground, as well as using evidence collected on the ground wherever available. Authoritative Russian authors Leonid Krylov and Yuriy Tepsurkaev—who carried out thorough research on the Soviet participation in the Korean War and cross-checked all kill claims contained in the official Soviet Air Force documents with those contained in US publications—have arrived at the conclusion that the Soviet MiG-15s had shot down (in a confirmed manner) some 150 F-86s. This figure also includes the aircraft damaged beyond repair that managed to land and also those examples which crashed on landing due to combat damages. In turn, as Krylov and Tepsurkaev claimed, the UN fighters in Korea managed to bring down as many as 283 Soviet MiG-15s.

The MiG-15's real strength in the Korean War was exactly in line with its design concept as a fighter originally tailored to intercept well-defended enemy bombers carrying nuclear bombs; this was especially evident in the operations against the USAF B-29 Flying Superfortress fleet. The first combats proved that the MiG-15 formations could easily penetrate through the B-29's fighter escorts, while its heavy-calibre guns were described as being effective in inflicting heavy damages to the four-engine bombers. The first B-29 (in fact, it was an RB-29 version used for reconnaissance) was claimed on 9 November 1950; the MiG-15 managed to inflict heavy damages on it and the aircraft crashed on landing in Japanese territory. On 14 November 1950, two more B-29s were heavily damaged and one of these was written off after emergency landing. On 1 December 1950 three more Superfortress kills were claimed, but in fact all of these managed to return to base despite the heavy damage. The first hike in the B-29 losses was reported on 12 April 1951, when as many as ten aircraft were claimed by the Soviet pilots. The detailed research of Krylov and Tepsurkaev, however, showed that four B-29s were shot down while three more examples managed to make emergency landings and were written off because of damages beyond repair. On 30 October 1951, the so-called 'Black Tuesday', the second hike in B-29 losses happened, with no less than twelve B-29s claimed gunned down plus four F-86s. However, Krylov and Tepsurkaev found out that the real B-29 losses in this combat accounted for three downed and six aircraft damaged beyond repair. After 'Black Tuesday' the B-29s were used for night missions only. There was one night victory achieved by the Soviet fighter force in late May 1952; the B-29 was tracked by ground searchlights and a MiG-15 piloted by Maj. Kalin mounted a successful attack, approaching unseen and firing from a close distance to guarantee destruction of the target.

The Cold War biography of the MiG-15 comprises many occasions when the fighters were scrambled to intercept Western aircraft that strayed into Soviet airspace on intelligence missions or simply due to a navigation mistake. The first MiG-15 victim in this typically Cold War style of encounters was an RB-29 flying in Soviet airspace in the Primorie region, in the Soviet Far East, not far away from the largest Soviet city in the region—Vladivostok. It was gunned down on 6 December 1950 by a pair of MiG-15s belonging to the 523rd IAP, stationed at the time in China. Then, on 13 July 1952, a B-29 was brought down by MiG-15s of the Soviet Pacific Fleet over Valentine harbour in the Sea of Japan, and another B-29 had the same fate on 7 October 1952 in Soviet airspace over the Kuril Islands chain (near Yury island).

On 18 November 1952 a four-ship MiG-15 formation from the 781th IAP, a fighter regiment assigned to the Soviet Pacific Fleet, was engaged in air combat by a formation of USN F9F-2 Panthers from VFA-781, operating off the aircraft carrier USS *Oriskany*, in an area over the sea near the Soviet city of Vladivostok. Two MiG-15s were gunned down in this encounter by the USN pilot, Lt Royce Williams, with their pilots declared missing in action; another MiG-15 crashed while returning to its base due to damage inflicted in combat.

The hot encounters continued in 1953, with an RB-50 reconnaissance aircraft intercepted over Kamchatka Peninsula by a pair of MiG-15s. The fighters attempted to force the RB-50 to land on Soviet territory, but the USAF aircraft opened fire with its defensive armament and tried to escape. The Soviet pilots were ordered to return fire and scored numerous hits into the RB-50, whose remains fell on the ground near Zhupalovo village. A similar encounter happened on 29 July that year near Gamova Cape, in the Sea of Japan, where a pair of MiG-15s from the VVS' 88th Guards IAP was scrambled to intercept another RB-50. As the Soviet pilots reported, the US gunners were the first to open fire, and the MiG-15s immediately returned fire. The RB-50 was shot down, and one of the MiG-15s, hit by the US gunners, had the same fate, its pilot managing to eject. The next encounter, on 7 November 1954, involved a B-29 attacked by a pair of Soviet MiG-15s over the Kuril Islands chain (Tanfilev Island), north of Japan. The B-29 was damaged and diverted to Japan; the Soviet intelligence sources then claimed that the bomber crashed on the territory of Hokaido Island.

In 1955, the Soviet MiG-15s continued to be active in the intercepts of US aircraft, with the first one happening on 18 April over Kamchatka Peninsula, attacking an USAF RB-47 on a reconnaissance mission in Soviet airspace. The attack was successful and the wreckage of the ill-fated RB-47 fell into the sea. The second encounter happened on 22 May, when two MiG-15s gunned down a USN P2V-5 Neptune maritime patrol aircraft while flying over the Sea of Japan. One month later, on 23 June, another P2V from VP-19 squadron followed suit in the airspace over the Bering Strait—it was heavily damaged by the MiG-15 fire and crashed on landing on St Laurent Island. In July that year the third P2V Neptune was gunned down over the sea near Nakhodka city, just north of Vladivostok, by MiG-15s from the 7th IAP, assigned to the Soviet Pacific Fleet. In this very strained situation, the Soviet MiG-15s were also involved in a friendly fire incident, shooting down a Tu-14 naval jet bomber over the sea near Nakhodka on 27 July 1956.

The Cold War in Europe also saw the active use of the MiG-15. The first occasion was reported on 16 June 1952, when Soviet MiG-15s assigned to the Baltic Fleet aviation service gunned down a Swedish PBY Catalina flying boat near Khiuma Island.

On another Cold War front in Europe, on the Balkans Peninsula, the Bulgarian MiG-15s were involved in shooting down of an El Al Airlines Lockheed L-049 Constellation passenger aircraft on 27 July 1955. The Israeli airliner deviated from its route over Yugoslavia due to a navigation mistake and strayed into Bulgarian airspace, flying towards the Greek border. The MiG-15 pilots mistakenly recognised the Constellation as a military transport and were ordered to open fire. The airliner was gunned down and its wreckage fell on Bulgarian territory, near the border with Greece; all fifty-eight people on board (fifty-one passengers and seven crew members) were killed in the accident.

## The MiG-17—an Affordable and Capable Fighter

The MiG-17 (NATO reporting name 'Fresco') had the distinction of being the most successful and widely-used first-generation Soviet-built jet fighter. Developed on the base of the proven MiG-15, it retained the general layout of its predecessor but introduced a host of aerodynamic performance improvements and better equipment—and yet it was as simple to produce, maintain and fly as the MiG-15. The MiG-17 was built in a mass manner in several variants; in addition to the fighter role, it was also widely used as a fighter-bomber and an advanced training aircraft in many local wars.

The chief goal of the design team at the OKB-155 was to improve the speed performance of the MiG-15, which was restricted to Mach 0.92 at altitudes between 900 and 5,000 m (2,952 and 16,400 feet). It was capable of reaching Mach 1 in dive, but only when flown by skilled test pilots. The MiG-15bis, powered by the VK-1 turbojet with a slightly higher power rating, had approximately the same speed performance.

In an effort to improve the airframe's aerodynamic performance, the MiG-15bis fuselage was modified with new, thinner wings with a 45° sweptback angle and an area that was increased to 22.6 m$^2$ (243 sq. feet), featuring three aerodynamic fences on the upper surface on each panel (the original MiG-15bis has two fences only). The wing panels were installed with anhedral of -3°. The empennage was also redesigned—the sweptback angle of the fin at the leading edge was increased to 56° and its area was also increased. The horizontal tail surfaces were also enlarged and the rudder received a small flexible plate—the so-called 'knife'—useful for aerodynamic balancing. The fuselage was longer by 90 cm (35.4 in) than that of the MiG-15bis, but the internal fuel tankage was reduced to 1,412 litres.

The new aircraft received the internal designation SI and an informal designation MiG-15bis45, denoting the increased 45° sweptback angle. It retained all instruments and avionics of the basic MiG-15bis unchanged. The SI prototype made its maiden flight on 14 January 1949. During the first flights it quickly became clear that its top speed was 40 km/h (26kt) higher than that of the MiG-15bis, and on 1 February it hit 1,114 km/h (601 kt) at 2,200 m (7,216 feet). On 20 March that year, however, the prototype was written off in a fatal crash, killing the test pilot I. Ivashtenko. This happened while the aircraft was in descent from 11,000 m (36,080 feet), suddenly entering into a steep dive and hitting the ground.

The factory tests continued almost one year later using the second example, designated as the SI-02, flown by the famous NII VVS test pilot Grigoriy Sedov.

The MiG-17 (initially designated as the MiG-15bis45) used the basic MiG-15 fuselage, mated to new, thinner wings with a 45° sweptback angle and increased area, featuring three aerodynamic fences on the upper surface. The first prototype—designated SI—made its maiden flight on 14 January 1949. This is the third MiG-15bis45 example, equipped with underwing external tanks each holding 400 litres of kerosene. (*Mikoyan & Gurevich OKB*)

In one of the sorties in 1950 he entered into a situation presumably similar to that encountered by his colleague, I. Ivashtenko, in the SI crash on 20 March 1949. Sedov was able to escape the dangerous flight regime (uncommanded pitch down) by entering climb and throttling back the engine for an additional speed loss. The cause of the sudden loss of control was defined as an elevator flutter that created excessive vibrations, destroying the elevator structure. Sedov was able to land his aircraft, which lacked nearly 40 per cent of the elevator surface. Post-flight analysis showed that the flutter developed at a speed of 1,020 to 1,044 km/h (550 to 563 kt). Another phenomenon encountered by Sedov in high-speed flight referred to the aileron reversal because of the insufficient stiffness of the wing structure.

A small batch of pre-series SI aircraft intended for flight testing was built at the GAZ-21 in Gorky, and after completing the factory testing phase the first one was submitted to the NII VVS for the state testing effort, which was eventually completed in 1951. During tests, LII pilots Sergey Anokhin and I. Kazmin went supersonic, managing to hit Mach 1.14.

A Ministry of Aircraft Industry order dated 1 September 1951 called for launching the new fighter type in production at six factories simultaneously. Compared to the standard MiG-15bis, the new version's more swept wings and other airframe improvements led to increased speed performance, with its top speed reaching 1,114 km/h (601 kt)—equating to Mach 0.97 at 10,000 m (32,800 feet)—while the SI's stability and controllability characteristics remained almost the same. At speeds between 720 and 750 km/h (388 to 405 kt), however, it suffered from slight oscillations around the yaw and bank axes. The manoeuvrability performance in the horizontal plane and the take-off/landing performance were slightly inferior to that of the MiG-15bis, but this was not seen as an issue at all.

As test pilots tended to comment, the MiG-15bis45 was very stable in high-altitude flight, able to perform turns with a slight loss of height even at its practical ceiling. It also demonstrated fairly good spin characteristics, tending to enter into inverted spin or spiral only in case of gross handling mistakes. The minimum speed of stable level flight with undercarriage and flaps up, and engine set at idle, was between 200 and 220 km/h (108 and 119 kt).

The new fighter, designated as the MiG-17, was initially launched in production in 1952 at the GAZ-1 in Kuybishev as well as at the GAZ-21 in Gorky, GAZ-153 in Novosibirsk, GAZ-292 in Saratov, and the GAZ-126 in Komsomolsk-on-Amur, while in 1953 the GAZ-31 in Tbilisi followed suit.

In 1953 the first series of improvements were introduced, such as ejection seats equipped with a curtain for the protection of the pilot's face, AGI-1 attitude indicator (artificial horizon), single-piece moving canopy, ASP-3NM gun-sight, non-reversible actuators for the elevator and equipment for use of the PPK-1 pilot anti-G suit. The VK-1 turbojet was replaced by the improved VK-1A, sporting the same thrust rating but boasting an extended time between overhaul and overall service life. The vanilla MiG-17 remained in mass production in the Soviet Union until 1955, with 5,497 examples rolling out the line at six plants.

The non-afterburner MiG-17 remained in mass production in the Soviet Union until 1955, with 5,497 examples rolling off the line at six plants. (*Author's collection*)

## MiG-17 and MiG-17F Specification

|  | MiG-17 | MiG-17F |
| --- | --- | --- |
| Dimensions: |  |  |
| Wing span | 9.60 m | 9.60 m |
| Length | 11.26 m | 11.26 m |
| Height | 3.80 m | 3.80 m |
| Wing area: | 22.60 m² | 22.60 m² |
| Weights: |  |  |
| Empty | 3,798 kg | 3,939 kg |
| Normal take-off | 5,200 kg | 5,340 kg |
| Maximum take-off | 5,930 kg | 6,069 kg |
| Fuel | 1,173 kg | 1,170 kg |
| Performance: |  |  |
| Max level speed at sea level | 1,060 km/h | 1,060 km/h |
| Max level speed at high level | 1,114 km/h | 1,145 km/h |
| Landing speed | 170-190 km/h | 170-190 km/h |
| Practical ceiling | 15,600 m | 16,600 m |
| Take-off distance | 940 m | 590 m |
| Landing distance | 850 m | 850 m |
| Range on internal and external fuel | 1,295 km | 1,240 km |
| Max G-load | 8 | 8 |

## MiG-17 Afterburner Version

The MiG-17F was the second variant produced in numbers, powered by the VK-1F afterburning turbojet. This new derivative of the VK-1A was ground-tested for the first time in late 1951, demonstrating a maximum thrust rating of 3.312 kN (7,450 lb st. or 3,380 kgf), which represented a 25 per cent increase compared to that of the VK-1A, while at military power it was rated at 2.548 kN (5,730 lb st. or 2,600 kgf).

The new engine was installed on a production-standard MiG-17, which received an improved fuel system to cope with the higher flow requirements imposed by the afterburner chamber. In the beginning, operation of the afterburner was limited to three minutes at up to 7,000 m (22,960 feet) altitude and ten minutes above 7,000 m (22,960 feet).

The new version, known internally within the OKB-155 as the SF, began flight tests on 29 September 1951. The factory tests were completed on 16 February 1952 and then it was handed over to the NII VVS for its state flight test effort. The afterburning engine provided the SF with a much-improved performance, especially in terms of level speed and rate of climb. At 3,000 m (9,848 feet) altitude, the maximum level speed hit 1,145 km/h (618 kt), while the rate of climb hit 75.8 m/s (14,917 fpm). The maximum Mach number was lifted up to 0.994 at 11,000 m (36,000 feet). During the flight test the aircraft demonstrated supersonic speed performance, getting up to Mach 1.03, but the test pilots reported excessive stick forces at this flight regime. The maximum altitude attained during the state testing was 16,600 m (54,448 feet), and the aircraft still had plenty of rate-of-climb reserves, but this level was set as the practical ceiling due to limitations related to the cockpit pressurisation, which was operating at its upper limit to provide working conditions for the pilot—who lacked a pressurised suit and helmet.

The new version, designated MiG-17F, was launched in production in late 1952 at the GAZ-21 in Gorky, and later on it was manufactured at the GAZ-126 and the GAZ-153. The last MiG-17Fs were rolled out in 1958, but from 1956 onwards all production went to export customers. The MiG-17F's production output in the Soviet Union accounted for 1,702 examples.

The radar-equipped MiG-17 prototype, internally designated as the SP-2, was developed in 1951. It featured the installation of the single-antenna Korshun air-intercept radar, developed by the NII-17 design bureau. This prototype was originally built as a MiG-15bis, but received a new wing with a 45° sweptback, an altered fixed canopy part and increased volume of the rear fuel tanks. This modification converted the MiG-15bis into a *de facto* radar-equipped MiG-17, with armament comprising two NR-23 cannons only.

The SP-2 was flown for the first time in its new guise in April 1950, with its joint state testing undertaken between 28 November and 29 December that year. The radar performance, however, proved to be very poor chiefly due to the manual target tracking, which overloaded the pilot during the intercept (target search, closure and sighting). As a consequence, the SP-2 was rejected for production.

The next radar-equipped version was the SP-6, which received the RP-1 Izumrud radar, integrated with the ASP-3NM gun-sight. This two-antenna radar set had a search antenna installed in the upper part of the intake lip and a tracking antenna in the centre-body. Its armament comprised three NR-23 cannons, each provided with 100 rounds. During the intercept, when the distance between the fighter and target reduced to below 2 km (1.1 nm), the tracking antenna switched on automatically, enabling accurate sighting. In clear-weather conditions the pilot used the ASP-3NM gun-sight only. Maximum detection range against a four-engine bomber was up to 9.5 km (5.1 nm), while small twin-engine bombers (such as the Il-28) were detected from 7.5 km (4 nm). The radar, however, was ill-suited for the interception of targets flying below 3,000 m (9,900 feet) due to ground clutter, and the minimum altitude of the fighter during intercepts was limited to 2,500 m (8,200 feet). Three radar-equipped MiG-17s, designated as SP-7s, were converted at the OKB-155's experimental plant in Moscow from existing MiG-17s built at the GAZ-21.

The new fighter, which received the in-service designation MiG-17P, was commissioned in service on 27 June 1953, and the type entered service with the IA PVO and the Soviet naval aviation's shore-based fighter regiments. Only 178 examples were built in 1952.

The VK-1F afterburning engine provided the MiG-17F gunfighter with a much improved performance, especially in terms of level speed and rate of climb. (*Author's collection*)

The last MiG-17Fs were rolled out in the Soviet Union in 1958, but from 1956 onwards all production was delivered to export customers only. (*Author's collection*)

The production-standard MiG-17Ps, rolled out at the GAZ-21, introduced a new canopy with an altered shape and increased-area air brakes. The radar increased the aircraft's empty weight by 220 kg (485 lb), and the radome of the search radar worsened the pilot's forward-downward view.

The MiG-17PF was the next radar-equipped version, powered by the VK-1F afterburning engine and armed with three NR-23 cannons; it was also equipped with the Sirena-2 radar-warning receiver (RWR) and the NI-50B navigation indicator. It was developed following the Council of Ministers decree dated 27 June 1952. The prototype—designated as the SP-7F—took to the air for the first time on 24 July 1952, and its factory testing phase of forty-six sorties was completed on 16 December that year. During the period between January and May 1953 it underwent its state testing effort, which was completed with a positive result, and the new derivative was then recommended for launching into production.

The radar-equipped MiG-17PF was heavier than its radar-less predecessor and therefore had a lower rate of climb and a longer time for performing a 360-degree turn in the horizontal plane, amounting to eighty-five seconds at military power and sixty-two seconds at afterburner.

The new derivative was commissioned on 27 June 1953 and launched in series production at the GAZ-21 in Gorky; it was also produced by Avia in Czechoslovakia (designated as the S-104) and by PZL in Poland (Lim-5P).

In January 1954 the further-improved SP-8 was tested; it was fitted with the new RP-5 Izumrud-5 radar set with better jamming protection, capable of tracking targets at up to 4 km (2.1 nm). The tests were successfully completed in April that year, with the new radar-equipped derivative recommended for production. It was built at the GAZ-31 in Tbilisi in 1955 and 1956, with the examples rolled out in 1956—going to export customers only.

The MiG-17PFU was an all-missile-armed fighter-interceptor. It saw its cannons deleted and received four K-5 air-to-air missiles—two under each wing, carried on APU-4 launch rails. This missile used the beam-riding guidance method, with the radar beam formed up by the modified RP-5 radar. The K-5 (NATO codename AA-1 'Alkali'), had a maximum range of 3 km (1.6 nm) and was suitable for use only against non-manoeuvring targets—bombers and reconnaissance aircraft at high altitude, in all weather conditions. The missile was tested on three SP-6 prototypes. The tests were successful and the aircraft was recommended for launching into production. It was built at the GAZ-21, which converted forty incomplete MiG-17PF airframes to the new standard in 1955.

The MiG-17R (SR-2 and SC-2S) was a reconnaissance derivative powered by the new VK-5F engine. In was developed in accordance with the Council of Ministers decree dated 3 August 1951. In addition to the engine, the list of novelties implemented in this new version included a new cannon mount, a photo camera suite and an audio recorder. It also introduced a powered elevator and an all-new instrument panel in the cockpit.

The new VK-5F afterburning turbojet was rated at 2.92 kN (6,612 lb st. or 3,000 kgf) dry and 3.773 kN (8,484 lb st. or 3,850 kgf) with afterburner. A VK-1F

The radar-equipped MiG-17P interceptor was developed in 1950, and its afterburner derivative, the MiG-17PF, took to the air for the first time on 24 July 1952. (*Author's collection*)

A close-up view of the MiG-17P/PF RP-1 Izumrud radar, integrated with the ASP-3NM gun sight. This rather primitive (according to today's standards) radar had a two-antenna set; its search antenna can be seen here in the upper part of the intake lip, while the tracking antenna dish was housed in the centre-body. (*Author's collection*)

The MiG-17PFU was a missile-armed/all-weather fighter-interceptor without guns and armed with four K-5 beam-riding air-to-air missiles. (*Mikoyan & Gurevich OKB*)

derivative, it had a higher thrust setting thanks to the increased temperature in front of the turbine due to the use of new heat-resistant alloys for the turbine blades and better cooling. The MiG-17R was armed with only two NR-23 cannons with 100 rounds each, as the single N-37D was removed in order to save weight. The reconnaissance equipment was represented by an AFA-BA-40R camera and a MAG-9 audio recorder, the latter used to record the pilot's accounts based on the visual information he acquired while flying in the target area—combined with his notes, written on a map. The camera was installed on a mount, enabling it to be pointed downwards or sideways (to the left, at 30° off vertical). The camera window was provided with a metallic cover to protect the lens from sand, stones, dust and dirt.

The SR-2 prototype was completed in May 1952 and made its maiden flight in June of that year. It underwent a protracted factory testing programme that lasted until January 1954, and in July that year the SR-2 was submitted for state testing, which was completed on 10 August that year. It completed the effort with sufficient grade, but the flight test report noted that its performance was practically the same as that of the MiG-17F, powered by the VK-1F, and that it would be suitable to recommend production of a new MiG-17F derivative featuring the recognisance equipment already tested on the SR-2. This new tactical-reconnaissance variant, dubbed 'SR-2S', was built and successfully tested, and then launched into production.

The most unusual MiG-17 derivative, dubbed 'SN', was built with an all-new armament, including cannons movable in the vertical plane and installed onto a SCV-25-MiG-17 nose mount. Its integration necessitated the introduction of side air intakes for feeding the engine. Due to the new nose, the fuselage length was extended by 1.069 m, and it got new main undercarriage wheels, an increased-length canopy for better view, new instrument panel, a new gun-sight and internal tankage increased by 50 litres. The movable gun mount with three 23-mm cannons was intended to provide the pilot with easier sighting conditions without the need to point the nose towards the targets (as is the case when firing fixed cannons). The new mount was therefore meant to enable the pilot to open fire earlier than the enemy, with the ability to point the cannons towards the enemy at a faster pace. The movable mount was able to move at 27° 26' upwards and at -9° 28' downwards by using an electric actuator.

The SP prototype was tested for the first time in 1953 by OKB-155 test pilot Georgiy Mosolov; it was then submitted for state testing on 15 February 1954, amassing 130 sorties and spending a total of 15,000 23-mm rounds in the process.

Flight tests showed that the SP had a maximum level flight speed 60 km/h (32 kt) lower than that of the production-standard MiG-17F, with a lower rate of climb and practical ceiling. The manoeuvring performance was also inferior compared to that of its predecessor—for example, the 360-degree turn at 10,000 m took seventy-seven seconds, which was fifteen seconds longer than the figure demonstrated by the vanilla MiG-17.

The cannon firings also brought some unpleasant surprises. It turned out that when all three cannons were fired in deflected up or down position, this resulted in flightpath deviations to the opposite side. It was also reported that it could be next to impossible to make accurate firing up, with the cannon deflected more than 10°, without using dampers to neutralise the momentum created by the recoil forces generated by the cannons. In the event, the use of the moving gun mount was considered to be ineffective and the programme was shelved.

The SN, which flew for the first time in February 1954, was a MiG-17 derivative with side air intakes, armed with 23-mm cannons installed in its redesigned nose, movable in the vertical plane. (*Mikoyan & Gurevich OKB*)

## MiG-17 Licence Versions

The licensed production of the MiG-17F in Poland was launched at PZL Mielec, while PZL Rzeszów commenced manufacture of the VK-1F engine. The Polish-made aircraft, designated as the Lim-5, had a more effective afterburner control system. The first aircraft was rolled out at PZL Mielec in November 1956, and until July 1960 a total of 477 examples were built. The Lim-5 was heavier than the MiG-17 but had a higher speed, reaching 1,154 km/h (622 kt). The Polish-built MiG-17PF derivative was designated as the Lim-5P; it was in production between January 1959 and December 1960, with 129 examples rolling off the line.

The Lim-5M was an improved MiG-17F equipped with brake parachute, optimised for use in the fighter-bomber role, with a strengthened undercarriage (and twin-wheel main units enabling use from soft, unpaved runways, which retracted in a wing-root extension also housing fuel tanks) and jet-assisted take-off boosters. The Lim-5M took to the air for the first time in the early 1960s and was in production between November 1961 and May 1962, with sixty examples rolling off the line at PZL Mielec.

The Lim-6 was a further-modified MiG-17F derivative, outfitted with an altered engine intake, brake parachute in a pod in the fin base and blown flaps. It took to the air for the first time in 1961, and its testing effort continued until March 1962. As many as forty examples were built, but it proved that the Lim-6's performance

The Lim-5 was a licensed version of the MiG-17F built at the PZL Mielec plant in Poland; this is an example operated by the Bulgarian Air Force in the ground-attack role. (*Author's collection*)

was inferior to the un-modified Lim-5, and that is why these aircraft were used in the attack and reconnaissance role only.

The Lim-6bis was a follow-on version of the Lim-6 that lacked most of the novelties implemented into its processor—such as the take-off boosters, twin-wheel main undercarriage units and wingroot fuel tanks. It retained the brake parachute container in the fin base and introduced additional pylons under the centre-wing section, capable of accommodating 16-round rocket packs. The Lim-6bis prototype was flown for the first time in mid-1962, while in 1963 most of the earlier-produced Lim-6s and some Lim-5Ms were modified to this new standard.

The Lim-6R was a reconnaissance derivative of the Lim-6bis, carrying its cameras in underwing pods plus an AFA-39 camera installed in the lower fuselage. It lacked a radar range-finder and was able to carry illumination bombs only.

The license production of the MiG-17F in China was launched in 1955, and the first example assembled at the plant in Shenyang (by using components supplied from the Soviet Union) was flight-tested in 1956. The type remained in production until 1959, with 767 examples rolling off the line and wearing the local designation J-5. Development of a radar-equipped derivative—locally made in China—was initiated in 1961. Designated as the J-5A, it took to the air for the first time on 11 November 1954, and was launched into production in the following year.

China also developed a twin-seat J-5 version, designated as the JJ-5, which was used to replace the Soviet-supplied UTI MiG-15 in the jet conversion role. Its prototype, powered by a WP-5D turbojet (a VK-1A copy), took to the air for the first time on 8 May 1968 and remained in production until late 1986; as many as 1,061 examples were built. The twin-seater was armed with one Chinese copy of the NR-23 cannon only.

The total MiG-17 production run, including the Polish- and Chinese-built examples, accounted to about 11,000 aircraft; as many as 8,085 of these were built in the Soviet Union.

## The MiG-17 in Service

The first production-standard MiG-17s delivered to the VVS were used for field testing in 1952 at Dzhankoy Airfield in the Crimea Peninsula, where the 62nd IAP was stationed. In 1953, thanks to the large-scale production, the MiG-17 was widely introduced with the VVS and the fighter regiments of the naval aviation arm, while from late 1953 the radar-equipped MiG-17P was delivered exclusively to the IA PVO regiments. The MiG-17F with afterburning engine was inducted in VVS service in early 1954, and the radar-equipped MiG-17PF interceptor was taken on strength by the IA PVO in late 1954.

The IA PVO MiG-17P/PFs saw a lot of operational use to intercept Western reconnaissance aircraft performing missions in close proximity to or inside Soviet airspace. Such an encounter took place for the first time on 4–5 January 1954, when eight MiG-17s were despatched to intercept an RAF Canberra reconnaissance aircraft flying at high altitude over the Caspian Sea; however, the aircraft reportedly failed to close to firing distance, and the target escaped untouched. There were also a few occasions when radar-equipped MiG-17P/PFs failed to detect their targets in instrument meteorological conditions. It also proved difficult for pilots to master real-world radar intercepts due to the workload-intensive nature of these missions and the importance of accurate guidance from the ground until detection of the target with its own radar. The guidance from ground-controlled intercept stations using voice commands required prolonged practice; this proved to be too cumbersome, with significant lags in issuing steering commands that led to the failure of the entire intercept process. Only after improving the ground guidance did the MiG-17P/PF become an effective interceptor that was able to bring down USAF, USN and RAF reconnaissance aircraft. The first occasion of a successful operation was reported on 8 May 1954, when a group of MiG-17PFs of the 1619th IAP managed to intercept and damage an RB-47 in the Murmansk area on the Kola Peninsula; the RB-47 eventually escaped to Finland.

The MiG-17P was the first Soviet aircraft to shoot down high-flying reconnaissance balloons. It happened in Ukraine in the summer of 1954, with the target floating at 10,000 m (32,800 feet) near the city of Tchernovtsi; the MiG-17P used only nine rounds. The next sortie—a few days later, flown by the same pilot, Capt. L. Savitchev—proved fruitless. The pilot expended the entire ammunition load of 150 rounds, but without any result as the balloon climbed out well beyond the reach of the 'Fresco's' canons.

There were other countries in the Soviet bloc that reported successful shoot downs of Western reconnaissance balloons, such as Bulgaria. Between January and September 1956, Major Todor Trifonov from the 19th IAP, flying the radar-equipped MiG-17PF, managed to bring down as many as four balloons, and three more were downed by other pilots from the same fighter regiment, home-based at Graf Ignatievo Airfield near Plovdiv.

The MiG-17s also saw a fair share of operational use in many Cold War encounters around the Soviet borders. The first encounter, noted above, was reported on 8 May 1954 over the Kola Peninsula, when a pair of MiG-17s from the 1619th IAP of the Northern Fleet was scrambled to intercept two B-47s; they were later reinforced by another MiG-17 from the 614th IAP. The MiG-17 attacks, however, proved fruitless, and both B-47s escaped undamaged. The next encounter was more successful—this time it happened in the Far East, where two MiG-17s from the 23rd IAP intercepted a USN P2V Neptune over the sea near the coastal city of Nakhodka. After the attack the USN aircraft fell in the sea near Ostrovnoy Island. The third such incident, on 27 June 1958, took place in Armenia, where a pair of MiG-17Ps intercepted a USAF C-118 transport flying in Soviet airspace, forcing it to land. On landing, however, the C-118 crashed and was consumed by fire; the crew members escaped just in time, and they were rescued. The next MiG-17 victim of the Cold War was also gunned down in Armenia, near the capital city of Yerevan, where a C-130 four-engine transport was intercepted and attacked on 2 September 1958. It was brought down on Soviet territory and all nineteen people on board perished. On 7 November the same year, an RB-47 was attacked over the Baltic Sea by a pair of MiG-17s. It was damaged but it managed to get to neutral waters; its fate is unknown. In 1960 the Soviet MiG-17s reported another success, bringing down an RB-47 just inside Soviet airspace over the Barents Sea. Three years later, in mid-1963, a pair of MiG-17Ps from the 156th IAP, an IA PVO regiment based at Mari-2 Airfield in Turkmenistan, were used to good effect in shooting down an Iranian Air Commander 560 piston-engined aircraft that entered into Soviet airspace from Iran; its remains fell on Iranian territory next to the border. In 1964, MiG-17Ps of the same regiment engaged an Iranian aircraft performing a geographic survey mission; it entered Soviet airspace and was intercepted again by a pair of MiG-17Ps, which forced it to land at an auxiliary airfield near Mari.

The Chinese People's Liberation Army Air Force's (PLAAF) copies of the MiG-17—designated J-5—saw use in anger against the Republic of China (RoC) air force in 1957. The biggest clash dated back from 24 September, when thirty J-5s encountered a large formation of RoC F-86Fs. The RoC fighters had the edge because they were armed with the new AIM-9B heat-seeking air-to-air missiles, and four J-5s hit by missiles were claimed, plus six more killed with guns. In 1957 PLAAF J-5s managed to bring down a USAF RB-57 reconnaissance aircraft.

The MiG-17 gained a fair share of its combat fame in the air-to-air role in the war in Vietnam between 1965 and 1973. There, the type was mainly used for intercepting USAF, USN and USMC fighter-bombers and attacking aircraft flying at subsonic speeds at low and medium level. In addition, the Vietnamese People's Air Force (VPAF) MiG-17s were also employed in air combats with their escorting supersonic fighters such as the F-8 and F-4, which, however, were forced to fly at subsonic speed—they thus lacked any manoeuvrability advantage when engaging the small and agile 'Fresco'.

The VPAF had two fighter regiments equipped with the type during the war, a mixture of Russian- and Polish-made MiG-17Fs, in addition to a number of Chinese-built J-5s. The MiG-17s operated in own airspace, in proximity to the guarded objects, and when attacking strike aircraft at low level, the Vietnamese pilots used hit-and-run tactics. The first victory in the Vietnamese skies was reported on 3 May 1965 against an USN A-4 Skyhawk attack aircraft, while the first loss in air combat was sustained on 17 June 1965. The last MiG-17 victory in Vietnam was achieved on 11 July 1972 against a USN F-4J fighter from VF-103 (operating off USS *Saratoga*). The most successful VPAF ace flying the MiG-17, Nguyen Van Bay, amassed seven kills under his belt, and three others ended the war with six kills. According to the official VPAF data, cited by the prominent war researcher Dr Istvan Toperscezer, the MiG-17 kills in the period from 1965 to 1972 numbered seventy-three. The MiG-17F force was also involved in one anti-shipping mission, despatching two aircraft to attack two USN destroyers— USS *Higbee* and USS *Oklahoma City*, shelling Vietnamese coastal targets—with 250-kg (550-lb) bombs. The former sustained serious damages from a direct hit (in the rear deck area), while the later sustained only minor damages.

## MiG-19—The Soviet Union's First Supersonic Fighter

Widely considered to be a breakthrough design by the time of its first flight and entry into service, the supersonic-capable MiG-19 was then plagued by a very problematic service; this resulted in numerous follow-on developments caused by a plethora of technological and political factors. Its air combat performance was highly appraised by the front-line at the time it was inducted in service in the Soviet Union with both VVS and IA PVO in the mid-1950s. However, the type never had the chance of becoming a long-lasting success and dominating the fighter fleet in either VVS or IA PVO service, as only about 2,000 examples were built in the Soviet Union compared to more than 10,000 MiG-21s. As a result, in the early 1960s the hastily-designed, produced and fielded-in-service MiG-19 was rapidly superseded in the air-superiority role by the famous and much more successful MiG-21, while in the air defence role it was superseded by the Su-15—even before overcoming its numerous teething troubles.

The basic idea behind the twin-engine MiG-19 dates back to 30 July 1950, when the Soviet leader Iosif Vissarionovich Stalin ordered the development of a new jet fighter type with a considerably better range performance that that of the just-introduced-into-VVS service MiG-15 and its improved derivative, MiG-17.

The development programme undertaken at the OKB-155 resulted in the building of a family of prototypes used to test the new fighter's powerplant (SM-1) and the host of new aerodynamic features (SM-2), the latter taking to the air for the first time on 24 May 1952. The MiG-19's first prototype that introduced the full set of new features was known as the SM-9/1; it made its maiden flight on 5 January 1953 in the capable hands of Mikoyan OKB's test pilot Grigoriy Sedov. During the initial series of test flights it already demonstrated a top speed of 1,400 km/h (755 kt), equating to Mach 1.33. The SM-9 completed its factory testing on 12 September that year, and on 30 September the prototype was submitted to the NII VVS to commence its state testing and evaluation effort. The conclusion report from the effort noted that the speed performance demonstrated by the SM-9/1 was much better than that of the MiG-17F—the top speed at 10,000 m (32,800 feet) proved to be 380 km/h (205 kt) faster, while the practical ceiling was higher by 900 m (2,952 feet). The report, approved by the VVS Commander-in-Chief (C-in-C), Aviation Marshal P. Zhigarev, recommend commissioning the SM-9/1 in service and assigning it the in-service MiG-19 designation. The order for launching the type into serial production was issued even before completion of the state testing effort—the relevant Soviet Council of Ministers decree was dated 17 February 1954. It called for launching the MiG-19 in production at two plants simultaneously—at Gorky (GAZ-21) and Novosibirsk (GAZ-153). The Ministry of Aviation Industry was obliged to produce as many as fifty aircraft and 100 engines by using the chief designer's work drawings—instead of series-production drawings. The Ministry of Defence was obliged to accept these aircraft.

In this way the MiG-19 gained the distinction of being the first supersonic Soviet fighter that entered mass squadron service with the Soviet and allied air

Aircraft SM-9/1 was the MiG-19 prototype featuring all the design novelties combined in a single airframe; it took to the air for the first time on 5 January 1953, flown by Grigoriy Sedov. Not long afterwards, it demonstrated a top speed of 1,400 km/h (755 kt). (*Mikoyan & Gurevich OKB*)

The first production MiG-19s rolled off the line at the Gorky-based GAZ-21 factory in March 1955. (*Mikoyan & Gurevich OKB*)

arms. The first production examples (NATO reporting name 'Farmer-A') rolled off the line at the Gorky-based GAZ-21 factory in March 1955; this was only twenty-five months after the SM-9's first flight.

The improved MiG-19S version (NATO 'Farmer-C') was designed in a crash programme aimed at addressing most of the handling problems demonstrated by the initial-production variant. The main design change was the introduction of an all-movable tailplane (all-movable horizontal stabiliser), used for the first time in the Soviet Union in an effort to achieve a better supersonic controllability. This design novelty was tested for the first time on the SM-9/2 and SM-9/3 prototypes, the former taking to the air for the first time on 16 September 1954, while the latter—armed with three 30-mm NR-30 cannons instead of the 23-mm NR-23s on the previous prototypes—followed suit on 27 November that year. By May 1955 Mikoyan OKB and NII VVS pilots amassed a total of fifty-eight flights on the improved prototypes, and their reports noted the excellent performance—including an impressive rate of climb of 180 m/s (35,424 fpm). The maximum speed achieved in vertical dive from 9,300 m (30,504 feet) equated to Mach 1.462.

In addition to the all-moving tailplane, the SM-9/2 and SM-9/3 featured interceptors (interlinked with the ailerons) installed onto the lower wing surface for better high-speed controllability in the roll axis, as well as irreversible boosters for deflecting the tailplane and the ailerons. The SM-9/2 was also armed with three NR-23 23-mm cannons and had a provision for two rocket packs. The ARU-2A was the main novelty in the control system—it was a device purposely designed for controlling the all-moving tailplane deflection by using two gearing ratios and also to adjust the stick forces, depending on speed and altitude. At high speed (where the control surfaces are highly effective), the stick push or pull caused less tailplane deflection than identical stick movements at low speed (when the control surfaces are less effective), and subsequently the aircraft demonstrated almost the same handling behaviour at supersonic and subsonic speed regimens of flight. The ARU-2A allowed the full use of the manoeuvrability performance of the new fighter, with the maximum permissible G-loads at altitude above 10,000 m (32,800 feet); in supersonic flight this was reported to have increased some 1.8 times compared to the same aircraft without the ARU-2A system.

The MiG-19S (using the SM-9/3 design as a pattern aircraft) had already superseded the MiG-19 at the production line in Gorky during August 1955, and the type became available for export to friendly states in the following year. The MiG-19S was the most numerous 'Farmer' variant, accounting for around 70 per cent of the total production—equating to about 1,400 examples. The total number of MiG-19s built in the Soviet Union amounted to 2,069 examples; 1,303

The improved MiG-19S gunfighter featured an all-movable horizontal stabiliser (the first in the Soviet Union) in order to get a better supersonic controllability. This is the SM-9/3T prototype, used to test the R-3S (K-13) heat-seeking air-to-air missiles. (*Mikoyan & Gurevich OKB*)

of them were produced at the GAZ-21 in Gorky and 766 more were rolled out at the GAZ-153 in Novosibirsk. As many as 105 MiG-19s were produced under licence in Czechoslovakia, wearing the local designation S-105—these rolled off the line at Aero factory in Vodochody, near Prague, between 1958 and 1961.

## Supersonic Design for the First Time

In its general design layout, the MiG-19 broke little new ground aerodynamically and structurally as it resembled the earlier Mikoyan OKB jet fighters. The air-defence-optimised fighter MiG-19 had a longer fuselage and larger, thin, high-aspect-ratio, sharply-swept wing, with a 55° sweep-back and 4° 30′ anhedral. The root thickness/chord ratio was 8.74 per cent, decreasing to 8 per cent at the tip.

One large fence was installed onto the upper side of each wing, and the horizontal tail surfaces were mounted in the base of the fin—instead on the top, as it had been in the MiG-17's design layout. The entire trailing edge inboard of the wing fence was occupied by single-piece Fowler flaps, while outboard of the wing fence was a half-span tabbed aileron. The airframe was cleared for +6-G manoeuvring. The MiG-19 was the first Soviet fighter to introduce a brake parachute from the outset, used for shortening the landing roll.

The MiG-19 also pioneered an all-new powerplant required for achieving supersonic performance—it was represented by a pair of RD-9B (originally designated as the AM-9) axial-flow turbojets, densely packed side-by-side in the rear fuselage; each of these was rated at 25.50 kN (5,732 lb st. or 2.599 kgf) dry and 32.36 kN (7,275 lb st. or 3,288 kgf) with afterburning. This engine was a direct successor of the AM-5, the first wholly Soviet-designed jet engine, with a two-stage turbine connected to a nine-stage axial-flow compressor via a single tubular shaft. The afterburner had three stages of reheat and its design incorporated ten adjustable nozzle flaps.

Interestingly, OKB-155 designers were compelled to use two engines simply due to the unavailability in the Soviet Union of a suitable 63 kN-class (14,000 lb st. or 6,400 kgf) turbojet in the mid-1950s. The single pitot-type intake in the nose is said to have caused a fairly large number of engine problems—for instance, if one of the engines failed, the other one usually followed suit immediately due to the airflow disturbance inside the intake. Another major RD-9B problem was the unstable and notoriously protracted starting up sequence due to the unreliable automatic control system, which often tended to overheat the engine during the start, requiring reversion to manual control.

The MiG-19 had very much different systems compared to its subsonic predecessor MiG-17, and thus could be regarded as a fairly good achievement for the post-Second World War Soviet aircraft industry, which was traditionally set to produce pretty simple and short-lived low-technology designs at a high rate. Fully in line with this concept, the sophisticated MiG-19 featured relatively short maintenance cycles—its airframe time between overhauls (TBO) was only 400 to 500 flight hours (depending on the production batch), or five years, while the RD-9B turbojets were required to be removed for refurbishment after every 100 flight hours. The airframe total life, as originally set up for the MiG-19S and MiG-19P, was 1,400 flight hours, while that of the MiG-19PM was 1,500 hours, or twenty years—whichever was reached first.

Widely considered as a hard-to-maintain and rather fastidious-to-fly fighter when compared not only to its predecessor MiG-17 but also to its successor, MiG-21, the MiG-19 is claimed to have possessed a pretty high air combat capability (though often underused and underestimated) by the time it entered squadron service. This was especially true regarding the aircraft's impressive low-level climb and turning performance—these proved to be definitely better than those of its predecessor, the MiG-17, and even exceeded the performance of its nominated successor, the single-engine MiG-21F-13. Furthermore, the MiG-19 offered a stable and well-armed weapons platform, and in the hands of experienced pilots it might have been a formidable foe for any Western tactical fighter or bomber type of the mid–late 1950s. The overall combination of these

A look inside the MiG-19S's crammed cockpit, full of 'steam gauges' and various switches and buttons. (*Author's collection*)

capabilities made the MiG-19S the most important tactical fighter of the late 1950s. However, the dominance of Mikoyan's supersonic gunfighter lasted for a very short period; this extended for a mere five years, and the 'Farmer' never had the chance of becoming a long-lasting success story like the MiG-17 or the MiG-21. It was, however, successfully produced, fielded into front-line service in large numbers and exported well during its second incarnation in China in the 1960s, 1970s and 1980s, as its production run even exceeded that in the Soviet Union (even when excluding the Q/A-5 attack derivative with side intakes). Over 2,000 single-seat and 664 two-seat examples were manufactured in China until the early 1980s, and a significant number of these were exported to at least eleven countries, whereas the Soviet-built MiG-19 saw export to at least thirteen countries (including China itself).

When entered into service, both the MiG-19 and MiG-19S—the former armed with three NR-23 23-mm cannons and the latter with three much more powerful NR-30 30-mm cannons—were considered as valuable air-superiority and air defence assets. The 'Farmer' was tailored for the then-modern reactive scrambles to climb rapidly to medium and high altitudes and towards potential hostile intruders—either NATO tactical fighters or medium/strategic bombers carrying nuclear weapons. The MiG-19S gunfighter climbed to 10,000 m (32,800 feet) in 1.8 minutes in full afterburner and 2.3 minutes at military power. The time taken to intercept a transonic target flying at 14,000 m (45,920 feet) was twenty-eight to thirty minutes from brake release, provided that the target had been detected by the ground-based radars at 320 km (172 nm) from the interceptor's airfield. The MiG-19S' three NR-30 cannons, mounted in the nose and wingroots, had a rate of fire of 900 rpm and were provided with a total of 210 rounds. The NR-30 was considered as a highly effective weapon to be employed not only against aerial targets but also for strafing soft and semi-hardened ground targets such as armoured personnel carriers and light tanks. The trio of NR-30s—aimed through the ASP-5N gyro gun-sight, coupled with the SRD-1M radar rangefinder—provided between 3.7 and 4.9 seconds of non-stop firing time at an effective range of 2,000 m (6,560 feet) when fired at above 8,000 m (26,240 feet). The weight of the three-cannon full burst accounted for 45 kg (99 lb), and the theoretical probability of kill (PoK) against the B-47 or B-57 jet bombers—as quoted in the MiG-19's combat employment manual—was between 0.54 and 0.735. This was achieved by simultaneous firing with the three cannons of a 1.2 to 1.5 second burst from 1,100 m (3,608 feet) distance in tail-on attacks.

For use in the air defence role, the cannons were complemented (albeit rarely) by a pair of underwing ORO-57K eight-round pods firing ARS-57M 57-mm rockets. The rocket was considered to be an effective weapon, particularly when fired from close distances—in tail-on, shallow climb attacks against non-manoeuvring large bombers or transport aircraft. The rockets were also advertised as being effective enough against a wide variety of soft or area ground targets. The hardpoints occupied by the rocket packs and the drop tanks could also be used for the carriage of free-fall bombs, with the total bombload reaching 1,000 kg (2,204 lb);

this comprised four 250 kg (550 lb) bombs, although the standard warload was only two bombs.

The MiG-19S' ASP-5N-B3 gyro gun-sight was regarded as a very precise device, especially when fed with range information derived from the SRD-1M radar rangefinder (also known as gun-ranging radar), which was accurate to about 30 m (100 feet). The SRD-1M provided the pilot with accurate enough information for firings against fighters at distances of up to 1,400 m (4,592 feet), against medium-sized bombers—up to 1,900 m (6,232 feet), while against heavy bombers the maximum firing range was 2,400 m (7,872 feet). The MiG-19S was also equipped with a Sirena-2 radar-warning receiver (RWR) intended to issue warnings when the aircraft was under attack from enemy fighters, with their radars/radar rangefinders on in the rear quarter.

## MiG-19SV—Tailored Against High-Altitude Targets

The MiG-19SV (SM-9V) was a lightened version purposely designed for high-altitude intercepts—mainly against RB-57 and U-2 reconnaissance aircraft flying deep inside Soviet airspace. It boasted uprated engines and the principal weight reduction was achieved by the removal of the two wingroot cannons. The list of the other weight-reduction measures included a reduced number of rounds for the nose-mounted canon, as well as the deletion of the cockpit armour, brake chute and radar altimeter. A flap setting of 10° was introduced instead of the usual 15°, and this was also used to increase lift above 15,000 m (49,212 feet) and speeds below Mach 0.9; the flap setting was reduced to 8° on production aircraft for a further increase of lift at altitudes above 18,000 m (59,055 feet). The aircraft also had an expanded-capacity oxygen system for the pilot wearing the VKK-2A pressure suit, capable of ensuring his survival in the event of a high-altitude cockpit depressurisation, which could cause sudden decompression and be lethal.

Thanks to the complex array of weight-reduction measures, airframe improvements and the use of up-rated engines, the MiG-19SV's service ceiling increased by 500 to 700 m (1,640–2,296 feet). The first MiG-19SV, converted from a production-standard aircraft at the plant in Gorky, took to the air for the first time in 1956 powered by the increased-thrust RD-9BF engines. These were fitted with fixed-area nozzles, and their military power (non-afterburning) rating was upped by increasing the turbine temperature and modifying the flame stabilisers. However, this method of boosting-up the thrust rating had a negative impact on the engine reliability, as its design proved somewhat overstressed. As a consequence, the hotter engines tended to cause overheating of fuselage structures and the systems, necessitating introduction of additional cooling intakes on the rear fuselage.

During the state testing effort, the MiG-19SV demonstrated a service ceiling of 18,500 m (60,695 feet), which was considerably lower than required by the VVS—20,000 m (65,616 feet)—while its top speed was 1,572 km/h (848 kt), equating to Mach 1.48 at 11,000 m (36,089 feet) altitude; in zoom climb the MiG-19SV reached a dynamic ceiling of 20,740 m (68,044 feet).

A small batch of MiG-19SVs was built for the IA PVO through conversion of production-standard MiG-19S airframes in a rushed programme; the service was designed to get some new capabilities to intercept high-flying aircraft.

## MiG-19P/PM—Radar-Equipped 'Farmers'

The MiG-19P ('P' for '*Perekhvatchik*', or 'interceptor') was a dedicated all-weather interceptor version designed for service in both the IA PVO and VVS forces. Its development was initiated by a Council of Ministers degree dated 15 August 1953. The project received the internal Mikoyan OKB designation SM-7, and the first prototype, SM-7/1, was built in July 1954. It took to the air for the first time, flown by Vladimir Nefyodov, on 28 August the same year.

The SM-7 had a redesigned and stretched front section to accommodate the twin-antennae RP-1 Izumrud-1 air-intercept radar, later replaced by the RP-5 Izumrud-2. Its search antenna was housed under a radome located in a lipped top of the intake, while the tracking antenna was installed inside the intake centre-body. The weight penalty imposed by the heavy air intercept radar necessitated the removal of the nose cannon. The lengthened nose housing the radar antennas and black boxes, combined with the large hood of the radar display in the cockpit, eventually caused a severe restriction of pilot's visibility—especially during the landing approach phase. A manoeuvring limitation of 3.5-G was imposed onto the MiG-19P (and later on to the MiG-19PM) in the beginning due to radar operability and reliability concerns—the chief reason was the rather primitive and unreliable vacuum tube technology available in the Soviet Union in the 1950s.

The heavier MiG-19P (NATO reporting name 'Farmer-B') had a reduced performance relative to the MiG-19S; its maximum level speed at high altitude fell from 1,452 km/h (783 kt) to 1,370 km/h (739 kt), and the service ceiling fell from 17,900 m (58,725 feet) to 17,250 m (56,580 feet).

The RP-5 air-intercept radar was a development of the RP-2 (tested before on the MiG-17P/PF) and had a scan capability of +/-60° in the horizontal plane (azimuth) and +26/-17° in the vertical plane (elevation), relative to the aircraft's centreline. Its detection range against medium-sized bomber targets was about 8 km (4.4 nm), and the tracking range did not exceed 4 km (2.2 nm). In service, the bulky RP-5 proved to be a notoriously unreliable piece of kit, thereby significantly affecting the MiG-19P's real-world all-weather operational capabilities. Some of the MiG-19P and -PM interceptors lacked the Sirena-2 RWR—especially those built for export.

The MiG-19P's three prototypes, designated as the SM-7/1, SM-7/2 and SM-7/3, were submitted to the NII VVS for their state flight-testing effort in the second half of 1954, but it proved to be a slow-going and protracted undertaking

The RP-5 Izumrud-2 radar system, equipping the MiG-19P and MiG-19PM all-weather interceptors (both of which are seen here), used a search antenna housed under a radome inside the lipped top of the intake, while the tracking antenna was installed in the intake centre-body. (*Author's collection*)

due to various design shortcomings popping out, causing frequent interruptions of the tests for introducing the necessary modifications.

The state test effort was completed in the second half of 1955, but the type was launched in production earlier that year, designated as the MiG-19P, destined for delivery to the PVO's fighter regiments. The production standard-machines were outfitted with a longer nose section, featuring a more streamlined intake centre-body radome and a relocated nose undercarriage unit; they also lacked the fuselage gun, while the pitot boom was relocated to the starboard wing and the gun camera was moved to the starboard. The initial-production aircraft were equipped with the RP-2, but later on the MiG-19P received the improved RP-5 Izumrud radar. The modified canopy was provided with an alcohol de-icing system, and the heavier MiG-19P used smaller, 540-litre external fuel tanks, providing a maximum range of 1,520 km (820 nm).

In addition to the two NR-30 cannons, the MiG-19P was also capable of using two ORO-57 rocket packs suspended under the wings, each containing eight 57-mm rockets that were usable against both air and ground targets.

In the mid-1960s the entire fleet of MiG-19P 'gunfighter-interceptors' was made missile-capable for engagements in visual meteorological conditions through an upgrade that enabled the carriage of two APU-26 launch rails for the R-3S (NATO AA-2A 'Atoll') air-to-air missiles, with the associated wiring

A MiG-19PM pilot wearing a GSh-3 protective helmet, posing in front of his mount. All 'Farmer' drives tended to note that the aircraft sported excellent low-level turning and climbing abilities. (*Author's collection*)

The MiG-19PM lacked guns and had no provisions for rocket pods, its armament comprising only four RS-2US beam-riding air-to-air missiles; these were only suitable for use against non-manoeuvring targets. (*Author's collection*)

and control boxes installed inside the airframe. The R-3S was, in fact, a slightly improved, reverse-engineered copy of the AIM-9B Sidewinder heat-seeking AAM boasting an effective range at low level of between 0.5 and 2 km (0.27–1.1 nm), extending at high level up to 9 km (5nm). The missile was tested for the first time on the SM-9/3T prototype, converted from a production-standard MiG-19S, with the APU-26 rails fitted at the hardpoints previously used for suspension of the external fuel tanks. The R-3S tests were carried out in February and March 1959, proving that its firings had no adverse effects on the aircraft's airframe, powerplant, systems or handling performance.

The R-3S's capability turned the MiG-19S into the PVO's best-armed interceptor of its time—with a weapons suite comprising a pair of NR-30 cannons, a pair of ORO-57K 57-mm rocket pods and a pair of R-3S AAMs. The last MiG-19P-equipped squadrons continued to serve with the IA PVO forces until 1979.

The MiG-19PM was the missile-armed interceptor version (NATO 'Farmer-E'). Its first prototype, dubbed the 'SM-7/2M' (in fact, it was a missile-armed SM-7/1 prototype), made its first flight in the new configuration in January 1956. The airframe of the MiG-19PM was different than that of the MiG-19P—the list of the new features included four APU-4 missile pylons under the wings, a longer fin fillet and a rudder fitted with a trim tab. Additionally, the MiG-19PM lacked guns and had no provisions for rocket pods, its armament comprising only four RS-2US (NATO code AA-1 'Alkali') beam-riding air-to-air missiles (AAMs).

The missile-armed 'Farmer-E' featured the RP-5-U radar (a slightly improved RP-5 derivative)—used to provide search, acquisition and automatic tracking of air targets to achieve the solution for a missile pursuit attack. The RS-2US missile had an effective range of between 2 and 5 km (1.4 and 2.8 nm) at low altitude, extending to 6.5 km (3.6 nm) at high altitude. Its launch weight was 85 kg (185 lb)—the warhead weighing 13 kg (28.6 lb)—and the maximum speed was only 1,650 km/h (891 kt). The first-generation RS-2US was extremely sensitive to the illuminating radar beam shape and the movements of the launch platform. The missile required uninterrupted target tracking by the MiG-19PM's radar until hitting its target, and it is said to have been prone to jamming—that is why the RS-2US proved effective only against non-manoeuvring bombers and transport aircraft. The RS-2US had a fairly low hit rate, necessitating the attack of all important targets with the entire on-board salvo (two or even four missiles). The lack of cannons is said to have considerably limited the MiG-19PM's usefulness, and the missile-carrying 'Fighter-E' was known as being entirely unsuitable for use against turning fighters.

The MiG-19PM was considerably heavier than the MiG-19S, and consequently it had a notably reduced performance, with a maximum speed of only 1,250 km/h (674kt). It was launched in production in early 1957 at the GAZ-153 factory in Novosibirsk.

## MiG-19S, MiG-19P and MiG-19PM Specification

|  | MiG-19S | MiG-19P | MiG-19PM |
|---|---|---|---|
| Dimensions: |  |  |  |
| Wing span | 9.00 m | 9.00 m | 9.00 m |
| Length | 12.54 m | 13.02 m | 13.02 m |
| Height | 3.88 m | 3.89 m | 3.89 m |
| Wing area: | 25.00 m$^2$ | 25.00 m$^2$ | 25.00 m$^2$ |
| Weights: |  |  |  |
| Empty | 5,172 kg | 5,468 kg | 5,673 kg |
| Normal take-off | 7,560 kg | 7,348 kg | 7,730 kg |
| Maximum take-off | 8,832 kg | 8,738 kg | 8,464 kg |
| Fuel | 1,800 kg | 1,800 kg | 1,800 kg |
| Performance: |  |  |  |
| - Max level speed at sea level | 1,150 km/h | 1,150 km/h | 1,150 km/h |
| - Max level speed at high level | 1,452 km/h | 1,370 km/h | 1,250 km/h |
| - Maximum Mach number | 1.6 | n/a | n/a |
| - Landing speed | 235 km/h | 235 km/h | 235 km/h |
| - Max rate of climb | 115 m/s | n/a | n/a |
| - Time to 10,000 m | 3 min | n/a | n/a |
| - Practical ceiling | 17,900 m | 17,250 m | 16,700 m |
| - Take-off distance | 515 m | 515 m | 515 m |
| - Landing distance | 610 m | 610 m | 610 m |
| - Range on internal fuel | 1,390 km | 1,474 km | 1,290 km |
| - Range on internal and external fuel | 2,200 km | 2,318 km | 1,520 km |
| - Max G-load | 8 | 8 | 8 |

## MiG-19—Experimental Variants

The SM-30 was among the most interesting experimental aircraft built on the MiG-19 base. It was designed as the principal component of a zero-length launch (ZELL) system, launched from a trailer. A Council of Ministers decree issued in 1955 ordered the development of the system at the Mikoyan OKB. The design work was completed in a prompt manner and the system was submitted for factory testing in autumn 1965.

The SM-30 system was intended for use in areas lacking normal airfields, such as extreme northern areas or those in close proximity to the battlefield, in case of a large-scale war. The aircraft used the MiG-19S airframe, which received some local strengthening in selected areas in order to sustain the sharply increased loads during the launch. The ventral fin was deleted as it was replaced by twin outward-canted fins to allow the aircraft belly to rest firmly on the launcher rail, elevated at 15°. The start was provided by a PRD-22 solid-fuel rocket booster, installed under the rear part of the belly, operating for 2.5 seconds.

The launch sequence included starting-up of the main engines, setting them up initially at full military power, and then engaging the afterburners—simultaneously igniting the rocket booster. The total thrust generated by the engines and the rocket booster sheared off the bolts attaching the aircraft on the launch rail and it lifted off. Launch acceleration was 4.5-G. Three seconds after separation from the launch rail a special mechanism unlocked the aircraft flight controls, while at the same time the rocket motor was jettisoned away, with the fighter finally set free to fly in normal mode. Upon completing the mission, the aircraft had to land at a suitable airstrip.

The SM-30/1, the first prototype of the system, was tested for the first time in remote-control mode, while the first flight in manned mode took place on 13 April 1957. As many as six launches were made in manned mode with partial combat loads, whereas the seventh one involved a fully loaded aircraft carrying two external fuel tanks—each holding 760 litres—and two ORO-57 pods for firing 57-mm S-5 rockets.

SM-30/1 was then handed over to the NII VVS to undergo its state testing effort; soon afterwards it was joined by SM-30/2, which featured a series of design refinements and a further strengthened fuselage. All the test pilots who flew the SM-30 reported that the take-off was easy, but they noted that they did not like the fact that the controls locked for the first three seconds after launch. The SM-30 retained the overall performance of its predecessor, MiG-19S, with a top speed of 1,450 km/h (782 kt), a practical ceiling of 17,500 m (57,414 feet) and a time to 10,000 (32,800 feet) of 1.1 minutes, while the range with external fuel tanks reached 2,200 km (1,186 nm).

In the event, the SM-30 was not developed into a fully-fledged ZELL combat aircraft as the programme was subject to termination before reaching production stage. The chief reason for this was the mass introduction of the high-altitude SAM systems to the PVO, such as the SA-75 (NATO reporting name SA-2 'Guideline'), which were deemed more suitable and flexible for providing air defence in remote areas lacking developed airfield networks.

The SM-50 and SM-51 were experimental aircraft equipped with rocket boosters in an effort to increase their practical ceiling. The high-altitude operating capability was needed to counter the overflights of US reconnaissance aircraft that maintained flight levels otherwise unreachable for the Soviet jet-powered fighters in service with the IA PVO regiments in the mid-1950s. The first prototype, SM-50, was based on a production-standard MiG-19S, powered by increased-thrust RD-9BM engines rated at 31.38 kN (7,098 lb st. or 3,199 kgf) each, while the self-contained rocket motor was housed with its fuel and oxidiser in a streamlined, jettison-able pod under the belly. The rear section of the pod contained the motor and the lower fuselage behind its nozzle was protected by a heat shield. Due to the lack of space, two fuel cells in the rear fuselage were removed, and their place was occupied by the heat shield and the rocket motor.

The SM-50 was equipped with the Kaskad intercept guidance system, and the airframe was stripped of all surplus equipment and systems in order to offset the

The SM-30 was a MiG-19S derivative designed as the principal component of a zero-length launch (ZELL) intercept system, launched from a trailer. (*Mikoyan & Gurevich OKB*)

weight increase caused by the rocket motor pod installation—the list of deleted items included the fuselage cannon, the rocket pack wing pylons, the forward airbrake panel, the signal flare launcher, the radio altimeter, the radar-warning receiver, the fire extinguishers and the brake parachute. In order to provide safe high-altitude conditions for the pilot, the SM-50 had an increased-capacity oxygen system and the pilot wore a pressure suit and helmet, which were useful in the event of a rapid decompression at stratospheric altitude.

The liquid-fuel rocket motor (also known as a rocket booster) had enough fuel to operate for 3.5–4 minutes at its minimum thrust rating of 12.75 kN (2,865 lb st. or 1,300 kgf) and two minutes at its maximum rating of 29.42 kN (6,613 lb st. or 2,299 kgf). The main difficulty for the pilot in managing the combined powerplant was choosing the right moment to ignite the rocket motor and following an optimum intercept trajectory in order to get into a good firing position for the 30-mm cannons—i.e. right behind the target and slightly below. It proved virtually impossible for the pilot to do this during the first attack due to the short rocket motor operation. The optimum trajectory was possible only in the event of using the Kaskad ground guidance datalink, but it was never tested.

The SM-50 began its factory flight tests in the beginning of December 1957, and continued the effort until the end of the year. The new combined powerplant demonstrated a notable improvement in the climb, speed and altitude performance as the SM-50 was able to climb out to 20,000 m (65,600 feet) in eight minutes,

The SM-50 prototype was based on a production-standard MiG-19S airframe, powered by increased-thrust RD-9BM engines and also featuring a self-contained rocket motor, with its fuel and oxidiser housed in a streamlined, jettisonable pod installed under the belly. (*Mikoyan & Gurevich OKB*)

had a sustained ceiling of 23,000 m (75,440 feet) and was able to get to 24,500 m (80,360 feet) in zoom climb. The state testing was carried out in early 1958, during which the SM-50 demonstrated a top altitude of 24,000 m (78,720 feet) and a maximum speed that equated to Mach 1.6, while the time for climbing out from ground level to its practical ceiling was 9.5–11 minutes. However, the SM-50 programme was considered too complex a development to get to operational condition, and it was shelved as a consequence.

The SM-51 experimental aircraft used the fuselage of the MiG-19P interceptor, boasting a rocket motor in an underbelly pack similar to that of the SM-50, and received the designation MiG-19PU. Powered by a U-19D self-contained rocket motor (requiring only attachment points and electrical supply from the carrier aircraft) and two up-rated RD-9BF turbojets, it was also subject to the same weight-reduction effort as that for the SM-50, including removal of the seat armour protection. It showed promising results during its testing, such as a top speed of 1,930 km/h (1,041 kt) and a practical ceiling of 24,000 m (78,720 feet). In the event, just like the SM-50, the SM-51 programme was shelved in favour of the mass deployment of new SAM systems capable of engaging high-altitude targets.

The SM-12 was the first Mikoyan OKB fighter fitted with a two-position intake shock cone, used for improving engine performance in supersonic flight by reducing the pressure losses inside the inlet duct. The rounded intake also proved to create excessive drag in supersonic flight and had to be replaced by a sharp-lipped design. The SM-12 prototype received a new lengthened nose section with a shape similar to that of the MiG-21F, and introduced an intake centre body housing a SRD-5A radar rangefinder. The aircraft was powered by RD-9BF up-rated engines, with maximum thrust rating at full afterburner of 32.34 kN (7,273 lb st. or 3,300 kgf), while the planned RD-9BF-2, further up-rated to 40.21 kN (9,038 lb st. or 4,098 kgf) was to be installed as soon as declared ready for use. The nose cannon was deleted. A batch of four SM-12s was produced at the GAZ-21 at Gorky and the first flight tests used two of these aircraft—SM-12/1 and SM-12/3. The SM-12/3 was powered by the R3-26 experimental turbojets, derived from the RD-9BF, each rated at 32.27 kN (7,251 lb st. or 3,290 kgf), had an improved control system and was equipped with an SIV-52 IR sight. During its flight tests, the SM-12/3 demonstrated a top speed of 1,930 km/h (1,040 kt) while the time to climb to the practical ceiling of 18,000 m (59,040 feet) was 3.2 minutes. The speed increase by 500 km/h (270 kt) was attributed chiefly to the much more efficient new intake design.

The SM-12/1 and SM-12/3 underwent their state testing effort between 17 March and 27 August 1957, amassing in excess of 150 sorties. The SM-12/3 showed even better performance, with a top speed of 1,926 km/h (1,039 kt) at 12,500 m (41,000 feet), but the practical ceiling proved to be lower than that of its predecessors—17,500 m (57,400 feet). In the event, this new MiG-19 version was judged to possess good combat capabilities that were broadly equal to that of the MiG-21 prototypes undergoing testing at the same time. The NII VVS recommended that it should be cleared for production after testing a production-standard SM-12 and removing all deficiencies. In the event, the SM-12 programme was shelved in favour of the much more modern and faster single-engine MiG-21F. The third and fourth SM-12 prototypes, SM-12/3 and SM-12/4, were retained in airworthy condition for use in various development programmes at the OKB-155. Both of these received pylons and black boxes to fire the new R-3S heat-seeking

A MiG-19S derivative, the SM-12 introduced a two-position intake shock cone, which was used for improving engine performance in supersonic flight by reducing the pressure losses inside the more efficient inlet duct. (*Mikoyan & Gurevich OKB*)

air-to-air missile and the SRD-5M Kvant radar rangefinder to be used in the testing programmes for the R-3S and the SRD-5M, wearing the new designations SM-12/3T and SM-12/4T.

The SM-12PM and SM-12PMU were prototypes for all-weather interceptors, powered by the R3-26 turbojets and featuring an increased-diameter intake with sharp lips and a conical centre-body, housing a larger radar antenna of the new TsD-30 radar. The cannons were deleted and both prototypes were armed with two K-5 beam-riding air-to-air missiles only. They also had a split titanium tailcone for nozzle adjustment, acting as convergent-divergent nozzle segments. The SM-12PM underwent its factory flight tests in 1958 and in the following year it continued with the state testing effort at the NII VVS. The prototype demonstrated a maximum speed of 1,720 km/h (928 kt), equating to Mach 1.60, while the practical ceiling was 17,400 m (57,072 feet) and the time to 10,000 m (32,800 feet) was four minutes; the range on internal fuel was 1,700 km (917 nm).

The SM-12PMU was a prototype similar to the SM-12PM but featuring a U-19U liquid-fuel rocket booster motor rated at 29.40 kN (6,612 lb st. or 3,000 kgf), intended for providing a better speed and altitude performance. The rocket motor was the same as that used on the SM-51; it was also armed with the improved RS-2US air-to-air missile and equipped with the Vozdukh-1 ground guidance datalink for remotely controlled intercepts. The SM-12PMU was flown for the first time in 1958, and during its state testing stage demonstrated a maximum speed that was the same as that of the SM-12PM—1,720 km/h (928 kt)—while the maximum altitude reached in zoom climb was 24,000 m (78,720 feet). Both the SM-12PM and SM-12PMU programmes remained in prototype form because of the availability of an all-weather version of the more modern MiG-21, equipped with the same radar and armed with the same missiles but boasting better speed and altitude performance.

## MiG-19—Operational Career

The MiG-19 saw little action in Soviet service, as it was used at the height of the Cold War to counter the threat posed by NATO high-altitude reconnaissance aircraft. Its first use in anger dated back to countering CIA Lockheed U-2 overflights between 1957 and 1960, albeit without any success. Furthermore, a MiG-19P was shot down by friendly fire (a missile launched from an SA-75 SAM system) near the city of Sverdlovsk on 1 April 1960; this occurred during the well-publicised shooting down of the U-2 piloted by Francis Gary Powers, who was performing a CIA spying mission to photograph a number of Soviet strategic objects. In fact, the first kill credited to the MiG-19 happened a month later—it was a USAF 55th SRW RB-47 ELINT aircraft gunned down in the Arkhangelsk area on 1 June 1960. The 'Farmer' claiming the kill belonged to the 171st Guards IAP and was flown by Capt. V. Polyakov. A month later, another RB-47 had the same fate. The Soviet air defence forces claimed at least two more US aircraft that entered the Soviet airspace as well as a number of US-launched reconnaissance aerostats, shot down by the IV PVO MiG-19Ps.

In Chinese service, the MiG-19's locally-built derivative J-6 saw much more use in anger, as its first kill was reported in 1964; it was a Nationalist China F-101 Voodoo, followed by another one of the same type in the following year. The J-6 frequently operated against Taiwanese aircraft, and Chinese sources claimed that as many as fifteen enemy aircraft were shot down between 1964 and 1971 in their own or disputed airspace. The J-6s of the Vietnamese Air Force saw much use during the Vietnam War, and the aircraft was employed in its originally intended role—against US jet fighter-bombers and enemy attack aircraft at low and medium level, mostly utilising the hit-and-run tactics. They claimed seven kills in 1972. Interestingly, China used its J-6 during the short but bloody invasion of Vietnam in 1979, whereas Vietnam put its J-6 in operational use during the occupation of Cambodia.

The MiG-19 proved once again that it was a capable dogfighter during the Israeli-Arab Wars, flown in the colours of both the Egyptian and Syrian air arms, which had on strength 100 and forty aircraft respectively in the mid-1960s. In addition, Egypt used its newly-delivered MiG-19s in the ground-attack role during its military operations in Northern Yemen in the early 1960s. It is interesting to note that Egypt and then Iraq opted in the 1970s and 1980s to acquire additional numbers of Chinese-made F-6s—apparently at a very low price—and these were almost immediately used in the ground-attack role during the war between Iran and Iraq. In the later stages of the war, however, the Iraqi F-6s were re-directed to the advanced training role. The most prominent F-6 operator, however, was Pakistan, which successfully used its aircraft during the 1971 war with India—seven Indian aircraft were claimed shot down and one damaged, whereas Pakistani losses amounted to four F-6s; some 650 air defence and 184 ground-attack sorties were flown during the course of the war. Other countries known to have used their MiG-19 in the ground-attack role are Cuba and Afghanistan. The former despatched its MiG-19s in action against opposition and CIA-run vessels (and on one occasion, in error, an East German tanker), while the later used its MiG-19s against the *Mujahedeen* opposition in the early 1980s. The MiG-19s and J-6s were also used in anger in a number of smaller and lesser-known local conflicts, and against the internal opposition forces in Africa.

# 2

# Second Generation

## MiG-21—The Soviet Union's Greatest Lightweight Fighter

The MiG-21 (NATO reporting name 'Fishbed') is known as one of the greatest aircraft of all time, firmly holding the title of the most widely used and widely operated post-war jet fighter, serving with no fewer than fifty air arms worldwide. Originally designed as a faster and lighter successor to the twin-engine/swept-wing MiG-19 (NATO reporting name 'Farmer'), it pioneered the concept of a single-engine lightweight and speedy tactical jet with a bare minimum of armament and mission avionics, designed to intercept subsonic and supersonic high-altitude bombers, fighter-bombers and cruise missiles in clear-weather conditions, performing tail-on attacks only.

Two alternative wing shapes were evaluated during the project definition phase for the new fighter. The first of these was a tapered swept wing with a swept angle of 55°—the same as that of the MiG-19—while the second one called for a delta-wing planform with a leading-edge angle of 57° and conventional horizontal tail surfaces. The swept-wing prototype was designated as the Ye-2, while the delta-wing prototype was initially designated as the Ye-1, but later as the Ye-4.

Design work on the delta-wing prototype commenced in September 1953, immediately after the receipt of the relevant authorisation from the Soviet government and the Ministry of Aviation Industry, which requested that the aircraft be submitted for its state flight-testing effort in March 1955. The Ye-1 was required to accelerate up to 1,750 km/h (944 kt), with the engine in afterburner mode for five minutes at 10,000 m (32,800 feet); this altitude was to be climbed to in 1.2 minutes and the practical ceiling was set at 18,000 to 19,000 m (59,000 to 62,300 feet). Range requirements called for 1,800 and 2,700km (971 and 1,456 nm) at 15,000 m (49,200 feet), with and without afterburning respectively, while take-off run and landing-roll requirements called for 400 and 700 m (1,312 and 2,296 feet) respectively. The new fighter was also required to be capable of operating from unpaved runways and performing a constant-speed vertical dive with airbrakes deployed. Its armament suite was set to include three NR-30 30-mm cannons aimed via an optical sight coupled to a radar rangefinder, installed inside the nose cone, plus sixteen air-to-air rockets in two packs suspended on

*The Ye-2 was a swept-wing, single-engine prototype sporting a wing similar to that of the MiG-19, with a swept angle of 55°. (Mikoyan & Gurevich OKB)*

underwing pylons. This rather unimpressive armament was originally optimised for use against non-manoeuvring bombers, allowing for a single attack run only. Furthermore, during the fighter's design phase, in order to save weight, one of the three NR-30 cannons was deleted.

The prototype with the delta-wing planform was designated as the Ye-4, and its general design concept was presented for the first time in April 1954. As was the case with its swept-wing predecessors, the Ye-2 and Ye-50, the delta-wing prototype began its flight-test programme powered by the interim RD-9B engine in an effort to speed up the definition of the flight characteristics and explore the specific features of the then-all-new and still-unknown planform. The Ye-4 featured a perfect-triangle planform with pointed wingtips, tracked slotted flaps and one-piece ailerons. The circular nose air inlet had sharp lips and in the beginning the armament comprised three NR-30 30-mm cannons, although in the course of the flight-testing effort one of these was removed. Other design alterations undertaken during the Ye-4's flight-test phase included the addition of fences on the wing—initially, two full-chord fences on the underside, but later replaced by three shallower fences added across the upper surfaces. The delta-wing prototype also received the more powerful RD-9I engine. The first Ye-4 made its maiden flight on 16 June 1955 with Grigoriy Sedov at the controls, and its so-called factory testing phase, undertaken by the OKB-155, continued until 20 September 1956. The performance demonstrated during these early tests, comprising of 107 flights, proved to be rather disappointing, however, with a maximum speed of only 1,290 km/h (696 kt) and a service ceiling of 16,400 m (53,800 feet). Nevertheless, the Ye-4 proved to be a valuable flying test-bed that was used to study the specific features of the then little-known delta-wing planform.

The Ye-5 (NATO reporting name 'Fishbed-A') was a follow-on delta-wing prototype based on the Ye-4's fuselage and wings, powered by the long-awaited

R-11-300 turbojet rated at between 51.99 kN (11,660 lb st. or 5,300 kgf) and 53.96 kN (12,100 lb st. or 5,500 kgf) with afterburning, while the internal fuel capacity was 1,570 litres. In the beginning, the Ye-5 received three aerodynamic fences across the upper surface of each wing, which improved stability in the roll axis at a high angle of attack (AoA) and also increased the roll rate.

Design work on the new prototype at the OKB-155 began after the Soviet Council of Ministers decree dated 28 March 1956, which required a delta-wing fighter capable of reaching 1,700–1,750 km/h (917 and 944 kt) maximum speed and 17,000–18,000 m (55,800–59,000 feet) practical ceiling.

The first example of the Ye-5, designated as the Ye-5/1, was flown for the first time on 9 January 1956 by the OKB-155 test pilot Vladimir Nefyodov; one year later the aircraft received its in-service designation—MiG-21. The more powerful engine—combined with a host of fuselage refinements to improve the aerodynamic performance (mainly for reducing drag)—resulted in a considerably increased maximum level speed, which even exceeded the designer's expectations. On 19 May 1956 the Ye-5/1 demonstrated 1,960 km/h (1,057 kt) maximum speed, corresponding to Mach 1.85 at 11,000 m (36,100 feet).

The first pre-production batch of five MiG-21s was built at the GAZ-31 in Tbilisi in 1957, and five more examples were reported to be in their final assembly phase by the year's end. The improved series-production version, known as the MiG-21F 'Fishbed-B', was designed following a Soviet government decree dated 24 July 1958 and the corresponding follow-on order issued by State Committee of Aviation Technique (the successor of the Ministry of Aircraft Industry) on 3 August 1958. The new lightweight fighter derivative of the Ye-5 was to be powered by an uprated R-11F-300 turbojet (which is why the letter 'F' in the designation was used to distinguish this specific version).

The improved engine, rated at 56.40 kN (12,650 lb st. or 5,749 kgf) with afterburner and 38.06 kN (8,536 lb st. or 3,880 kgf) at military power, retained the compressor, combustion chamber and turbine of its predecessor almost unchanged, and added an improved afterburner section. The boosted afterburning rating promised a significant increase in performance, reflected in the performance requirements decreed for the MiG-21F, which needed to deliver 2,300 to 2,500 km/h (1,241 to 1,348 kt) maximum level speed and 21,000 to 22,000 m (68,900 to 72,200 feet) practical ceiling. Ferry flight range requirements called for 1,400 km (755 nm) range on internal fuel and up to 2,000 km (1,079 nm) with an external tank, while flight endurance was to be no less than 1.5 and 2.25 hours respectively. The time for climbing to 20,000 m (65,600 feet) was required to be eight to ten minutes; the take-off run length was to be up to 450 m (1,476 feet) and the landing roll 450 to 850 m (1,476 to 2,788 feet).

The new version of the lightweight fighter, converted from existing MiG-21 airframes built at the GAZ-31, was set for submission for its state testing effort with the NII VVS in the fourth quarter of 1959. As many as twelve series-production examples were ordered for manufacture in Tbilisi, replacing the original MiG-21 version, already launched there, on the assembly line.

The first MiG-21F prototype, designated as the Ye-6/1, initially utilised the delta-wing design, inherited unchanged from the Ye-5 and featuring three aerodynamic fences. The second prototype, the Ye-6/2, introduced a modified wing design configuration, retaining only one fence—the change improving the aerodynamic performance and simplifying the manufacturing process. The pointed wingtips were also removed, the wing chord was increased at the rear and the aileron span was reduced. In the event, this successful wing design was retained almost unchanged on the follow-on MiG-21 versions built until the mid-1980s.

Other modifications introduced into the Ye-6/2's design included a new circular air intake with sharp lips and a two-shock conical centre-body that slid axially in three positions: fully retraced at speeds up to Mach 1.5; intermediate for speeds from Mach 1.5 up to Mach 1.9; and fully forward for speeds exceeding Mach 1.9.

The Ye-6 also received a brake parachute housed in a bay on the port underside of the rear fuselage, and introduced a dorsal fin that joined the dorsal spine and the fin; the Ye-5's two ventral strakes were replaced by a single ventral fin on the Ye-6.

The avionics suite included the ASP-5N gyro lead-computing gunsight, intended to be offered together with an optional SIV-52 forward-looking infrared system for night visual intercepts, ARK-54I automated direction finder (ADF), MRP-56I marker beacon receiver and the KKO-3 oxygen equipment set.

The Ye-6/1 made its maiden flight on 20 May 1958 with Vladimir Nefyodov at the controls, and during initial tests it demonstrated a very promising performance, reaching 2,181 km/h (1,176 kt)—corresponding to Mach 2.05 at 12,050 m (39,500 feet). This prototype, however, had a very short life, as it was lost on its seventh flight on 28 May 1958, crashing onto the runway at Zhukovskiy during an engine flame-out landing approach. The engine failed while the aircraft was flying at 18,000 m (59,000 feet), and the pilot attempted an emergency landing by gliding the unpowered fighter back to the airfield. Nefyodov lost both lateral and longitudinal control at the very end of the unpowered approach, just before touching down with the hydraulic system inoperative, while the back-up electrically driven pump (used to maintain pressure in the hydraulic system) proved ineffective. Following an ill-fated attempt at a flared landing, the Ye-6/1's undercarriage hit the runway hard, turned upside down and caught fire. The pilot was quickly recovered from the wreckage, but died from severe burns and other injuries in the hospital later the same day.

The second and third MiG-21F prototypes, designated as the Ye-6/2 and Ye-6/3 respectively, continued the type's flight-test efforts and introduced a plethora of design refinements and improvements, such as a larger air intake cone, duplicated hydraulic system, additional fuel cells housed in the wings and the fuselage, auxiliary air inlets on both sides of the nose to prevent compressor stalls, an all-new SK ejection seat with blast protection for the pilot during bail-out, an increased-area fin and a larger ventral fin. The Ye-6/2, featuring a cleaner wing and two cannons with 30 rounds each, took to the air for the first time on 15 September 1958, while the Ye-6/3 followed suit in December 1958.

The sixty-one factory test flights demonstrated that the MiG-21F's practical ceiling was 20,100 m (65,920 feet) whilst maintaining Mach 1.1, and the maximum level speed in afterburner was Mach 2, equal to 2,100 km/h (1,133 kt) at 15,000 m (49,200 feet). There were expectations that further design refinements would allow the maximum speed to be increased, initially to 2,300 km/h (1,241 kt) and then to 2,500 km/h (1,348 kt). The time for climbing from sea level to the practical ceiling of 20,700 m (67,900 feet) in afterburner was eight minutes and twenty-five seconds, while at military power rating the practical ceiling was 14,500 m (47,560 feet).

In April 1959 the MiG-21F was submitted for state testing with the NII VVS, and the effort was completed in November the same year. The final flight-test report noted that the MiG-21F had demonstrated good handling characteristics and stable engine operation; the aircraft was also judged as being simple to control, with its design features allowing operations from Class II airfields (i.e. capable of being operated from unpaved runways).

Serial production of the MiG-21F was launched at the GAZ-21 in Gorky in 1959. The first example took to the air on 8 February 1960, and the production run in 1960 and 1961 accounted for seventy-nine examples. After that the MiG-21F was replaced by the follow-on 'Fishbed' derivative, boasting a guided missile armament and a plethora of small airframe improvements. In addition, the GAZ-31 added ten more MiG-21Fs, all of which were rolled out in 1959.

## MiG-21F-13—A Basic Clear-Weather-Only Fighter

The MiG-21F-13 (NATO reporting name 'Fishbed-C') was a basic, lightweight, daytime, short-range, clear-weather interceptor and tactical fighter. Its principal armament of two R-3S heat-seeking air-to-air missiles was carried on two APU-28 rail launchers (later replaced by the APU-13) attached to BD3-58-21 adaptor beams, one under each wing. The R-3S (K-13) air-to-air missile was a reverse-engineered copy of the US AIM-9B Sidewinder heat-seeking AAM, with an effective range at low altitude of 0.5–2 km (0.3–1.1 nm), which at high altitude extended to 9 km (4.9 nm).

The MiG-21F-13 also retained one internal NR-30 30-mm cannon on the starboard side, with only 30 rounds. The alternative ordnance in the fighter-interceptor role consisted of two UB-16-57UM rocket packs, each loaded with 16 S-5M 57-mm rockets instead of the R-3S missiles. For ground attacks the MiG-21F-13 was cleared to carry two UB-16-57UM rocket packs, each containing 16 S-5 57-mm rockets, two ARS-212 or ARS-240 (S-24) missiles or 250/500-kg high-drag, high-explosive bombs.

The MiG-21F-13 was designed from the outset to intercept transonic/supersonic bombers and fighter-bombers at altitudes up to 20,000 m (65,600 feet). Interceptions were limited to rear-hemisphere attacks only, using the rudimentary SRD-5M Kvant radar rangefinder with a range of 0.5–7 km (0.27–3.8 nm).

The Ye-6/3 prototype pictured here is armed with two 16-round 57-mm rocket packs and fitted with a 490-litre underfuselage drop tank. (*Mikoyan & Gurevich OKB*)

The Ye-6/2 prototype received APU-13 launchers for the R-3S heat-seeking missile on the wingtips; these necessitated wing modification, with outer sections leading edge sweep reduced to 48°. However, in the event this proved to be an ill-suited configuration.
(*Mikoyan & Gurevich OKB*)

The Kvant provided information on missile launch and gun-firing distances; the associated ASP-5ND gun-sight was used to assist accurate aiming during gun- and rocket-firing runs on both air and ground targets.

The first MiG-21F-13s for the frontline units of the Soviet Air Force's Frontal Aviation arm were taken on strength in 1961. During series production, a plethora of improvements were adopted; these included additional internal fuel tanks in the fuselage and the wings as well as an increased-chord fin. Total internal fuel capacity reached 2,550 litres; in addition, the centreline pylon was modified to carry one 490-litre drop tank. The MiG-21F-13 also received a limited reconnaissance capability thanks to the installation of an AFA-39 camera in a bay aft of the nose wheel.

In December 1959 a decree for discontinuing MiG-21F production at GAZ-21 was issued by the State Committee for Aviation Technique as the aircraft was to be quickly superseded by the MiG-21F-13 'Fishbed-C'. As many as 532 MiG-21F-13s for the Soviet Air Force rolled off the line at the GAZ-21 in Gorky, but this model remained in production for less than three years before being replaced in 1962 by the MiG-21PF radar-equipped interceptor. MiG-21F-13 production for export customers began in 1962 at the GAZ-30 *Znamya Truda* in Moscow; later, its licence production was handed over to the Aero Vodochody Company in Czechoslovakia, where the type received the local designation S-106. In early 1961 the MiG-21F-13 production licence was also provided to the People's Republic of China (PRC), with two pattern aircraft and a number of component knocked-down kits delivered there. In the event, the Chinese licence-production programme proved to be a failure due to China's abrupt split with the Soviet Union.

## MiG-21P/PF—A Radar-Equipped All-Weather Interceptor

The MiG-21PF 'Fishbed-D' was the first production-standard all-weather interceptor derivative of the family, equipped with the RP-21 Sapfir-21 air-intercept radar and sporting a series of fuselage and powerplant improvements. It was originally designed as an integral component of the MiG-21P-13 air-intercept system ('P' stood for '*Perekhvatchik*', or 'Interceptor', and the '13' stood for the K-13 missile system with the R-3S heat-seeking missile), launched by a Council of Ministers decree dated 24 July 1958 and the subsequent State Committee for Aviation Technique order dated 2 August 1958. Both of these government authorisations called for development of an all-weather (i.e. capable of operating at night and in adverse weather) interceptor based on the MiG-21F design. The fighter and its weapons-control system were required to be submitted for state flight testing in the fourth quarter of 1959.

The design work was completed in early 1959 and the new 'Fishbed' derivative, bearing the prototype designation Ye-7, introduced a vastly modified fuselage with a longer nose and a much larger intake centrebody accommodating the large radar antenna, which measured 500 mm in diameter, while at the same time retaining

The MiG-21F-13 was a basic daytime short-range interceptor and tactical fighter with a principal armament of two K-13 (R-3S) heat-seeking missiles carried on the underwing pylons and a single NR-30 30-mm cannon with only thirty rounds. (*Author's collection*)

A close-up scan of the MiG-21F-13's crammed cockpit. (*Author's collection*)

the airflow rates of 65 kg/s (143 lb/s) required for the normal engine operation. The dielectric nose cone was installed with an axis pointing 3° downwards relative to the aircraft's longitudinal axis in order to provide maximum pressure recovery at high AoA. The large parabolic antenna was housed inside the notably enlarged nose cone that moved continuously forward and aft to provide optimum engine working conditions at different speeds and altitudes.

This new 'Fishbed' derivative dispensed with the cannon armament altogether in a bid to compensate for the weight increase caused by the radar installation while retaining the performance as per the technical specification. The bulky and heavy ASP-5ND gun-sight was replaced by the much simpler and lighter PKI-1 collimator gun-sight to enable bomb and napalm tank drops, as well as rocket firings and visual aiming of the R-3S missiles when the radar was switched off. Other avionics components included the RSIU-5V UHV coms radio, ARK-54I ADF, MRP-56I marker radio receiver, KSI-1 heading system, SRO-2M IFF transponder and the SOD-57M air traffic control transponder. The interceptor prototype also received the KAP-1 single-axis autopilot, providing authority in the roll axis.

The interceptor was designed from the outset to cope with fast, high-altitude targets; in addition to the radar it boasted dedicated guidance equipment, represented by the Lasour-1 integrated on-board automated system, to receive intercept information, datalinked from the ground control station of the Vozdukh-1 intercept operations control system. Intercept commands (such as heading, altitude and speed), generated by the system's analogue computer, were received by the Lasour-1 equipment and displayed on the respective instruments using bugs, while lamps were used to issue discrete commands such as afterburner on, zoom climb, and switching on the radar when entering into the terminal attack phase.

In 1958 and 1959 the OKB-155 rolled out three interceptor prototypes; the first of these, designated as the Ye-7/1, took to the air for the first time on 10 August 1959 in the capable hands of Mikoyan test pilot Piotr Ostapenko. It had ballast in place of the radar and was almost fully dedicated to testing the new inlet design.

The MiG-21P was the first all-weather interceptor derivative of the 'Fishbed' family, equipped with the RP-21 air-intercept radar housed within a movable cone in a widened nose section. (*Mikoyan & Gurevich OKB*)

The Ye-7/1, however, had a very short life, as it was lost on 28 November 1959—only three months after its first flight—due to a supersonic stall and a subsequent spin, caused by the loss of directional stability at the maximum permissible Mach number. However, the test pilot, Igor Kravtsov, managed to eject safely. The reason for the loss of directional stability was attributed to the notably altered nose fuselage shape with a large centrebody, the changes having created an additional lateral force at high speed, which, in turn, caused the aircraft to yaw excessively and depart from controlled flight.

The second prototype, the Ye-7/2—flown for the first time on 1 February 1960, also by OKB-155's Piotr Ostapenko—featured a set of aerodynamic modifications introduced in a bid to improve directional stability, such as an increased-area fin, a ventral fin and the KAP-1 autopilot. The Ye-7/2 was dedicated to testing the TsD-30 radar set but also proved to be a short-lived aircraft; just like the Ye-7/1, it was lost while undergoing its factory flight-test programme. While on its 72nd flight on 5 June 1960, the Ye-7/2 suffered engine failure and was destroyed in the subsequent attempt to land with a flamed-out engine. It touched down 200 m (656 feet) before the end of the runway, and test pilot Igor Kravtsov was lucky to survive the crash.

The Ye-7/3, powered by the uprated R-11F2-300 engine with a maximum afterburner rating of 60.03 kN (13,464 lb st. or 6,120 kgf), took to the air for the first time in May 1960 and was more successful than its two predecessors. In addition to the uprated engine, it introduced a modified tail-end as well as a broader fin (which became the production standard by 1961), while the brake parachute housing was relocated to the base of the fin, just above the jet pipe. The nose wheel steering mechanism was deleted and the aircraft received a dorsal fuel tank at the rear of the cockpit. The Ye-7/3 was used for initial testing of the TsD-30 radar and the Lasour datalink, operating against real-world airborne targets. It also tested an improved version of the radar, designated as the TsD-30T, which could provide target range information necessary for calculating the R-3S missile's launch envelope (i.e. maximum and minimum permissible launch ranges at different closure speeds and altitudes).

The Ye-7/4, also powered by the uprated R-11F2-300, dispensed with the nose wheel steering, incorporated an enlarged fin and introduced the new KAP-2 autopilot, operating in the roll axis only, while the pitot boom was relocated to a new position atop the inlet and on the centreline. The Ye-7/4 also added a new dorsal tank and wing tanks, housing an additional 380 litres of jet fuel. It was also earmarked to test the further-improved TsD-30TP radar and commenced its factory flight tests in August 1960. Together with the Ye-7/3, which was modified in the same fashion, it was used for completing the Ye-7's state testing programme, which finally began on 30 June 1961. The state testing effort, undertaken by the NII VVS together with the OKB-155, was completed in late July 1961.

The maximum speed recorded by the Ye-7 was 2,175 km/h (1,173 kt) and the practical ceiling was 19,000 m (62,300 feet), while range proved to be 1,600 km (863 nm) with two R-3S missiles and internal fuel and 1,900 km (1,025 nm) with a centreline drop tank. Flight endurance in level flight at 19,000 m (62,300 feet), on internal fuel, was eight minutes, extending to twelve minutes when using a centreline drop tank. Maximum flight endurance at optimum speed and altitude with a drop tank reached 2.27 hours.

The radar-equipped interceptor initially received the new in-service designation MiG-21P, and its production was launched at the GAZ-21 following a State Committee for Aviation Technique decision dated March 1960; however, it was very soon superseded by the improved MiG-21PF version, featuring an additional 170-litre tank on the top of the fuselage, just behind the cockpit, as well as two 105-litre tanks in the wings. The first production-standard MiG-21PF fighter took to the air on 28 June 1961, and in December that year it received the improved TsD-30TP radar (designated as the RP-21 when installed on the series-production MiG-21PF).

Other modifications, incorporated in the first series-production fighters (designated as the MiG-21PF but bearing the internal OKB-155 designation Type 76), included a reduction in the volume of the dorsal tank by some 80 litres (due to the larger 'black boxes' of the new radar), provision for using the K-51 weapons system with the RS-2US (AA-1 *Alkali*) AAM, and introduction of the SRZO-2M IFF interrogator/transponder system.

In March 1962 the MiG-21PF received a further-improved subversion of the TsD-30TP radar, and was used to test-fire RS-2US missiles; the trials programme, completed in September 1962, proved that the beam-riding missile could be used as an all-weather weapon, replacing the R-3S in bad-weather intercepts. The

The MiG-21PF was a classic representative of the first-generation interceptors of the 'Fishbed' family—fast and light, armed with just two air-to-air missiles and capable of carrying air-to-ground ordinance of up to 1,000 lb (2,200 kg). (*Author's collection*)

fifteenth aircraft from the sixteenth production batch was the first to be equipped to fire the RS-2US.

As many as thirty MiG-21PFs were rolled out at the GAZ-21 in 1961, and sixty more followed suit in the first ten months of 1962. The MiG-21PF's sub-variants, destined for export customers, were produced at GAZ-30 in Moscow between 1964 and 1968.

The Ye-7SPS was another improved prototype of the radar-equipped interceptor featuring the new SPS blown flaps system (boundary layer blower), which provided a useful increase in lift during landing approach. The SPS was installed on a production-standard MiG-21PF that was then handed over to the OKB-155 for testing purposes. The new version was powered by the R-11F2S-300 engine, rated at 60.76 kN (13,640 lb st. or 6,194 kgf), which was modified to supply bleed air in the slot in front of the simple hinged flaps. The new interceptor version, designated as the Ye-7SPS, also introduced the RV-UV radar altimeter and an increased-area brake parachute, the latter housed inside a cylindrical fairing at the base of the rudder. The new brake parachute was cleared for deployment before touchdown to further shorten the aircraft's landing roll.

The modified MiG-21PF, featuring the SPS system, underwent its state testing with the NII VVS in the first half of 1962. The blown flaps bestowed a notable improvement in landing performance: in combination with the more effective cruciform brake parachute, this novelty enabled the landing roll to be shortened to 480 m (1,574 feet), while the landing speed decreased to 249 km/h (134 kt). A significant reduction in the take-off run was achieved by use of two SPRD-99 assisted take-off solid-fuel boosters, each developing 24.52 kN (5,500 lb st. or 1,323 kgf) of thrust for ten to seventeen seconds.

The improved interceptor derivative equipped with the SPS system was designated as the MiG-21PFS (Ye-7SPS, Type 94), and it entered series production at the GAZ-21 in 1962. During the production run the MiG-21PFS received a plethora of additional improvements such as a larger nose wheel and a more effective braking system, as well as a still-broader-chord tail fin, extending forward a further 450 mm to further improve directional stability at high speeds.

The MiG-21PFM 'Fishbed-F' combined the MiG-21PFS' basic design with the new KM-1 (SK-3) ejection seat, and this was the definitive configuration retained on all subsequent derivatives. The new version had a two-piece canopy with fixed windscreen and sideways-hinged (to starboard) main section instead of the MiG-21PF/PFS's single-piece canopy, which acted as a blast shield during ejection. The introduction of a considerably simpler and therefore more dependable ejection system was made due to reliability concerns regarding the complex SK-2 system, which had a large number of mechanisms and pyrotechnical cartridges in order to form a blast shield, separate the pilot from the seat at the appropriate moment and deploy the rescue parachute. The new KM-1 crew escape system enabled safe ejections at zero altitude and a minimum speed of 130 km/h (70 kt) during take-off run and landing roll. The new ejection seat was used for the first time on the Ye-7M, which entered production under the MiG-21PFM designation but still bore the internal designation Type 94. This new derivative also had its internal fuel capacity reduced by some 100 litres compared to that of the initial-production MiG-21PF. In the 1970s, a proportion of MiG-21PFMs had their R-11F2S-300 engines replaced by the more powerful R-13-300.

The Ye-7M was submitted for its state flight testing on 29 December 1962 and was used for trialling the new K-51 guided missile system with the RS-2US radar beam-riding missile. The new derivative successfully completed its state flight tests in 1964 and was recommended for entry into service with the Soviet Air Force.

The RS-2US (K-5) used by the MiG-21PF/PFS/PFM was a 1950s-vintage guided weapon originally designed for use with the RP-5 air-intercept radar of the MiG-19PM, and it was only effective against non-manoeuvring targets. The effective range at low altitude was 2.5–5km (1.3-2.7 nm), while at high altitude it extended to 6.5 km (3.5 nm).

The RP-21M radar equipping the MiG-21PFM used a single parabolic conical-scan antenna housed in the nose centrebody. It featured a 15-km (8.1-nm) detection range against a fighter-sized target and the tracking range was 10 km (5.4 nm), while against bombers these ranges increased to 20 km (10.8 nm) and 15 km (8.1 nm) respectively.

A pilot, wearing a GSh-3 protective helmet, posing in the MiG-21PFM's cockpit, dominated by a large, hooded radar display. (*Author's collection*)

## Second Generation

The MiG-21PF/PFS/PFM's time to intercept a target flying at 16,000 m (52,500 feet) was eight minutes from the initial take-off run. Owing to their weak armament of only two short-range AAMs, both the MiG-21PF and PFM variants were nicknamed the 'Peaceful Doves' in the Soviet Union and Warsaw Pact.

The MiG-21PF/PFS/PFM was produced at the GAZ-21 for the Soviet Air Force between 1961 and 1968.

## MiG-21PF/PFM's Export Versions

Derivatives of the MiG-21PF/PFM/FL for export were produced at the GAZ-30 between 1964 and 1968, with peak rates of thirty aircraft per month. The aircraft supplied to the Warsaw Pact countries and some other close allies of the Soviet Union featured an equipment/avionics configuration close to that of their Soviet counterparts, known as the A-variant of the respective 'Fishbed' derivative (i.e. Type 94A or MiG-21PFMA).

The derivative, sold to a number of developing countries, was designated as the MiG-21FL and featured a considerably more sanitised avionics suite; this primarily concerned the radar, designated as the R-1L (export version of the TsD-30T) but replaced in 1965 by the R-2L (export version of the TsD-30TP),

A selection of air-to-ground weapons cleared for use by all MiG-21 versions can be seen here in front of this MiG-21bis, including UB-16-57 and UB-32M rocket packs and OFAB-100-120 high-explosive/fragmentation bombs. (*Author's collection*)

which lacked some of the operational modes of the original radars used by the VVS and had somewhat reduced detection ranges.

Bearing the internal design bureau designation Type 77, the MiG-21FL, powered by the R-11F-300 engine, featured the MiG-21PF's SK ejection seat and upwards-opening canopy, plus the smaller (later enlarged) fin. It lacked the Lasour datalink as well as the RS-2US missile and S-24 rocket capability. The radar installed on Indian Air Force MiG-21FLs was the R-2L and the radio was an improved RSIU-5T version, but no Soviet-made IFF was supplied as this system was installed locally in India. The MiG-21FL was flight-tested for the first time in the second half of 1963 and the following year it underwent its state testing and evaluation with the NII VVS. This derivative was also produced under licence in India by Hindustan Aeronautics Limited (HAL) at Nasik, using component knocked-down kits supplied by the GAZ-21 in Gorky. A number of MiG-21FLs assembled at the plant in Gorky were operated by the Soviet Air Force and the type was exported to a number of developing states such as Algeria, Afghanistan, Egypt, Iraq and Syria.

## Ye-8—The Radically Reworked Interceptor

A Ye-8 programme was formally launched in 1960, following a Council of Ministers decree dated 30 May that tasked the OKB-155 with commencing the design of a radically improved MiG-21PF derivative to be equipped with the all-new S-23 weapons control system. Designated as the Ye-8, it was to include the all-new Sapfir-23 air-intercept radar and the K-23 AAM, featuring semi-active radar homing (SARH) and infrared (IR) homing derivatives.

Due to the large diameter of the radar antenna's reflecting dish, the Ye-8's nose was completely redesigned to house the radar, while the inlet was moved under the forward fuselage and fitted with sharp-edged lips swept-back at 55° in plan view. The aircraft's aerodynamics were also improved by adding foreplanes (also known as destabilisers), which spanned 2.6 m. Installed horizontally just below the fuselage centreline, these foreplanes freely pivoted in subsonic flight, remaining aligned with the local airflow, while in supersonic flight they locked into neutral position, causing a two-fold increase in lift at Mach 2 and moving the lift vector forward, resulting in improved supersonic manoeuvrability. At 15,000 m (49,200 feet) the new aerodynamic feature enabled a maximum sustained turn with 5-G load factor (in such conditions, the production-standard MiG-21 was limited to 2-G only). In order to improve the supersonic directional stability, the ventral fin was considerably enlarged; it hinged sideways when the undercarriage was in the extended position, and was stowed horizontally towards the right.

The radically reworked Ye-8 interceptor prototype had a large radar antenna, an underfuselage intake and a more powerful R-21-300 turbojet, but was plagued by powerplant troubles during the early stages of its flight-test programme. These problems eventually caused the loss of the first prototype, the Ye-8/1, on 11 September 1962.

The Ye-8 also introduced integral fuel tanks without flexible cells, occupying five compartments in the fuselage and four in the wings, with a total volume of 3,200 litres; there was also provision for carriage of a 600-litre centreline tank. The cockpit was set to introduce the then-new KM-1 ejection seat, with the canopy featuring a fixed forward section and a movable rear section hinged to starboard. The Ye-8 introduced a new engine, the R-21F-300, a vastly improved derivative of the R-11F-300 featuring an increased-diameter compressor inlet to supply greater airflow in order to achieve increased thrust ratings. It also sported a new afterburner design, with convergent/divergent multi-flap nozzle, which projected well beyond the rear of the fuselage. The new engine had a slightly increased weight and its rating at military and afterburner power settings increased to 46.20 kN (10,362 lb st. or 4,710 kgf) and 70.60 kN (15,873 lb st. or 7,197 kgf) respectively.

The Ye-8's wings, main undercarriage legs, fin and tailplanes were all inherited from the MiG-21PF unchanged, with the tailplanes mounted 135 mm lower. The radically reworked prototype introduced a new, taller and strengthened nose undercarriage leg that retracted to the rear, provided with a larger tyre and new brake unit; the main undercarriage legs were also equipped with larger tyres and boasted improved brakes.

The Ye-8/1 was the first prototype of the radically reworked 'Fishbed' version, lacking the radar and the KM-1 ejection seat (replaced by the MiG-21PF's original

The radically-reworked Ye-8 interceptor prototype featured a nose large enough to accommodate a large radar antenna, underfuselage variable-area intake and a more powerful R-21-300 turbojet. This advanced 'Fishbed' derivative was plagued by powerplant maturity troubles in the beginning of the flight test programme that eventually caused the loss of the first prototype—the Ye-8/1—on 11 September 1962. (*Mikoyan & Gurevich OKB*)

SK seat but without blast protection for the pilot). It made its maiden flight on 17 April 1962, with Georgiy Mosolov at the controls. The test effort, however, turned out to be a rather problematic undertaking after the fourth flight due to engine problems, such as frequent compressor stalls and flame-outs. During forty test flights the R-21F-300 experienced no fewer than eleven flame-outs (with subsequent mid-air restarts), and the engine had to be changed two times—the twenty-first and twenty-fifth flights. On 11 September 1962, during the fortieth flight and supersonic acceleration at 10,000 m (32,800 feet), flying straight and level at Mach 1.7, the Ye-8/1 experienced an uncontained engine failure at the sixth compressor stage. Parts of the disintegrated disc caused severe damage to the starboard wing, both hydraulic systems and the fuel tanks, resulting in an on-board fire and rapid roll with violent deceleration. The pilot managed to eject but barely survived, having sustained numerous injuries from the airflow after ejecting and receiving additional injures upon impact with the ground, which resulted in Mosolov spending more than a year in hospital.

The Ye-8/1's crash, however, combined with the unreliable and still immature engine, eventually put an end to this otherwise promising programme; in the mid-1960s, the Ye-8/2 was utilised as a ground test platform for a number of novel design features intended for the newly developed MiG-23 swing-wing fighter.

## MiG-21R—For Tactical Recce Missions

The MiG-21R (Type 94R; NATO codename 'Fishbed-H') was a MiG-21PFM derivative tailored for tactical reconnaissance, but which retained the full all-weather interceptor capability of its predecessor. Its development was launched following a Council of Ministers decree issued in October 1963. The airframe/powerplant design was originally based on that of the MiG-21PF with minimum alterations, with the reconnaissance-gathering mission equipment housed in a large underfuselage pod carried on the centreline pylon. The MiG-21R was able to carry underwing drop tanks, which further increased the fuel capacity and extended mission radius.

The MiG-21R became the first 'Fishbed' version to feature four underwing hardpoints instead of the two on all previous MiG-21s; all the hardpoints were plumbed for carriage of 490-litre drop tanks or two tanks and two R-3S AAMs for self-defence.

The first two prototypes of the reconnaissance 'Fishbed', which received the new prototype designation Ye-7R, were manufactured at the GAZ-21 at Gorky in cooperation with the OKB-155, using production-standard MiG-21PF airframes. The new derivative was initially designated as the MiG-21PR and the first prototype took to the air in 1964. The following year, both the MiG-21PRs were submitted for their state testing effort with the NII VVS. Series production at the GAZ-21 was launched in 1965, with the first production-standard aircraft, eventually designated as the MiG-21R, being rolled out in early 1966. The type stayed in production at the GAZ-21 in Gorky until 1971.

A wider 340-litre dorsal tank was introduced on the production-standard MiG-21R, an addition that marginally increased the aerodynamic drag while increasing the internal fuel capacity to 2,800 litres. The MiG-21R also sported the MiG-21PFM's broad fin and the cruciform brake parachute, the latter housed in a pod at the base of the fin. The aircraft was also the first member of the 'Fishbed' family to receive an AoA sensor on the starboard side of the fuselage, which was used to feed information to the newly introduced AP-155 three-axis full-authority autopilot and also to an AoA indicator in the cockpit. The PVD-5 pitot boom, located above the nose, was moved to the right for better pilot visibility. A back-up pitot probe was installed in front of the cockpit on the starboard side.

The MiG-21R was the first member of the 'Fishbed' family to introduce four underwing pylons, modified to carry additional fuel tanks for extending range when the aircraft was operating with the large underfuselage pod housing specialised recce equipment.

The MiG-21R retained the RP-21M air-intercept radar and added an SPO-3 radar-warning receiver (RWR) with 360-degree coverage in the horizontal plane. Its receiver antennas were housed in small cylindrical pods on the wingtips, while the 'black boxes' were housed in the underfuselage pod and the indicator was installed in the cockpit.

The MiG-21R retained the entire air-to-air and air-to-ground ordnance selection of its predecessor, the MiG-21PFM, except for the GP-9 gun-pod. However, the reconnaissance 'Fishbed' had a reduced manoeuvring limitation (from 8.5-G to 6-G) because of the four underwing drop tanks and the sensitive electronic

The MiG-21R was the first of the 'Fishbed' family to introduce four wing pylons, two of which were plumbed to carry additional fuel tanks for extending range when operating with the large underfuselage pod housing specialised recce equipment. (*Author's collection*)

equipment housed in the centreline pod. Furthermore, its maximum speed at high altitude was reduced to 1,700 km/h (917 kt), equating to Mach 1.6; this limitation was imposed in order to maintain enough directional stability when equipped with the underfuselage pod and underwing tanks, thus avoiding unwanted oscillations in yaw that resulted in poor-quality photographs. The MiG-21R was required to take off in afterburner mode only due to the heaver configuration than that of its fighter predecessors.

Another reconnaissance version, dubbed 'MiG-21RF', was purposely built for Egypt; it lacked the reconnaissance pod and featured an internally mounted pack of three A-39 cameras on a common frame located under the cockpit and covered by a sideways-hinged panel with camera windows.

There were no fewer than four non-interchangeable versions of the MiG-21R's reconnaissance pod, designated as the D-, N-, R- and T-series, designed for daylight photo-reconnaissance, night-time photo-reconnaissance, electronic intelligence (ELINT) and TV-reconnaissance respectively; in addition, there was a dedicated pod for radiation contamination monitoring.

The R-series of ELINT pods were equipped with the SRS-6 and the SRS-7M or the Romb-4A and Romb-4B ELINT systems and a single AFA-39 camera. Its sub-version, supplied in the late 1960s to Warsaw Pact allies, incorporated a single AFA-39 camera installed in a forward oblique position, and the Romb-4A and Romb-4B systems for intercepting radar and communication electronic emissions, recorded on MS-81 wire recorders, while the ASO-2I chaff/flare dispensers were used for self-defence.

The D-series of daylight photo-reconnaissance pods weighed some 285 kg and contained a battery of six AFA-39 cameras and one AShTShAFA-SM camera. One of the AFA-39 cameras was installed forward-facing in the pod's nose, while the other six were vertically mounted. The D-series pod also housed an SPO-3R RWR and two ASO-2I countermeasures dispensers, usually loaded with PRP-2I-15 chaff cartridges.

The N-series pods for night-time photo-reconnaissance were equipped with one UA-47 camera featuring two lenses, inclined at 160° left and right, and 152 FP-100 illumination flares. The camera was operated at between 300 and 1,000 m (980 and 3,300 feet) while the aircraft was flying at between 750 and 1,100 km/h (405 and 593 kt); the 80-mm-wide film was enough for shooting 152 pairs of frames.

The T-series of pods were equipped with the Bariy-M TV-reconnaissance system and were used only by the Soviet Air Force, operating in conjunction with a truck-mounted ground receiver station for real-time reception of the video image.

The MiG-21R's radiation monitoring pod was equipped with the Yeir-1M system for taking air samples and detecting particulate constituents when flying in contaminated atmospheres.

# The MiG-21S/SM/M/MF/SMT Family Line

The MiG-21S 'Fishbed-J' (Type 95) was another tactical fighter version; its development commenced in 1963 following the Council of Ministers decree issued in the first half of 1962, with a requirement for the development phase to be completed in a little more than three years. During that time, the Vympel Design Bureau was tasked with developing the vastly improved R-13M heat-seeking missile, derived from the R-3S. The first MiG-21S prototype entered flight testing in late 1963, and in 1964 it was joined by another example. One of these was based on the MiG-21PF, and the other on the MiG-21PFM; both were subsequently handed over to undergo state testing and evaluation with the NII VVS in 1964.

The MiG-21S featured the MiG-21R's basic airframe with four underwing pylons. The enlarged dorsal tank gave a straight line from the top of the canopy to the front of the fin, while the pitot boom above the air intake was offset to starboard. In order to be more capable of operating from unpaved runways, the new derivative also received a strengthened undercarriage.

The MiG-21S retained the R-11F2S-300 engine and the AP-155 autopilot with automatic levelling capability, engaged in the event of pilot disorientation. The most important new component incorporated into the MiG-21S's new mission suite was the vastly improved RP-22S Sapfir-21 air-intercept radar, which used a twist-Cassegrain antenna and featured the monopulse target direction-finding method. This method provided notably better resistance to both passive and active jamming compared to the conical scanning as used by the RP-21MA. The RP-22S was a more powerful system that boasted some 150 per cent greater target detection and tracking range compared to that of its predecessor. Bomber-type targets were typically detected at 30 km (16.2 nm) and tracked at 15 km (8 nm), while against fighter-sized targets the RP-22S's maximum detection range reached 18 km (9.7 nm) and its tracking range was up to 11 km (5.9 nm).

The new radar was introduced together with the new R-3R (AA-2B) semi-active radar homing (SARH) missile, which had a range of 0.8–7 km (0.5–3.8 nm); it was used for all-weather intercepts and was suitable against non-manoeuvrable targets. After launch, the fighter was free to manoeuvre within a limited space, keeping the target within the radar's gumball limits (30° up/down and left/right) as the R-3R homed onto the reflected signal from the target, continuously tracked by the RP-22S. The radar's range-finding function provided the pilot with information about the maximum and minimum missile launch ranges at different altitudes and closing speeds (displayed on a mechanical needle display on the ASP-PF-21 gun-sight). It also supplied range information for the employment of the GSh-23L 23-mm cannon against air targets and for firing both the gun and rockets against ground targets. The SPO-10 Sirena-2 RWR was also incorporated into the mission suite of some MiG-21S aircraft. It had antennas looking back from the top of the fin, and the cockpit indicator provided the rough direction of any radars 'painting' the aircraft, with 45° precision in azimuth.

The gun-sight was the new ASP-PF-21 lead-computing gyro unit, enabling more precise firing against air targets with the GSh-23L cannon (carried in the GP-9 conformal gun-pod) as well as generating better aiming information for using the cannon, rockets and bombs against ground and sea targets. The gunsight, however worked at manoeuvring with up to 2.75-G, thus limiting the ability to aim the GSh-23L cannon in a turning dogfight. The MiG-21S also incorporated an improved Lasour-M datalink for receiving steering commands from a ground-based intercept control station.

The armament of this vastly improved 'Fishbed' derivative was enhanced in 1974 with the addition of the R-13M (K-13M, NATO AA-2C) heat-seeking missile, an enhanced derivative of the R-3S missile that incorporated a more sensitive, nitrogen-cooled infrared seeker and boasted better agility and an extended range; it also bestowed some reduced manoeuvring limitations on the launch platform. The MiG-21S was the first 'Fishbed' derivative capable of carrying a total of four AAMs—typically a combination of two R-3Ss or two R-13Ms and two R-3Rs, or two missiles on the inner pylons and two 490-litre drop tanks on the outer pylons.

The new 'Fishbed' derivative entered series production at GAZ-21 in 1965, and the plant rolled out an initial batch of twenty-five aircraft in the same year, even before completion of the type's state flight testing programme. The MiG-21S remained in production until 1968.

The MiG-21S's export derivative (also known as 'Fishbed-J'), designated as the MiG-21M (Type 96), was the first member of the 'Fishbed' family to receive the 23-mm GSh-23L built-in cannon, housed in a neat ventral pack between frames eleven and sixteen and provided with 200 rounds in a belt around the fuselage. It also incorporated an improved ASP-PF gun-sight together with an SSh-45-1-100S gun-camera, but retained the MiG-21PFM's RP-21M downgraded conical-scan radar since the more advanced RP-22S system was not yet cleared for export. The MiG-21 underwent its state testing and evaluation programme with the NII VVS in 1968; that same year the first nine examples were rolled out at the GAZ-30 in Moscow. The type was in production until 1971, while in India its local assembly was carried out between 1973 and 1981 under the designation 'Type 88'.

The MiG-21SM (Type 95M; later re-designated Type 15) and its export derivative, MiG-21MF (Type 96F), inherited the MiG-21S' basic airframe and systems, but this was combined with the new R-13-300 turbojet. This engine was a follow-on development of the R-11-300-series with increased thrust, developing 65.33 kN (14,652 lb st. or 6,660 kgf) at maximum afterburner rating and 39.93 kN (8,973 lb st. or 4,070 kgf) at military power rating, and featured a fully variable afterburner.

The MiG-21SM and MF derivatives can be easily distinguished from the MiG-21M thanks to the presence of small deflector plates installed under the auxiliary engine inlet. The underwing pylons also received the BD3-6021D adaptor beams for carrying the MBD-2-67 multiple bomb racks and the UB-32 32-round rocket packs for firing 57-mm rockets. During the 1980s the weapons control system of many of the exported MiG-21MF aircraft was modified to give it the capability of firing the highly agile R-60 and R-60MK AAMs.

The MiG-21M was the export derivative of the MiG-21S, a heavier version equipped with four weapon pylons for carrying ordinance. It was also the first to introduce the ventral GSh-23L gun pack, with 200 rounds. (*Author's collection*)

The MiG-21SM/MF also received a rear-view periscope fitted on top of the canopy, and the new PVD-7 pitot boom with vanes for AoA and sideslip angle measurement, used to provide data for precise gun-aiming calculations. The mission suite also included the SPO-10 Sirena-3M RWR, SRO-2 IFF transponder, SRZO-2 interrogator-transponder, the SOD-57 ATC transponder and the Lasour-M datalink equipment. The MiG-21MFs built for use by the air arms of developing countries continued to be equipped with an export version of the old RP-21MA radar. Both the MiG-21SM and MiG-21MF featured a built-in GSh-23L gun-pack and an improved ASP-PFD-21 gun-sight. The internal fuel tanks had a total capacity of 2,650 litres.

The MiG-21SM made its maiden flight in 1967 and remained in production at the GAZ-21 in Gorky for the VVS between 1968 and 1974. Production of the MiG-21MF for export customers began at the GAZ-30 in Moscow in 1969 and continued until 1974; in the first year of manufacture as many as ninety-six examples were rolled out, all of which were promptly exported to Egypt. Between 1974 and 1976 the MiG-21MF was also produced at the GAZ-21 in Gorky, where a total of 231 of the type were built.

The MiG-21SMT 'Fishbed-K' (Type 50) was a derivative with a massively increased internal fuel capacity, reaching 3,100 litres, while the MiG-21MT was its export derivative with a sanitised mission suite. Both introduced very large dorsal spines that extended from the cockpit to halfway along the fin and then

The MiG-21MF was the export derivative of the MiG-21SM; it was widely exported in the early/mid-1970s and saw a lot of combat in local conflicts worldwide. (*Author's collection*)

tapered to join up with the parachute housing, and which provided maximum possible tankage. The three-cell dorsal conformal tank package accommodated 900 litres of fuel. In addition, the new R-13F-300 engine received an emergency afterburning mode, rated at 68.08 kN (15,268 lb st. or 6,940 kgf). Flying at low level at speeds close to Mach 1, this new, enhanced afterburning mode provided a thrust increase of some 18.59 kN (4,180 lb st. or 1,895 kgf) compared to the baseline R-13-300. The MiG-21SMT's take-off weight with full internal tanks and two missiles was 8,900 kg (19,616 lb), while the maximum take-off weight with air-to-ground ordnance under the wings and a centreline drop tank reached 10,100 kg (22,260 lb).

Directional stability issues were experienced at high AoA because the considerably enlarged spine distorted airflow around the fin, eventually prompting Mikoyan OKB designers to rework the spine tank; the volume was reduced to 600 litres, reducing in turn the total fuel capacity to 2,950 litres. The MiG-21SMTs already produced in 1971 by the GAZ-21 in Gorky retained the original big spine throughout their service life, while the examples assembled in 1972 and 1973 featured a smaller dorsal tank. In total, as many as 281 MiG-21SMTs rolled off the line between 1971 and 1973 (distributed over fifteen production series), including 116 big-spine examples.

Only fifteen export-standard MiG-21MTs (Type 96T) were produced at GAZ-30 in Moscow in 1971, but these big-spine 'Fishbed-Ks' were never exported and instead were used by the VVS—initially by one of the squadrons of the 234th

The big-spine MiG-21SMT was, in fact, plagued by some controllability and stability issues due to the huge dorsal tanks, disturbing the airflow around the fin at high AoA; however, it proved suitable for use in the low-level nuclear delivery role. (*Author's collection*)

Guards IAP (Fighter Regiment) at Kubinka, near Moscow, for air displays. Later, they were handed over to serve with one of the squadrons of a fighter-bomber regiment stationed in East Germany.

## MiG-21bis—The Last of the Line

The MiG-21bis (known also as Ye-7bis and Type 75) was the last mass-produced version of the 'Fishbed'. It was purposely redesigned in order to be better suited for high-G manoeuvring dogfights at low and medium levels, where previous versions had demonstrated a number of shortcomings and were hampered by a plethora of operating limitations in terms of maximum speed and G. This new-style air combat, experienced for the first time in the late 1960s in the Middle East, required from the 'Fishbed' more power, more fuel, better weapons (i.e. missiles able to be launched during high-G manoeuvres) and better sighting systems, as well as improved stability and controllability characteristics and reduced low-level speed restrictions. In the event, the MiG-21bis, developed as a successor to the MiG-21SMT, successfully integrated a 1960s-technology airframe with a 1970s analogue avionics suite and a further uprated powerplant, combined in the mid–late 1970s with modern, lightweight dogfight missiles.

The main feature of this last production derivative was the Tumanskiy R-25-300 engine, derived from the R-13F-300 and optimised for low-level operations. It was

The last of the long 'Fishbed' family line, the MiG-21bis sported a better equipment outfit, more power and strengthened airframe optimised for low-level air combat and ground-attack missions. (*Lubomir Slavov*)

rated at 40.20 kN (9,038 lb st. or 4,098 kgf) dry and 67.20 kN (15,653 lb st. or 6,850 kgf) at full afterburner, increasing to 97 kN (21,790 lb st. or 9,888 kgf) at the emergency afterburner setting—which was permitted for up to three minutes at low altitude. Pilots often noted, however, that the more powerful and heavier MiG-21bis was much less agile than the MiG-21F-13 and PF/PFM versions, claiming that the last 'Fishbed' derivative 'behaved like a bull' in the air, while flying the lighter MiG-21PF/PFM was 'like riding a stallion'.

The MiG-21bis' flight tests showed that the new and considerably more powerful engine significantly boosted the aircraft's low-level performance; for example, the climb rate was improved by some 1.6 times, and at Mach 0.9 at low level it reached some 235 m/s (46,250 fpm) with emergency afterburner on. At the same time, the MiG-21bis retained some of the chief design shortcomings of its predecessors, such as the limited operational radius and radar performance, lack of beyond-visual-range missiles, poor pilot visibility (particularly in his six o'clock), mediocre slow-speed handling characteristics and high pilot workload during all phases of flight.

Air-to-air ordnance initially consisted of the new R-13M and the R-55 heat-seeking missiles (the latter an RS-2US derivative equipped with a heat-seeking homing head), but in the mid-1970s the R-55 was rapidly superseded by the much better R-60, and eventually the R-60M in the early 1980s. Thanks to the APU-60-2 twin-round launcher rails suspended on the inner pair of underwing pylons, the MiG-21bis was capable of carrying up to six R-60/R-60Ms or a combination of two R-3Rs/R-13Ms and four R-60s. It also retained the GSh-23L internal gun-pack with 200 rounds, later increased to 250 rounds. The aircraft's fuel system was also improved by the introduction of an enlarged dorsal tank package (essentially the same as that installed on the late-production MiG-21SMTs), resulting in an internal fuel capacity of 2,880 litres.

The MiG-21bis airframe incorporated a number of structural changes and was stressed to 8.5-G in order to be better suited for low-level dogfighting. The nose inlet diameter was increased to 900 mm as opposed to the 870 mm of its predecessors, to satisfy the increased airflow requirements of the more powerful R-25-300 engine, but the nose centrebody remained unchanged.

The new 'Fishbed' version retained the RP-22S Sapfir-21S radar with a marginally improved look-down capability and received the improved ASP-PFD-21 gun-sight. The MiG-21bis derivative, built for developing countries, was equipped with the old-generation Almaz-23 conical-scan radar, an improved RP-21MA derivative, upgraded to guide R-3R SARH missiles.

A proportion of the production-standard MiG-21bis' also received the Polet-OI flight/navigation suite with the SAU-23ESN automatic flight-control system (incorporating an autopilot with three-axis stabilisation capability) and the RSBN-5S tactical navigation and instrument landing system—an important asset in bad-weather operations; particularly so given the MiG-21bis' limited fuel capacity.

There was also a MiG-21bis production-standard sub-variant without the Polet-OI and RSBN-5S systems, but featuring the Lasour-M (ARL-SM) datalink equipment for remotely controlled intercepts. Some aircraft also had an additional gun camera mounted in a non-standard 'scabbed-on' fairing in the nose, by the side of the PVD-18 pitot boom. There were no different Soviet Air Force designations for these MiG-21bis sub-variants, but the one equipped with the RSBN-5S was given the NATO codename 'Fishbed-N', while the Lasour-M-equipped machine was known as the 'Fishbed-L'.

Design of the MiG-21bis commenced at the Mikoyan OKB in 1971, and in February 1972 it entered service with the VVS; as many as thirty-five aircraft were delivered during the first production year. The MiG-21bis was built at the GAZ-21 at Gorky only; production continued until 1985, with as many as 2,030 examples rolling off the line or delivered in the form of component knocked-down kits for assembly by HAL Nasik in India.

Soviet Air Force examples bore the internal Mikoyan OKB designation Type 75, while the examples built for export to the Warsaw Pact member states were designated as the Type 75A, and those for the developing world were known as the Type 75B. The MiG-21bis was also manufactured under licence in India by HAL Nasik between 1979 and 1987—as many as 220 examples were assembled there, with a gradually increasing local content of airframe parts and systems; the internal design bureau designation of this specific MiG-21bis sub-variant was Type 75L. Initially, six completed MiG-21bis aircraft were delivered to India, followed by sixty-five kits for local assembly; finally, 220 more were built at HAL in Nasik using locally manufactured parts.

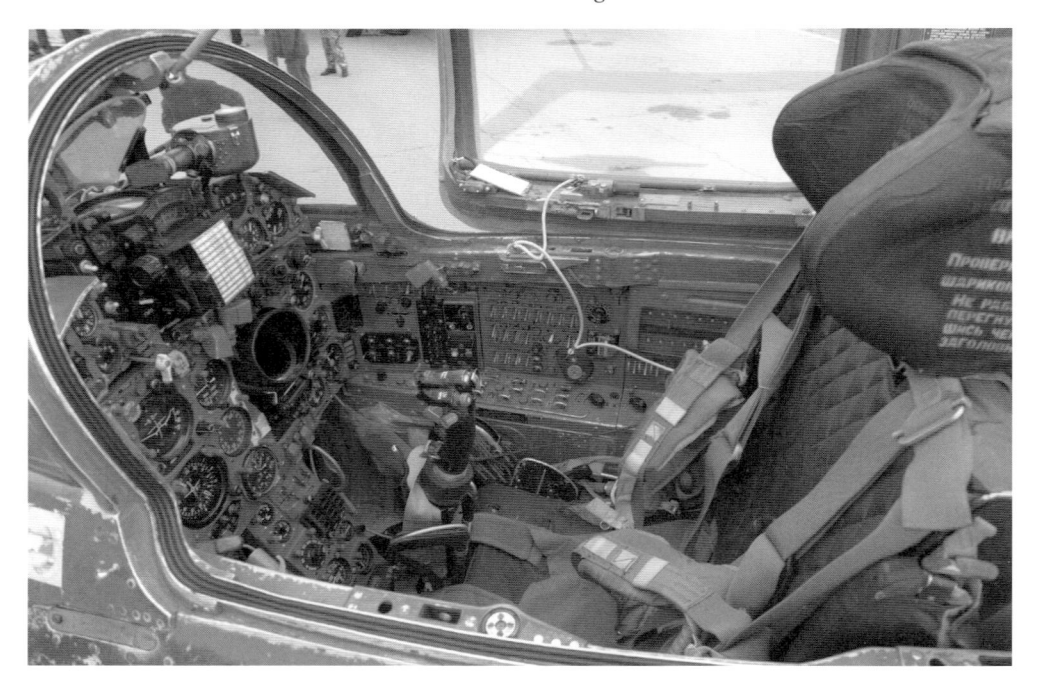

The MiG-21bis cockpit offers the 'Fishbed' driver a crammed and work-intensive environment during sorties typically lasting between thirty and forty minutes. (*Author's collection*)

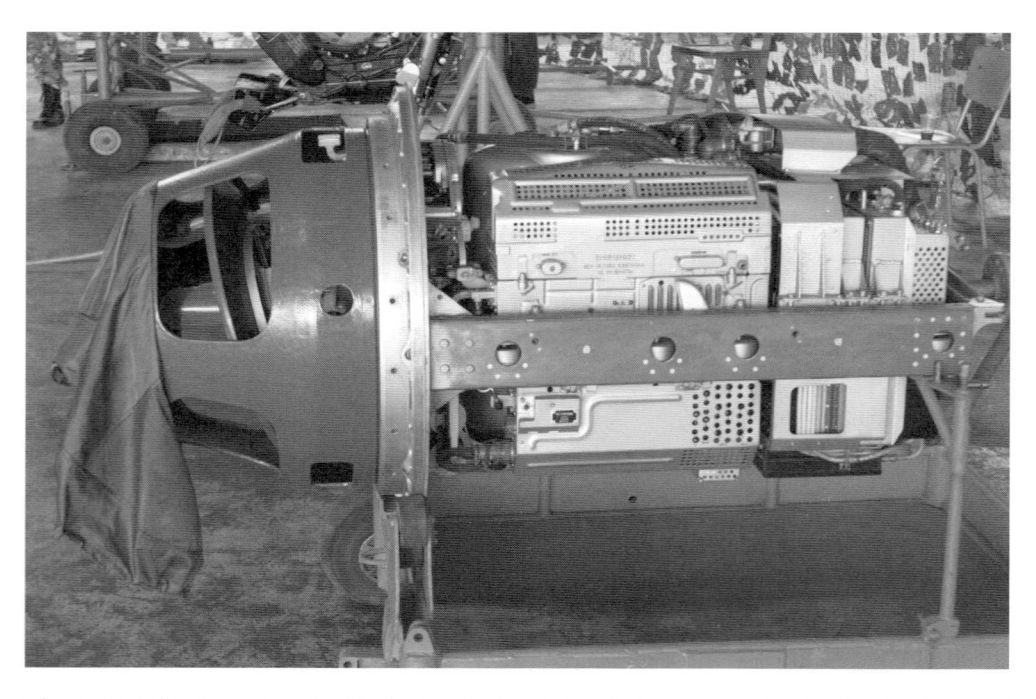

The MiG-21bis is equipped with the RP-22 Spafir-21 air-intercept radar, lacking look-down/shoot-down capability. (*Author's collection*)

## MiG-21bis Heat-Seeking Air-to-Air Missiles

|  | R-3S | R-13M | R-60 | R-60MK |
|---|---|---|---|---|
| Maximum low-level range/rear quarter | 2.5 km (1.55 m) | 3.5 km (2.17 m) | 2 km (1.24 m) | 2.2 km (1.37 m) |
| Maximum high-level range/rear quarter | 7 km (4.35 m) | 13km (8.07 m) | 8 km (4.97 m) | 8 km (4.97 m) |
| Minimum range/rear quarter | 1 km (0.62 m) | 0.9 km (0.56 m) | 0.2 km (0.12 m) | 0.2 km (0.12 m) |
| Maximum G of the launch aircraft | 2 | 3.7 | 7 | 7 |
| Maximum G of the target | 3 | 5 | 8 | 8 |
| All-aspect capability | None | None | None | Limited |
| Weight | 76.6 kg (169 lb) | 90 kg (198 lb) | 43.5 kg (96 lb) | 44 kg (97 lb) |
| Warhead weight | 11.3 kg (24.9 lb) | 11.3 kg (24.9 lb) | 3 kg (6.6 lb) | 3.5 kg (7.7 lb) |

## MiG-21 Two-Seat Derivatives

Development work on the MiG-21 two-seater began following the Council of Ministers decree dated 11 November 1959, under the initial OKB-155 designation UTIMiG-21F and factory designation Ye-6U or Type 66. This new version utilised the MiG-21F-13 basic airframe and powerplant and was required to have a 2,000 to 2,200 km/h (1,078 to 1,187 kt) maximum speed, 20,000 m (65,600 feet) practical ceiling and 1,400 km (755 nm) range on internal fuel. The take-off run with two R-3S missiles was not to exceed 700 m (2,296 feet) and the landing roll was to be below 1,200 and 600 m (3,936 and 1,968 feet), without and with the brake parachute respectively.

The two-seater introduced a redesigned nose section, at frame eighteen, by inserting the second cockpit (occupied by the instructor), which, as expected, caused a reduction in the internal fuel tankage. In a bid to at least partially compensate for this, a new flexible tank was added between frames fourteen and twenty-two, and consequently the internal fuel volume increased to 2,350 litres.

Both of the MiG-21U cockpits were provided with SK ejection seats lacking the blast protection function; instead the front cockpit had a fixed windscreen, while the single-piece moving main part of the canopy for both cockpits hinged to starboard. The cockpits were separated by a transparent screen and the instructor, sitting in the rear cockpit, had a very poor forward view, especially during take-off and landing.

MiG-21U's first prototype, known as the Ye-6U/1, made its maiden flight on 17 October 1960. (*Mikoyan & Gurevich OKB*)

The two-seater retained the MiG-21F-13's ASP-5ND gyro lead-computing gun-sight and the SRD-5 radar range-finder, but the NR-30 cannon was deleted. Just like the single-seater, the intake centrebody had three working positions—at the rear for flight at speeds below Mach 1.5, in the middle for Mach 1.5 to Mach 1.9, and fully forward at speeds exceeding Mach 1.9. The weapons suite included two R-3S AAMs on underwing pylons and one GP-A-12.7 conformal gun-pod on the centreline, housing an A-12.7 12.7-mm machine-gun with 60 rounds. In the air-to-ground role the two-seater was capable of carrying two free-fall bombs, each weighing up to 500 kg, or two 16-round packs for 57-mm rockets on the underwing pylons. The two-seater also retained the provision for using two assisted-take-off SPRD-99 rocket boosters.

The main undercarriage units were provided with KT-92 large-diameter (800 mm) braking wheels, while the airbrake was of single-piece type, installed on the centreline, and the brake parachute was housed in the underside of the fuselage, between frames thirty and thirty-two. The pitot boom was moved to the centreline position above the nose intake. The MiG-21 two-seater was equipped with the KAP-2 autopilot from the outset, its purpose being to improve stability in the roll axis.

The two-seater's first prototype, designated as the Ye-6U/1, was built in 1960 and made its maiden flight on 17 October the same year in the capable hands of Mikoyan test pilot Piotr Ostapenko. In March 1961 the Ye-6U/1 was handed over for its state testing and evaluation programme to the NII VVS at Akhtubinsk, followed in July that year by the second two-seat prototype, the Ye-6U/2. It featured a balance weight of some 40 kg (88.16 lb), installed in the centre-body, next to frame two, in order to improve the lateral stability; it also boasted an increased internal fuel capacity of 2,340 litres. The vastly improved KAP-2 autopilot had altitude and speed correction functions. The SOD-57 air traffic control transponder was also added to the two-seater's avionics suite.

The two-seater's state testing programme, carried out by the NII VVS, proved to be a very quick and straightforward undertaking. The concluding flight-test report, approved by the VVS C-in-C in August 1961, noted that the two-seater sported the same manoeuvrability, stability and controllability as that of the MiG-21F-13 and the MiG-21PF, but also retained the chief shortcoming of high rudder forces at speeds in excess of Mach 1.4, making the aircraft's handling more difficult. The MiG-21U was cleared for operations from Class-II paved runways no shorter than 2,000 m (6,560 feet). The NII VVS test team also recommended in its final report that the MiG-21U's design should be further improved by adding the new SK-3 (KM-1) ejection seats, a KAP-3 three-axis autopilot and the SPS blown flaps system for reducing the landing speed.

In 1962 the MiG-21U two-seater entered series production at GAZ-31 in Tbilisi under the internal designation Type 66, while the NATO codename assigned was 'Mongol-A'. The first three production-standard examples were rolled out in 1960 and as many as 180 MiG-21Us were produced at the GAZ-31 in Tbilisi between 1962 and 1966. A number of these aircraft (beginning with the seventh example of the sixth production batch) were built with the SPS blown flaps system, but they never achieved operational status as all the aircraft built at the GAZ-31 retained the old R11F-300 engine, which lacked the bleed air capability. During the production run the MiG-21U's design was improved by the addition of an underrudder brake parachute housing and an enlarged-area fin.

The MiG-21U was also produced at the GAZ-30 in Moscow for export customers between 1964 and 1968, with no fewer than 230 examples being built. A significant proportion of these featured the improved airframe design with the enlarged-area fin and parachute housing at the base of the fin.

The MiG-21US (Type 68; NATO codename 'Mongol-B') was an improved two-seater derivative sporting a number of novelties already implemented in the design of the MiG-21PFM. It was powered by the uprated R-11F2S-300 engine and featured the SPS blown flaps system; it also introduced KM-1M ejection seats (designated as the KM-1U for the front and the KM-1I for the rear cockpit), a further-improved KAP-2 autopilot and the definitive increased-area fin, 5.32 m$^2$ (57.2 sq. feet) in area. The MiG-21US also boasted an increased fuel capacity of 2,450 litres and had a brake parachute container at the base of the fin. The instructor's canopy received a periscope on a metal top rail in a bid to improve the view forward during take-off and landing: its upper mirror was automatically raised when the landing gear was extended and retracted with the retraction of the landing gear.

The MiG-21US prototype was flight-tested for the first time in 1965, and in 1966 it superseded the MiG-21U on the GAZ-31 production line in Tbilisi, with as many as 347 examples produced there until 1971.

The MiG-21UM (Type 69), known to NATO as the 'Mongol-C', was the definitive two-seater derivative of the type. It retained the basic airframe and systems design of the MiG-21US but incorporated the uprated R-13-300 engine, although a number of early production examples retained the R-11F2S-300.

It also introduced an entirely new flight/nav. equipment suite borrowed from the MiG-21S, including the AP-155 three-axis full-authority autopilot and the ASP-PFD-21 gun-sight, while the equipment in the nose bay was installed in an easily removable rack.

Externally, the MiG-21UM could be distinguished from its predecessor by the presence of a DUA-3A AoA sensor on the port side of the nose (installed for the first time in 1972). Some aircraft also featured a large blade antenna on the top fuselage, just in front of the fin, used by the ARK-10 ADF.

The MiG-21UM took to the air for the first time in 1968 and remained in production at GAZ-31 in Tbilisi between 1971 and 1985, with as many as 1,133 examples rolling off the line in fifteen years.

The MiG-21US improved two-seater featured the R-11FS-300 engine and blown flaps in order to reduce landing speed. (*Author's collection*)

A late-series MiG-21UM two-seater operated by the Bulgarian Air Force until the end of 2015. (*Lubomir Slavov*)

A look inside the front (left) and rear cockpits of a late-production MiG-21UM. (*Author's collection*)

# MiG-21 Specification

## MiG-21 dimensions

| MiG-21 variant | Wingspan | Length (excluding pitot boom) | Height | Wing area, gross |
|---|---|---|---|---|
| MiG-21F-13 | 7.154 m | 13.4 6 m | 4.10 m | 23.0 m² |
| MiG-21PFM | 7.154 m | 14.10 m | 4.125 m | 23.0 m² |
| MiG-21SM | 7.154 m | 14.185 m | 4.125 m | 23.0 m² |
| MiG-21SMT | 7.154 m | 14.10 m | 4.125 m | 23.0 m² |
| MiG-21bis | 7.154 m | 14.10 m | 4.125 m | 23.0 m² |
| MiG-21UM | 7.154 m | 13.46 m | 4.10 m | 23.0 m² |

## MiG-21 weights

| MiG-21 variant | Empty | Normal | Max. take-off | Max. warload |
|---|---|---|---|---|
| MiG-21F-13 | 4,819 kg | 7,100 kg | 8,376 kg | 1,000 kg |
| MiG-21PFM | 5,383 kg | 7,750 kg | 8,238 kg | 1,000 kg |
| MiG-21SM | 5,998 kg | 8,330 kg | 9,400 kg | 2,000 kg |
| MiG-21MF | 5,350 kg | 8,150 kg | 9,400 kg | 2,000 kg |
| MiG-21SMT | 5,700 kg | 8,400 kg | 10,100 kg | 2,000 kg |
| MiG-21bis | 5,450 kg | 8,725 kg | 10,400 kg | 2,000 kg |
| MiG-21UM | 5,380 kg | 8,000 kg | 8,376 kg | 1,000 kg |

## MiG-21 performance

| MiG-21 variant | Max. speed sea level | Max. speed high level | Service ceiling | Range | Rate of climb |
|---|---|---|---|---|---|
| MiG-21F-13 | 1,200 km/h | 2,175 km/h | 19,000 m | 1,420 kg | 138 m/sec |
| MiG-21PFM | 1,200 km/h | 2,175 km/h | 19,000 m | 1,670 km | 125 m/sec |
| MiG-21SM | 1,200 km/h | 2,230 km/h | 18,000 m | 1,240 km | 120 m/sec |
| MiG-21SMT | 1,200 km/h | 2,175 km/h | 17,000 m | 1,300 km | 120 m/sec |
| MiG-21bis | 1,200 km/h | 2,175 km/h | 17,500 m | 1,225 km | 235 m/sec |
| MiG-21UM | 1,200 km/h | 2,175 km/h | 17,700 m | 1,210 km | 130 m/sec |

| MiG-21 variant | Time to climb to height | Take-off run | Landing roll | Design load factor |
|---|---|---|---|---|
| MiG-21F-13 | 19,000 m in 13.5 min | 900 m | 900 m | 7 G |
| MiG-21PFM | 18,000 m in 8 min | 900 m | 750 m | 8.5 G |
| MiG-21SM | 17,500 m in 9 min | 900 m | 550 m | 8.5 G |
| MiG-21SMT | 16,800 m in 9 min | 950 m | 550 m | 8.5 G |
| MiG-21bis | 17,000 m in 8.5 min | 830 m | 550 m | 8.5 G |
| MiG-21UM | 16,800 m in 8 min | 900 m | 550 m | 7 G |
| * With one 490-litre centreline drop tank ||||| 

| Main production (1958–85) ||||
|---|---|---|---|
| MiG-21 variant | Number built | First flight | Production Period/Factory |
| MiG-21F | 10<br>83 | 1958 | 1958/GAZ-31<br>1959–60/GAZ-21 |
| MiG-21F-13 | 539<br>513<br>194 | 1959 | 1960–62/GAZ-21<br>1962–64/GAZ-30<br>1961–72/Aero Vodochody |
| MiG-21PF | 525 | 1960 | 1961–65/GAZ-21 |
| MiG-21PFM | 944 | 1963 | 1963–66/GAZ-21 |
| MiG-21FL | 233 | 1961 | 1961–65/GAZ-21* |
| MiG-21R | 448 | 1964 | 1966–71/GAZ-21 |
| MiG-21S | 145 | 1964 | 1966–68/GAZ-21 |
| MiG-21SM | 349 | 1967 | 1968–71/GAZ-21 |
| MiG-21SMT | 281 | 1970 | 1971–73/GAZ-21 |
| MiG-21M | n/a | 1968 | 1968–71/GAZ-30 |
| MiG-21MF | n/a<br>231 | 1970 | 1971–73/GAZ-30<br>1975–76/GAZ-21 |
| MiG-21MT | 15 | 1971 | 1971/GAZ-30 |
| MiG-21bis | 2,013 | 1971 | 1972–85/GAZ-21 |
| MiG-21U | 180<br>230-plus | 1960 | 1962–66/GAZ-31<br>1964–68/GAZ-30 |
| MiG-21US | 347 | 1965 | 1966–70/GAZ-31 |
| MiG-21UM | 1,133 | 1968 | 1970–85/GAZ-31 |
| * Supplied as component knocked-down kits for local assembly at HAL Nasik in India ||||

## MiG-21—Operational History

The MiG-21 saw its baptism of fire in the war between India and Pakistan in September 1965. Eight serviceable Indian Air Force MiG-21F-13s, equipping 28 Squadron, were used to fly combat air patrols (CAPs), in the vicinity of two forward Pakistan Air Force (PAF) airfields in Punjab, but no air-to-air combats were reported. The type had more contact during the next war with Pakistan in December 1971. Equipping eight Indian Air Force squadrons at the time, the 'Fishbed' saw active use in both the air-to-air and air-to-ground roles. There were a few air combats involving the MiG-21, the first of these taking place on 6 December, when a MiG-21FL shot down an F-6 attack aircraft, using the GP-9 gun-pod. On 12 December, during the first-ever reported clash between double-supersonic fighters, Indian MiG-21FLs managed to gun down a Pakistani F-104A Starfighter, again using the GP-9 gun-pod. On the last day of the war, 17 December, four more F-104As were claimed in air combats with the MiG-21FL, all of these on the account of 29 Squadron, without any losses of their own. There was one MiG-21 air combat loss that occurred during a combat with Pakistani F-86F Sabres, while several 'Fishbeds' returned to base with combat damage inflicted by the Pakistani anti-aircraft artillery (AAA).

The MiG-21 was introduced into service with the Vietnamese People's Air Force (VPAF) in mid-1965. The type equipped one squadron of the 921st Fighter Regiment (FR) at Noi Bai, which initially had a mixture of MiG-21PFs and MiG-21F-13s. The first use in anger of the type was reported in February 1966, and the first aerial victory was scored the following month—gunning down a Ryan AQM-34 'Firebee' reconnaissance drone flying at 18,000 m (59,000 feet).

According to Soviet sources citing the recollections of the VPAF's Soviet military advisor, Colonel Vladimir Babich, in April and May 1966 only RS-2US AAMs were employed by the VPAF MiG-21PFs in attacks against US aircraft, but reportedly without any success due to the very tight G-load manoeuvring restrictions and design deficiencies of the radar-beam-guided missile. As many as fourteen RS-2US missiles are said to have been launched in combat, all of which reportedly failed to hit their intended targets. The S-5 57-mm rocket was another air-to-air weapon used in combat by the VPAF MiG-21F-13s and MiG-21PFs in 1965 and early 1966 because R-3S heat-seeking missiles had yet to be delivered.

The first R-3S heat-seeking missiles were delivered from April–May 1966, but their initial supply was very limited, and, as a consequence, only the pair leaders were armed with them—wingmen continued to use the two 16-round 57-mm rocket packs. The first occasion on which this new tactic was employed was 7 May 1966, when a pair of VPAF 'Fishbeds' attacked an F-105 Thunderchief formation at low altitude. One Thunderchief was hit by an S-5 rocket, but it subsequently managed to escape further attacks and returned to base. The first VPAF 'Fishbed' victory against US manned aircraft was reported on 5 June 1966, when two F-4 Phantom IIs were downed by R-3S missiles. The VPAF's first MiG-21 combat loss was reported on 26 April 1966, when an aircraft was downed by an F-4 using air-to-air missiles, and the second 'Fishbed' loss followed on 14 July 1966.

The most practical MiG-21 tactics devised by the VPAF, with assistance from Soviet advisers, called for the use of hit-and-run attacks, penetrating at high speed through the fighter escort and attacking the strikers, forcing them to drop their bombs *en route* to their intended target. The VPAF had between twenty and thirty operational MiG-21s in 1966 and 1967, and the preferred method of their combat employment called for launching one or two pairs, vectored by GCI, to intercept from behind US formations flying on known routes. So small and fast was the 'Fishbed' that its pilots were often able to mount unseen high-speed attacks on the US Air Force (USAF) and US Navy (USN) integrated strike packages of fighter-bombers and escorting F-4s, heading to targets around Hanoi and Haiphong.

The year 1967 was a very difficult time for the VPAF's small 'Fishbed' community, as five aircraft were lost during Operation *Bolo*, a large-scale counter-air operation launched by the USAF. A total of seven kills were claimed by the USAF, but VPAF and Soviet data confirmed only five losses sustained on 2 January 1967. Two days later, two more 'Fishbeds' were reported to have been downed by USAF F-4s, with one pilot ejecting and another one killed. After this heavy blow the VPAF 'Fishbed' force was immediately grounded, but it resumed combat operations four months later by adopting more effective hit-and-run tactics, preferably with high-speed attacks from the rear and above, followed by a prompt exit from the attack. The updated tactics were used for the first time on 31 April 1967, with two 'Fishbed' pairs managing to down a total of four F-105s. A week earlier, however, a MiG-21 loss was reported in air combat with USAF F-4Cs.

A classic North Vietnamese propaganda photo from the early 1970s, depicting a trio of prominent VPAF fighter pilots in front of a row of MiG-21PF/PFMs; on the right is the VPAF's top ace, Nguen Van Coc, with nine kills. (*Author's collection*)

November and December 1967 continued to be rather busy months for the VPAF 'Fishbeds'; their claims for the period comprised one RB-66 (but this has not been confirmed by official US war losses records), an F-105 on 12 December and, six days later, three more F-105s from a formation approaching Hanoi. A unique F-102A Delta Dagger loss was reported by the USAF on 3 February 1968; it turned out that this aircraft was downed by the top VPAF ace Nguen Van Coc. Four days later the same pilot downed a USN F-4B, this being his eighth kill of the war.

Between 1969 and 1971 there were no air-to-air combats over North Vietnam, following the Americans' unilateral cessation of all bombing operations effective from 1 November 1968. There were, however, many intercepts of AQM-34 Firebee recce drones, with the VPAF claiming no fewer than ten in 1970 and one in 1971. In addition, there were some sporadic clashes in the air north of the 20th Parallel in 1970, with one F-4 (this has not been confirmed by US war loss records) and one HH-53B Combat SAR helicopter claimed by the VPAF 'Fishbed' force on 28 January; one MiG-21 was also reported lost in combat on that day.

A new phase of the war in early 1972 began with no success for the VPAF 'Fishbed' community, as the type amassed painful losses but no victories at all until late April. By that time, the VPAF had two 'Fishbed' fighter regiments—the 921st FR, equipped with the MiG-21MF (delivered in 1969), and the newly formed 927th FR, equipped with the older MiG-21PF and PFM interceptors.

On 10 May 1972, Operation *Linebacker I* was launched, with mass and sustained bombings by USAF and USN aircraft against important military, infrastructural and industrial targets north of the 20th Parallel. The small VPAF fighter force was stretched to the limit trying to counter the large-scale bombing raids, and faced stiff resistance from US fighters employing improved air combat tactics. In the spring and early summer months of 1972, the VPAF continued to suffer numerous and painful losses in air combat and also due to the heavy bombing of its ground infrastructure.

Despite the significant losses, the VPAF fighter force retained basic operating capabilities and the service commenced training a dozen pilots in night intercept tactics, seeking to challenge the B-52 Stratofortresses' bombing of targets in the north. There were, however, no chances to intercept a B-52 during Operation *Linebacker I*, as it was stopped on 22 October 1972 by US President Richard Nixon. Operation *Linebacker II*, which commenced on 17 December 1972, saw a resumption of the bombing campaign, in an attempt by President Nixon to force North Vietnam back to peace talks.

The bombings hit all the main VPAF airfields and a number of industrial centres, with B-52s heading for targets in the Hanoi area. An attempt by the MiG-21s to engage the B-52s took place on 18 December, when VPAF pilot Pham Tuan scrambled but failed to make contact with the enemy. On 27 December the same pilot was lucky at last, reportedly managing to penetrate the F-4 fighter escort and reach a three-strong bomber formation. The MiG-21MF was flying at 1,200 km/h (647 kt) at 10,000 m (32,800 feet) as Tuan launched two R-3S heat-seeking missiles in salvo against one of the B-52s from 2,000 m (6,560 feet) distance, immediately disengaging, breaking sharply and entering into a steep dive. The bomber was confirmed as a loss by the USAF, although US sources denied that the B-52 was downed by a Vietnamese MiG-21 and instead claimed that the loss was caused by a SAM hit. The second B-52 victory claimed by the VPAF was reported on 28 December, when pilot Vu Xuan Thieu managed to break through the American fighter escort and unleash his missiles, but his aircraft was lost and he died. It was guessed by Soviet military advisers who examined the aircraft wreckage that the MiG-21MF had rammed the B-52, while another version of events says that the fighter took hits from debris falling off the exploding bomber.

According to Soviet Air Force Major-General Mikhail Fesenko (who worked as military adviser to the VPAF commander-in-chief), in 1972 the North Vietnamese MiG-21 force amassed as many as 540 combat missions and suffered thirty-four losses, while the total number of victory claims, scored together with the MiG-17 and MiG-19 fleets, accounted for eighty-nine US aircraft downed in the course of 201 air combats. It is noteworthy, however, that there was a considerable difference between the kill claims of the warring parties. For instance, the VPAF kill claims list (as cited by prominent VPAF wartime operations researcher Dr Istvan Toperczer) comprised of no fewer than 320 US aircraft, with 134 own losses admitted in air combats. In contrast, US claims (as per the US Navy official study) comprised 193 kills and ninety-one own losses or probable losses (six of these losses were on account of Chinese fighters that downed US aircraft after the latter had strayed into Chinese airspace). At the same time, there were some twenty-two aircraft in the official US losses list for which no VPAF claims have been made at all. In the event, only sixty-four US losses were confirmed by both warring parties.

The 'Fishbed' entered service with the Egyptian Air Force (at the time known as the United Arab Republic Air Force) in 1963, and by the middle of the decade the fleet numbered about sixty MiG-21F-13s, supplemented not long after by forty-five to fifty MiG-21PFs. The Syrian Air Force received its first MiG-21F-13s in 1961 and by 1966 it operated some forty-five 'Fishbeds'. In 1965 the radar-equipped MiG-21PF was inducted into Syrian service, with an initial batch comprising fifteen examples plus six to eight two-seaters for use by both the F-13 and PF-equipped squadrons. The Iraqi Air Force was the third Arab air arm to receive the then-modern 'Fishbed', with around sixty MiG-21F-13s delivered between 1963 and 1966, together with some sixty MiG-21PFs and a few MiG-21U two-seat trainers. The Iraqi MiG-21s were the first of the type in the Arab world to see use in anger, flying a number of ground-attack sorties against Kurdish separatists in the northern and eastern parts of the country.

The Syrian MiG-21s' first use in anger dated from April 1967, as the type participated in a series of air combats against Israeli Air Force (IAF) fighters, reporting six losses and no victories at all in the initial encounters. In fact, this series of battles proved to be a prelude to an even more disastrous episode in the MiG-21's service in the Arab world—namely the Six-Day War in June 1967. It began with a sudden Israeli air attack against a number of Syrian, Egyptian and Iraqi airfields;

these surprise attacks destroyed a large proportion of the Egyptian and Syrian MiG-21s on the ground. The success of the Israeli mass attack against the Egyptian forward airfields was undeniable; the Israeli jets faced very little resistance while mounting their devastating strikes on the first day of the war, 5 June 1967. A few MiG-21s that were able to take off to fight the attackers were promptly shot down, although a small number of surviving Egyptian MiG-21s were later used to attack the advancing Israeli ground forces, mostly deploying 57-mm rockets.

The Syrian air arms had fewer than twenty fully operational 'Fishbeds' at the onset of the Six-Day War, and a small proportion of these were used for escorting fighter-bombers and intercepting Israeli jets attacking Syrian airfields. No fewer than eighteen aircraft (both operational and non-operational examples) were destroyed on the ground by the Israeli strikes during the first day. As a consequence only six Syrian 'Fishbeds' are reported to have survived intact and continued fighting on 5 June and the following days.

The period between the Six-Day War and the October 1973 War (also known as the Yom Kippur War) saw a large number of clashes between fighters in the air, in which the Arab MiG-21s fought against Israeli jets with varying degrees of success. Egypt rapidly restored its 'Fishbed' inventory thanks to a massive supply of new and second-hand aircraft from the Soviet Union, while Algeria also provided a number of MiG-21s. The first air combats over Sinai occurred barely one month after the end of the Six-Day War, and the first Israeli Mirage IIICJ was claimed on 15 July 1967, at the expense of two Egyptian MiG-21s reported lost in the same dogfight.

By the end of 1968 the Egyptian air arms already operated a fleet of about 115 MiG-21s, and these aircraft were soon thrown into operations against Israel. The first large-scale air clash took place on 23 October 1968, with three Mirage IIICJs claimed by the Egyptians—although Israeli sources denied such losses.

The official start of the so-called War of Attrition was announced by Egypt on 14 March 1969; it saw sporadic air and ground combat operations aimed at inflicting damage on the Israeli defensive positions built alongside the western

This Iraqi Air Force MiG-21F-13 (serial '534') defected to Israel on 12 August 1966, flown to the country by Capt. Monir Radfa. (*Author's collection*)

bank of the Suez Canal, and Egyptian aircraft took an active part in the attacks. Meanwhile, the improved MiG-21PFM entered Egyptian service at the beginning of 1969; it was the first radar-equipped interceptor version sporting the GP-9 gun-pod, a welcome complement to the R-3S missiles. It was useful at very close distances (less than 1,000 m (3,300 feet)), where the R-3S was impossible to launch. In late 1969 the vastly improved MiG-21M—with four missile launch rails and a GSh-23L built-in gun-pack—was taken on strength.

At the same time, the Egyptians commenced training in new-style low-level interception and air combat tactics in a bid to challenge the Israeli tactical superiority. In February and March 1970 eighty MiG-21MFs were delivered from the Soviet Union, sporting a more powerful engine and better radar. In this new environment the clashes between the Israeli and Egyptian fighters continued, but with varying success for both parties. The biggest air battle from this period, where the Egyptian MiG-21s scored three widely publicised and acknowledged kills, took place on 11 September 1969. Two of these confirmed kills were Mirage IIIs flown by prominent Israeli aces Giora Rom and Shlomo Weintraub, but five MiG-21s and three other aircraft were lost in the same combat.

Soviet air combat data about the War of Attrition period showed that from July to December 1969 the United Arab Republic Air Force's losses were seventy-two combat aircraft, fifty-three of which were lost due to enemy action and a large proportion of which were MiG-21s. In total, the War of Attrition saw no fewer than fifty group air battles fought over both sides of the Suez Canal, claiming sixty Egyptian and thirty Israeli aircraft (according to Colonel Vladimir Babich). In turn, Israel admitted only four losses of its own in air combat—and only in those instances when the pilots were captured or found dead on Egyptian territory.

The onset of the October 1973 war saw the Egyptian air arm operating a fleet of about 200 MiG-21s of various versions and, just before the war, reinforcements from other Arab countries were taken on strength. In addition, Pakistani instructors and North Korean volunteers flew the MiG-21s in combat, while Algeria deployed two squadrons, equipped with the MiG-21F-13 and MiG-21PF respectively, to

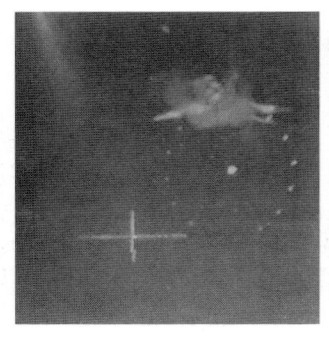

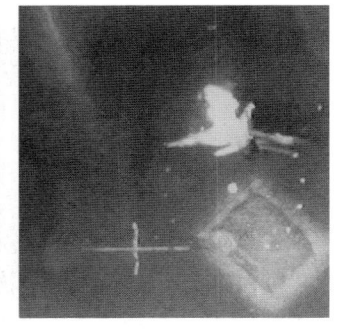

A gun-camera sequence showing the destruction in the air of an Egyptian Air Force MiG-21, hit by 30-mm rounds fired by an Israeli Mirage III fighter. (*Author's collection*)

Egypt. In addition to the air defence and escort missions, the Egyptian MiG-21s flew a large number of attack missions, armed with two 500-kg or four 250-kg bombs or 57-mm rocket packs.

The war broke out on 6 October with massive air attacks by the Egyptian Air Force, successfully enacting surprise tactics and facing little opposition in the beginning. Only one aircraft from the first wave was reported lost, and by the end of the day the number of losses reached just ten jets. The next day the IAF entered into decisive play, attacking the major Egyptian air bases in the Nile Delta. Massive air battles developed at low and medium altitudes as large numbers of Egyptian MiG-21s were scrambled to repulse the attack. The MiG-21s continued flying attack sorties on the second day, and the Algerian 'Fishbed' force that had been deployed to Egypt saw combat for the first time.

The biggest air battle took place on 14 October, day nine of the war, as sixty-two MiG-21s stood against an Israeli attacking force of about 120 F-4E Phantom IIs and A-4 Skyhawks, which had been launched in three waves against the large air base at al-Mansurah. In fact, this air battle proved to be the most successful action of the Egyptian air arm during the war—and indeed its entire history—as it claimed no fewer than twenty victories at the expense of six losses of its own.

At the outbreak of the war, the Syrian air arm had some ten MiG-21 squadrons on strength, the majority of which were equipped with older 'Fishbed' versions such as the F-13 and PF/PFM. The first Syrian war operations saw the MiG-21 flying escort missions for fighter-bomber formations launched in two waves to attack the Israeli positions. During the second wave of day one, the first air clashes took place. At the same time, the IAF launched a counteroffensive aimed at destroying the Syrian SAM sites; this proved to be a failure, and MiG-21s on CAP also assisted in repelling an F-4E anti-SAM attack, claiming two Israeli jets and reporting two own losses. In total, twelve Israeli jets were claimed on the second day of the war by the Syrians against fourteen of their own losses.

Day five of the war on the Syrian front saw nineteen Israeli claims and sixteen for the Syrians and Iraqis, and on this day the Syrian fighter force adopted the principal air defence responsibility over the frontline since the surviving SAM units had run out of missiles. The same day, reinforcements from Iraq arrived in the form of eleven MiG-21MFs. The Israeli attacks against the Syrian airfields continued, with eight MiG-21s destroyed on the ground and one F-4E claimed by an Iraqi MiG-21 pilot. There were mass air battles fought over the frontline areas, with a number of Syrian MiG-21s claimed shot down while scoring only one victory—the downing of an A-4.

Day six was even more difficult for the struggling Syrian fighter force, and the Iraqis also continued to suffer painful losses—including at least two MiG-21s. They also claimed no fewer than four Israeli aircraft, but in fact only one or two were damaged in air combats and no kills were scored at all in the morning battles. Four more MiG-21s were downed in the afternoon of that hot day and another Iraqi 'Fishbed' was lost to Syrian AAA.

The MiG-21 itself also suffered from a number of design shortcomings when employed in the low-altitude manoeuvring air combat role, as the type was never designed for such operations. In fact, when flown by skilled pilots, the 'Fishbed' sported an impressive turning performance, especially when facing the Mirage III and F-4E. The improved training and better tactical skills were also among the major factors that contributed to the considerably increased kill ratio of the Egyptian and Syrian 'Fishbeds' in the October 1973 war.

The next notable use of the MiG-21 in anger took place during the 1979 war between Egypt and Libya. The Egyptian 'Fishbeds' were employed in the fighter-bomber escort role and clashed with Libyan Mirage V fighters, reporting one loss. In another air combat during that war, a pair of MiG-21MFs armed with US-supplied AIM-9P Sidewinder missiles clashed with two Libyan MiG-23MS aircraft and gunned down one of the 'Floggers'.

The Syrian MiG-21s were involved in a new series of air combats in July 1979, when the war between Israel and neighbouring Lebanon broke out. This time, however, the Syrians faced a vastly superior foe, as the IAF introduced both the F-15A Eagle and F-16A Fighting Falcon fourth-generation fighters.

At that time, the Syrian air arm had a fleet of about 200 MiG-21s—most of them MFs, armed with the improved R-13M missile. The most fierce air battles before the full-scale war took place in May 1982, with no fewer than twenty MiG-21s lost. During the clashes before the June 1982 war in Lebanon, only one A-4 was claimed shot down by the Syrian 'Fishbeds'. During the 1982 war, MiG-21 losses continued to mount due to the overwhelming Israeli superiority and poor Syrian tactics. On 9 June, during the famous Israeli air attack against the Syrian SAM batteries in the Bekaa Valley, no fewer than ten MiG-21s were claimed in air combat, and another example was lost due to friendly fire. On 10 June 14 more MiG-21s were claimed lost in air combat; the 'Fishbeds' scored one kill only, downing an F-4E with cannon fire. On 11 June six more MiG-21s were lost in air combat, claiming another F-4E. This episode put an end to the MiG-21's use in the 1982 war.

By 1980, the Iraqi Air Force/Air Defence Force operated some ninety MiG-21MFs, plus a handful of MiG-21F-13s and two-seaters, serving with five fighter squadrons, as well as a small number of MiG-21Rs. During the war with Iran, the MiG-21 was pitted against the technologically superior F-4D Phantom II and F-14A Tomcat, while the nimble F-5E Tiger II was regarded as a less serious opponent. The only chance the Iraqi MiG-21 pilots had when fighting against the F-4 and F-14 was if they enjoyed the element of surprise in close encounters—but this proved to be a very rare occurrence.

Even before the war, on 10 September 1980, two MiG-21Rs were lost while on a reconnaissance mission inside Iranian airspace, downed by an F-14A, and four days later four more 'Fishbeds', also flying over Iranian territory, were gunned down by F-4s. After war broke out on 22 September 1980, Iraqi losses continued to mount, with three 'Fishbeds' claimed by the Iranian fighter force on the first day, while the second day of the war saw Iraqi MiG-21s claiming two F-5Es.

At the beginning of the war, Iraqi MiG-21s also flew low-level attack missions against ground targets, most often armed with 250-kg general-purpose bombs.

During the following phases of the war, the MiG-21 was mainly used as a point-defence interceptor, tasked with protecting Baghdad (the capital) and the northern part of the country from the attacks of Iranian fighter-bombers. In early 1981 the Iraqi MiG-21s received considerably better air-to-air weapons in the form of the French MATRA Magic Mk 1 heat-seeking missile, and became operational with this weapon in March 1981. The new missile replaced the rather antiquated R-3S and proved more successful in combat. Within one week in May 1981, two F-4Es, two F-5Es and one AH-1J Cobra attack helicopter were claimed by the Iraqis, who lost only one MiG-21; soon afterwards, two more F-4s and F-5s were claimed shot down by the Magic Mk 1 missiles. The Iraqi MiG-21s also used AIM-9B Sidewinder AAMs obtained from Jordan in 1983, managing to shot down two F-5s, one F-4D, one C-130H Hercules transport aircraft and a Bell 214 helicopter with this new weapon.

In 1983 the Iraqi MiG-21 inventory was reinforced with the arrival of some forty Chinese-made F-7Bs, which were obtained with the help of Saudi funding. A batch of twenty-five MiG-21bis' was also taken on strength in the same year, followed not long after by another batch of the same 'Fishbed' derivative, already armed with the R-60 agile dogfight missile.

The Iraqi inventory of some 120 MiG-21s and F-7Bs failed to have any impact during the 1990–1991 Gulf War. The only known instance of air combat occurred on 17 January 1991, with four MiG-21s acting as decoys to divert an F-14A combat air patrol while two more 'Fishbeds' attempted to attack an F/A-18A Hornet formation from USS *Saratoga*, which was launched on a mission against the H-3 airfield complex in the western part of Iraq. The attacking MiG-21 pair, however, had the bad luck of flying directly into the main strike package, and consequently both the MiG-21s were immediately shot down by the Hornets.

## Soviet MiG-21s in Action

The prime MiG-21 operator in the 1960s and 1970s was the Soviet Air Force's Frontal Aviation branch, which had thousands of 'Fishbeds' in frontline service, but the type saw little use in anger. Among the few instances when Soviet MiG-21s were employed in the air-to-air role during the Cold War era was an interception on 23 November 1973, when Captain Gennadiy Yeliseev from the 982nd IAP (stationed at Vaziani Airfield in the Soviet Republic of Georgia) downed an Iranian Air Force jet (believed to be a McDonnell Douglas F-4 fighter) that had strayed into Soviet airspace. The MiG-21SM initially launched two R-3S missiles, but they failed to hit the target. Since the distance between the interceptor and the target was too close for firing two more missiles and the Iranian jet was just about to cross the border line back into its own territory, Captain Yeliseev instead committed to ram the target, killing himself during the mid-air collision while the two crew members of the downed jet (an Iranian student pilot and a US instructor) managed to bail out safely.

At the beginning of the Soviet campaign in Afghanistan in 1979, the MiG-21 was the principal combat jet, with no fewer than thirty-seven examples deployed to perform air defence and ground attacks. The 115th Guards IAP, a fighter regiment stationed at Kokaity in Uzbekistan, deployed to Bagram Airfield on 27 December 1979, with one of its squadrons equipped with twelve MiG-21bis and two MiG-21UMs. The 136th APIB, a fighter-bomber regiment stationed at Chirchik in Uzbekistan and operating MiG-21PFMs, re-roled as fighter-bombers and followed suit in early January 1980. Both of these units were reassigned to the 34th Air Corps; shortly afterwards this transformed into the 40th Air Army, purposely established for operations in Afghanistan and headquartered at Bagram. In February 1980 another squadron drawn from the 115th Guards IAP was initially deployed to Bagram, but four months later it moved to Kandahar.

The 136th APIB was initially ordered to deploy its three squadrons to Kokaity and commenced flying its first patrols in Afghan airspace on 25 December 1979, with the aim of protecting the columns of Soviet ground forces entering the country. The principal area of operations for the fighter-bomber regiment covered the main roads used by the Soviet vehicle columns. 'Fishbeds' flying these patrols were each armed with a pair of UB-32 rocket packs and also carried a centreline fuel tank. The first combat sorties using weapons against the enemy forces on the

The MiG-21 had a long and productive career with the Soviet Air Force, serving in the advanced and lead-in fighter training role between the late 1960s and early 1990s. (*Aviatsia i Kosmonavtika*)

ground were reported on 9 January 1980; a Soviet armoured vehicle and truck column fell under attack by Afghan *mujahedeen* fighters. The first air strikes were mounted by the quick-reaction alert (QRA) pair, scrambled from Kokaity, followed by a formation consisting of pilots from the regiment's command section. Each of the 'Fishbeds' unleashed sixty-four S-5 57-mm rockets against *mujahedeen* fighters, who were on foot and mounted on horses.

One of the regiment's squadrons deployed to Kandahar in Afghanistan in early January 1980, while the second one was ordered to return home and undertake conversion to the more capable MiG-21SM; the third squadron remained at Kokaity for operations in the northern provinces of Afghanistan until the second half of February, when it too was ordered to deploy to Bagram. The 136th APIB continued operating the MiG-21SMs, re-roled as fighter-bombers until April 1981; no combat losses were reported. The 115th IAP, home-based at Kokaity, Uzbekistan, and equipped with the MiG-21bis, was then deployed to Afghanistan in 1980.

Due to the lack of significant air threats in Afghanistan, the two deployed fighter squadrons of the 115th Guards IAP were soon re-roled in the ground-attack role; clashes with the *mujahedeen* had become increasingly intensive in the months following the Soviet intervention, with the result that Soviet troops on the ground needed more and more air support. The main ground-attack weapons used by the MiG-21bis in the early stages of the war in Afghanistan were the OFAB-250-270 250-kg (550-lb) high-explosive/fragmentation bombs, up to four per aircraft, most often dropped from a steep 60° dive in two passes by using the MiG-21's ASP-PFD-21 gunsight in manual mode. The workload on the Soviet MiG-21s in Afghanistan was pretty high, with 200–250 hours' annual utilisation per aircraft, which translated to 400–450 sorties—most of them dedicated to real-world ground attacks. The simple and robust MiG-21, which lacked sophisticated avionics and systems, demonstrated good reliability in austere wartime operating conditions, and the fleet availability rate (represented by the percentage of combat-ready aircraft) was maintained at between 85 and 90 per cent.

The 115th IAP suffered two combat losses and saw the end of its combat deployment in Afghanistan in June 1981. Its three squadrons were replaced by two squadrons drawn from the 27th Guards IAP, home-based at Uch-Aral in Kazakhstan, each with sixteen to eighteen aircraft including several two-seaters. The new squadrons were deployed to Bagram and Kandahar, and on 15 June 1981 the 27th Guards IAP reported its first combat loss; a MiG-21UM two-seater was shot down in the notorious Tora-Bora cave area in the mountains next to the border with Pakistan. The aircraft was downed when flying at low altitude, killing one of the pilots, while the other crew member ejected and was captured on the ground before being sent to Pakistan and subsequently released. A second loss occurred shortly after the first one—the pilot managed to eject and was promptly rescued. The third loss during the regiment's combat deployment took place on 27 May 1982—a MiG-21bis exploded in the air during an attack diving run (most likely hit by anti-aircraft fire from the ground), killing the pilot.

The MiG-21bis of the Soviet Air Force's 115th IAP, stationed at Kokaity in Uzbekistan, only 50 km (27 nm) from the border with Afghanistan, continued flying combat sorties from its home base on an occasional basis until the late 1980s. (*Author's collection—Aviatsia i Kosmonavtika*)

The next Soviet MiG-21 unit rotating through Afghanistan was the 145th IAP, home-based at Ivano-Frankovsk (now in the Ukraine). It commenced its year-long combat deployment with two squadrons in mid-June 1982, stationed at Bagram and Kandahar, while a four-ship QRA flight was kept at Shindand, in the southern part of the country. The deployment judged itself as lucky because the 145th IAP suffered no pilot losses during its thirteen months of virtually non-stop combat operations and thousands of ground-attack combat sorties; only one MiG-21bis was reported downed near Bagram on 18 August 1982, but the pilot ejected and was quickly rescued.

The 927th IAP, home-based at Beryoza in Byelorussia, was the last Soviet 'Fishbed' fighter unit deployed to Afghanistan. A two-squadron fleet of twenty-eight single-seaters and four two-seaters arrived in theatre in late June 1983. After four days of joint operations with their predecessors, the 927th IAP commenced its independent combat work, amassing on average three to four combat sorties per aircraft each day. The bombing missions were usually flown by eight–to-twelve-ship groups in order to ensure reliable destruction of the targets. The formations featured mixed ordnance loads, most often represented by the OFAB-250-270 bombs, S-24 rockets or UB-32 rocket packs. The 927th IAP's intense combat work saw some 10,000 sorties and 12,000 flying hours amassed during its twelve-month Afghanistan deployment, lasting from June 1983 to June 1984.

The 115th IAP, having moved back to Kokaity, Uzbekistan, only 50 km (27 nm) from the border with Afghanistan, continued flying combat sorties from its home base on an occasional basis after its withdrawal from Afghanistan in mid-1981.

The great worldwide operational career of the MiG-21 is coming to an end; however, there are a few remaining operators around the world who plan to continue flying the type until the late 2010s. (*Author's collection*)

From time to time it received orders to pound targets situated in the northern provinces of Afghanistan, and it continued flying this type of combat mission until 1989. The MiG-21bis operating from the home base typically carried one 800-litre centreline drop tank and were armed with two 500-kg or four 250-kg high-explosive bombs. Due to the considerably strengthened *mujahideen* air defence, all dive attacks commenced from 8,000 m (26,200 feet), with bombs released at 5,000 m (16,400 feet), followed by an immediate pull-out and climb up to a minimum safe altitude of 3,000 m (9,840 feet) above ground level in order to avoid ground fire.

## Tu-128—A Heavyweight Arctic Guardian

The Tupolev Tu-128 (NATO reporting name 'Fiddler') was the first true long-endurance (or 'loitering') supersonic fighter-interceptor fielded in the Soviet Union. Based on a 1950s-vintage experimental bomber design, it was a heavyweight interceptor with restricted manoeuvrability, boasting a powerful radar and long-range air-to-air missiles. The Tu-128 was optimised from the very beginning for operating over the Soviet Union's vast Polar territories in order to be able to stop the large formations of US strategic bombers approaching across the North Pole; the type had a faithful service in this demanding niche role in the 1960s and 1970s.

During the unstable and very tense 1950s, at the peak of the Cold War, the Soviet Union's air defence system saw a rapid development, including the mass fielding into service of radar-equipped, missile-armed fighter interceptors and surface-to-air (SAM) missile systems. At the time, the Soviet Union was still recovering from the colossal damage inflicted by the Second World War, and its huge military machine still lagged behind the USA in many very important areas— such as in nuclear weapons and strategic bomber development. In this clearly unfavourable situation, the Soviet military planners tended to rely extensively on the development of the country's air defence system. The newly-introduced SAM systems, operating in layered air defence schemes, together with subsonic and (later) supersonic fighter-interceptors, were seen as a promising weapon used for setting up effective defensive belts around all the important urban and industrial centres in the Soviet Union.

This so-called 'static' or 'positional' air defence concept, however, proved entirely unsuitable for covering the enormous northern border of the huge country, which spans no less than nine time zones. It was simply impossible to establish dependable SAM belts in the remote border areas that were capable of stopping the USAF bombers on their ingress routes passing over the North Pole. Likewise, the thousands of short-legged jet fighters equipping the PVO fighter aviation force in the 1950s, such as the MiG-17 and MiG-19, were only useful for point

Andrey Tupolev (1888–1972) was the founder and Chief Designer (and Designer General from 1956) of the Tupolev Design Bureau (Tupolev OKB); he was among the most productive and distinguished Soviet aircraft designers working between the early 1930s and late 1960s. (*Tupolev OKB*)

defence, being ill-suited for providing reliable anti-bomber cover in the remote northern regions, where only a handful of airfields were available for air defence purposes. The only practical way to perform the task in an effective manner called for fielding purposely-designed loitering fighter-interceptors with long enough endurance and range, rendering them suitable to defend vast territories lacking an airfield network—including a significant portion of the Polar Ocean adjacent to the Soviet borders.

The subsonic Yakovlev Yak-25 was the first of the class to be inducted in IA PVO service in the late 1950s, but it was also considered to be a short-legged and slow design, and therefore not fully suitable for the demanding task of countering the US jet-powered strategic bombers.

In an effort to get the needed range and loitering time, the IA PVO Commanding Officer, Marshal Yevgeniy Savitskiy, decided to follow a non-conventional plan and use an existing supersonic bomber design as a base. It was to be equipped with a powerful radar and armed with long-range air-to-air missiles. The only suitable design at the time was available at the Tupolev OKB, also known as the OKB-156 (Experimental Design Bureau No. 156). This experimental supersonic bomber aircraft—codenamed '98'—was originally intended to be used in the anti-ship role and had a two-man crew—a pilot and a navigator-operator. In 1957 Marshal Savitskiy was given a presentation of model '98' during a meeting organised at the Tupolev OKB, where he suggested that this should be developed into a heavyweight fighter using the baseline design of the already flight-tested machine.

The initial design work at the OKB-156 was performed without a formal government assignment and funding, instead using company internal resources. The new fighter received the '128' code and Vladimir Yeger was appointed as the chief designer for the new project. The end result of the design effort by the Tupolev OKB was a heavyweight fighter interceptor with the in-service designation Tu-128. It became the most notable representative of the second-generation loitering fighters fielded in service by the IA PVO, tasked mainly with protecting the skies of Siberia and the Far East, intercepting nuclear-armed USAF bombers *en route* to targets that were predominantly situated in the European part of the Soviet Empire.

The twin-jet fighter inherited the basic fuselage of the experimental bomber, albeit with some redesigned sections and mated to all-new sharply swept wings. The mid-set wings featured a slight anhedral and a swept angle of 56°, using a set of low-thickness profiles, straight trailing edge and a considerably increased chord on the inboard panels. The fuselage was redesigned by using the area rule in order to reduce transonic drag and increase the maximum speed, while the navigator's cockpit was moved behind the pilot's one. This design solution enabled the nose to be used for accommodating the bulky and heavy electronic boxes of the air-intercept radar, which was purposely designed for the new fighter by the OKB-156. The reshaped fuselage with a pronounced waist gave a better lift-to-drag ratio at subsonic cruise speeds, thus increasing the aircraft's subsonic range. The shoulder-type air intakes for the afterburning turbojets were also extensively redesigned and received moving half-cone shock bodies driven forward and aft, in order to vary the cross section according to the flight regime. At supersonic speeds the moving half-cone bodies were used to focus the shock waves on the intake lip and reduce the air intake area. Engine jet pipes were positioned side-by-side in the bulged tail.

In order to shorten the landing roll—an important consideration when operating from packed ice- and snow-covered runways—the new heavy interceptor received a brake chute, while the approach speed was reduced thanks to the use of slotted flaps. Likewise, in a bid to further improve the take-off and landing performance, the wings received slotted flaps and interceptors that could also be used as air brakes. The wide track main undercarriage units were also modified to receive four-wheel bogies each, retracting into large fairings onto the winds trailing-edges. The new fighter-interceptor inherited a good many systems from the Tu-16 bomber, and this trend was especially evident in the flight/navigation instrumentation suite.

The development of the new loitering fighter-interceptor for the PVO aviation force was formally launched by Soviet Council of Ministers decree issued on 4 July 1958. It ordered the Tupolev OKB to develop the Tu-128-80 air intercept complex. It was an integrated weapons system consisting of the Tu-28 fighter-interceptor, powered by two Lul'ka AL-7F-1 turbojets and equipped with powerful air-intercept radar; it was to be armed with the K-80 air-to-air missiles and had on-board equipment allowing the interceptor to be guided by the Vozdukh-1 ground-based remote-control intercept system.

The aircraft was required to accelerate to between 1,700 and 1,800 km/h (917 and 971 kt) and have a flight duration at subsonic speed of 800 to 1,000 km/h (431 to 540 kt) of no less than three and a half hours. This heavyweight intercept complex was intended to be pitted against subsonic aircraft flying at up to 21,000 m (68,880 feet). A derivative, powered by the then-designed VD-19 turbojet (an

The experimental supersonic bomber, dubbed 'Project '98', was used by the Tupolev OKB as a basis for development of the Tu-128 'Fiddler', a heavyweight interceptor with restricted manoeuvrability boasting a powerful radar and armed with long-range air-to-air missiles. (*Tupolev OKB*)

engine with a higher thrust rating than that of the AL-7F-1), was also under consideration, expected to reach a maximum speed of 2,000 km/h (1,080 kt).

The new K-80 missile was designed by the OKB-4 (later on known as the Molnya OKB) in two versions. The first one was equipped with an IR seeker while the second one sported a radar seeker. The new RP-S Smerch radar set, designed by the OKB-339 (later on renamed as Phazotron NNIR company), was required to have a detection range of no less than 60 km (32 nm) against bomber-sized targets.

The Tu-28 was a non-manoeuvrable aircraft made capable of shooting down manoeuvring targets thanks to its agile long-range missiles, capable of turning at a high-G rate when fired against turning aircraft. The aircraft itself was limited to turning with up to 2.4-G, while the missile was capable of pulling up to 15-G; later, the capability was expanded to 21-G. The weapons control system enabled the Tu-28 to conduct missile engagements against targets flying 3,000 m (9,840 feet) higher than the interceptor—in this case the pilot was required to pull up at a 20-degree pitch in zoom climb towards the target just before launching its missiles.

The Tu-28 was made capable of carrying four K-80 missiles under the wings. Two of these, carried inboard, were equipped with IR seekers, and the other outboard-fitted two were equipped with semi-active radar-homing (SARH) seekers. The latter type was useable in head-on intercepts, while the former was made capable of deployment in tail-on intercepts and in situations where dense electronic countermeasures would render the radar-guided missiles ineffective.

The concept of operations of the long-range loitering interceptor called for performing the intercepts at a distance of up to 1,500 km (809 nm) from the protected objects, with up to 3.5 hours loitering time inside its assigned combat patrol area. Moreover, it was not over-reliant on ground control when compared with its short-legged predecessors, which were equipped with small radars with limited range. The powerful radar was able to provide information for accurate-enough missile guidance onto the tracked target during the terminal phase of the intercept. This method of performing the intercept made it possible for the Tu-28-80 system to use a simplified derivative of the integrated on-board automated guidance equipment, receiving guidance information datalinked from the ground control stations of the Vozdukh-1 intercept operations control system. The Tu-28-80 was also required to team up with the Tu-126 Airborne Early Warning and Control (AEW&C) aircraft operating over the remote northern and far eastern parts of the Soviet Union, where the PVO forces lacked any extensive ground-based early warning and command-and-control infrastructure. According to the calculations of the design team at the Tupolev OKB, the Tu-128-80 intercept complex had a 76–77 per cent probability of hitting its intended targets during a typical intercept mission.

The Tu-28 was intended to be manned by a crew of two—a pilot and a navigator/weapons system operator. The latter had to play the main role in the mission, providing guidance cues to the pilot (using voice commands) during the

The Tu-128 was optimised from the very beginning for operating over the Soviet Union's vast Polar territories. It was a non-manoeuvrable aircraft made capable of shooting down manoeuvring targets thanks to its agile long-range missiles, capable of turning at a high-G rate when fired against turning aircraft. (*Tupolev OKB*)

intercept and also handling all navigation tasks over featureless terrain or over the sea. As a rule, the pilot was granted a low workload in order to remain in a good working condition during the entire long-endurance mission.

The design of the new aircraft was approved in June 1959 and the mock-up was accepted in early 1960. The first Tu-28 prototype was completed in January 1961 and made its maiden flight on 18 March that year in the hands of Tupolev OKB test pilot Mikhail Kozlov, with K. Malkhasyan flying in the rear cockpit as the test navigator. The first supersonic flight was reported on 24 April the same year.

In June 1961 the first two prototypes took part in the big traditional flypast at Tushino Airport in Moscow. Each of the aircraft carried two K-80 missiles and an underfuselage pod containing test-recording equipment. The Soviet media outlets were officially tasked to disseminate false information about the new aircraft shown at Tushino for the first time, so they referred to it as a new-generation multi-role supersonic bomber. Likewise, Western experts studying the photos obtained during the Tushino flypast assumed that the underfuselage pod carried by the new Tupolev twin-engine design could house a multi-role radar. Nobody on the ground, however, had realised that it was only the thirty-first sortie of the new aircraft, although the missiles suspended under the wings could provide some clues about its true purpose.

The set-up of the serial production of the new heavy fighter-interceptor was undertaken in a very rushed manner, going in parallel with the progress of the design and development works. This decision carried a huge technical risk—if major design issues were encountered with the prototypes, it would incur costly changes on the production line. At the same time, the Soviet air defence forces were overstressed by the frequent reconnaissance operations around its borders being undertaken by aircraft from NATO countries, including—from time to time—intentional airspace violations to probe the USSR's reaction capabilities. This uneasy situation motivated PVO commanders to insist on the delivery of the new long-range interceptor as soon as was possible. The production of the first batch of four production-standard aircraft was initiated at the GAZ-64 in Voronezh in late 1959, well before the first flight of the Tu-28 prototype.

The flight test effort went in a pretty smooth manner, with the Tu-28 confirming all performance expectations. The first missile launches against aerial targets were made in September 1962 at the NII VVS range near Akhtubinsk. The first aerial target shot down by the new interceptor was a remotely-piloted Il-28 bomber, while in October the same year the Tu-28 brought down a Yak-25RV flying at high altitude, showing its capability to be effectively used against the Lockheed U-2. In November 1962, for the first time in the Soviet Union, the Tu-28 demonstrated a successful head-on missile engagement—downing an Il-28 target drone with a SARH-guided K-80 missile.

The aircraft involved in the flight-testing effort amassed a total of 799 sorties, reaching completion in mid-1964. The Tu-28 was eventually judged to have met the PVO expectations, and it was commissioned into service in a prompt manner immediately after completing the flight testing and evaluation programme. The original Tu-28-80 air intercept system designation was changed to the Tu-128S-4 by a Council of Ministers decree dated 12 December in 1963. The aircraft itself was designated as the Tu-128, while the Kh-80 air-to-missiles got the new in-service designations R-4R (equipped with SARH seeker) and R-4I (equipped with IR seeker).

The Tu-128S-4 air intercept system was capable of performing all-aspect intercepts against targets with closure speed between 200 and 1,600 m/s (656 and 5,248 fps). The initial intercept guidance after take-off was undertaken by using the Put-4P on-board equipment, which received steering commands from a ground intercept control station. These commands (such as heading, speed or altitude) were displayed on to the flight/navigation instruments in the pilot's cockpit, and he had to follow the cues until target detection by the aircraft's own radar, operated by the navigator in the rear cockpit. There were some other discrete remote-control commands received on-board; for example, these were used for switching on the pre-launch heating of the vacuum tubes in the missiles' electronics or directing the aircraft's radar antenna dish towards the target in order to facilitate an easier detection. The radar featured a maximum detection range of 50 km (27 nm), while the R-4-series of air-to-air missiles were made capable of hitting targets flying at between 800 and 21,000 m (2,624 and 68,800 feet) and at up to 25 km (13.5 nm) in head-on encounters. Armed with four R-4 missiles, the Tu-128 was able to fly at a maximum level speed of 1,665 km/h (898 kt), while in clean configuration its maximum speed hit 1,910 km/h (1,030 kt). The maximum range was 2,565 km (1,383 nm), while the practical ceiling reached 15,600 m (51,168 feet). The Tu-128 was capable of intercepting air targets at a distance of up to 1,170 km (631 nm) from the take-off airfield or the protected object, with two hours and forty minutes loitering (combat air patrol endurance) in the air.

The Tu-128 was made capable of carrying four K-80 long-range missiles under the wings—two inboard, fitted with IR seekers, and two more outboard, featuring semi-active radar-homing seekers. (*Tupolev OKB*)

The Tu-128S-4 air-intercept system was officially commissioned by the PVO in a Soviet Council of Ministers decree dated 30 April 1965, with the first production aircraft taken on strength the same year. As many as fifteen Tu-128s were delivered in 1965, with thirty-seven more examples following suit in 1966. The first aircraft were delivered to the IA PVO's combat training and aircrew centre (148th TsBPiPLS) at Savastleika, northeast of Moscow, while the first front-line unit, the 518th IAP in Talagi, took its first Tu-128s on strength in October 1966.

The initial PVO plans called for the 'Fiddler' to be introduced in as many as twenty-five fighter regiments between 1966 and 1970. In fact, only six regiments took the new, long-legged interceptor on strength. Typically, the IA PVO regiments had three squadrons equipped with nine to twelve aircraft each.

The GAZ-64 plant in Voronezh rolled out as many as 198 Tu-128s, the last of which was handed over to the IA PVO in 1971.

## Tu-128's Trainer Version

There were initially no plans for designing a dedicated training version of the new interceptor, but during the aircrew conversion-to-type training for the first front-line regiments, it turned out that there the process was plagued by some serious issues. Most (if not all) of the IA PVO pilots converting to the Tu-128 had previous flying experience accumulated on lightweight fighters only, such as the MiG-17, MiG-19 and Su-9. As a consequence, they were ill-prepared to fly the much heavier Tu-128, which featured rather complex handling characteristics. In addition, the

As many as 198 Tu-128s were produced at the GAZ-64 plant in Voronezh, with the last of these handed over in 1971. (*Tupolev OKB*)

navigator/WSO faced the challenge of handling an air intercept system comprising very complex avionics and weapons. That is why, after losing several Tu-128s in accidents, the IA PVO command authorities requested that the Tupolev OKB developed a dedicated training derivative. The design work on this new version commenced in September 1966 and was completed as late as 1970. Initially, four production-standard Tu-128s were converted into trainers and designated as Tu-128UTs, commissioned in September 1971. The trainers received a new cockpit in the nose, replacing the radar, while retaining the navigator's cockpit—albeit with a simplified set of equipment only useful for navigation tasks, although the underwing pylons were retained for carrying R-4T training rounds. The two-seater received the nickname *Pelican* due to its unique appearance, as its reshaped nose resembled the goitre of a Pelican bird. In addition to the first four-strong batch, ten more Tu-128UTs were built through conversion of standard Tu-128s.

## The Improved Tu-128A

The first design work on a radically improved Tu-128 version had already commenced as the baseline Tu-128 was launched into production in 1961. The new version would be equipped with the RP-SA Smerch radar and was armed with longer-legged missiles; the new radar had a maximum detection range of 100 km (54 nm), with a lock-on range of up to 50 km (27 nm). It was to be armed with the improved K-80A missiles, featuring a maximum launch range of 32 km (17 nm). The new aircraft version, designated as the Tu-128A, was to be powered

The Tu-128UT trainer received a new cockpit in the nose for the instructor, replacing the radar, while retaining the navigator's cockpit—albeit with a simplified set of instruments. (*Tupolev OKB*)

by the new VD-19 afterburning turbojets, but this new powerplant required extensive fuselage redesign (especially for the rear fuselage) as well as adding larger intakes to satisfy the higher airflow requirements. The new version was expected to have a maximum speed of 2,000 km/h (1,079 kt), but experiments using a Tu-128LL testbed showed that the real speed increase was only 110 km/h (60 kt). In the event, this little gain was the prime cause for the cancellation of the Tu-128's re-engining effort.

In the second half of the 1960s the upgrade initiatives at the OKB-156 continued, but this time the aim was to boost the maximum altitude for attacking targets up to 25,000 m (82,000 feet), while the maximum closure speed of the missiles with the target was to increase from 2,000 km/h (1,080 kt) to 3,000 km/h (1,618 kt), together with an expansion of the missile's acceptable launch region. There were also plans for another re-engining effort to encourage the interceptor's maximum speed to hit 2,100 km/h (1,133 kt) while at the same time also extending its range.

In the event, the package of novelties implemented in the upgraded interceptor system proved to be a rather modest one. The design and development works were carried out at a slow pace until the end of the 1970s. The improved interceptor—designated as the Tu-128S-4M—was commissioned in service with the IA PVO as late as in 1979. There were no newly-built aircraft and the entire existing fleet was cycled through the upgrade to the Tu-128S-4M standard, with the work undertaken at the VVS aircraft repair plants. During the upgrade process, the aircraft received a new radar, new electronic systems and strengthened pylons for carrying the new R-4RM and R-4TM missiles.

There were several non-built projects for follow-on of the Tu-128. Known by their internal Tupolev OKB designations '138' and '148', they had introduced

A scan of the Tu-128 pilot's cockpit. (*Tupolev OKB*)

more powerful radars and advanced aerodynamic layouts such as variable-geometry wings that would enable new flight profiles and multi-functional use. Such multi-functional capability, however, proved to be unrequired in the Soviet Air Force as it had already selected the Su-24 swing-wing frontal bomber; the IA PVO leadership was not interested in getting this capability either.

## Tu-128 and Tu-128M Specification

|  | Tu-128 | Tu-128M |
|---|---|---|
| Dimensions: Wing span Length Height | 17.53 m 30.06 m 7.15 m | 17.53 m 30.06 m 7.07 m |
| Wing area: | 96.94 m$^2$ | 96.94 m$^2$ |
| Weights: Empty operating Normal take-off with four AAMs Maximum take-off | 25,960 kg 40,000 kg 43,000 kg | 25,960 kg 40,000 kg 43,260 kg |
| Performance: Max level speed at high level with missiles Max level speed at high level clean Landing speed Practical ceiling, clean Take-off distance Landing distance Intercept range Loitering time | 1,665 km/h 1,910 km/h 290 km/h 15,600 m 1,350 m 1,050 m 1,170 km 2.75 hours | 1,665 km/h 1,910 km/h 290 km/h 15,600 m 1,350 m 1,050 m 1,130 km 2.6 hours |

## The Tu-128 in Service

The first PVO regiment to take the Tu-128 on strength was the 518th IAP at Talagi Airfield, where the aircraft underwent the field testing programme in October 1966. The next regiment to be equipped with the Tu-128 was the 445th IAP at Kotlas, which commenced operations with the new type in 1967. Both regiments provided their aircraft and aircrews for participation in the famous 1967 flypast at Domodedovo Airport, near Moscow. The type was then also used to re-equip the regiments at Anderma (72nd Guards IAP), Semipalatinsk (356th IAP), Belaya (350th IAP) and Omsk (64th IAP). It is noteworthy that upon taking the Tu-128 on strength, these units were re-designated simply as Aviation Regiments (*Aviatsiony Polk* or AP), as the word 'Fighter' ('*Iztrebitel'ny*') was deleted from their official designation. The reason was that the Tu-128 can hardly be considered as a fighter in the true meaning of the word.

The Tu-128 pilot conversion training had its specifics, especially for drivers with previous experience on lightweight fighters, who were only used to a control stick. In the Tu-128 this was replaced by a control column similar to that used on all other heavy aircraft types. Another specific feature of the Tu-128, making its handling very specific and difficult for drivers with low experience, was related to the high inertia experienced by the pilot on the landing approach, which made the aircraft's behaviour totally different to those of the agile lightweight fighters. The take-off also had its own share of difficulties. In order to convert to the Tu-128, in the 1960s and the early 1970s the pilots were required to have logged at least 400 hours on lightweight fighters and possess a first-class rating—i.e. to be trained for combat missions in all weathers, day and night.

The Tu-128 was successfully deployed as the long arm of the Soviet air defence system in the northern territories, and played a very important role in protecting the vast borders of the country occupying one-sixth of the Earth. The long-range interceptor had frequent encounters with various NATO aircraft performing reconnaissance and patrol missions. The biggest troubles were caused by the USAF SR-71 flying next to the Soviet borders, with Tu-128s having been despatched to shadow the Blackbird from their own territory, flying at a parallel heading and at a distance of about 5 km (2.7 nm). The Tu-128 force also saw use against Western reconnaissance balloons (free-floating aerostats) at high altitude. The 'Fiddlers' were frequently despatched to intercept and shoot down both NATO balloons fitted with reconnaissance equipment and also Soviet scientific-research balloons that veered off-course. The anti-balloon operations necessitated the use of a special derivative of the IR-guided R-4T missile.

The aircraft was successfully operated from forward airfields with packed snow- and ice-covered runways at forward operating airfields beyond the Polar Circle. During its entire service the type proved itself as a reliable aircraft, whereas its initial design concept of combining a non-manoeuvrable long-endurance launch platform armed with long-range manoeuvrable air-intercept missiles proved a definitive success.

The improved interceptor, designated as the Tu-128S-4M, was commissioned in service with the IA PVO in 1979, and the last examples remained in operational use until 1988. (*Tupolev OKB*)

In the late 1970s the upgraded Tu-128M force was already considered to be obsolete, but all six regiments equipped with the type continued to use it until the mid–late 1980s; the last flight operations were conducted in 1988. All of the regiments eventually replaced the faithful Tu-128M with the MiG-31, which had similar loitering performance but boasted a much more capable look-down/shoot-down radar and longer-range missiles, combined with all-altitude supersonic performance.

## Su-9—Sukhoi's First Supersonic Interceptor

The Sukhoi OKB (also known at the time as the OKB-51), started developing swept-wing and delta-wing fighters in accordance with the general initiative of the Soviet government dating from October 1953, which called for an accelerated development of a new generation of Mach 2-capable fighter types. Powered by the AL-7F engine, the Sukhoi's swept-wing prototype—designated as the S-1—hit 2,170 km/h (1,170 kt), and in early 1958 the VVS command authorities saw it as a more capable design, sporting better performance than that of the MiG-21 prototypes. The delta-wing T3 prototype made its maiden flight on 26 May 1956 in the hands of the Sukhoi OKB test pilot Nikolay Makhalin.

The swept-wing S1 and delta-wing T3 prototypes proved to be faster by 150–200 km/h (81 to 108 kt), and demonstrated a higher practical ceiling by 1,000–1,500 m (3,280–4,920 feet), compared to their Mikoyan OKB counterparts, the Ye-2 and Ye-4 respectively. Furthermore, the S1's design maturity was judged to be better than that of the Mikoyan OKB aircraft. The swept-wing prototype was also considered suitable for use in the fighter-bomber role thanks to its heavier warload, while the delta-wing T3 was eventually developed into a pure fighter-interceptor sporting all-missile armament and powerful radar. Both aircraft featured a cylindrical body with a nose air intake and were powered by the same turbojet—the Lul'ka AL-7F, designed by the OKB-165. In this way, the heavyweight Sukhoi fighter design eventually evolved into the swept-wing Su-7 fighter-bomber for the VVS (optimised for delivery of tactical nuclear bombs) and the delta-wing Su-9 missile-armed fighter-interceptor for the Soviet Air Defence Forces (PVO).

The delta-winged prototype made its first public appearance at the flypast at Tushino Airfield in Moscow on 24 June 1956. During the testing it demonstrated promising performance, as its maximum speed in level flight hit 2,100 km/h (1,133 kt) and a service ceiling reached 18,000 m (59,040 feet). For its use in the air intercept role, it received the Almaz-3 radar and was armed with two K-7L or K-6V radar beam-riding air-to-air missiles.

A Soviet Council of Ministers decree dated 25 August 1956 tasked all Soviet fighter design bureaus with increasing the operational ceiling of their new aircraft, apparently in order to be capable of countering the new US reconnaissance aircraft such as the Lockheed U-2—which had been successfully used for spying missions deep into Soviet airspace. A subsequent Ministry of Aviation Industry order called for increasing the operational ceiling of the S-1 and T-3 prototypes to 21,000 m (68,880 feet) by installing an up-rated AL-7F derivative dubbed 'AL-7F-1' and removing all non-essential systems. The new engine had a larger diameter, and the tail section was widened in a bid to accommodate it. The wing received a dogtooth on each panel, generating powerful vortices at high AoA and performing the function of an aerodynamic fence in this manner, while the aileron area was reduced.

In an attempt to avoid aircraft production delays in case of developmental problems with the new engine and air-to-air missiles, the initial production aircraft built at the GAZ-153 in Novosibirsk were ordered to be powered by the existing AL-7F engine, and the first fifteen examples were set to receive NR-30 30-mm cannons instead of air-to-air missiles.

The first prototype of the improved delta-wing fighter was flown for the first time on 10 October 1957, with Sukhoi OKB test pilot Vladimir Ilyshin in the cockpit. It was dubbed 'T43-1', powered by the AL-74-1 and provided with a new nose section with a two-position centre body shock-cone (extending full forward at Mach 1.35 and above and retracting full aft at lower speeds). On 30 October, during the third test flight, Ilyshin hit 21,500 m (70,520 feet), and three days later he attained a maximum speed of 2,200 km/h (1,187 kt), equating to Mach 2.06.

The next task in the development programme called for installing an air-intercept radar on board the T43, a challenge to the design team due to the small size of the intake centrebody. The TsD-30 radar was small enough to be accommodated inside the small space available in the nose. It was designed to detect and track air targets and also to provide guidance to the K-5M (RS-2US) beam-riding air-to-air missile.

A Council of Ministers decree dated 16 April 1958 set the final configuration of the aircraft and mission suite. In line with the new tradition of developing aircraft-missile systems, the OKB-51 was ordered to develop an air-intercept

Pavel Sukhoi (1895–1975), OKB-51's founder and first Chief Designer, promoted to Designer General from 1956. (*Sukhoi OKB*)

The delta-wing T3 supersonic prototype – the predecessor of the Su-9 - made its maiden flight on 26 May 1956. (*Sukhoi OKB*)

system incorporating the aircraft itself, to be equipped with an air-intercept radar and air-to-air missiles capable of operating in conjunction with the Vozdukh-1 automated ground control intercept system. The decree also called for the development of two different variants of the system; the first one, dubbed 'T3-51', was to feature the T-3 aircraft equipped with the TsD-30 radar and two to four K-5M air-to-air missiles. The second was to be turned into a more sophisticated version, dubbed 'T3-8'; this was to be equipped with the Oryol radar and armed with two K-8M air-to-air missiles. In addition, the OKB-51 was tasked to develop a two-seat trainer version of its delta-winged interceptor.

The T3-51 was a simpler version and had to be developed the first, followed by the more capable derivative with the powerful Oryol radar. In fact, both intercept systems were developed and tested almost simultaneously between 1958 and 1960. The T3-51 prototype retained its OKB-51 internal designation, T43, used from the very beginning for the AL-7F-1-engined delta-wing prototype. The Council of Ministers decree called for a very compressed development timeline, with the flight testing set to commence in the third quarter of 1958. Due to the high importance of the programme, as many as six aircraft were to be submitted simultaneously for participation in the state testing effort with the NII VVS—this was instead of two, which had been the established practice earlier. In addition to the first T43, the other five aircraft used the already constructed airframes of the first production T3 aircraft built at the GAZ-153 at Novosibirsk. Two of these were modified at the factory and three more at the Sukhoi OKB's experimental

The first prototype of the improved delta-wing fighter—dubbed 'T43-1'—was flown for the first time on 10 October 1957, and soon afterwards it demonstrated a maximum speed of 2,200 km/h (1,187 kt), equating to Mach 2.06. A production-standard Su-9 is pictured here, armed with four radar-beam-riding RS-2US (K-5) air-to-air missiles, on display at the Soviet Air Force Museum in Monino, near Moscow. (*Boris Lilov*)

factory in Moscow. All of the T43s received the new KS-2 ejection seat, enabling a safe bail out at a maximum speed of 1,000 km/h (540 kt). The prototypes were equipped with both the TsD-30T radar and the Lasour datalink, and were armed with K-51 (RS-2US) air-to-air missiles.

The first aircraft modified in Novosibirsk was the T43-2, which was flown for the first time in May 1958. By late July that year all six examples were completed and test-flown, while on 30 August the fleet was declared ready to be submitted to the NII VVS for the state testing effort. In this way, the Sukhoi OKB had managed to meet the tight deadline set out by the Council of Ministers decree, but the state testing effort had commenced with a delay of some three months due to numerous shortcomings found during the acceptance of the aircraft; these had to be fixed before the aircraft were handed over to the NII VVS. On 20 October 1958 a serial-production standard T43 aircraft was lost due to radar cone disintegration and a subsequent engine flame out. The production test pilot was unable to relight the engine and attempted an unsuccessful emergency landing in a field, destroying the aircraft and killing himself.

The state testing effort commenced on 3 December 1958 and had two phases; the first was completed in May 1959, and the second one took place between June 1959 and April 1960. In general, the testing effort proved very difficult due to the very high complexity of the aircraft and its systems. The engine and intake control system were the sources of many troubles, such as surges when the engine was throttled back at a speed above Mach 1.8, or when in climb at an altitude above 15,000 m (49,200 feet) and exceeding Mach 1.5. The movement of the nose cone was extended to cope with the problem, and it received a new electro-mechanical control system for continuously adjusting its position forward and aft depending on the speed and altitude.

During a test flight on 20 June 1959, the T43-6 prototype was lost due to unknown reasons. The crashed prototype was promptly replaced in the test campaign by another aircraft from the serial production, designated as the T43-11; this joined the fleet in August that year. The second phase of the state testing effort was set to evaluate the performance of the overall combat system, with missile launches to be conducted against MiG-15 target drones at medium altitude; there were no high-altitude missile tests due to the lack of suitable target drones. The two phases of the state test programme included 407 sorties, and the effort was officially completed on 9 April 1960. The test completion report noted that all basic characteristics set out in the government decree had been achieved. The air-intercept system was able to destroy air targets flying at speeds between 800 and 1,600 km/h (431 and 863 kt), and at altitudes between 5,000 and 20,000 m (16,400 and 65,600 feet); the probability of target destruction was found to be between 0.7 and 0.9, while the maximum intercept radius was 430 km (232 nm).

The field testing effort was carried out in the autumn of 1960 at the PVO combat training centre at Krasnovodsk, on the coast next to the Caspian Sea. The new aircraft was commissioned in IA PVO service by a Council of Ministers decree dating from 15 October 1960. It received the Su-9 (NATO reporting name 'Fishpot-A') designation, while the radar was designated as the RP-9U and the missile as the RS-2US. The overall air-intercept system was designated as the Su-9-51. The new aircraft was shown in public for the first time during the 9 July 1961 parade in Tushino, with the formation performing a fly-by with pilots from the 148th TsBPiPLS from Savastleika.

In early 1961 the Su-9 underwent a flight test campaign aimed at evaluating the spin characteristics, flown by the prominent LII test pilots Sergey Anokhin and Alexander Shterbakov. They found that the aircraft could enter a spin only due to a gross pilot mistake or in case of intentional entry.

The series production of the Su-9 was launched immediately after the completion of the factory testing in 1958, and the new type was rolled out at the GAZ-153 until 1962. In parallel with the Novosibirsk production line, it was also launched in production at the GAZ-30 in Moscow, with the first two pre-series examples rolled out in mid-1959. The full-scale series production was launched in 1960 and continued until 1961. The total production run at the two plants accounted for 888 single-seat and 126 two-seat aircraft.

During the improvement process, the Su-9 received strengthened armament in the form of K-55 heat-seeking missiles, an RS-2US derivative fitted with an IR seeker borrowed from the K-13 (R-3S) missile. The tests proved to be a very protracted undertaking due to problems encountered with the then-very new missile, and they were only completed in 1967. The new missile was commissioned in service under the R-55 designation, and the improved radar, capable of providing targeting and launch information, was designated as the RP-9UK.

From 1966–1967 two production-standard Su-9s were used in a programme to test bomb deployment—mainly involving the FAB-250 250-kg (550-lb)

The Su-9-51 air-intercept complex was formally commissioned in IA PVO service on 15 October 1960. (*Sukhoi OKB*)

high-explosive bombs—and in the late 1960s the aircraft was tested with the UPK-23-250 gun-pods, installed under the fuselage, using the pylons previously occupied by external fuel tanks. The results from the UPK-23-250 tests were promising, but the pod was not used by the front-line IA PVO units because the Su-9 suffered from a notably shortened range when flying without external tanks.

## Su-9 Specification

| Dimensions:<br>Wing span<br>Length with Pitot probe<br>Height | 8.54 m<br>18.06 m<br>4.82 m |
|---|---|
| Wing area: | 26.20 m$^2$ |
| Weights:<br>Empty operating<br>Normal take-off with four AAMs<br>Maximum take-off<br>Fuel in internal tanks | 8,342 kg<br>11,422 kg<br>12,512 kg<br>3,100 kg |
| Performance:<br>Max level speed at sea level<br>Max level speed at high level<br>Practical ceiling<br>Rate of climb at low level<br>Take-off distance<br>Landing distance<br>Range on internal fuel<br>Range on internal and external fuel | 1,150 km/h<br>2,230 km/h<br>20,000 m<br>200 m/s<br>1,200 m<br>1,250 m<br>1,350 km<br>1,800 km |

## U-43—The Two-Seat Su-9 Derivative

The two-seat Su-9 derivative, which was to be built in accordance with the Council of Ministers decree dated 16 April 1958, was delayed due to the lack of engineering capacity at the OKB-51. At the time the entire engineering potential at the Sukhoi OKB was directed at the development of the two T-3 single-seat derivatives, which were to be submitted for testing in a very compressed timeframe. The two-seater's development started as late as March 1959, following a new Council of Ministers decree ordering development of a conversion training derivative of the T-43. Internally dubbed 'U-43' at the OKB-51, it received a tandem cockpit with a fuselage lengthened by 600 mm due to the insertion of a fuselage plug, accommodating the rear cockpit for the instructor and retaining the fuel capacity untouched. Student and instructor were accommodated in separated cockpits

In the mid-1960s the Su-9 was considered as a pretty capable interceptor, fielded in mass use to equip no less than twenty-seven IA PVO regiments. (*Sukhoi OKB*)

with individual canopies hinged to open upwards. The two-seater retained the full mission avionics fit of its single-seat predecessor, including the TsD-30 radar and the Lasour datalink; both cockpits also had hooded radar displays. In contrast to the single-seater, the two-seater was armed with only two K-5MS missiles instead of four. Adding the second cockpit caused an increase in weight by some 630 kg (1,388 lb) compared to the single-seater.

The two-seater was built using the fuselage of a production-standard Su-9 single-seater originally assembled at the GAZ-30. It made its maiden flight on 25 January 1961, and by May that year the U-43 completed its factory tests. The only shortcoming noted by the test pilots was the poor visibility from the rear cockpit. The U-43 commenced its state tests at the NII VVS in September 1961 and completed the effort by 23 December, amassing eighty-three sorties.

In February 1962 the U-43 was modified to provide better visibility for the pilot in the rear cockpit, and it took to the air for the first time in its new guise on 23 March that year. In April it underwent a short military testing phase to evaluate the functionality of the novel design solutions. In the event, the rear view was judged as sufficient and the two-seater was recommended to be launched in production. Designated as the Su-9U (NATO reporting name 'Fishpot-B'), it was launched in production in late 1961.

## The Su-9 in IA PVO Service

The Su-9 proved to be a brand new world for the IA PVO in the early 1960s as it was much more complex and effective than the previous fighter types operated by the service, such as the MiG-15, MiG-17P/PF and MiG-19P/PM. However, it also featured more difficult handling, and in this situation only pilots with the 2nd Class rating (i.e. with no less than 400 hours of flying experience, including in the day in instrument meteorological conditions and in the night in visual meteorological conditions) were allowed to convert to it. In fact, this strict rule was not respected all the time due to the urgency of the front-line units to convert to the new type. When combined with the unreliable systems and engine, this urgency is said to have led to a very poor flight safety record during the Su-9's induction in service with the IA PVO front-line units in the first half of the 1960s.

In June 1961 the first production-standard aircraft were delivered to the leading unit—the 813th IAP, an IA PVO regiment based at Tolmachevo, near Novosibirsk (Western Siberia), not far away from the GAZ-153. The same month a few aircraft were handed over to the 148th TsBPiPLS at Savastleika. The centre's pilots were also used to ferry the aircraft from the GAZ-153 to the front-line units converting to the new type. By early June the centre had taken eight aircraft on strength, logging seventy-two flights in about thirty hours, providing conversion-to-type training for six pilots from the front-line units (813th IAP); three more also began their training. The initial pilot conversion courses were undertaken without use of two seaters, the first of which was taken on strength in 1962. Each front-line unit initially received one Su-9U for use in continuation training and check rides. Due to the shortage of two-seaters, the front-line units continued using the obsolete UTI MiG-15 for instrument and handling technique checks. In addition to Tolmachevo, among the initial IA PVO regiments that converted to the Su-9 were those stationed at Krasnovodsk, Ozernoye, Baranovichi, Kilp-Yavr and Karshi.

By the mid-1960s the Su-9 was operated by no fewer than twenty-seven IA PVO regiments. However, its induction into service between 1961 and 1963 saw a very high attrition rate, with most of the accidents caused by the engine (due to failures in the automatic compressor control and the fuel system), electrical system and hydraulic booster failures. A significant proportion of the accidents suffered by the Su-9 units were attributed to pilot and technician mistakes, as it was a complex aircraft with many systems that needed skilled handling in the air and servicing on the ground.

The low reliability and time between overhauls (TBO) of the AL-7F-1 turbojet were among the main problems during the Su-9's initial operation. The engine had a TBO of only 250 to 350 hours, which led to frequent changes and grounding of the aircraft in the front-line units while waiting for delivery of overhauled or new engines. The low reliability of the Su-9's systems required a series of modifications to be performed by factory teams in the field. This type of improvement work continued on a regular basis in the early years of the type's IA PVO service, with a huge number of improvements made to the engine, fuel, electrical and hydraulic systems. In contrast to the reliability issue, the Su-9's handling performance was described as good and the aircraft lacked any unwanted specifics during transonic acceleration. Furthermore, the Su-9 had decent acceleration thanks to the combination of the powerful engine and the low-drag airframe.

There were some negative pilot comments, however, referring to the Su-9's excessive acceleration after take-off, which necessitated a prompt landing-gear retraction; this also had to be made below 600 km/h (324 kt). The pilots were required to maintain a high angle of climb after undercarriage retraction, and the aircraft also featured a rapid deceleration when the engine was throttled back in high-speed flight. Landing the Su-9 also proved to be a relatively difficult task due to the very high approach and touchdown speeds.

The combat training syllabus required the Su-9 drivers to master several typical intercept profiles, comprising of attacks against low-speed/high altitude targets (such as the U-2), medium-altitude/subsonic targets (such as the B-47 and B-52 heavy bombers) and high-altitude/high-speed small-sized targets (such as the AGM-28 Hound Dog cruise missile). The list of the practice targets used in these intercept training missions included the Yak-25RV (replicating the U-2), the Tu-16 (replicating the US subsonic bombers) and Su-9 itself (replicating the AGM-28 Hound Dog missile). The most difficult typical intercept was that performed against the U-2 or similar high-altitude targets flying at 500 to 600 km/h (270 to 324 kt) at the Su-9's operational ceiling. The interceptor was required to initially climb to the base altitude of about 10,000 m (32,800 feet), to accelerate to Mach 1.6 in level flight and then enter a climb, maintaining an instrument speed no lower than 1,100 km/h (593 kt), equating to Mach 1.9 at altitudes near the practical ceiling. In fact, the pilot had to maintain a speed equating to no lower than Mach 1.7, since at lower speeds the Su-9 was not able to maintain level flight. At the same time, the pilot was tasked with following the guidance instructions from the ground intercept control officer, and the intercept had to be carried out quickly because the closure speed between the interceptor and the target was so high.

In the late 1960s the Su-9 became an effective interceptor, manned and maintained by trained crews and boasting a reliable-enough mission avionics suite. The type saw a sporadic use for intercepting aircraft violating Soviet airspace, with the most well-known instances occurring on 9 April and 1 May 1960. The first date saw two Su-9s from the 739th IAP (based at Karshi, Uzbekistan) scrambled in a rushed manner against a Lockheed U-2 high-altitude reconnaissance aircraft operating out of Peshawar, Pakistan, which was performing a spying mission in Kazakhstan, deep inside Soviet territory (the nuclear proving ground near Semipalatinsk, the air defence proving range at Sari-Shagan and the space launch centre at Tur-Taram). However, the Su-9 pilots lacked the training to perform this complex type of intercept because the aircraft had been introduced with their regiment only a month ago. The pair scrambled to intercept the U-2 eventually failed to do the job, as the pilots proved unable to get to the target's altitude due to the inappropriate climb profile they had followed. Consequently, the failure to intercept the U-2 caused a big scandal as the Su-9's poor performance was held up as the main cause of this mission's failure. An industry/PVO commission was immediately despatched to the regiment to investigate the failure and find the reasons for it. This commission included Sukhoi and NII VVS test pilots, who flight-checked the Su-9 at Karshi and demonstrated that the aircraft was well-capable of getting to 20,000 m (65,600 feet) by using the special climb profile, which, at the time, was unknown to the regiment's pilots. A group of four NII VVS pilots, participating in the state testing effort of the Su-9, were then ordered to stand on QRA for a couple of weeks at Akhtubinsk in an effort to counter the expected U-2 overflights; on 26 April they were relieved by a front-line Su-9 squadron, deployed in a rushed manner to Akhtubinsk.

During the next U-2 mission on 1 May 1960, its route passed next to the big site of Sverdlovsk, in the Ural region. A Su-9 was present by chance at Sverdlovsk for a refuelling stop during its ferry flight from Novosibirsk to its new home at Baranovichi, Byelorussia. Its pilot, Capt. Igor Mentykov, was ordered to intercept the intruder, and due to his lack of missiles he was ordered to ram the target. Mentykov lacked the pressurised suit and helmet required for such a high-altitude intercept, but he was nevertheless ordered to launch and intercept the target. In the event, Capt. Mentykov failed to get into position to ram the U-2, but the US aircraft's mission on that day ended near Sverdlovsk as it took a hit by a missile fired by an SA-75 (SA-2 'Guideline') SAM system.

The third known instance of combat deployment of the Su-9 happened in the late 1960s, when a pair belonging to the 976th IAP at Kurdamir was scrambled to intercept two Iranian fighters that strayed into Soviet airspace. The Su-9s managed to get into firing position and the leader launched a RS-2US missile, but this failed to hit its intended target.

The Su-9s were also used against free-floating balloons sailing in Soviet airspace. On one occasion in 1969, a 179th Guards IAP (stationed at Stryi Airfield in Ukraine) Su-9 was launched to attack a balloon at 26,000 m (85,280 feet). The pilot was able to climb to 22,000 m (72,160 feet) and launch an RS-2US missile that inflicted damage to the lower half of the target. The balloon, however, remained aloft, and it had to be downed by another fighter.

The Su-9 already began to be replaced by newer types during the late 1960s, with the first three regiments of the 14th PVO Army, situated in extreme northern territories, taking the heavyweight Tu-128 'Fiddler' on strength; in the early 1970s, all the other Su-9-equipped regiments were reequipped with Su-15s and MiG-25Ps. The Su-9 remained in mass front-line use with the IA PVO until the late 1970s, and the last regiments equipped with the type continued flying it until 1981, when they converted to the MiG-23P and MiG-23ML.

## Su-11—A Capable Interceptor with No Luck

The next delta-wing interceptor developed by the Sukhoi OKB used the basic fuselage and powerplant inherited from the T-43 (Su-9), but it was to be equipped with more powerful Almaz radar with the large antenna housed in the intake centre-body of an enlarged nose. A resolution of the Ministry of Aviation Industry and VVS dated 18 December 1957 called for the first ten aircraft of this version (dubbed 'T47') to be produced in 1958. These were to be used as a stop-gap solution, equipped with the Almaz radar but armed with cannons instead of air-to-air missiles.

The first T47 was built by Sukhoi in late 1957 by using the second series-production T-3, which received an enlarged nose section, new radar, NR-30 cannons and two ORO-57 rocket packs for firing 57-mm rockets. The aircraft made its maiden flight on 6 January 1957 with V. Mosolov in the cockpit. The second prototype, intended for development testing of the K-7 air-to-air missile, had an improved aerodynamics thanks to the introduction of a dogtooth on each wing, and took to the air for the first time on 21 February 1958. By mid-1958, however, the development of the interceptor equipped with the Almaz radar and armed with 30-mm cannons and K-7 missiles was shelved in favour of another equipment and armament selection.

In the second half of 1958 the Sukhoi OKB commenced the development of a new derivative of the T47 interceptor; it would be equipped with the new Oryol radar, originally designed by the OKB-339 for the Yak-27K long-range fighter-interceptor. This new and more capable version was to be armed with the K-8M air-to-air missile, available in two versions. The first one was equipped with a semi-active radar homing (SARH) seeker and the second sported an infrared (IR) seeker suitable for day and night use. The radar and the two K-8M versions were capable of rear-hemisphere (tail-on) attacks only. The first design work on the new aircraft began in the second half of 1958, and the first two T47 prototypes and several production-standard aircraft were employed in the test programme, equipped with the new radar and missiles. The first prototype lacked the radar and featured only the enlarged cone and the widened nose section for aerodynamic trials and missile launches. Designated as the T47-3, it took to the air for the first time on 27 December 1958. The new enlarged nose section caused performance degradation, represented by a reduction in the practical ceiling, maximum speed, range and acceleration performance. Two more T47s joined the flight testing in early 1959, plus another three in the middle of the year. The T47-5, which began flight testing in May 1959, was equipped with the Oryol radar and K-8M missiles, while the T47-4 got its radar in January 1960.

In August 1959 all the T47s were submitted to the NII VVS for the state testing effort, the preliminary phase of which included forty intercept sorties—intended for evaluation of the radar performance—and ten missile launches. The first phase of the state testing effort took place between November 1959 and April 1960, which included an evaluation of the combat performance with the IR-guided missiles that involved three aircraft. By April 1960 two more aircraft were made available for use in the evaluation of the radar-guided missile. One of these (T47-8) introduced a more powerful AL-7F-2 engine in order to improve the slightly degraded performance and also sported an improved fuel system with a total capacity of 4,195 litres. All the T47 prototypes were involved in the second stage of the state test effort, which commenced on 26 April 1960. By the end of the summer the T47s were modified to the standard pioneered by the T47-8, which enabled the new fighter to show an acceptable range performance.

The state test effort was completed in late May 1961, and on 8 June that year the type's test report completion protocol was signed. The prototypes amassed 475 flights during the state testing, and the total number of test sorties logged during the factory and state test effort was more than 700. The new fighter-interceptor was officially commissioned in service by a Council of Ministers decree dated 5 February 1962. The aircraft received the Su-11 in-service designation (NATO reporting name 'Fishpot-C'), while the radar was designated as the RP-11 and the missile as the R-8MR (the version equipped with SARH seeker) and R-8MT (the version equipped with an IR seeker). The overall air intercept system was designated as the Su-11-8M.

## Su-11 Specification

| | |
|---|---|
| Dimensions: Wing span Length with Pitot probe Height | 8.54 m 18.23 m 4.70 m |
| Wing area: | 26.20 m$^2$ |
| Weights: Normal take-off with four AAMs Maximum take-off Fuel in internal tanks | 12,647 kg 13,990 kg 3,440 kg |
| Performance: Max level speed at sea level Max level speed at high level Practical ceiling Take-off distance Landing distance Intercept range Rate of climb at low level Range on internal fuel Range on internal and external fuel | 1,150 km/h 2,340 km/h 18,000 m 1,260 m 1,710 m 350 km 200 m/s 1,260 km 1,710 km |

The series production was launched in late 1961, and it was set to supersede the Su-9 at the production line at GAZ-153 in Novosibirsk, with as many as forty aircraft planned to be built by the end of that year. The first production-standard Su-11 was flight-tested for the first time in July 1962. However, this example was sadly soon lost, crashing during its factory testing due to engine failure. The NII VVS test pilot V. Andreev attempted to perform a flamed-out landing, but the aircraft was destroyed and the pilot was killed. This was a very difficult moment

The first Su-11, dubbed 'T47', made its maiden flight on 6 January 1957, but the series production of the type was not launched until 1962. (*Sukhoi OKB*)

The Su-11 was equipped with the Oryol radar and armed with the K-8M air-to-air missile, available in two versions—the first with a semi-active radar homing seeker and the second sporting an infrared seeker suitable for day and night use. (*Boris Lilov*)

The Su-11 was put into limited production (with only enough aircraft for three regiments), and served in the front-line role from 1964 to 1980. (*Sukhoi OKB*)

for the programme as the IA PVO Commanding Officer, Marshall Evgeniy Savitski, was very upset from the poor reliability performance of the Su-9, and he considered its successor, Su-11, as an unreliable aircraft too. In addition, the influential OKB-115 chief designer Alexander Yakovlev also attacked the Sukhoi's single-engine fighter concept, claiming that his Yak-28P twin-engine design was a much more dependable and safe design. As a consequence, the IA PVO and Aviaprom leadership took the decision to build the Su-11 in very small numbers, as it was to be promptly superseded at the GAZ-153 production line by the Yak-28. In this manner, the Su-11 remained in production until early 1965, with only 112 examples built.

The first production Su-11s were taken on strength by the 393rd Guards IAP, stationed at Astrakhan Privoljskiy Airfield, in mid-1964; the new type underwent its field trials here. The other two front-line regiments slated to convert to the Su-11 took their aircraft in the first half of 1965—these were the 790th IAP at Khotilovo, north of Moscow, and the 191st IAP at Yefremovo Airfield. In service, the Su-11 proved to be a reliable aircraft thanks to the long series of modifications implemented during the flight tests, with the AL-7F-2 also showing a fairly good reliability. The type remained in front-line service with the IA PVO until 1980.

## Su-15—Sukhoi's Last Delta-Winged Interceptor

The Su-15 (NATO reporting name 'Flagon') was the last representative of Sukhoi's delta series of the Su-9/11 family, sporting the most modern radar, a better armament suite and an improved overall performance. It was also the

This is the only Yak-23U two-seater built; previously preserved at the Yakovlev Design Bureau (also known as the OKB Yak or Yakovlev OKB) premises, now it is on display at the Technical Museum Vadima Zadorojnogo in Arakhangelskoe, near Moscow. (*Author's collection*)

A Bulgarian Air Force Yak-23 single-seater in its original paint scheme on display at the Aviation & Air Force Museum at Kumovo Air Base, near Plovdiv. The best Soviet straight-wing jet fighter saw brief operation in the Soviet Air Force; then, in the early 1950s, most of the 310 built examples were handed over to the friendly states in Eastern Europe such as Bulgaria, Czechoslovakia, Poland and Romania. (*Author's collection*)

A production-standard Yak-25 twin-engine loitering fighter; it is armed with two NR-37L 37-mm cannons, with fifty rounds each, in the lower fuselage, while in overloaded mode its capacity could be increased to 100. Aiming was possible by using either the RP-6 radar-sight or the ASP-3NM optical gun-sight. (*Yakovlev OKB*)

The Yak-28's interceptor derivative—dubbed Yak-28P—took to the air for the first time on 5 March 1958, powered by R-11-300 afterburning turbojets. It introduced the K-8M-1 missile system, comprising an Oryol-D air-intercept radar and two R-8M-1 air-to-air missiles, equipped with IR or SARH seeker heads. This example is preserved at the Technical Museum Vadima Zadorojnogo in Arakhangelskoe, near Moscow. (*Author's collection*)

The UTI MiG-15 two-seater was in production at several plants, with the last examples flying in military service around the world until the late 1980s. (*Author's collection*)

The MiG-17 was a mass-produced, simple and pretty affordable combat aircraft that was mass-produced. It initially served as a fighter, and later in its career, since the late 1950s, it had been re-roled as a fighter-bomber. It continued operating with the Soviet air arm until the late 1960s, while the Eastern European air arms continued operating it in the ground-attack role until the mid-1980s. (*Author's collection*)

The MiG-17PF was a dedicated fighter-interceptor equipped for bad-weather intercepts, capable of firing its two 23-mm cannons at air targets without visual aiming, using the radar to track the target and calculate a firing solution. (*Author's collection*)

The MiG-19S was a supersonic fighter armed with a trio of NR-30 cannons holding a total of 210 rounds, featuring an effective range of 2,000 m (6,560 feet). This is a North Korean Air Force example—most likely Chinese-built—armed with eight-round packs for firing 57-mm rockets. (*Author's collection*)

The gun-less MiG-19PM had a stretched nose section to accommodate the twin-antenna RP-5 Izumrud radar, and it was armed with four RS-2US (K-5) air-to-air missiles. (*Author's collection*)

The lightweight MiG-21F-13 was designed from the outset to intercept transonic/supersonic bombers and fighter-bombers at altitudes up to 20,000 m (65,600 feet), with interceptions limited to rear-hemisphere attacks only in a single attack run, firing the cannon or launching the heat-seeking air-to-air missiles. (*Author's collection*)

The radar-equipped MiG-21PF was originally designed as an integral component of the MiG-21P-13 air-intercept system, capable of operating at night and in adverse weather and comprising the aircraft and the K-13 (R-3S) heat-seeking air-to-air missile. Later on it was complemented by the RS-2US beam-riding missile. (*Author's collection*)

The MiG-21PFM combined the MiG-21PF's basic design with the new KM-1 (SK-3) ejection seat and an improved RP-21M radar, but it retained the weak armament options of its predecessor MiG-21PF— only two R-3S (K-13) or RS-2US (K-5) air-to-air missiles. (*Author's collection*)

The MiG-21M was the first member of the 'Fishbed' family to receive the 23-mm GSh-23L built-in cannon, housed in a neat ventral pack and provided with 200 rounds accommodated in a belt around the fuselage. (*Author's collection*)

The MiG-21MF retained the MiG-21M's fuselage but sported an increased-thrust R-13-300 engine and an improved equipment standard. It was a dedicated export derivative of the MiG-21SM built only for the Soviet Air Force. (*Author's collection*)

The big-spine MiG-21SMT had an increased internal fuel capacity, and its take-off weight (with full internal tanks and two missiles) reached 8,900 kg (19,616 lb). The maximum take-off weight with air-to-ground ordnance under the wings and a centreline drop tank increased to 10,100 kg (22,260 lb). (*Author's collection*)

16. The MiG-21bis was the last single-seat 'Fishbed' production derivative, re-engined and with a redesigned airframe in order to be better-suited for high-G manoeuvring dogfights at low and medium levels, combined with a 1970s analogue avionics suite. This aircraft is armed with R-60 and R-13M heat-seeking air-to-air missiles and carries a 490-litre, jettisonable external tank under the fuselage. (*Lubomir Slavov*)

Despite the redesign effort, the MiG-21bis, launched in production in 1972, retained some of the chief design shortcomings of its predecessors, such as the limited operational radius and radar performance, lack of beyond-visual-range missiles, poor pilot visibility (particularly in his 6 o'clock), mediocre slow-speed handling characteristics and high pilot workload during all phases of flight. (*Author's collection*)

The improved two-seater MiG-21UM, flown for the first time in 1968, introduced an entirely new flight/navigation avionics suite borrowed from the MiG-21S single-seater, including the AP-155 three-axis full-authority autopilot and the ASP-PFD-21 gun-sight. (*Author's collection*)

The two-seat radar-less MiG-21UM was rolled out at the GAZ-31 aircraft plant in Tbilisi between 1971 and 1985; as many as 1,133 examples were manufactured and the last of these are set to continue soldiering on until the early 2020s. (*Author's collection*)

A late-series Su-15TM distinguishable thanks to its ogival nose cone, which was installed in order to create better working conditions for the Taifun-M (RP-26) radar and remove the unwanted reflections from the dielectric nose cone. (*US DoD*)

The fully-armed Su-15TM with an R-98R missile under the starboard wing, an R-98T under the port wing and a pair of R-60 'pocket' air-to-air missiles suspended on inner underwing pylons. (*Author's collection*)

The MiG-23MS was an export derivative of the MiG-23M with a notably reduced mission avionics performance; its radar was the RP-22 Sapfir-21 inherited from the MiG-21bis. This is an ex-Egyptian Air Force aircraft operated in the aggressor role by the USAF's 4477th Test and Evaluation Squadron, stationed at Tonopah AFB, Nevada. (*USAF*)

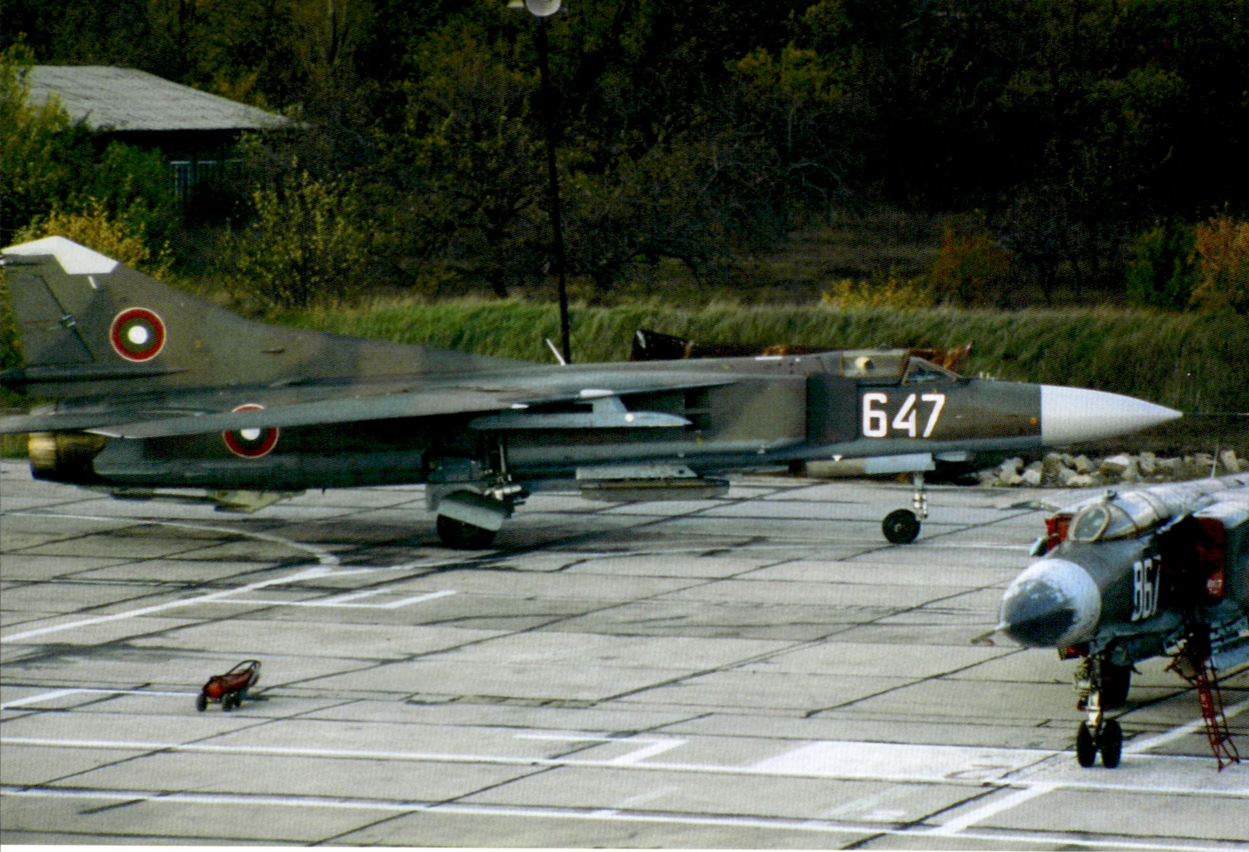
647

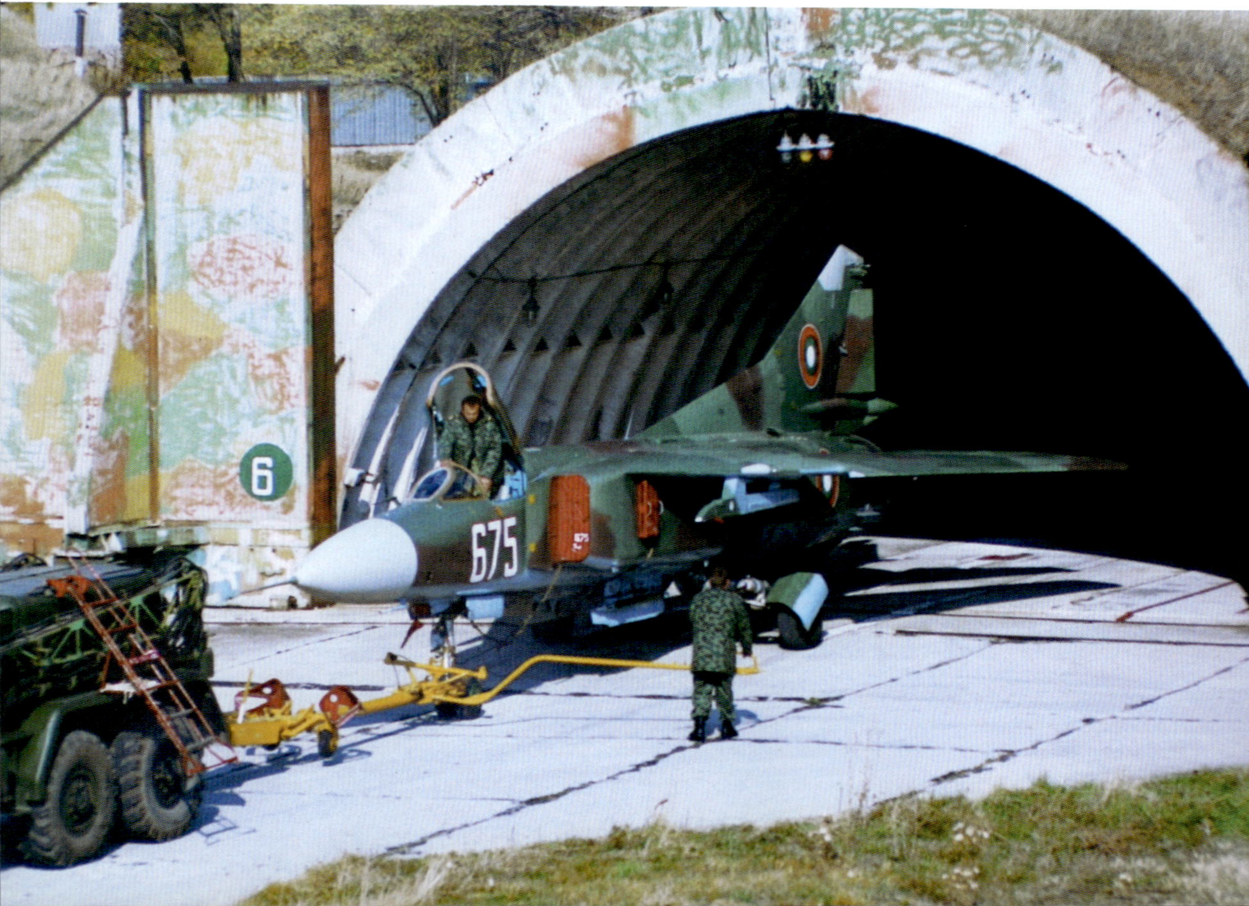
6
675

The MiG-23MLA introduced the ASP-17ML HUD/gun-sight and 26ShI IRST, useful for silent (emission-free) intercepts; in 1981 the new R-24R/T air-to-air missile, which boasted much improved range, warhead, fuse and ECM resistance compared to that of the R-23R/T, was added to its arsenal. (*Author's collection*)

*Opposite above:* The MiG-23MF was the most numerous export derivative of the MiG-23M, sharing the same airframe, general systems and powerplant, but equipped with a slightly different mission avionics set. (*Author's collection*)

*Opposite below:* The MiG-23MF sported the much-improved Sapfir-23D look-down/shoot-down radar and the TP-23 infrared search-and-track sensor. It was armed with R-23R/T BVR missiles and R-13M WVR missiles, complemented later on by the much more capable R-60. (*Author's collection*)

The MiG-23ML/MLA's overall combat effectiveness was about 20 per cent better than that of the MiG-23M/MF thanks to the better performance and more capable radar and IRST. (*Author's collection*)

The list of aerodynamics features introduced with the MiG-23MLD mid-life upgrade delivered to the Soviet Air Force included vortex generators on the pitot boom, and notched leading-edge roots were added to act as vortex generators and energise the flow over the wings in order to delay the stall. This aircraft carries a full combat loadout of two R-24 BVR and two R-60 WVR air-to-air missiles, while the wings are set in a full forward position to enable low-speed flight. (*US DoD*)

The MiG-23MLD (export), pictured here, retained the MiG-23MLA's basic airframe and powerplant, combined with new flight/navigation and mission avionics. The 23-22 version (delivered to Bulgaria and seen here) was almost identical in avionics and equipment to the Soviet Air Force's 22-18 mid-life upgrade, while the 23-19 (delivered to Syria) was a sanitised version. (*Author's collection*)

The MiG-23UB two-seater lacked radar and retained the capability to use the R-3S and R-13M heat-seeking missiles in addition to a selection of air-to-ground ordinance. (*Author's collection*)

The MiG-25PU combat trainer operated by the Soviet Air Defence Forces was made capable of carrying up to four R-40T/TD heat-seeking BVR air-to-air missiles, but this configuration was never used for operational missions. (*Andey Zinchuk*)

31. This is an export-standard MiG-25PD operated by the Libyan Arab Air Force, seen here armed with a pair of R-40 missiles and a quartet of R-60 air-to-air missiles. (*USN*)

A MiG-25PU two-seater captured by the camera while taking off from Monchegorsk airfield for a training flight with its engines set at full afterburner mode. *(Andrey Zinchuk)*

*Above*: A MiG-25PD seen on landing roll with a pair of brake parachutes deployed for shortening the roll length. (*Vestink Vozdushnogo Flota*)

*Below*: This MiG-29, serialed '10', is an early production example owned by OKB MiG and used for display purposes. It was shown for the first time at Farnborough Air Show in September 1988, stealing the show; it was lost at the Paris air show on June 8 1989, with OKB MiG test pilot Anatoliy Kvochur performing a spectacular last-moment ejection at ultra-low level after an apparent engine failure. (*RSK MiG*)

The MiG-29 features an all-swept wing configuration that was selected by the MiG design team, with wide ogival LERXs and outward-canted tailfins, installed on booms on the outer side of the widely-spaced engines. (*Author's collection*)

A pair of humpbacked MiG-29s (9-13 sub-version) belonging to the Russian Air Force's 4th Combat Training and Aircrew Conversion Centre at Lipetsk. (*Andrey Zinchuk*)

A German Air Force MiG-29 pictured during the launch of an R-27R1 beyond-visual-range missile while on a training deployment to the USA. (*USAF*)

Thanks to the combination of the high-lift aerodynamic configuration, wing high-lift devices and afterburning thrust/weight ratio exceeding 1.1 during operations at normal take-off weight, the MiG-29's take-off run is exceptionally short—it takes only 820 feet (250 m) to become airborne. When military-power mode is used, the take-off run is 700 to 800 m (2,296 to 2,624 feet). (*Krasimir Grozev*)

The MiG-29's Klimov RD-33 has a pretty good efficiency in cruise flight and impressive afterburning rating, but it suffers from some notable shortcomings such as low TBO and the production of a pronounced smoke trail on transient modes of operation, between idle and military-power settings. (*Lubomir Slavov*)

This is the first of two MiG-29K prototypes built in the late 1980s, used as the baseline for developing the new-style, shipborne 'Fulcrums' built for the Russian and Indian naval air arms. (*RSK MiG*)

The MiG-31 'Foxhound' is a huge heavyweight fighter with restricted manoeuvrability and maximum take-off weight reaching 46,200 kg (101,820 lbs); at landing it uses two brake parachutes to reduce the distance needed for a full stop. (*Andrey Zinchuk*)

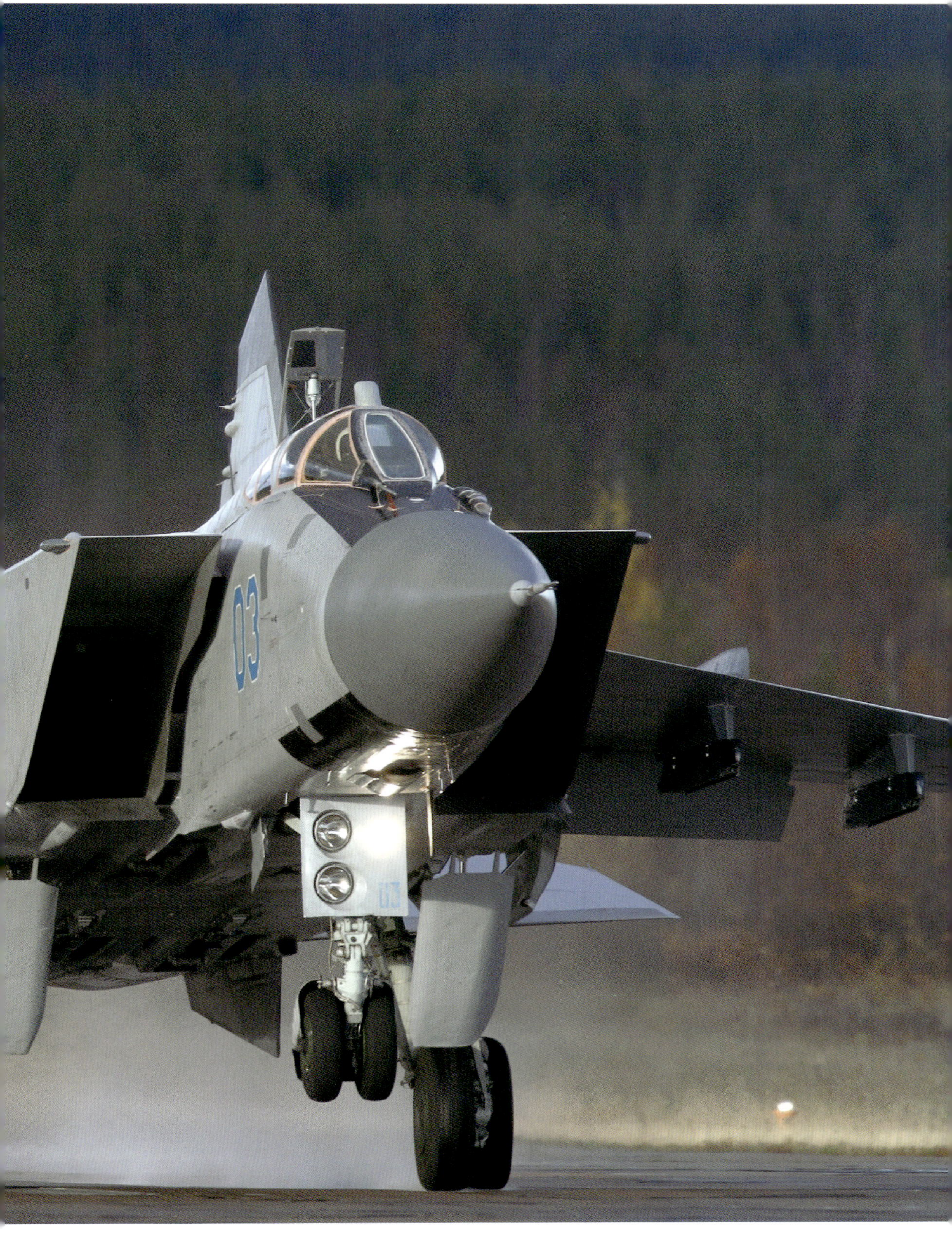
03

A Russian Air Force MiG-31BM armed with four R-33 air-to-air missiles, captured by the camera while performing a patrol mission over the Barents Sea. (*Andrey Zinchuk collection*)

About 500 MiG-31s of all variants were produced between 1977 and 1994 in Gorky. The type has never been exported, despite the marketing effort initiated immediately after the end of the Cold War and lasting until the mid-1990s. (*Andrey Zinchuk*)

A pair of Chinese People's Liberation Army Air Force Su-27SKs demonstrate loadouts of four R-27 BVR missiles and two R-73 missiles each (containing training rounds). s(*Author's collection*)

A Su-30 two-seat long-endurance interceptor operated by the Flight Research Institute, seen while taking fuel from an Il-78 tanker during the flying display at MAKS-2001 air show. (Author's collection)

*Above*: A clean Russian Air Force Su-27S comes into landing with its dorsal airbrake deployed. After the break-up of the Soviet Union in 1991, the 'Flanker-B/C' fleet inherited by Russia numbered about 300 examples. (*Andrey Zinchuk*)

*Below*: The 'Flanker' routinely uses twin brake parachutes for shortening its landing roll, which is especially useful when operating from ice or snow-covered short runways. (*Andrey Zinchuk*)

A Su-27SM and a Su-30 heavyweight fighter seen taking off in a tight formation. The colourful example flying as a wingman is among the five improved Su-30 two-seaters with air-to-air missiles, taken on strength between 1994 and 1996 by the Russian Air Defence Forces and originally operated by the 148th TsBPiPLS at Savastleika airfield, north of Moscow. (*Andrey Zinchuk*)

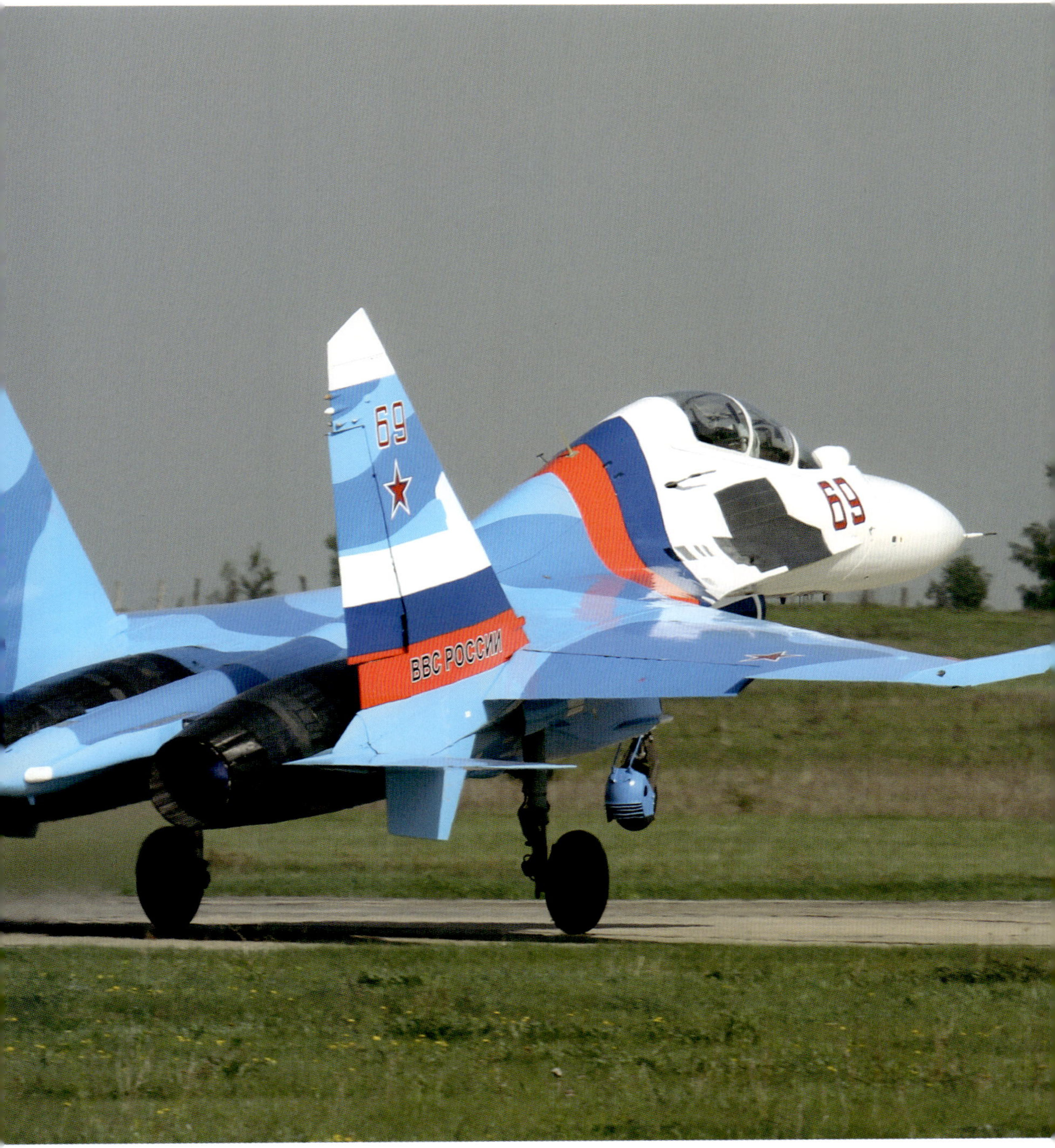
69
ВВС РОССИИ
69

A Su-33 shipborne fighter demonstrating take-off at full afterburner. (*Andrey Zinchuk*)

A well-adorned Russian Naval Aviation Su-33 of the 279th KIAP, seen just after lift-off from the runway of its home base at Severomorsk-3, near Murmansk, on the Kola Peninsula. (*Andrey Zichuk*)

A look inside the MiG-23MLD's cockpit—hardly an ergonomic layout, typical for all 1970s-vintage Soviet combat aircraft. They were crammed with instruments and switches and incurred a pretty high workload on the pilot. (*Author's collection*)

first Soviet fighter-interceptor made capable of attacking targets flying as high as 23,000 m (75,440 feet).

The Su-15 design concept derived from a series of experimental aircraft that were used to test some major design novelties. The P-1, a two-seat interceptor with side air intakes, was the first of them. Flown for the first time on 12 July 1958, its development was terminated in September 1958 due to the serious development problems shown by its Lul'ka AL-9 engine. The T5 was the second experimental aircraft in this series that contributed to the development of the Su-15, using the proven T3 layout with a nose intake but adding a new rear fuselage section modified to accommodate two Tumanskiy R-11F-300 engines arranged side-by-side. It made its first flight (with Vladimir Ilyshin at the controls) with the new powerplant on 18 June 1959, and completed the testing in the following June. The third experimental aircraft in the series, dubbed 'T49', was based on the Su-11 airframe; it was intended to test an unusual radar/intake arrangement. The modified nose contained a radar cone protruding forwards, with air intakes on the sides just aft of the radome. It took to the air for the first time on 10 January 1960, but it had a brief career due to being damaged in an incident soon after its flight tests commenced.

Based on the promising test results demonstrated by the three prototypes, in 1960 the OKB-51 proposed a new interceptor aircraft to the IA PVO leadership; the aircraft would be used as a component of the Su-15-40 air-intercept system, also including the K-40 air-to-air missile. The Soviet Council of Ministers issued a decree for launching the Su-15's development nearly two years later, on 5 February 1962. This document, however, obliged the OKB-51 to simply develop an improved Su-11 derivative, free from the deficiencies found during its state testing and evaluation, and equipped with the Su-11's mission suite, including a slightly improved Oryol-D58 air-intercept radar and K-8M1 missiles; the designation of the new intercept system was to be the Su-11-8. The second stage of the Su-15's development programme was set to see the introduction of the new Smerch-AS radar and the improved K-8M2 missiles.

In the event, OKB-51's head, Pavel Osipovich Sukhoi, decided to proceed with a much more promising new design dubbed 'T-58D', with two engines fed by side intakes. It made it possible for the interceptor to be outfitted with a large radar antenna capable of guiding missiles for all-aspect intercepts. Powered by two R-11F2S-300 afterburning turbojets—each rated at 60.97 kN (13,688 lb st. or 6,215 kgf)—the new design retained the Su-9/11's wing, empennage, main undercarriage units, cockpit canopy and most of the general systems unchanged, while introducing an all-new fuselage with side intakes. It is noteworthy that the side intake design was used for the first time in the Soviet Union on this particular Sukhoi design.

The first prototype, T58D-1, made its maiden flight on 30 May 1962 at Zhukovskiy (Ramenskoye) Airfield in the capable hands of Sukhoi's famous test pilot Vladimir Ilyushin. The prototype design saw some minor changes during the factory testing period, such as moving the brake parachute container to the base of the fin and increasing the fin area for improving the longitudinal stability.

The T-58D-1 lacked radar and other mission systems and was used mainly for performance testing.

The new interceptor was initially earmarked to receive the Su-11's Oryol-58D radar, renamed later as the 'RP-15' (with an enlarged-diameter antenna providing some 35-per-cent-longer detection range compared to the original version) and it was installed on the T58D-2 prototype in an enlarged nose. It was flown for the first time on 4 May 1963, again with Vladimir Ilyushin in the cockpit. In June that year the T58D-2 was submitted for undergoing its state testing with the NII VVS at Akhtubinsk; this effort was completed within one year.

The third prototype, T58D-3, was flown for the first time on 2 October 1963; this example introduced a series of fuselage design alterations intended for improving the performance, with a new rear-fuselage shape. This new rear fuselage was used for housing more fuel on the production-standard aircraft, with the total tankage reaching 6,860 litres. The T58D-3 was used for testing the RP-15M weapons control system and the new R-98 missiles, as well as the SAU-58 automated flight control system conceived for the new 'Flagon' derivatives.

On 30 April 1965 the Su-15-98 air-intercept complex (or system), consisting of the Su-15 aircraft and the R-98R/T missile, was commissioned in the IA PVO service by a Soviet Council of Ministers decree. The aircraft received the NATO codename 'Flagon-A'.

The Su-15-98 air intercept system was purposely designed to work in conjunction with the Vozdukh-1 automated ground control intercept (GCI) system to perform all-aspect intercepts with so-called 'instrument guidance' from the ground, providing the pilot with steering cues until they detected the target with their own radar. Due to the lack of R-98 missiles in the beginning of Su-15 deployment, the aircraft delivered to the first front-tine regiments continued use of the older R-8M-1.

The T49 prototype pioneered a twin-engine configuration packed side-by-side and fed by air intakes on the sides, just aft of the radome. This arrangement enabled the nose section to receive a larger radar antenna for long-range target detection and tracking compared to the then-common configuration with pitot-type nose intake. (*Sukhoi OKB*)

The first production-standard Su-15 example, built at the GAZ-153 plant at Novosibirsk, took to the air for the first time on 6 March 1965, and the full-scale manufacturing of the new type was launched in 1966. The Su-15 continued in production until 1970, and all production-standard aircraft were fitted with improved RP-15M radars that boasted a better resistance to jamming.

In 1969 the aircraft in the eleventh production batch received an increased-area cranked wing, with sweepback at the outer section reduced to 45°—with an attachment at the end, beyond the aerodynamic fence, 2.65 m (8.7 feet) from the aircraft's centre-line. This change was introduced in order to reduce the Su-15's take-off and landing speeds, and also to reduce induced drag in flight. The new wing design was tested for the first time in 1966. Another novelty for further improving the take-off/landing performance on the original Su-15, which was described as being very poor (as its landing speed exceeded 300 km/h [162 kt]), called for the installation of the UPS blown flaps system. It was initially set to work at a 20° deflection angle for take-off and a 45° for landing, using bleed air taken from engine compressors. However, it turned out that the engine power rating was clearly insufficient to provide enough bleed air at the intended flaps settings, prompting their reduction to 15° and 25° respectively. The modified engine feeding the UPS system was designated as the R-11F2SU-300. Later on, the up-rated R-13-300, used to power the much-improved Su-15TM, made it possible for full flap deflection to be used, causing a further reduction of the type's take-off and landing speeds and thus simplifying the handling characteristics and reducing pilot workload.

## Su-15—Technical Description

The Su-15 had a mid-wing airframe with a delta wing, with a structure made of D16, D19 and V95 aluminium alloys, with the heavy loaded parts made of 30KhGSA and 30KhGSNA high-tensile strength steel alloys. The fuselage was of semi-monocoque structure, and had two parts at frame thirty-four. The front part contained the radar, front undercarriage unit, cockpit and a group of three fuel tanks. The rear fuselage featured two engines accommodated side-by-side and four air brake panels.

The cockpit was equipped with the KS-4 ejection seat. Designed by the Sukhoi OKB, it was capable of providing safe ejection of the pilot from ground level to 20,000 m (65,600 feet), and at instrument speeds between 140 and 1,200 km/h (76 and 647 kt). The ejection sequence started with jettisoning of the canopy.

The wings had a 60° sweepback on the leading edge, angle of incidence of 0° and anhedral of -2°. From the eleventh production series, the wings received extension at their ends, beyond the aerodynamic fence, with a sweepback angle of 45°—which increased the span to 9.34 m (30.64 feet). The wing mechanisation comprised blown flaps and ailerons. The wing structure contained compartments to accommodate the main undercarriage units, fuel tanks, landing lights and antennas.

The third T58D prototype, dubbed 'T58D-3', on display at the Russian Air Force Museum in Monino, near Moscow (*Boris Lilov*)

This is one of the first production-standard Su-15s, rolled out at the GAZ-153 in 1966. (*Sukhoi OKB*)

The Su-15-98 air-intercept complex—consisting of the Su-15 aircraft, RP-15 radar and R-98R/T missiles—was officially commissioned in service in April 1965. (*Sukhoi OKB*)

The empennage consisted of a tailfin with a rudder fastened to fuselage frames thirty-five and forty-three and an all-moving tailplane. Both the fin and the tailplane had a sweep angle of 55°.

The undercarriage was of tricycle type, with the front unit retracting forward into the fuselage and provided with twin-controllable wheels. The main undercarriage units, retracting inwards into the wings, were provided with single braking wheels. A brake parachute container was accommodated in the fin base.

The Su-15's mechanical flight control system used irreversible BU-49 boosters for actuation of the elevator, rudder and ailerons. The Su-15TM used the more powerful BU-220 and BU-250 boosters.

The Su-15 used four independent hydraulic systems, operating at a 210 to 215 kg/cm$^2$ (2,986 to 3,058 psi) pressure and using the AMG-10 hydraulic fluid. Two of these systems were used for feeding the port and starboard boosters, and the other two for operation of the undercarriage, flaps, air brakes, air intake ramps, radar antenna. The improved Su-15M had three hydraulic systems because the Taifun radar antenna used electrical rather than hydraulic steering.

The three independent pneumatic systems, working at a pressure of 200 kg/cm$^2$, were used for braking the wheels, cockpit pressurisation and also for emergency lowering of the undercarriage and flaps. The electrical system used an AC voltage of 115 V/400 Hz and a DC voltage of 27 V.

The full-scale manufacture of the Su-15 was launched at the GAZ-153 in Novosibirsk in 1966. (*Sukhoi OKB*)

## The Enhanced-Performance Su-15T/TM

The Su-15 derivative equipped with the Smerch-AS radar was dubbed 'T-58T' and developed in accordance with a Council of Ministers decree dated 1962. The new radar, however, was ready as late as in 1968, when it received the new name '*Taifun*' ('Typhoon'). A derivative of the extremely-powerful RP-25 Smerch-A radar equipping the MiG-25P, Taifun's installation onto the Su-15 necessitated some design changes to the forward fuselage. The modified aircraft was also powered by R-13-300 turbojets (originally designed for the MiG-21SM) and was flown for the first time on 31 January 1969, with Vladimir Krechetov at the controls. The new engines, rated at 40.20 kN (9,039 lb st. or 4,097 kgf) dry and 64.71 kN (14,550 lb st. or 6,596 kgf) with afterburner (a 10 per cent increase compared to the R-11F2SU-300), required larger intakes to cope with the increased airflow requirements. The pair of R-13-300s provided better performance—particularly at take-off and landing, due to the use of the full blown flaps setting—combined with slightly better acceleration and range performance. The aircraft, which received the new service designation Su-15T ('T' denoting 'Taifun'), also introduced the SAU-58 automatic flight control system and an RSBN-5S tactical aid for navigation, better radios, an upgraded Lasour-SM intercept guidance datalink and a Sirena-3 RWR.

The first production Su-15Ts were rolled out in 1970 and 1971, even before completion of the type's state testing effort. At the time, however, the new radar demonstrated serious deficiencies, and the aircraft's production had been stopped after rolling out only ten examples. Later, it was considered that the Taifun should be replaced on the Su-15T by its improved derivative, Taifun-M, which had a two-times-greater detection and tracking range compared to that of the original RP-15M Oryol-DM. This new Su-15 derivative was designated as the Su-15TM

A close-up view of the R-98MT heat-seeking air-to-air missile hanging under the Su-15's starboard wing. (*Sukhoi OKB*)

(NATO 'Flagon-E'), and was launched in production in December 1971. The first aircraft to roll off the line at the GAZ-135 was used in the state flight test programme of the Taifun-M radar, which was initiated in 1970. Upon entry into service, the new radar received the RP-26 designation.

The Su-15TM interceptor, armed with K-98M (R-98M) air-to-air missiles, was formally commissioned in IA PVO service in January 1975, when the series production run was close to completion. The R-98MR was the SARH version and the R-98MT was the IR-guided version, using the same body, motor and warhead.

The new radar, combined with the R-98M missiles with a maximum range of 24 km (12.9 nm) when launched head-on, made the Su-15TM capable of intercepting air targets flying at speeds between 500 and 1,600 km/h (269 and 863 kt) in the rear hemisphere (tail-on attacks), at altitudes between 500 and 24,000 m (1,640 and 78,720 feet); in the forward hemisphere (head-on attacks), these figures were 500 and 2,500 km/h (269 and 1,348 kt), and 2,000 to 21,000 m (6,560 and 68,880 feet) respectively. The minimum head-on range was 4 km (2.15 nm), while the minimum tail-on range was only 1.8 km (1 nm).

The radar was able to detect targets flying up to 9,000 m (29,520 feet) above the Su-15TM, while the R-98M missiles were able to reach targets flying up to 4,000 m (13,120 feet) higher than the launch platform in head-on attacks and up to 6,000 m (19,680 feet) in tail-on attacks. The intercept radius against a target at 10,000 m (32,280 feet) was 510 km (275 nm) in head-on and 340 km (183 nm) in tail-on attacks. The missile weighed 292 kg (644 lb) and had a warhead weighing 40 kg (88 lb).

The production-standard Su-15TM was equipped with the new and much more capable Taifun-M radar (also known as the RP-26), and the machines from the eighth production series onwards introduced an ogival nose cone. (*Sukhoi OKB*)

The Su-15TM's sophisticated SAU-58 system facilitated automatic flight during the intercept, beginning immediately after take-off and without any pilot involvement. The aircraft simply had to follow the intercept profile calculated by the Vozdukh-1M ground station, with commands received by the on-board Lasour-SM equipment and fed into the autopilot. After launching the missiles and exiting from the attack, the flight continued in the automatic mode, as the autopilot, fed by information derived from the RSBN-5S navigation system, was able to return the aircraft to the pre-programmed airfield and perform the landing approach down to about 60 m (200 feet); at this point the pilot was required to take over and perform the final approach, flaring, touchdown and braking hands-on.

The Taifun-M radar operations, however, proved problematic due to its much higher pulse power compared to that of the old Oryol-58DM, creating sensible reflections from the dielectric nose cone inherited from the original Su-15. In order to avoid the unwanted reflections displayed on the radar scope, the radome shape was changed to ogival, and the new design was introduced on the Su-15TMs from the eighth production series on; this sub-version received the NATO reporting name 'Flagon-F'.

During the aircraft's service with the IA PVO, the Su-15 and Su-15TM fleets received additional armament for close-quarters engagements, represented by two R-60 (AA-8 'Aphid') air-to-air missiles on additional wing pylons. In addition, two UPK-23-250 gun-pods, aimed through a simple K-10T collimator sight, could be carried under the fuselage. Both of these modifications were undertaken in the early 1970s to boost the Su-15's overall combat potential.

In the late 1970s and the early 1980s, the IA PVO commenced training its interceptor force for attacking low-flying targets, but the lack of look-down/shoot-down radar on the Su-15TM led to the invention of new tactics, calling for attacks from below, in an effort to provide the radar with suitable conditions and without picking up ground clutter. In order to be made suitable for such a

A look inside the Su-15TM's cockpit. (*Dmitri Sribniy*)

type of intercept in automated mode, the Su-15TM force received the modified SAU-58-2 automatic control system, integrated with a low-altitude radar altimeter. In this way the modified Su-15TM was made capable of performing an intercept receiving Vozdukh-1M steering commands while flying at a minimum altitude of 200 m (660 feet) and still remaining below target altitude. However, pilots had never liked this kind of remotely-controlled intercept, necessitating hands-off flying at high-speed and at ultra-low altitude; as a consequence, this type of operational training was never used in a mass manner. Nevertheless, the experience gained during the SAU-58-2 testing was utilised at a later stage, during the development of the terrain-following modes of the Su-24 swing-wing low-altitude frontal bomber.

In 1973 a newly-built Su-15TM received the more powerful R-25-300 engines, an R-13-300 derivative, rated at 69.6 kN (15,626 lb st. or 7,094 kgf) at the so-called 'emergency afterburner' mode, permitted for up to three minutes of operation. Use of such an engine on the Su-15TM, re-designated as Su-15bis, was expected to improve the acceleration, speed and rate-of-climb performance at altitudes up to 4,000 m (13,120 feet), as well as increasing both the practical ceiling and head-on intercept range. The re-engined sole prototype of the Su-15bis was flight tested between 3 July and 20 December 1972, and the effort was successfully completed. However, the series production of this version was shelved due to a lack of engines—all R-25-300s produced at the Ufa-based plant No. 26 were intended for installation on the new MiG-21bis version, built at the time in large numbers (for domestic use and export) at the GAZ-21 in Gorky.

## Su-15 and Su-15TM Specification

|  | Su-15 | Su-15TM |
|---|---|---|
| Dimensions:<br>Wing span<br>Length with Pitot probe<br>Height | 8.616 m<br>21.44 m<br>5.00 m | 9.34 m<br>21.44 m<br>5.00 m |
| Wing area: | 34.56 m² | 36.60 m² |
| Weights:<br>Empty operating<br>Normal take-off<br>Maximum take-off<br>Internal fuel<br>Internal and external fuel | 10,355 kg<br>16,700 kg<br>17,350 kg<br>5,600 kg<br>6,580 | 10,760 kg<br>16,700 kg<br>17,900 kg<br>5,550 kg<br>6,530 |
| Performance:<br>Max level speed at low altitude<br>Max level speed at high altitude<br>Practical ceiling, clean<br>Take-off distance<br>Landing distance<br>Max G-load<br>Range on internal fuel<br>Range on internal and external fuel | 1,200 km/h<br>2,230 km/h<br>18,100 m<br>1,150 m<br>950 m<br>5<br>1,305 km<br>1,600 km | 1,200 km/h<br>2,230 km/h<br>17,540 m<br>1,150 m<br>1,250 m<br>5<br>1,210 km<br>1,780 km |

## Su-15 Radars

The basic Su-15 'Flagon-A' was equipped with the Oryol-58D (NATO 'Skip Scan'), a further development of the basic Sokol radar equipping the Yak-25 and Yak-27 from 1954. It had a larger parabolic antenna—950 mm (37.4 in) in diameter—providing an increase in the detection range against a Tu-16 bomber to 40 km (21.6 nm). The Oryol-D58M was an improved derivative boasting better resistance to jamming.

The Su-15T's Taifun was a downscaled version of the Smerch-A radar, designed by the OKB-339 and introduced for the first time by the MiG-25P, adapted to fit inside the Su-15T fuselage. The series-production Su-15TMs were outfitted with the improved Taifun-M (PR-26 or N004). It maximum detection range against a

A Su-15TM operating at low altitude over the Baltic Sea, armed with two R-98 missiles and two UPK-23-250 gun-pods—a typical QRA loadout in the 1980s. (*Swedish Coast Guard/Air Patrol*)

bomber-sized target at high altitude was up to 70 km (37.8 nm), while against a fighter-sized target it was reduced to 55 km (29.7 nm). The maximum tracking range was up to 45 km (24.3 nm). At low altitude the radar exhibited a notably reduced performance, with a maximum range of detection of bomber-sized targets of 12 km (6.5 nm); against fighter-sized targets it was 10 km (5.4 nm). The maximum low-level tracking ranges were up to 10 km (5.4 nm) as well. The radar picture was provided to a large hooded display in the centre of the instrument board.

## Su-15 Two-seat Variants

The conversion and continuation trainer version of the Su-15, designated as the U58T, was built in 1969; its development was initiated shortly after the decision of launching the single-seat Su-15. The U58T only differed from the single-seater by having a two-seat cockpit, retaining the weapons control system unchanged. The second cockpit for the instructor was accommodated to the rear of the existing one and this necessitated lengthening the fuselage by 45 cm (17.7 in), with the capacity of the front fuel tank having to be reduced by 900 litres; to compensate for this, an additional fuel tank was accommodated in the rear fuselage, giving a total fuel tankage of 6,110 litres. The cockpits had separate rearwards/upwards-hinged panels over each seat. The rear cockpit was provided with a retractable periscope to give the instructor forward vision during the approach.

At a later stage, in order to accelerate the development process, an unarmed prototype was built, designated as the U58T; it lacked the radar and missile-carrying capability. This became the production standard and the radarless two-seater was made capable of carrying two inert missiles on underwing pylons.

This is the antenna dish of the Oryol-58D (RP-15) radar as installed on the Su-15. (*Sukhoi OKB*)

The U58T took to the air for the first time on 26 August 1968, flown by Yevgeniy Kukashev. It was found that that the design changes to insert the second cockpit had imposed some performance penalties; for instance, the maximum speed was reduced to 1,850 km/h (998 kt) and the practical ceiling decreased to 16,700 m (54,780 feet).

The unarmed two-seater completed the state test efforts on 3 July 1970 and was commissioned with the IA PVO, wearing the official designation S-15UT (NATO codename 'Flagon-C'). Its manufacture was launched at that year at the GAZ-153, with the last examples rolled out in 1972.

The U58B was a two-seater with the standard weapons system inherited from the Su-15 single-seater. It was flown for the first time on 20 June 1970, but the testing programme was stopped soon after encountering problems with an unacceptable forward shift in the centre of gravity, which was caused by the presence of the heavy radar in the nose. Its testing effort was stopped soon after its first flight, and it was later used as a ground instructional airframe.

The U58TM was a two-seat trainer developed by using the Su-15TM's airframe, powerplant and systems; just like the U58T, it lacked the single-seater's radar, weapons and other mission equipment. Unlike the Su-15UT, which had an extended fuselage compared to the Su-15 single-seater, the new two-seater retained the Su-15TM's fuselage unchanged, and it was made capable of using the R-98MT and R-60 heat-seeking air-to-air missiles as well as two UPK-23-250 gun-pods suspended under the fuselage (with 250 rounds each).

The U58TM's prototype was flown for the first time on 23 April 1976 at the GAZ-153 in Novosibirsk; it completed its state testing effort in November

The Su-15UT improved two-seater was commissioned in service in July 1970 and remained in production until 1972. (*Sukhoi OKB*)

1976 with a recommendation to launch into production. Tests showed that the maximum speed of the R-13-300-powered two-seater was 1,875 km/h (1,011 kt) and that the practical ceiling was reduced to 15,500 m (50,840 feet).

When commissioned in IA PVO service, the improved two-seater was given the designation Su-15UM (NATO reporting name 'Flagon-G'). Its production run continued from 1976 to 1979 as the Su-15UM, and it was was the last 'Flagon' version to be manufactured at the GAZ-153. A total of 1,290 examples of all Su-15 versions rolled off the production line in Novosibirsk between 1966 and 1979.

## The Su-15 in Service

The field testing effort of the Su-15 was undertaken between September 1967 and July 1969, using ten aircraft operated by one of the squadrons of the 611th IAP at Dorokhovo, 70 km (37 nm) west of Moscow. A ten-aircraft formation (of which nine were from Dorokhovo and the tenth was a black-painted T6-1 prototype) participated in the famous flypast on 9 July 1967 at Domodedovo Airfield, near Moscow.

In IA PVO service the new type gradually replaced the Yak-25, Yak-28P, Su-9 and Su-11. The unit to take on strength the 'Flagon-A' and two-seat 'Flagon-C' was traditionally the 148th TsBPiPLS at Savastleika, where the type was used for the training of an initial instructor cadre, who, in turn, was then tasked with conversion training of pilots from the front-line regiments taking the new type.

Two Soviet pilots wearing VKK-6 pressure suits and GSh-6 pressure helmets, pictured posing in front of a Su-15UM two-seater in a classic Soviet-style propaganda set-up. (*Author's collection*)

By 1990 as many as seven IA PVO regiments stationed in the European part of the Soviet Union still operated the Su-15TM, with a total inventory of 230 aircraft (with ninety more stationed in the Asian part). However, the type was in the process of being gradually replaced by newer and much more capable interceptors such as the MiG-31 and Su-27, while all early production Su-15s were replaced in the early 1980s by the MiG-23P, boasting a look-down/shoot-down radar for operations against targets flying at ultra-low level. After the Soviet Union's dissolution from late 1991 until early 1992, two Su-15TM-equipped regiments remained in the newly-independent state of Ukraine and continued operations for a while.

The type's operational career featured three well-publicised highlights in typical Cold War situations. In two of them, the 'Flagon' faced Korean Air Lines (KAL) aircraft that had veered off course; this had grave consequences, as both encounters saw the use of air-to-air missiles. On the first occasion, on 20 April 1978, a KAL Boeing 707-321B performing Flight 902 (KAL 902)—flying from Paris, France to Seoul, South Korea via Anchorage, Alaska—violated Soviet airspace. When the Korean aircraft passed over the Kola Peninsula at 9.19 p.m. (Moscow time), PVO scrambled a pair of Su-15TMs from the 431st IAP based at Afrikanda Airfield, near Murmansk. The aircraft flown by Capt. Alexander Bosov intercepted the Boeing, but the KAL plots failed to respond to Soviet ground control or the interceptor that escorted their aircraft. By that time, fighters from three other IA PVO regiments were directed to intercept the KAL airliner as it approached the Soviet Northern Fleet bases, which housed ballistic missile-armed submarines. After the failure to get a response from the Korean Air crew, the Su-15TM pilot was ordered to open fire. At 9.42 p.m. Capt. Bosov launched two R-60 missiles; one of these scored a hit that caused decompression of the fuselage, but the Boeing 707 remained airborne and reduced its altitude to 2,000 m (6,560 feet), preparing for an emergency landing. It was being simultaneously pursued by another Su-15TM, whose pilot was ordered to gun it down; however, in the event he proved unable to detect and attack the airliner. The crew of the damaged Boeing somehow managed to fly across the whole Kola Peninsula at low altitude while searching for a suitable place for emergency landing. Finally the pilot, Kim Chang Ky, managed to bring the plane down on the ice of the frozen Korpijarvi Lake in Karelia, approximately 140 km (76 nm) from the Finnish border. A total of twelve crew members and ninety-seven passengers were on board Flight 902 and casualties among them during the emergency landing on the ice surface accounted for two passengers killed.

The second occasion of 'Flagon' involvement in a Cold War-style clash with a foreign civil aircraft was reported on 18 July 1981. It was a Su-15TM from the 166th IAP—home-based at Sandar, in present-day Azerbaijan—that was scrambled to intercept a Canadair CL-44 transport aircraft belonging to Transporte Aéreo Rioplatense SACL, a cargo airline registered in Argentina. The transport, used for illegal shipment of Israeli-made defence equipment to Iran, entered Soviet airspace from Iran. 'Flagon' pilot Capt. Valentin Kulyapin detected the target and

In 1990, at the end of the Cold War, the Soviet Air Defence Forces had a fleet of 230 Su-15s operated by some seven regiments, with ninety more stationed in the Asian part of the Soviet Union. (*Dmitriy Pichugin*)

drew closer to it, but then the CL-44 turned toward the Iranian border. Kulyapin was ordered to shoot it down, but he was not able to deploy missiles against the slow-flying CL-44 because of the close distance. In an effort to stop the intruder from crossing the border back, he decided to ram the target; the Su-15 went under the CL-44 and hit a horizontal tail surface with its fuselage. Capt. Kulyapin realised that his aircraft had also sustained serious damage during the hit and ejected successfully. His parachute brought him safely to the ground, but all on board the mortally damaged CL-44 perished upon impact with the ground.

The third event perhaps had the worst consequences of the entire Cold War period, caused by the fog of the conflict. It took place on 1 September 1983 and once again involved a KAL aircraft; this time it was a Boeing 747 on Flight KAL007 from New York to Seoul, via Anchorage. The airliner strayed from its route and entered deep Soviet airspace, remaining there for 2.5 hours before being fired at by a Su-15TM from the 777th IAP at Sokol Airfield (at Sakhalin island), flown by Maj. Gennadiy Osipovish. He was ordered to bring down the Boeing 747, which was suspected by the Soviet command authorities of being a US reconnaissance aircraft on a probing mission. Maj. Osipovish consequently launched two R-98 missiles at it. The damage inflicted on the target was considerable, and its remains fell into the sea near Moneron Island, west of Sakhalin Island, killing all 269 passengers and crew on board.

During the Cold War, the Su-15s were also used on numerous occasions to intercept free-floating air balloons (aerostats), presumably launched by Western intelligence agencies; these entered Soviet territory from the east and exited it

The 'Flagon' recorded its participation in three notable Cold War incidents, downing civil aircraft flying without authorisation inside Soviet airspace. The worst of these was the shooting down of the Korean Air Lines Boeing 747 on 1 September 1981, resulting in the deaths of all 269 people onboard. (*Sukhoi OKB*)

over the Pacific coast. There were also a few occasions when scientific balloons were downed; these were used by both Western and Soviet civil organisations. The last achievement in this business was reported on 2 September 1990, when a Su-15TM from the 431st IAP, stationed at Afrikanda Airfield, brought down a civil research-scientific balloon from the Pirog-5-series, launched on 27 August that year from the European Space Range at Kiruna, Sweden. Equipped with modern space surveillance equipment, it was flying at 12,000 m (39,370 feet) over the Kola Peninsula when it was destroyed by two R-98TM missiles.

The twin-engine Su-15 had a pretty good flight safety record when compared to the other IA PVO fighters from that time. According to an article published in the Russian air and space magazine *Aviatsia i Kosmonavtika* (issue 5–6, 1992), during its first decade of service, between 1967 and 1976, the 'Flagon' fleet amassed 547,055 flying hours, and thirty-seven aircraft were lost. This means that the loss rate was 6.76 per 100,000 flying hours, while the overall loss rate for the entire in-service period of the type amounted to 6.2—compared to 10 for the MiG-25 and 11.5 for the MiG-31 fleets.

## Yak-28P—Yakovlev's Mediocre Interceptor

The supersonic Yak-28 (NATO reporting name 'Firebar') was built in several versions—for use in the fighter-interceptor role as well as bomber, air reconnaissance and electronic warfare aircraft. All of these versions utilised a common supersonic platform, featuring shoulder-mounted wings and tandem twin-wheel main undercarriage units, following the general configuration pioneered by the Yakovlev OKB on the subsonic Yak-25.

The family development began with the '125' prototype, using the Yak-25 airframe and powered by two AM-9A afterburning turbojets, which were to be used for both the tactical bomber and reconnaissance aircraft versions. The lightweight axial-flow engine, weighing only 700 kg (1,543 lb), had a pretty good rating—32.373 kN (7,273 lb st. or 3,300 kgf) with afterburner—and a very small cross-section to reduce transonic drag. It was tested for the first time in 1952, but developmental problems precluded its use, and the '125' prototype was consequently initially powered by the non-afterburning AM-5 engine.

The formal development of the aircraft's fighter version at the Yakovlev OKB commenced following a Soviet Union Council of Ministers decree dated 10 June 1954. It obliged the OKB-115 to develop a two-seat, long-range supersonic fighter-interceptor, provisionally designated as the Yak-2AM-11, powered by two AM-11 afterburning turbojets. Later, this aircraft had to be used as a baseline for developing dedicated bomber and reconnaissance versions. It was expected that the new AM-11 turbojets—a follow-on AM-9 development with increased thrust rating—would be ready for installation on the new aircraft by early 1955. This engine was rated at 39,240 kN (8,816 lb st. or 4,000 kgf) dry and 49.05 kN (11,020 lb st. or 5,000 kgf) with afterburner. However, the development troubles encountered by

Mikulin's OKB-300 experimental design bureau incurred a significant delay on the AM-11 programme, forcing the Soviet aviation industry leadership to cancel the Yak-2AM-11's development altogether in March 1955, instead redirecting the Yakovlev OKB efforts to developing an alternative version powered by the older AM-9AK. The new aircraft, designated as the Yak-26 (also known under the internal OKB-115 designation '123'), was required to be capable of reaching a maximum speed of 1,400 km/h (755 kt) and a practical ceiling of 16,700 m (54,776 feet), while the maximum range was to extend to 2,200 km (1,187 nm).

In order to reduce wave drag, the airframe received a new wing configuration personally proposed by the OKB-115 chief designer and founder, Alexander Yakovlev. It had a thinner wing, and this meant the configuration deviated from the specification set out by the VVS; however, Yakovlev insisted on using it in a bid to achieve a design that was as simple and as lightweight as possible.

The prototype aircraft was built and took to the air in the first half of 1956; it completed its series of factory testing flights in June that year. In July it was submitted to the NII VVS to commence its state testing programme, which was conducted between 27 July and 28 August 1956. The new aircraft demonstrated a maximum speed of 1,230 km/h (663 kt) and a practical ceiling of 16,000 m (52,480 feet). At the same time, the design suffered from numerous deficiencies, leading to frequent sortie cancellations; in the event it proved able to complete only twenty-seven out of 110 planned test and evaluation sorties. Among the chief issues revealed during the testing by the NII VVS were the lack of stability at high-angle-of-attack flights, the poor visibility from the navigator's cockpit in the nose, the high control forces and the unintentional banking and loss of aileron effectiveness in high-speed flight. The aircraft suffered from an inadequate reaction to aileron deflection at altitudes between 4,000 and 6,000 m (13,120 and 19,680 feet), as the airflow forces reached their maximum and the aircraft tended to bank to the direction opposite to the command inputs by the pilot. This phenomenon—known as 'aileron reversal'—was caused by the insufficient wing stiffness due to its low thickness. This is why the testing commission at the NII VVS eventually decided to stop any further testing, instead requesting that the aircraft '123' should receive an all-new wing design with increased stiffness in order to avoid the aileron reversal effect.

The prototype received its new strengthened wings in late 1956, in addition to an adjustable elevator and more powerful RD-9B engines—rated at 37.28 kN (8,375 lb st. or 3,800 kgf)—and a redesigned canopy, navigator cockpit entry door and ejection seats. The wing leading edge received an aerodynamic tooth used to generate vortices that provided warnings when the aircraft got near to critical AoA, but this novel addition also increased drag.

The second Yak-26 prototype was built in 1967. It was a bomber version with a mission suite including the Lotos radar and an OPB-11 bomb sight. This aircraft was used for the investigation of the aileron reversal effect, and in October 1957 tests of the weapons system were commenced, with bomb drops made at both subsonic and supersonic speeds.

The first fighter derivative (developed on the '123' base) was the Yak-121—a two-seat aircraft equipped with the Sokol-M radar and armed with two NR-30 30-mm cannons and twenty-four ARS-57 57-mm rockets. The first Yak-121 (equipped with the wing and engine nacelles as those used on the Yak-26-1 and using the existing Yak-25M fuselage) completed its factory trials in May 1956. It demonstrated a maximum speed of 1,235 km/h (666 kt) at 10,000 m (32,800 feet), which fell short of that requested by the VVS specification—1,400 km/h (755 kt). The aircraft also suffered from aileron reversal, which imposed speed restrictions at low and medium level.

Initially, even before completion of the flight tests, the cannon-armed Yak-121 was intended to be produced in a batch of twenty-five examples, receiving the in-service designation Yak-27; it was then to be modified to fire air-to-air missiles. However, these plans were shelved due to numerous design shortcomings, and eventually only ten examples were built at the GAZ-292 in Saratov. These aircraft were utilised in the testing campaign of the K-8 air-to-air missile.

The modified Yak-27K, using the airframe of the second production-standard example, commenced its factory flight testing in January 1957, powered by the RD-9F turbojets and equipped with the Sokol-2K air-intercept radar. Its armament suite comprised just two K-8 air-to-air missiles. The testing was carried out in a smooth manner and the prototype shot down two Il-28 radio-controlled target drones with the new K-8 missile. The overall flight performance, however, proved clearly inferior to that of the Sukhoi Su-9, a single-engine delta-wing fighter also armed with the K-8 missile. Based on the test results, the VVS C-in-C, Marshal Konstantin Vershinin, had recommended shelving the Yak-27 in favour of the much-more-capable Su-9 and cancelling the production plans for fourteen Yak-27s that were to be built at the GAZ-292. In this way, Marshall Vershinin effectively put an end to the plans for the Yak-27 production; nevertheless, three years later the OKB-115 resumed the development work to create a new long-range, all-weather, missile-armed two-seat fighter.

The Yak-26 prototype aircraft was built and took to the air in the first half of 1956; it completed the series of factory testing flights in June that year. The third prototype is shown here, designated as the 123-3. (*Yakovlev OKB*)

This time, however, the new model used the fuselage of the Yak-28 supersonic bomber, powered by R-11-300 afterburning turbojets and featuring a shoulder wing; it took to the air for the first time on 5 March 1958. The Yak-28's interceptor derivative, dubbed 'Yak-28P', was armed with the K-8M-1 missile system, comprising the Oryol-D radar and two R-8M-1 air-to-air missiles, equipped with heat-seeking or SARH guidance, plus their associated launcher units. The missile pylons were mounted under the wing, outboard of the engine nacelles, while the pilot's and navigator-operator's cockpits received a common canopy.

The fuselage was an all-metal semi-monocoque structure of a basically oval section, with its load-bearing members made of forty-two frames, additional semi-frames, beams, spars and stringers. The skin used the D16V and B95TV aluminium alloy sheets. The cantilever shoulder-mounted variable-thickness wing had two consoles, each with a basic sweepback of 45° and a basically constant chord, with a dogtooth in the leading edge outboard of the engine nacelle. The outer wings featured extendable leading edges, which also ran between the fuselage. The wing had a -6° anhedral from the root and +2° incidence. A single fence was mounted on upper surface of each wing, between the fuselage and engine nacelle. The wings used TsAGI P-53 and S-12S symmetrical aerofoil profiles and the skin was made from the D16TV alloy. Each wing panel was provided with a short trailing-edge flap and a shot aileron, with a tab outboard of the nacelle of each wing.

The empennage was a cantilever all-metal structure, with a variable-incidence stabliser midway up the fin. The fin sweepback was 54° and that of the horizontal stabiliser was 55°. The rudder was provided with a trim tab. The dorsal fin faired into the spine along the top of the fuselage. The tail also featured a shallow ventral stabilising fin.

As all other Yak-28 versions, the interceptor featured a bicycle-type undercarriage with two twin-wheel units in tandem, which retracted into the fuselage. The

The first Yak-28P prototype is seen here, armed with two R-8M air-to-air missiles. (*Yakovlev OKB*)

forward unit, deflecting at up to 40° left and right, was installed under the cockpit, and the rear one was installed further aft, to a point immediately in front of the ventral fin. Small balancer wheels were mounted near each wingtip, retracting rearwards under the wing; their fairings were made integral with the leg.

The prototype aircraft were powered by R-11AF-300 afterburning turbojets, rated 38.7 kN (8,703 lb st. or 3,945 kgf) dry and 60.6 kN (13,615 lb st. or 6,177 kgf) with afterburner, housed in nacelles with oval-shaped intakes that were later changed to a circular shape. The improved Yak-28PD had an improved mission suite and was powered by the up-rated AM-11AF2-300, while the fuel tankage increased to 6,570 litres. Each engine nacelle was fitted with a centrebody-shock cone driven forward and aft automatically to provide optimum operating conditions for the engine, depending on the current speed, angle of attack and horizontal stabiliser deflection angle. Each engine was equipped with intake anti-icing, an adjustable all-regime nozzle and oxygen system for emergency relight in order to provide reliable high-altitude start-up. The fuel was accommodated in six fuselage tanks.

The crew of two was accommodated in tandem cockpits under a common long, transparent blister canopy. The cockpits were pressurised and equipped with ejection seats with a minimum operating altitude of 130 m (427 feet). The common canopy was rearwards-sliding. The aircraft had powered controls in the pitch and bank channels, while the yaw channel was unpowered, using mechanical linkages only.

The type's state testing effort with the K-8M-1 and K-98 air-to-air missile systems continued until 1965. However, production commenced in 1962, three years before the completion of the effort, at the GAZ-153 in Novosibirsk. As many as 435 aircraft were rolled out there by 1967, but the type was never

A close-up view of the R-8M radar-guided missile suspended under the Yak-27P's port wing. (*Yakovlev OKB*)

commissioned in IA PVO service despite being inducted into squadron service. The chief cause for this paradox was related to its poor performance, which eventually proved to be well below specification despite the many improvement attempts. These attempts continued after the start of the serial production by means of the installation of the further up-rated R-11AF3-300 engines, which enabled the Yak-28P to hit 2,400 km/h (1,294 kt) in level flight. In order to further improve its transonic acceleration, the Yak-28P got a more pointed nose, and the new lengthened dielectric fairing design was later on retrofitted on all examples produced beforehand. The armament was also strengthened by adding two R-3S (AA-2 'Atoll') short-range heat-seeking missiles carried on another pair of wing inboard pylons. This improved version was submitted for state testing with the NII VVS in 1966 and it was simultaneously launched into production at the GAZ-153.

The Yak-28-64 was a prototype with a considerably reduced drag thanks to the accommodation of the engines within the fuselage, and the use of rectangular variable-area side intakes while retaining the fuselage nose, cockpit, undercarriage, empennage and flight controls unchanged. It was similar in layout to the Sukhoi Su-15, with ailerons moved closer to the wingroots in order to avoid the reversal effect and increase the low-level speed. Its armament comprised two R-8M-1 missiles carried on inboard pylons, while two new-generation heat-seeking missiles were to be carried outboard. In addition, two external fuel tanks were to be carried under the fuselage in order to extend range and endurance. Flight tests, however, showed that the Yak-28-64's performance was close to that of the production-standard Yak-28, and consequently the design work on the new version was stopped.

The Yak-28U two-seat trainer featured two individual single-seat cockpits in tandem, each provided with its own canopy. (*Yakovlev OKB*)

One copy of the Yak-28-64 was built; it featured side-by-side engines packed in a rear fuselage resembling the Su-15. (*Yakovlev OKB*)

In order to further improve its transonic acceleration, the Yak-28P received a more pointed nose; the new lengthened dielectric fairing design was later retrofitted to all examples that had been previously produced. *(Yakovlev OKB)*

## Yak-28P Specification

| Dimensions:<br>Wing span<br>Length<br>Height | 13.00 m<br>21.70 m<br>4.30 m |
|---|---|
| Wing area: | 35.25 m$^2$ |
| Weights:<br>Normal take-off<br>Maximum take-off | 15,980 kg<br>18,400 kg |
| Performance:<br>Max level speed at sea level<br>Max level speed at high level<br>Max Mach number<br>Practical ceiling<br>Take-off distance<br>Landing distance<br>Range on internal fuel<br>Range on internal and external fuel<br>Max G-load | 1,050 km/h<br>1,840 km/h<br>1.74<br>16,000 m<br>1,300 m<br>1,200 m<br>2,150 km<br>2,700 km<br>3 |

The Yak-28U (NATO reporting name 'Maestro') was a two-seat trainer derivative used for conversion and continuation training of pilots flying all bomber, reconnaissance, EW and fighter versions. It lacked a mission suite and was equipped with two individual single-seat cockpits in tandem, each provided with its own canopy. The front canopy was sideways-hinged to starboard, while the rear one was made rear-sliding. The bomb bay was used to accommodate an additional fuel tank housing 1,350 litres of kerosene. The Yak-28U prototype, known at the time within the OKB-115 as model '129U', was flown for the first time in 1962, and its state testing effort was carried out at the NII VVS between 23 November 1962 and 15 March 1963. The trainer version was launched in production at the GAZ-153 in Novosibirsk in 1963, with 183 examples built.

The Yak-28P was operated by about ten IA PVO regiments, most (if not all) of them deployed to extreme northern locations in the Soviet Union. The VVS also operated the type for a short period, with two squadrons assigned to the 35th IAP, a fighter regiment of the 16th Air Army, stationed at Zerbst Airfield in East Germany. The type remained in operation with the 35th IAP between 1965 and 1974.

The Yak-28P saw a somewhat limited production run and proliferation, equipping only ten front-line interceptor regiments deployed to extreme northern locations in the Soviet Union. (*Yakovlev OKB*)

# 3

# Third Generation

## MiG-23—The Soviet's First Swing-Wing Fighter

The third fighter generation in the Soviet Union was conceived in the second half of the 1960s. By that time, there were enough new technologies already available (or expected to be available in the foreseeable future) to bring a drastic increase in combat effectiveness, in areas such as new aerodynamic layouts, more powerful engines, long-range fire-control radars and new-generation beyond-visual-range (BVR) air-to-air missiles.

However, it became clear that it was very difficult to integrate all of these sophisticated new technologies into an effective and reliable air-superiority fighter; the Mikoyan OKB's effort to bring the main representative of this generation to the front line proved to be a protracted, painful, and very expensive undertaking.

Five main design requirements were identified by the VVS and the industry research institutes in the early/mid-1960s, during the project definition phase of Mikoyan's new generation fighter. The first of these called for a significant increase in low-level speed; the second called for an effective improvement in pilot comfort during high-speed low-level rides; the third for a considerable range increase; the fourth for a huge advance in the take-off and landing performance, which would allow the use of shorter runways; and the fifth called for the integration of a powerful weapons control system to provide the much needed beyond-visual-range (BVR) missiles—this was considered essential for the air-superiority role in the 1970s. Both the McDonnell Douglas F-4 Phantom II and the Dassault Mirage F1 were viewed as the primary future opponents of the Soviet third-generation fighters in the air-superiority area.

As the first swing-wing or variable-geometry (VG) wing combat aircraft to be flown in the former Soviet Union, the MiG-23 proved to be much more complex in terms of airframe construction, engine, general aircraft equipment, mission avionics and weapons than its nimble and short-legged predecessor, the MiG-21. Compared to its delta-wing predecessor, the MiG-23's much higher level of airframe/powerplant/systems and mission avionics sophistication and integration is said to have resulted in a more-than-threefold increase in its overall theoretical air combat effectiveness. The trade-off, however, was a huge rise in the aircraft's acquisition

This MiG-23MS was a simplified export version lacking beyond-visual capabilities. This particular aircraft—pictured in flight, armed with R-3S heat-seeking air-to-air missiles—belongs to the Libyan Arab Air Force. (*US DoD*)

price, direct operating costs and maintenance requirements; as might be expected, this created huge difficulties during the type's development, testing and introduction into service with the VVS (Voenno-Vozdushniye Sily—Soviet Air Force).

## First Steps Towards the Third Generation

The aircraft was intended to be the successor to the MiG-21 with the VVS's Frontal Aviation (FA) arm, and initial design work on the project began in accordance with a 3 December 1963 decree from the Soviet Council of Ministers and the Central Committee of the Communist Party of the Soviet Union, which ordered that the prototype of the new generation combat aircraft should be submitted for joint state testing in late 1965.

The Mikoyan OKB—which was the principal design house for front-line combat aircraft in the Soviet Union at the time—assembled a pair of teams tasked to work in parallel on two different air-superiority fighter designs. The first was conceived with short take-off and landing (STOL) characteristics, using lift jets, whereas the second one was planned to use the then-revolutionary new VG wing design.

# The 23-01 STOL Prototype

The STOL project was known within MMZ Zenith (as the Mikoyan Design Bureau was officially known before 1970) as Aircraft 23-01, and alternatively under the draft designations of MiG-23UVP and MiG-23PD. It took shape as a supersonic design with a normal aerodynamic layout, employing a fixed delta wing and a conventional all-moving tailplane. Its chief designer was Vano A. Mikoyan, and power was supplied by a Tumanskiy R-27-300 'main' turbojet rated at 51.01 kN (11,440 lb st. or 5,200 kgf) at military power and 71.61 kN (16,060 lb st. or 7,300 kgf) with afterburner. It also featured a pair of Kolessov RD-36-35 lift jets rated at 23.030 kN (5,170 lb st. or 2,348 kgf) each, installed in the centre fuselage in a vertical position and useful for take-off and landing. Fed by intakes on the upper fuselage, the lift jets were only introduced with the idea of reducing the take-off and landing speed; they were never deemed capable of providing a true vertical take-off and landing capability. The maximum design speed of Aircraft 23-01 was intended to be between Mach 2.0 and 2.3.

The wing was fitted with a powerful blown flaps system, which, in combination with the lift jets, was intended to shorten the take-off run and landing roll considerably. The engine intakes were of semi-circular cross-section, with Mirage-III-style shock cones positioned carefully away from the fuselage in order to avoid boundary layer ingestion problems.

Aircraft 23-01 was planned as the prototype of an operational air-superiority fighter, and thus was intended to be armed with a built-in GSh-23 twin-barrel gun and two K-23R semi-active radar homing (SARH) air-to-air missiles or two K-23T heat-seeking missiles under the wings.

The aircraft made its maiden flight on 3 April 1967 but flew only fourteen times before its development programme was cancelled. The chief reasons were disappointing flight test results, which proved that a STOL-design concept with lift jets was unsuitable for use in an operational land-based combat aircraft. The

The single 23-01 prototype, with the intake for its lift engines opened and carrying dummy K-23T/R missiles under the wings. (*Mikoyan & Gurevich OKB*)

complex propulsion system meant that the jet efflux produced by the lift engines interacted with the ground to alter the aircraft's trim during take-off and cause a suction effect during the final landing approach. This made the pilot's workload extensive, for in order to prevent these potentially dangerous effects he was required to increase the main engine thrust to military power and even use the afterburner just before touching down. In addition, the lift jets imposed a significant weight penalty, which reduced the internal fuel and weapons load; understandingly, this was deemed unacceptable for the new generation combat aircraft.

Aircraft 23-01 made its last flight during the Domodedovo air show on 9 July 1967, and soon after it was passed to the Moscow Aviation Institute to be used as a ground instruction aircraft. Seen by the Western intelligence agencies for the first time at Domodedovo, Aircraft 23-01 was given the NATO code name 'Faithless'.

## VG Concept

Aircraft 23-11 with VG wing design was eventually viewed by both the Mikoyan OKB and VVS leadership as promising much better performance than the technologically complex STOL design.

Development of the VG wing prototype was ordered by the prominent Minister of Aircraft Industry Pyotr Dementiev in 1965. The resultant design was quite different to its lift-jet-equipped STOL forebear; the forward fuselage was of a vertical oval shape, fairing back to a rectangular-shaped cross-section. The low-drag canopy was similar in appearance to that used in the MiG-21, but hinged at the rear and faired into the fuselage spine, giving the pilot little spare headroom and limiting his field of view down and to the rear.

The principal load-bearing structural member was the main carry-through box in the top of the fuselage, made by welding thick plates of the special VNS-2 steel alloy; it was also used as fuel tank No. 2. The wing pivots were placed near the outer edge of the fixed wing glove and provided a range of sweep angles in an arc of 56°. The three main wing sweepback settings were 16°, 45° and 72°.

Each wing panel featured an extensive array of high-lift mechanisation devices on the leading and trailing edges. The airbrakes were in a four-petal configuration, located on the rear fuselage and moved forward in relation to the tail surfaces. When the landing gear was selected up, the large ventral fin rotated down and locked in a vertical position; when landing gear was selected down, the fin pivoted to the right, to the horizontal (stowed) position.

Aircraft 23-11 was powered by one Tumanskiy R-27F-300 turbojet fed by air entering through rectangular intakes with perforated variable-intake ramps, similar to those used on the F-4 Phantom II. The R-27F-300 turbojet—rated at 50.88 kN (11,440 lb st. or 5,187 kgf) dry and 76.31 kN (17,160 lb st. or 7,779 kgf) at full afterburner—was a scaled-up derivative of the widely-used R-11/13/25-300 turbojet series that powered various MiG-21 variants. Thanks to the new materials and manufacturing technologies used in it, the R-27F-300

The 23-11/1 prototype of the MiG-23, armed with K-23 missiles under the wing gloves. Upon entry into service, this BVR missile was re-designated as the R-23. (*Mikoyan & Gurevich OKB*)

had specific fuel consumption 25 per cent less than that of its predecessor. Fuel was carried in three fuselage tanks with capacities of 1,920, 820 and 710 litres respectively, and three integral tanks in each wing with capacities of 62.5, 137.5 and 200 litres.

The undercarriage was very tough and highly effective, with its main units also used as compressed air bottles—these were folded into a small space and left the underside of the fuselage free for carrying large centreline stores. However, this design (combined with the intakes, which were susceptible to foreign objects ingestion) made operations from unpaved, icy or snow-packed airstrips very difficult or almost impossible. Furthermore, the MiG-23 was known to be rather unstable during its landing roll on wet runways.

The first Aircraft 23-11 prototype's armament was intended to initially consist of four K-23 BVR air-to-air missiles carried on pylons under the wings and under the fuselage. Designated as 23-11/1 and appropriately serialed '231', it was rolled out in May 1967 and made its maiden flight on 9 July that year in the capable hands of Alexander Fedotov, the famous Mikoyan OKB chief test pilot. During that flight—performed at Zhukovskiy Airfield, near Moscow—the VG wings remained fixed in the full forward position, being moved to full backward position for the first time on 12 June; this was the second flight on the new aircraft. During the third test flight in the 23-11/1, Fedotov went supersonic, reaching Mach 1.2 at 72° wings sweep.

After the forty-fifth flight in late 1967, the twenty-five-hour life of the R-27F-300 expired, and the aircraft was grounded for the installation of a new engine and new equipment, such as an AP-155 three-axis autopilot. The 23-11/1's factory flight test programme was completed successfully in July 1968 after ninety-seven sorties, and shortly afterwards the aircraft was handed over to the Soviet Air Force Museum at Monino, near Moscow. The first VG prototype was followed in 1969 by two more, designated 23-11/2 and 23-11/3, which were equipped with the Sapfir-23 radar set and powered by the up-rated R-27F2-300 engine.

The 23-11/2 prototype posing with an unlikely loadout of K-23T missiles under the wing gloves and R-23R under the fuselage. In fact, the underfuselage pylons were only used for short-range heat-seeking air-to-air missiles. (*Mikoyan & Gurevich OKB*)

However, the brand-new and rather complex radar, which had been tested for the first time in the air when installed on a Tu-104 test-bed, was still a notoriously unreliable piece of hardware, and it caused many technical problems during the MiG-23's protracted flight test programme. Later, four more prototypes were involved in the trials—the 23-11/4 (first flight in 1969, used as the prototype for the fighter-bomber variant), 23-11/5, 23-11/6 and 23-11/9.

The public debut of the revolutionary new Soviet combat aircraft took place during the famous Domodedovo flypast held on 9 July that year, at which both the STOL and VG prototypes were displayed in flight. By that time it was apparent that Aircraft 23-11 would become the basis for the development of a high-performance fighter-interceptor to replace the MiG-21. Alexander Fedotov used the flypast—which marked the thirteenth flight of the first VG prototype - to a good effect, demonstrating the wings moving forward and backward at speeds between 400 and 800 km/h (216 and 431 kt) while rolling the aircraft.

A total of nine VG prototypes were built, and seven of them participated in the type's factory flight testing, which commenced in July 1967 at Mikoyan's own flight test facility at the Ministry of Aircraft Industry's (MAI) airfield at Zhukovskiy (also known as Ramenskoye), southeast of Moscow.

# New Design Features

The Aircraft 23-11 design team, led by A. A. Andreev, was given the fairly difficult task of designing a modest fighter-sized aircraft that employed the then-new VG wing concept, which was effectively unknown in the Soviet Union at the time. In 1964 this approach was considered by the aviation industry and military leadership as a promising new technology that would satisfy a multitude of conflicting main design requirements for the new generation of fighter and strike aircraft planned to enter mass service in the early 1970s. The new Mikoyan OKB fighter was initially conceived as a pure high-speed interceptor only, and would have no particular capability for high-G turning air combats—which were out of fashion by that time.

Aircraft 23-11's basic design concept called for a fighter-interceptor type with high-mounted (shoulder-type) wings, and in the event it was strongly influenced by the design of the then-revolutionary General Dynamics F-111 tactical fighter. The fuselage of semi-monocoque construction had a cigar-like shape with a pointed nose and rectangular cross-section behind, with rounded angles. The movable wing panels were hydraulically-driven and manually controlled, with three main sweep angles set up by the pilot using a small lever located beneath the throttle. A wings position of 16° (fully spread) was used for take-off/landing and low-speed cruise (limited to Mach 0.7); a mid-sweep of 45° was used for basic fighter manoeuvring, low-level intercepts and high-speed cruise; and a position of 72° (fully aft) was used for high-speed dashes at low level and high-level intercepts. The wings were liberally endowed with high lift devices such as full-span four-section trailing-edge flaps, leading-edge slats and two-section spoilers, all designed in an effort to provide the short take-off and landing performance required by the VVS specification. There were no ailerons on the wings in an attempt to prevent twisting the thin movable panels in high-speed flight; instead, spoilers were introduced for roll control at 16° and 45° sweep settings, operating in conjunction with the left and right tailerons (i.e. the tailplane, which was used for both pitch and roll control; for the latter the tailerons moved differentially), whereas at 72° sweep only the tailerons were used for roll control. After landing, the spoilers were also brought into play to increase drag and kill residual lift. A brake chute further shortened the landing roll.

The tailfin was made fairly big, extending into a long dorsal fillet halfway to the cockpit. A ventral fin was added to improve directional stability at high speeds, and to prevent it scraping the runway during take-off and landing, the design team chose a solution in which the fin hinged to a root section and folded sideways.

## Early Testing Troubles

In early May 1969, the first example of the initial production 'Flogger' variant (designated as the MiG-23S and fitted with the S-21M weapons system borrowed from the MiG-21S/SM) was built at the *Znamya Truda* factory in Moscow (final assembly line was located at the LMZ facility in the small of town of Lukhovitzy, near Moscow). It took to the air for the first time on 21 May 1969, piloted by Alexander Fedotov. Later on during the same year, a small number of MiG-23Ss were handed over to the both parties who formed up the MiG-23's Joint State Test Team—one of them based at the MAI's test centre at Zhukovskiy, near Moscow, and the other at the NII VVS (Soviet Air Force's flight test-research centre) at Akhtubinsk, in the southern part of the Russian Federation. This stage of the MiG-23 test programme commenced in July 1969 and continued until mid-1973.

A total of eleven MiG-23s (including some two-seaters) were involved in the protracted joint MAI/VVS testing effort, amassing just over 1,300 sorties.

The MiG-23S was an interim variant that was externally similar to the prototype, but equipped with a weapons control system based on the Sapfir-21 (also known as RP-22SM) radar with an ASP-PFD-21 lead computing gunsight, both borrowed from the MiG-21S/SM. The Sapfir-23 radar, purposely designed for the 'Flogger' by the OKB-339 in Moscow (later known also as NIIR-Phazotron Company), was delayed for some time due to severe developmental problems, so existing hardware was used as a stop-gap solution. The RP-22SM radar was housed in a purposely-designed conical radome, and the aircraft lacked the IRST sensor. The MiG-23S could carry four AAMs only—usually two SARH R-3Rs and two IR-homing R-3Ss. In addition, the proven GSh-23L 23-mm twin-barrelled gun with 200 rounds was available in a ventral pack.

The Del'ta-NM bullet-shaped pod used to guide the Kh-23 (AS-7 'Kerry') radio-command guided air-to-surface missile was built into the root of the starboard underwing pylon. In the ground-attack role, the MiG-23S was made to carry two Kh-23 missiles under the wing, two to four 16-round 57-mm rocket packs, S-24 240-mm rockets or up to 2,000 kg (4,408 lb) of iron bombs, napalm tanks or cluster bombs.

The initial production MiG-23Ss were powered by the R-27F-300 turbojet rated at 67.62 kN (15,300 lb st. or 6,893 kgf) dry and 78.5 kN (17,641 lb st. or

The MiG-23S was a simplified, early version equipped with the RP-22 radar (borrowed from the MiG-21bis). (*Dmitriy Srubny*)

8,002 kgf) with afterburner. Follow-on aircraft used the up-rated R-27F2M-300 derivative, rated at 64.53 kN (15,000 lb st. or 6,578 kgf) dry and 98.0 kN (22,000 lb st. or 9,989 kgf) with afterburner.

However, the flight test programme encountered a number of safety-related problems. For example, both the Mikoyan OKB and VVS test pilots discovered that the MiG-23S (and later on its successor, the MiG-23M) generally displayed fairly dangerous behaviour at high angles of attack combined with a certain sideslip, and the aircraft was judged as prone to spinning in particular circumstances. Such qualities were considered hazardous for flight safety by the time the aircraft entered mass service with the VVS. In addition, the centre fuselage welding joints and the wings often developed cracks, requiring urgent structural strengthening measures.

Two MiG-23Ss were lost within a week during the flight test programme in September 1970. The first of these crashed near Zhukovskiy due to a still-unknown cause; the aircraft exceeded the maximum speed limit and disintegrated in the air, killing the Mikoyan OKB test pilot Mikhail Komarov. The most probable cause was pilot incapacitation due to interrupted oxygen supply, but no cause was ever confirmed. The second MiG-23S crashed near the airfield at Akhtubinsk after entering a flat spin during a low-altitude air combat demonstration; it was manoeuvring at high AoA, but supposedly still within the design limits. The fatal combination of a certain AoA and sideslip caused the departure from controlled flight, killing NII VSS test pilot V. Zhukov. Not long afterwards, an experienced VVS instructor pilot from the Lipetsk-based combat training centre was killed when his MiG-23S spun out in similar circumstances. In another accident, the VVS's Moscow District Commander, General Odintzov, managed to eject at the last possible moment before his spinning MiG-23S hit the ground.

The first production-standard MiG-23Ss—with airframes cleared for only 4-G manoeuvring—entered service with the Lipetsk-based VVS 4th TsBPiPLS (aircrew combat training and conversion centre) and with the 979th IAP (fighter regiment), at Shtutchin, Byelorussia. A total of sixty or so MiG-23Ss are reported by Russian sources to have left the *Znamya Truda* factory in 1969 and the early 1970s. These saw only a brief front-line service career with the 4th TsBPiPLS at Lipetsk and the 979th IAP at Shtutchin. However, the huge amount of problems that were caused by the unreliable airframe and equipment prevented the MiG-23S's employment as a fully-fledged weapons system. The unstable take-off and landing performance (especially on the final landing approach), combined with the notoriously poor yaw controllability, was listed amongst the chief handling problems of the MiG-23S, which, in the event, led to a considerable attrition.

## MiG-23 *Edition 1971*

In late 1970 the MiG-23S was swiftly replaced on the production line by another interim variant of the 'Flogger', which continued in production into 1971; it was known simply as the 'MiG-23' (more colloquially known as the 'MiG-23 *Edition 1971*'). It was equipped with the initial production version of the Sapfir-23 radar, capable of providing guidance to the new R-23R (AA-7 'Apex') semi-active radar-homing (SARH) BVR missile. This unreliable radar was the Sapfir-23L (Lyogkii, lightweight) pulse radar; an interim solution, it lacked the definitive look-down/shoot-down capability that had originally been conceived for the MiG-23M. The mission avionics suite also incorporated the TP-23 IRST and ASP-23D gun-sight/HUD for displaying target data derived from the radar, replacing the head-down radar scope used on the MiG-23S.

This variant was powered by the R-27F2-300 turbojet, rated at 67.62 kN (15,300 lb st. or 6,893 kgf) dry and 98 kN (22,000 lb st. or 9,990 kgf) with afterburner. The MiG-23 *Edition 1971* introduced a redesigned fuselage in which the tail surfaces were moved aft 86 cm (33.8 in), giving the rear fuselage a very different look. Ribbed airbrakes were introduced and another fuel tank (tank No. 4), holding 470 litres (133 Imp. gal.), was inserted into the rear fuselage.

The *Edition 1971's* improved wing design, known as the *Edition 2 wing*, had its area increased by 20 per cent, or 5 m$^2$ (170 sq. feet). This was urgently needed in order to achieve an acceptable wing loading, which in turn would not only affect the aircraft's take-off/landing characteristics, but also considerably influence its range. The wing area increase led to a change in normal sweep settings of 2° 40', so the main positions became 18, 47° 40' and 74° 40'. For convenience, however, all cockpit indicators and manuals remained unchanged.

A pronounced leading-edge dogtooth was added, but the leading-edge slats were deleted in order to simplify the wing manufacturing process, thus accelerating the type's launch into production. The dogtooth discontinuity—a jagged forward-pointing portion—created a powerful vortex at high AoA, for example, when pulling G. However, subsequent testing revealed that the *Edition 2* wing was a source for potentially dangerous control and stability problems at high AoA, making take-off and landing difficult due to sharply reduced stall margins.

On 14 March 1972 a MiG-23 was lost during the testing of the new increased-area wing. The cause was traced to a structural failure of the fuselage main tank (designated as tank No. 2), which acted as the principal airframe load-bearing element while pulling 7.3-G; some sources say that the aircraft had already begun to disintegrate at 4.2-G. The initial design load factor of the MiG-23 had been set at 8-G. Luckily, the Mikoyan OKB test pilot, Aviard Fastovets, managed to eject safely from the disintegrating fighter.

Eighty (or slightly fewer) MiG-23s of this interim variant were manufactured in 1971. They served briefly with several front-line VVS fighter regiments, such as the 168th IAP at Starokonstantinov, Ukraine, before being assigned to the training role in 1978. The MiG-23 survivors were utilised for advanced and lead-in fighter training with a training regiment of the Tchernigov VVAUL, replacing the MiG-23S in this role at Pevtsi Airfield. However, their demanding handling characteristics (combined with poor maintenance) led to considerable attrition.

## MiG-23M/MF—The Most Numerous Variant

In 1972 the *Znamya Truda* plant began production of the definitive first-generation 'Flogger'—the MiG-23M. First flown in June 1972 (again in the capable hands of Alexander Fedotov), it sported the much-improved Sapfir-23D look-down/shoot-down radar and was armed with R-23R/T BVR missiles and R-60/R-13M WVR missiles.

The MiG-23M became the first VVS Frontal Aviation fighter to serve in large numbers that boasted a powerful radar with look-down/shoot-down (LD/SD) capability and IRST sensor. This enabled operations in a dense ECM environment, where the radar was rendered inoperative. The MiG-23M's weapons suite comprised a pair of R-23R/T SARH/IR-guided BVR air-to-air missiles and a pair of the then-revolutionary new R-60 (AA-8 'Aphid') dogfight missiles.

This variant was produced in the largest numbers of all the so-called first generation 'Floggers', and in the mid-1970s it became the VVS's most important air-superiority fighter.

The MiG-23M was powered by a considerably up-rated R-27 derivative—the Tumanskiy R-29-300 (*izdeliye 55A*), rated at 81.35 kN (18,400 lb st. or 8,293 kgf) dry and 122.50 kN (25,500 lb st. or 12,488 kgf) at full afterburner. It also introduced plumbed pylons under the movable wing panels for carrying optional 800-litre drop tanks. These tanks could be only used at 16° sweep, and for wing movement to 45° and 72° the pilot was required to jettison the tanks first. The MiG-23M featured the new SAU-23A three-axis automatic flight control system/autopilot and the Polyot-1I-23 navigation system.

The 'Flogger-B' was fitted with the definitive *Edition 3* wing, a design which retained the *Edition 2*'s overall dimensions but had leading-edge slats to improve the take-off and landing handling characteristics. The type's production at *Znamya Truda* plant gathered speed, and in 1974 it reached an impressive rate of thirty-plus airframes per month—up to as many as forty airframes at peak times.

The first production MiG-23Ms were equipped with the Sapfir-23L radar, succeeded shortly afterwards by the Sapfir-23D and in 1975 by the definitive Sapfir-23D-III. Later, the Sapfir-23D was brought to the D-III standard during field upgrades undertaken by factory teams.

The mass introduction of the MiG-23Ms was quite a painful undertaking for the VVS, because the new fighter demanded better-educated pilots and technicians than those for the MiG-21. This was due to the complex handling characteristics at the three different wings settings and the highly sophisticated airframe, powerplant, navigation and weapons control system.

The difficult and time-consuming process of expanding the G-factor and AoA envelope began in the mid-1970s; in the event, it took a lot of hard and bloody development work undertaken by Mikoyan OKB and VVS test pilots, while the design team was tasked with expanding the envelope and providing sufficient spin-safe handling qualities.

The initial mass production of the wing pivots and No. 2 centre-fuselage steel tank—the MiG-23's principal airframe load-bearing structural elements—was of

A MiG-23M captured in flight with a loadout comprising two R-23 and two R-60 air-to-air missiles, with wings set at the maximum sweptback position of 72°. (*US DoD*)

The MiG-23MF was the export derivative of the MiG-23M, in production between 1978 and 1983. (*Author's collection*)

low quality, and cracks often occurred on the MiG-23S/M/UBs produced in the early and mid-1970s. In addition, there were many wing sweep mechanism failures (mostly pivot structural failures), which prompted VVS command authorities to impose a temporary 5-G restriction that effectively prevented combat squadrons from practicing basic fighter manoeuvres until 1977. Until clearance was received for high-G manoeuvring, for almost four years the main combat employment *modus operandi* of the MiG-23M-equpped VVS regiments was all-aspect BVR intercepts.

Later in the same decade, the welding technology and quality control were considerably improved. The wing pivots were greatly strengthened, allowing the 'Flogger-B'-equipped VVS regiments to begin practicing close air combat in addition to the standard BVR and WVR intercepts. However, the poor high-AoA handling characteristics remained a limiting factor, despite the 1979 fleet-wide installation of the SOUA stick pusher.

The APU-60-2 double-rail launchers were introduced for the first time on aircraft No. 3201. The follow-on production batches (from aircraft No. 3701 onwards) could use the Kh-23 or Kh-23M radio-command (beam-riding) guided missiles with the associated Del'ta-NG illumination pod carried on the port underfuselage pylon. In addition, all VVS MiG-23Ms were wired to carry a single 10-kT-yield RN-24 nuclear free-fall bomb (later complemented by the 30-kT adjustable-yield RN-40) on a special adaptor under the fuselage.

The MiG-23M had an important secondary ground-attack capability, for which it could carry a warload of up to 3,000 kg (6,614 lb)—including free-fall and cluster bombs, napalm tanks, S-24 240-mm rockets and 16-round 57-mm rocket packs.

The first production MiG-23Ms entered service with the 4th TsBPiPLS in 1973, soon followed by front-line fighter regiments. In 1975 the 16th Air Army, stationed in East Germany, controlled as many as four regiments that converted to the new fighter, a total of twelve squadrons operating some 150 'Floggers'. In the mid–late 1970s, a small number of IA PVO regiments also converted to the MiG-23M.

The MiG-23M's export derivative was designated as the MiG-23MF, and it was available in two sub-versions; the first one (*izdeliye 2A or* 23-11A) was built for the Warsaw Pact states (Bulgaria, Czechoslovakia, East Germany, Poland, Hungary and Romania), and the second (*izdeliye 2B or* 23-11B) for a host of Third World client states (such as Syria, India and Cuba). The *izdeliye 2A* was virtually undistinguishable from the MiG-23M, perhaps with small differences in the communications and IFF equipment only. The *izdeliye 2B* subversion was very different in both radar (as it lacked the ECM-resistance features and often had downgraded performance) and communications equipment (the Lasour-SMA on-board automated datalink was deleted on some aircraft).

All export versions were equipped with the Sapfir-23D-III, re-designated for the export customers as Sapfir-23E. Until 1981 the aircraft were delivered with the R-13M close air-combat missiles instead of the much more agile R-60. The MiG-23MF was in production at *Znamya Truda* between 1978 and 1983.

The MiG-23MF, armed with BVR air-to-air missiles, was deemed too advanced and therefore non-suitable for export to untrusted Third World countries during the early and mid-1970s. The Soviet political and military leadership maintained that there would be unavoidable leaks of sensitive technical information that would compromise this new and very promising air defence fighter (as indeed was the case with the MiG-25P hijacked in 1972 by the young IA PVO pilot Lieutenant Victor Belenko, who flew to Japan). This eventually happened, as a number of MiG-23s (MS and BN versions), exported to Egypt in 1974 were handed over to the United States and China for technical evaluation after only four years in service.

As a result, a purely political decision was taken in late 1972 or early 1973 by the MAI and VVS leadership to develop a substantially downgraded export version of the MiG-23M. It would employ the same basic airframe and powerplant, but it would have the equipment and weapons system taken from the MiG-21S/SM—it included the Almaz-23 radar and ASP-PFD-21 gun-sight. The resultant MiG-23MS version (NATO 'Flogger-E') could easily be distinguished from the MiG-23M/MF thanks to its short nose radome, which housed a downgraded export version of the RP-22SM radar. The undernose IRST was deleted. The sanitised MiG-23M derivative was armed with up to four R-3S and R-3R air-to-air missiles only, although the improved R-13M heat-seeking air-to-air missile was added later.

The MiG-23MS was in production at the *Znamya Truda* plant between 1973 and 1978. Initially, a small batch was taken on strength by the large conversion training centre for foreign pilots located at the Lugovoye/Frunze in the former

This Soviet Air Force MiG-23MS was used for conversion training of pilots from customer nations for the type, such as Libya, Iraq, Syria and Algeria; it was operated by the 715th UAP (training aviation regiment), stationed at Lugovaya Airfield in modern-day Kazakhstan. (*VVS*)

The MiG-23MS was an export derivative of the MiG-23M intended solely for export to Third World countries; as such, it was equipped with downgraded radar and weapons. This is an ex-Egyptian Air Force example, handed over in the late 1970s to the USAF and operated until the late 1980s in the aggressor training role by the 4477th Test and Evaluation Squadron—colloquially known as the 'Red Eagles Squadron'—stationed at Tonopah, Nevada. (*USAF*)

Soviet Republic of Kyrgyzstan; the formal training unit was designated as the 715th UAP (training aviation regiment). The type was then exported to Syria (up to fifty-four aircraft, the first delivered in October 1973), Iraq (eighteen), Egypt (eight, delivered in 1974), Algeria (number and delivery timetable unknown) and Libya (fifty-four, delivered between 1974 and 1976).

## The Refined MiG-23ML

The MiG-23ML (*Type 23-12*, known within NATO as 'Flogger-G') was a much-improved and considerably lightened MiG-23 fighter derivative. It was purposely designed in the mid-1970s in an effort to eliminate the MiG-23M's most obvious design shortcomings (such as airframe and powerplant strength and reliability, manoeuvrability, and radar performance).

Thanks to the removal of No. 4 fuselage fuel tank and an extensive fuselage redesign, the MiG-23ML *(Lyogkiy, 'Lightweight')* was 1,250 kg (2,770 lb) lighter than its predecessor. It had somewhat refined aerodynamics to reduce drag, a new flight control system for better handing, an up-rated powerplant, and a completely redesigned mission avionics suite, with the new SUV-2ML weapons system for

The MiG-23ML was a lightened fighter 'Flogger' version with a more powerful engine, shorter nosewheel strut and a more capable radar. This is a prototype aircraft wearing an overall light-grey camouflage. (*Mikoyan & Gurevich OKB*)

improved reliability and enhanced combat capability. Externally, the MiG-23ML was distinguishable from the M variant by its much smaller dorsal fin and the lowered nose attitude when on the ground, which was due to the redesigned main undercarriage units.

The R-35F-300 turbojet was a growth derivative of the R-27F2M-300. It had a dry rating of 83.82 kN (18,849 lb st. or 8,544 kgf) and a maximum afterburner rating of 128.08 kN (28,800 lb st. or 13,056 kgf). The turbojet featured a compressor with increased-airflow (by 110 kg/s [242 lb per second]) and a turbine inlet temperature increased by 70°. These improvements enabled the new engine to have a lower specific fuel consumption (sfc) than its predecessor. At maximum afterburner, its sfc was 1.96, versus 2.09 kg/kgf.h for the R-27F2M-300. The new powerplant enabled the MiG-23ML's theoretical thrust-to-weight ratio to exceed 0.83 (0.77 for the MiG-23M), but in real-world conditions the ratio proved to be lower due to engine 'detuning' that was introduced to reduce thermal loads and extend the time between overhauls; it also increased the R-35F-300's specific fuel consumption.

During its initial years of service, the R-35F-300 suffered from many reliability problems due to turbine blade failures and combustor chamber cracking. Reliability subsequently improved, enabling extension of time between overhauls

(TBO) for the late-production engines to 450 hours. However, like its R-29-300 and R-27F2M-300 predecessors, it was strictly limited to only ten hours in total in military power and afterburner settings. The R-35F-300's hydro-mechanical control system (the same as that in the R-27F2-300 and R-29-300) was extremely effective and the pilot could slam the throttle from flight idle to full afterburner without worrying about engine failure, surge or compressor stall; it took only three to four seconds to change from idle to military power.

The structural weaknesses revealed during the MiG-23ML's initial service were considerably strengthened (particularly the wing pivot mechanism) so that the MiG-23ML could be cleared for manoeuvring with a maximum load factor of 8.5-G at speeds below Mach 0.85 and 7.5-G above Mach 0.85. The SOUA stick pusher device permitted the pilot to exploit the full AoA envelope of his mount; at 16° sweep the AoA limit was set at 20–22°, and at 45° and 72° sweep it increased to 28–30°.

At 1,000 m (3,280 feet), a MiG-23ML armed with two R-23 missiles had a maximum rate of climb of 215 m/s (42,323 fpm), reduced to 145 m/s (28,523 fpm) at 5,000 m (16,604 feet) and to 125 m/s (25,606 fpm) at 13,000 m (42,651 feet) altitude and at a speed of Mach 2. The acceleration time from 600 to 1,000 km/h (324 to 540 kt) was twelve seconds at full afterburner at 1,000 m (3,280 feet) altitude. The time taken for a 360° turn at 1,000 m (3,280 feet) was twenty-seven seconds, at an average of 6.5-G, entry speed of 900 km/h (486 kt) and final speed of 540 km/h (291 kt). The maximum rate of turn (instantaneous rate) was 16.7° per second (average rate of turn was 14.1° per second), achieved at the corner speed of 780 km/h (421 kt) and 27° AoA. The time taken from brake release to 15,000 m (49,212 feet), while accelerating to Mach 2.1 at full afterburner, was 4.3 minutes. According to data released from the Mikoyan OKB, the MiG-23ML/MLA's overall combat effectiveness was about 20 per cent better than that of the MiG-23M.

The Sapfir-23ML radar—officially known as N003—was among the MiG-23ML's newest features. It was considerably better than the Sapfire-23D-III—more reliable and with a much-improved look-down/shoot-down performance. In addition, the MiG-23ML featured the new more capable Type 26Sh IRST. The MiG-23ML's much-improved weapons control system enabled the use of the R-23R and R-23T BVR missiles in the same mission; usually the former was carried on the starboard wing pylon and the latter on the port. The MiG-23ML's weapons suite was enriched with UPK-23-250 23-mm gun-pods, with two carried on the underwing pylons. The aircraft also retained the capability of carrying a single nuclear bomb.

The MiG-23ML's navigation suite was represented by the new Polyot-21-23, which was significantly better than its predecessor; the same was true for the Lasour-23SML datalink, SAU-23AM flight control system and the RV-5R Reper-M radar altimeter.

The MiG-23ML's prototype (known as the 23-12/1) took to the air for the first time on 21 January 1975, with the Mikoyan OKB test pilot Aviard Fastovetzs in the cockpit. The new type swiftly entered mass production the same year, replacing the MiG-23M on the production line. However, export customers

The MiG-23MLA was a further refined version of the short-fin fighter 'Flogger', based on the MiG-23ML airframe and engine but boasting more capable avionics. (*Author's collection*)

continued to receive newly-built MiG-23MFs for seven more years. No fewer than 1,100 copies of the MiG-23ML and its further-improved derivative (known as the MiG-23MLA) were built for domestic use and export between 1978 and 1983. The VVS received its last fighter 'Flogger-Gs' in 1981.

A further-improved MiG-23ML derivative (utilising the same airframe and powerplant, but with a better mission avionics suite and equipment) was flown for the first time in 1977. Dubbed 'MiG-23MLA', it replaced the MiG-23ML on the production line later in the same year. This version had the improved Sapfir-23MLA (N003) radar with slightly better range, reliability and ECM resistance. The new radar had a frequency spacing feature that enabled group search-and-attack operations, something that could not be performed effectively by the MiG-23M because of mutual interference between the radars within a group. In such search-and-attack operations the fighters operated in four-ship formations, at 7–9 km (3.7–5 nm) lateral separation and 16–17 km (8.6–10 nm) distance.

The list of new features introduced on the MiG-23MLA also included the ASP-17ML HUD/gun-sight and 26ShI IRST. Most importantly, in 1981 the new R-24R/T air-to-air missile was included; it had a much-improved range, warhead, fuse and ECM resistance compared to the R-23R/T.

The search performance of the new IRST was limited by its field of scanning, which was restricted compared to the radar—only 60° in azimuth and 15° in elevation—and its maximum tracking rate was 6° per second. The average low-level detection range against receding fighter-sized targets (in tail-on aspect) with afterburner on was around 10 km (5.4 nm), and at high level the range could increase to 25 km (13.5 nm). Typical high-level detection range of a fighter-sized target with engine operating at military power was around 15 km (8 nm), and maximum detection range for a bomber-sized target at high altitude approached 45 km (24.3 nm).

Externally, the MiG-23MLA was virtually identical to the ML variant, and this version, which entered mass production in 1978, was available for sale to foreign customers from 1981. In most cases, the newly-exported aircraft were used to complement the previously-delivered MiG-23MFs; this was the case with the trio of Warsaw Pact countries—Bulgaria, Czechoslovakia and East Germany. A sanitised MiG-23MLA derivative was subsequently sold in the first half of the 1980s to Angola, Cuba, Iraq, North Korea and Yemen.

## MiG-23M/MF and MiG-23MLA Specification

|  | MiG-23M/MF | MiG-23MLA |
| --- | --- | --- |
| Dimensions: |  |  |
| Wing span at 16° | 14.00 m | 14.00 m |
| Wing span at 72° | 7,78 m | 7,78 m |
| Length without probe | 16.71 m | 16.70 m |
| Height | 4.82 m | 5.77 m |
| Wing area: |  |  |
| - at 16° sweptback | 37.27 m$^2$ | 37.35 m$^2$ |
| - at 72° sweptback | 34.16 m$^2$ | 34.16 m$^2$ |
| Weights: |  |  |
| Empty operating | 10,890 kg | 10,850 kg |
| Normal take-off | 15,700 kg | 14,700 kg |
| Maximum take-off | 18,400 kg | 17,800 kg |
| Performance: |  |  |
| Max level speed at sea level | 1,350 km/h | 1,350 km/h |
| Max level speed at high level | 2,500 km/h | 2,500 km/h |
| Max operating Mach number | 2.35 | 2.35 |
| Take-off speed | 280 km/h | 280 km/h |
| Landing speed | 240 km/h | 240 km/h |
| Practical ceiling, clean | 17,500 m | 18,500 |
| G limits | +8.0 | +8.5 |
| Rate of climb at low level | 195 m/s | 215 m/s |
| Take-off distance | 500 m | 500 m |
| Landing distance | 700 m | 750 m |
| Ferry range clean | 1,450 km | 1,950 km |
| Ferry range with external tanks | 2,380 km | 2,820 km |

## MiG-23MLA—Technical Description

The fuselage of semi-monocoque construction was made of two parts—nose and tail, joined together at frame twenty-eight. The tail part of the fuselage comprised afterburner, tailplane mounting and four petal-type ribbed airbrakes.

The variable-geometry wing was made of two parts. The fixed wing glove had a sweep of 70°. The movable wing panels featured sweep angles that were fully and continuously variable from 18.5° to 74.5°. The three main wing positions used in flight, for which controllability and stability performance were fully explored, were 16°, 45° and 72° (precise swept values being 18° 40', 47° 40' and 74° 40'). The wings had a number of high-lift devices—full-span, four-section trailing-edge flaps deflected at 25° for take-off and 50° for landing, leading-edge slats deflected at 20° and two-section spoilers.

The all-moving tailplane had a sweep angle of 55° 40' and was mounted to frame thirty-one. Deflection of the tailerons was from −28° 30' to +8° 30′ symmetrically for pitch control and +/-10° differentially for roll control. A large folding ventral fin was used to improve the high-speed yaw stability; when the undercarriage was down, the ventral fin was stowed to port.

The tailfin was fastened to fuselage frames twenty-nine and thirty-one, and had a rudder mounted on a damping device with deflection of 25° left and right. At the top of the tailfin in a dielectric housing were the antennas for the radio, SO-10M RWR and RSBN-6S tactical radio-navigation system. A brake parachute container was mounted at the fin base and the parachute itself had an area of 21.00 m$^2$ (226 sq. feet).

The landing gear was of classic three-unit type. The nose unit retracted rearwards and had a double 520 x 125-mm KT-152 wheel. The main units were designed to fit into a tight space and were fitted with a single KT-105 wheel (840 x 290 mm). Disc brakes were used and brake control was pneumatic.

The aircraft control system of hydro-mechanical type had channels for pitch, yaw, roll, speed brakes activation and wing movement.

The two independent hydraulic systems—the main and the booster—had a working pressure of 210 kg/cm$^2$ (2,986 psi). The booster hydro system was also responsible for feeding the SPK-1 wing sweep system. Two independent pneumatic systems were used for brake control emergency landing gear and fin retraction, canopy operation and pressurisation, brake parachute opening, wing seals, radar compartment pressurisation and air conditioning of the equipment in avionics compartments. The main undercarriage legs were also used as pressurised air tanks.

AC voltages of 36 V, 115 V and 380 V/400 Hz, and a DC voltage of 28 V were used in the electrical system, which was powered by the GSR-ST-18/7KTS starter-generator.

The powerplant consisted of one Soyuz R-35F-300 turbojet (*Izdeliye 77*) with a maximum dry thrust of 83.88 kN (18,849 lb st. or 8,550 kgf) and maximum thrust with afterburning of 128.98 kN (28,800 lb st. or 13,148 kgf). The engine start-up was provided by an on-board TS-11 turbo-starter.

Fuel was carried in three fuselage tanks and four cells in each movable wing panel, giving a total internal volume of 3,000 litres. Two additional tanks under the wings, holding 800 litres each, were only used at wing sweep position 16°, and one more 800-litre (176-Imp. gal.) drop tank was carried under the fuselage. The MiG-23MLA had a centralised pressure refuelling system.

Communications equipment encompassed one R-862 UHF radio set plus one R-855 emergency radio installed in the pilot's survival kit in the ejection seat. Navigation equipment comprised the Polyot-21-23 system, incorporating an RSBN-6S tactical radio aid to the navigation/automatic landing system, SKV-2NM-2 gyro reference system, DV-30K and DVS-10 air data sensors, ARK-15M ADF and a MRP-56 beacon receiver. Other avionics included the SOD-59 air traffic control transponder, a SRZO-2 IFF unit (interrogator-transponder), a RV-5R Reper-M radar altimeter, SPO-10M Sirena-3 RWR and the on-board set of the Lasour-SML command datalink for the Vozdukh-1M ground-based remote intercept control system.

The KM-1M ejection seat of Mikoyan's own design granted safe ejection throughout the entire envelope, at a minimal speed of 130 km/h (70 kt), including ground level. The cockpit was pressurised and air conditioned above 2,000 m (6,561 feet), as was the avionics compartment.

## The MiG-23P Specialised Interceptor

The MiG-23P (retaining the NATO 'Flogger-G' designation), formally known within the IA PVO as *izdeliye 6*, was ordered by the Soviet Air Defence forces as an interim, low-cost, stop-gap solution to counter the threat from low-altitude targets.

It possessed the genuine look-down/shoot-down radar capability deemed necessary to counter the threat posed by NATO's new-generation, low-altitude, tactical fighter-bombers (especially the then-new F-111, successfully used at low level in Vietnam between 1968 and 1972), strategic bombers (such as the then-new B-1B) and air-launched cruise missiles. The new interceptor drew on the basic MiG-23ML fuselage and powerplant but featured a considerably altered mission avionics suite, tailor-made to work with PVO's advanced remote intercept-guidance systems. It was used to replace both the Su-9/11 and MiG-19P/PM, which were used in relatively large numbers in the late 1970s with the IA PVO. Externally, it could be distinguished from the MiG-23ML/MLA by the different antennas endowing the fin tip.

The MiG-23P ('*Perekhvatchik*', 'Interceptor') was equipped with the much-improved SAU-23P autopilot/automated flight control system with a new-generation digital computer, which provided reliable, fully-automated and sufficiently remote guidance during an optimised flight path intercept using the Lasour-M equipment. The aircraft could automatically follow a course to its target, receiving steering information from the GCI ground station of the Vozdukh-1 system, without pilot intervention except for engine control. The initial production aircraft were equipped with the ASP-23P gun-sight/HUD, replaced in follow-on production MiG-23Ps by the much more modern ASP-23ML-P (DtZM-P). The weapons suite, initially comprising R-23T/P and R-60 missiles, was enriched in the early 1980s with the more capable R-24R/T and R-60M.

The MiG-23P proved to be the most popular and numerous PVO interceptor to feature look-down/shoot-down capability, which was urgently needed during the late 1970s and early 1980s. The MiG-23P's Sapfir-23P (N006) radar set was an improved Sapfir-23ML derivative, although it was initially unreliable and required much maintenance.

The MiG-23P proved to be the most durable 'Flogger' derivative in Russian service after dissolution of the Soviet Union in 1991. The last two MiG-23P-equipped IA PVO fighter regiments—one of them based at Kursk-East (472nd IAP) and the other one at Barnaul—operated the type until early 1998. Interestingly, thanks to the powerful radar and the fairly low frontal aspect radar-cross section with wings fully swept back (much lower than that of the Su-23P), the MiG-23P, flown by experienced pilots, proved to be equal if not better in the BVR mock air combats than the newer Su-27. The ready availability of surplus airframes suitable for cannibalisation meant that the combat-capable rate maintained in the last MiG-23-equipped regiments in the 1990s was much better than that of those equipped with the Su-27 and MiG-31.

## MiG-23MLD—The Ultimate Fighter 'Flogger'

The MiG-23MLD (*Type 23-18*, NATO 'Flogger-K') resulted from a comprehensive upgrade programme in 1982, which was aimed at enhancing the MiG-23ML/MLA's overall air combat capability. Initially, the Mikoyan OKB proposed a newly-built MiG-23MLD derivative ('*Dorabotannyi*', meaning 'upgraded' or 'improved'), known as the Type 23-19 (some sources say Type 23-16), lacking the original aerodynamics improvements. In the event, VVS command authorities proved reluctant to order newly-built MiG-23s and opted instead for a large-scale upgrade programme for the majority of its ML/MLA fleet. It was brought to the enhanced-capability standard with significant aerodynamics and avionics improvements.

The resolution for commencement of the upgrade programme was passed in 1981 and was finally approved by the VVS's Chief Aviation Engineer in May 1982. The first aircraft (factory number 0390315446) was converted at the *Znamya Truda* plant, while the subsequent conversion of 560 VVS MiG-23ML/MLAs (including a small number of MiG-23Ps) was carried out at three VVS maintenance facilities located in Moscow (Kubinka), Tchuguev and L'vov between May 1982 and May 1985.

The primary aim of the 23-18 programme was to enhance control at high AoA, which had been identified as the MiG-23M/ML's chief shortcoming and could be traced as far back as the MiG-23S/M. This prevented the full use of an aircraft's theoretical manoeuvrability potential in close air combat. To solve this, a host of aerodynamics features was introduced; vortex generators (thin steel plates) were fitted on the pitot boom, and notched leading-edge roots (also known as Lambda-shaped leading edge root extensions) were added to act as vortex generators and energise the flow over the wings in order to delay the stall.

The Soviet MiG-23MLD (23-18) was a mid-life upgrade of the existing MiG-23ML/MLA inventory, and the only export customer to get it was Bulgaria; its air arm took five such aircraft on strength after the end of the Cold War, in exchange for three MiG-25s. (*Author's collection*)

The flight-control system incorporated the SOS-3-4 synthetic stick-stop device/ signals limiter, which was borrowed from the MiG-29 to restrict G, AoA and pitch rate in order to reduce the probability of departure from controlled flight. The SOS-3-4 also featured automatic slats employment, depending on AoA, speed and altitude, giving improved stall protection and better turning ability at high AoA; this considerably improved the slow-speed handling and manoeuvring characteristics required for close air combat in the 1980s. The strengthened wing pivots allowed a new sweep position of 33°, which was intended to reduce the turn radius and to facilitate rapid deceleration during close air combats. On the negative side, the 33° wing sweep had a notably poor effect on acceleration characteristics and made handling a great deal more complex. In the event, all combat manuals continued to specify the 45° position, and 33° sweep was used primarily by experienced 'Flogger' drivers.

To enhance survivability, a pair of six-round downwards-firing chaff/flare dispensers was installed in the stretched underfuselage centreline pylon. These were complemented by the massive BVP-50-60 30-round upward-firing chaff/ flare dispensers.

The MiG-23MLD's weapons suite was enriched with the R-24R/T missiles and the aircraft could employ a pair of the B8M1 20-round rocket pods to fire 80-mm rockets of the S-8 family, fitted with a variety of warheads. The

A scan into the MiG-23MLD's cockpit. (*Author's collection*)

MiG-23MLD had a maximum bomb load of 2,000 kg (4,409 lb), usually comprising four FAB-500 500-kg (1,102-lb) general purpose (GP) bombs or ZAB-500 500-kg napalm tanks. Other bombing configurations comprised up to 16 FAB-100 100-kg (220-lb) GP bombs carried on four multiple ejector bomb racks, up to four FAB-250 250-kg (551-lb) GP bombs or two RBK-500 cluster bombs. The MiG-23MLD, like its MiG-23M and MiG-23ML/MLA predecessors, could employ Kh-23 and Kh-23M air-to-surface missiles and a single RN-24 or RN-40 nuclear bomb.

The MiG-23MLD's much-improved mission avionics suite centred on the Sapfir-23MLA-II radar (known also as N008) with an improved maximum detection range, reliability, ECM resistance and look-down/shoot-down capability over rough terrain. It also had a newly-added close air combat mode with vertical-scan capability in a narrow sector in front of the aircraft. The new radar's maximum detection range against a bomber-sized target at medium/high level exceeded 70 km (38 nm).

Other important new avionics suite components included the SPO-15L Beryoza radar-warning receiver that replaced the old SPO-10, and the new A-321 Klystron digital tactical radio navigation/automatic landing system that replaced the RSBN-6S. In addition, the MiG-23MLD received the improved SAU-23-18 automatic flight control system, the all-new MRK-32-25 nose undercarriage leg steering device and an enhanced-capability SARP-12-24 crash-resistant flight data recorder.

## Newly-Built MiG-23MLD Derivatives for Export

A couple of export MLD derivatives were produced between 1982 and 1984 at the *Znamya Truda* plant. They featured the new avionics and self-defence systems of the VVS aircraft but lacked the aerodynamic and flight control improvements of the 'true' MiG-23MLD, and they had the older-generation IFF systems. These aircraft were the only newly-built MiG-23MLDs; a total of sixty-six aircraft in two sub-versions were built at *Znamya Truda's* final assembly branch in Lukhovitzy between 1982 and 1984.

Externally, the MiG-23MLD's export derivatives could be distinguished from the upgraded Soviet MiG-23MLDs only by the radomes built into the leading edges of the wing gloves, covering the forward-facing wide-band antennas of the new SPO-15L Beryoza RWR (radar-warning receiver) and the lack of vortex generators on the pitot boom.

The first of these export derivatives—known as the Type 23-19—was purposely designed for export to Syria, and fifty aircraft were delivered from late 1982, together with a huge stock of the new R-24R/T BVR missiles.

The Type 23-19B retained the original MiG-23MLA's Sapfir-23MLAE (N003E) radar with downgraded capability compared to the VVS standard version, and perhaps lacked ECM resistance (a reduced number of pre-selected operating frequencies). During their main overhauls in the late 1980s, a proportion of the Syrian 'Floggers' received additional survivability enhancements in the form of fences housing pairs of 32-round ASO-2V chaff/flare dispensers, mounted symmetrically on the rear fuselage beside the fin.

One Syrian MiG-23MLD defected to Israel in October 1989. The Israeli Air Force pilots who tested the aircraft found its avionics (including the ASP-17ML HUD symbols) relatively easy to use, and the N003E radar was judged to be significantly more powerful than their intelligence had reported previously. As Israeli comparative flight tests using the MiG-23MLD have shown, the swing-wing fighter demonstrated—somewhat surprisingly—that it had better acceleration than the escorting F-16 two-seaters.

The second MLD export sub-variant was known under the Mikoyan internal designation Type 23-22A. Its mission avionics suite was virtually identical to that of the original Type 23-18; no significant differences have yet been discovered, with even the wiring for use of a nuclear bomb being retained.

Only sixteen aircraft of this sub-version were built in 1983 and 1984, intended for export to Bulgaria. The second batch of eight MiG-23MLDs (Export) assembled in November and December 1984 represented the very last fighter 'Floggers' to come from the *Znamya Truda* plant. The aircraft serialed '219' (factory number 29600327219) was the final MiG-23 fighter to be assembled at Lukhovitzy: it underwent its functional check flights on 22 December 1984 and was delivered to the Bulgarian air force in February 1985.

Several further-improved MiG-23MLD configurations were built in the early–mid-1980s, but none reached production. They were designed in an effort to cure a

Only sixty-six new MiG-23MLDs were built, with fifty of these delivered to Syria (known as 23-19) and the rest going to Bulgaria (designated as the 23-22), as seen here. These fighters retained the MiG-23MLA fuselage (i.e. lacking the aerodynamic refinements of the Soviet MiG-23MLDs), but boasted improved avionics and equipment. (*Author's collection*)

This is the Syrian Air Force MiG-23MLD (23-19) that defected to Israel in 1989 and was then tested by the Israeli Air Force. (*Israeli Air Force*)

major drawback of the fighter 'Flogger'—the absence of any ECM system (built-in or pod-mounted) for self-protection. As the Bekaa Valley clashes in 1982 clearly demonstrated, such equipment is a vital component of the mission avionics suite of an air-superiority fighter. In 1982 the Mikoyan OKB was ordered to develop new MiG-23 versions equipped with self-protection jammers. One proposal was the MiG-23MLDG (Type 23-57), featuring a built-in Gardeniya-1 jammer with rear-facing transmitting antennas built into the fin. Another derivative, known as the MiG-23MLS (Type 23-47), was offered to export customers equipped with the older SPS-141 Siren jammer. Mikoyan OKB sources also refer to another MiG-23 derivative fitted with ECM system—it was the MiG-23MLG (Type 23-37), equipped with the Gardeniya-1 active jammer too.

## MiG-23MLD Specification

| | |
|---|---|
| Dimensions: | |
| Wing span at 16° | 14.00 m |
| Wing span at 72° | 7,78 m |
| Length without probe | 16.70 m |
| Height | 5.00 m |
| Wing area: | |
| - at 16° sweepback | 37.35 m$^2$ |
| - at 72° sweepback | 34.16 m$^2$ |
| Weights: | |
| Empty operating | 10,230 kg |
| Normal take-off | 14,700 kg |
| Maximum take-off | 17,800 kg |
| Performance: | |
| Max level speed at sea level | 1,400 km/h |
| Max level speed at high level | 2,500 km/h |
| Max operating Mach number | 2.35 |
| Cruise speed | 990 km/h |
| Take-off speed | 280 km/h |
| Landing speed | 240 km/h |
| Practical ceiling, clean | 18,600 |
| G limits | +8.5 |
| Rate of climb at low level | 225 m/s |
| Take-off distance | 500 m |
| Landing distance | 750 m |
| Ferry range clean | 1,950 km |
| Ferry range with external tanks | 2,820 km |

This MiG-23MLD (export) is, in fact, the last single-seat 'Flogger' that rolled out the assembly line at the LMZ plant in December 1984. Here it is seen armed with a loadout of one R-24R (carried under the starboard wing glove but not visible on this photo), one R-24T (seen here under the port wing), and two R-60 close air combat missiles. (*Author's collection*)

## Two-Seat 'Floggers'

The MiG-23's two-seat version appeared some six months after the single-seater, as its development was approved in November 1967. It was a straightforward development of the MiG-23S, intended for pilot conversion and weapons training and powered by the same R-27F2-300 turbojet rated at 98.0 kN (22,000 lbs or 9,990 kgf) with afterburner and 66.9 kN (15,000 lbs or 6,820 kgf) dry. The only major design difference was the presence of the second cockpit where the equipment bay had been located—the equipment bay had itself moved to a redesigned nose. The two cockpits were covered by separate upward-hinging canopies, the rear one having a retractable periscope built into the roof to give a better view on approach.

The two-seater could perform the air-to-air role, equipped with the S-21M weapons control suite that originally was centred on the Sapfir-21M radar and armed with R-3S and R-13M missiles. The type also retained the single-seater's GSh-23L gun with 200 rounds, Kh-23/23M guided air-to-surface missiles, 57-mm or 240-mm rockets, and up to 3,000 kg (6,614 lbs) of bombs, carried on four hardpoints.

To compensate for the decreased fuel capacity, an additional fuel tank (No. 4) with a capacity of 470 litres was placed in the rear fuselage; this was the same solution implemented in the MiG-23 and MiG-23M.

The first prototype of the MiG-23UB two-seater took to the air for the first time on 10 April 1970. (*Mikoyan & Gurevich OKB*)

The MiG-23UB was equipped with the SAU-23UB flight control system and Polyot-1I-23 navigation system, comprising RSBN-6S tactical aid to navigation, a SKV-2N2 reference gyro and a DV-30 and DV-10 air data system. The back seater had a sophisticated system to simulate emergencies for the student pilot in the front cockpit.

The MiG-23UB prototype—dubbed '23-51/1', coded 251 and fitted with the Edition One wing—made its maiden flight on 10 April 1970 in the hands of test pilot Mikhail Komarov.

Serial production was launched at the Irkutsk Aviation Plant (IAZ) in 1970. From 1971, the production aircraft received the 'clawed' Edition Three wing, compatible with the carriage of outboard underwing fuel tanks on non-swivelling pylons. Early production aircraft also featured the Sapfir-21M radar, but the production run was limited and all subsequent batches lacked the radar. It was replaced by ballast blocks under a conical metal fairing. Additionally, from 1979 onwards the MiG-23UBs that were delivered to MiG-23M/ML-equipped regiments of the Soviet Air Force had their flight-control systems upgraded with the SOUA AoA limiter (most of the aircraft were retrofitted with the AoA limiter in-service) to constrain the AoA to within the 28-degree mark.

The MiG-23UB was in production for the Soviet Air Force and the Soviet Air Defence Forces until 1978, and continued to be manufactured for export until 1985. More than 1,000 aircraft were produced; some 760 of these were delivered to the VVS and IA PVO, and the rest went to export customers.

A scan of the front cockpit of a late-production MiG-23UB. (*Author's collection*)

The production-standard MiG-23UB two-seater lacked a radar and was only able to use heat-seeking missiles (in addition to the GSh-23L 23-mm cannon) in the air-to-air-role. (*Author's collection*)

## MiG-23 Radars

The MiG-23S variant was equipped with the RP-22SM pulse radar featuring a twist-Cassegrain antenna, as found on the MiG-21S. Maximum detection range approached 18 km (9.8 nm) and tracking range was up to 11 km (6 nm). The radar enabled use of the R-3R (AA-2C 'Atoll') SARH missile, which was suitable for tail chase engagements only and had a range of 0.8 and 7 km (0.43 and 3.8 nm). The R-3S (and later the improved R-13M) heat-seeking air-to-air missiles were useful only for clear-weather visual intercepts.

The MiG-23MS was exported to a number of Arab client states in the 1970s, and was equipped with a sanitised RP-22 version (borrowed from the MiG-21bis) provided with only one carrier frequency, a design with no electronic countermeasures (ECM) resistance. The RP-22's detection range reached 25 km (13.4 nm) and its tracking range reached 17 km (9.2 nm).

The Sapfir-23L was a simplified initial version of the definitive powerful pulse radar set developed for the MiG-23 by OKB-339 in Moscow (now known as the NIIR-Phazotron company); initial design work dated back to 1963. The L version, however, lacked the look-down/shoot-down (LD/SD) capability, so it could only provide guidance to R-23R SARH missiles fired against medium and high-altitude targets flying above 1,000 m (3,280 feet). The radar used a twist-Cassegrain antenna 800 mm (31.5 in) in diameter and had a continuous-wave target illuminator channel to provide SARH missile guidance in a single-target track mode.

The Sapfir-23D (known to NATO as 'High Lark II') was the first of the family endowed with LD/SD capability. It was followed in 1975 by the Sapfir-23D-III (*Izdeliye 323D-III*)—the definitive version of the first-generation Sapfir-23 family, which was fitted to MiG-23Ms built from 1975. It was considered advanced technology for the Soviet micro-electronics industry of the time, although by Western standards it was a somewhat old-fashioned piece of hardware. The analogue-technology Sapfir-23D-III was a pulse radar working in the 3-cm wavelength (carrier frequency of about 9 GHz) and capable of LD/SD engagements utilising the rather unreliable 'envelope detection' technique—reportedly taken by OKB-339 designers from the F-4J's AWG-10 radar captured in Vietnam in 1967. The maximum detection range of a well-tuned Sapfir-23D-III against fighter-sized targets in look-up mode/head-on engagement approached 45 km (25 nm); in look-down mode/tail-on engagement it was between 10 km (5.4 nm) and 20 km (10.8 nm). The detection range of bomber-sized targets was 55 km (30 nm) in look-up mode/head-on and tail-on engagements, while in look-down mode/tail-on engagement it was between 15 km (8 nm) and 20 km (10.8 nm). The minimal speed of the target in the LD/SD mode was about 60 km/h (32 kt).

The Sapfir-23ML (N003) radar equipping the MiG-23ML was a considerably improved and lightened version. It was soon followed by the further-improved Sapfir-23MLA, which was 170 kg (375 lb) lighter than the Sapfir-23D-III due to the use of new-generation micro-elements and other weight-reducing measures.

Its maximum detection range of a typical bomber-sized target in look-up mode approached 65 km (35 nm), reduced in LD/SD mode to below 20 km (11 nm).

The MiG-23P was equipped with the N006 radar, based on the N003 but with a slightly improved LD/SD capability—it was urgently required for countering the cruise missile and low-level strike aircraft operations that gained particular importance in the late 1970s. The new radar was used in conjunction with the ASP-17ML-P sight/HUD.

The MiG-23MLD was equipped with the much-improved Sapfir-23MLA-II radar (also known as the N008). Fifty per cent of this version's black boxes differed from those in the Sapfir-23MLA, and some digital memory was incorporated into the main computer. It weighed 360 kg (794 lb) and its peak emitting power was 60 kW, with an average emitting power of 1 kW. In the close air combat mode, the N008 could send commands to 'slave' the R-60, R-60M, R-13M and R-73 seeker heads towards the acquired target. The pre-launch acquisition mode extended 12° up/down and left/right relative to aircraft's nose (up to a 45° angle of slew for the R-73).

A close look at the N003 radar equipping the MiG-23MLA. (*Author's collection*)

## Maximum Ranges of the N008 Radar

|  | Bomber-sized target | Fighter-sized target |
| --- | --- | --- |
| Search range at high altitude | 75 km (40.5 nm) | 52 km (28 nm) |
| Tracking range at high altitude | 52 km (28 nm) | 39 km (22 nm) |
| Search range at low altitude (LD/SD mode)—rear/forward quarter | 23 km/23 km (12.5 nm/12.5 nm) | 23 km/14 km (12.5 nm/7.6 nm) |
| Tracking range at low altitude (LD/SD) mode—rear/forward quarter | 23 km (12.5 nm) | 15 km/9 km (8.2 nm/4.9 nm) |
| Scan field –azimuth × elevation | 60° × 6° |  |
| Auto track field–azimuth × elevation | 112° × (-44° to +56°) |  |
| Beam width–azimuth × elevation | 2.4° × 2.4° |  |

*Note*: The scan field of 60 × 6 degrees can be steered up to 60 degrees left and right in azimuth to expand the searched volume

## 'Flogger' Air-to-Air Missiles

The MiG-23M's basic weapons were two R-23R or R-23T beyond-visual-range (BVR) missiles. The aircraft was limited to carrying only one R-23 variant in a single mission, as each variant required different black boxes for the fire control system.

The R-23, initially known as the K-23, was developed at Factory No. 134 by a design team led by V.A. Pustyakov. The design requirements called for a missile capable of destroying bomber-sized targets at a maximum distance of 18 km (9.8 nm) and flying 4,000 m (13,123 feet) above the launch platform (snap-up capability). The K-23 was built in two versions—one with a SARH seeker (*Izdeliye 340)* and one with an IR seeker (*Izdeliye 360)*. Both of these were fitted with the same expanding-rod warhead weighing 26 kg (57.2 lb) and with a lethal radius of 8 m (26 feet). The SARH version's monopulse seeker gave it a fairly good ECM resistance compared to the F-4E's AIM-7E-2. The IR version employed a seeker with a liquid-nitrogen-cooled detector that required lock-on before launch, and it could be slaved onto the target by the radar or IRST sensor. The missile's 'brochure' probability of kill (PoK) was rated at 0.8–0.9.

Both the IR and SARH K-23 variants were commissioned into VVS service together with the MiG-23M in January 1974, and were designated R-24T and R-23R respectively. In real-world combat conditions, the R-23R was reasonably effective against high-altitude reconnaissance aerostats often encountered over

Eastern Europe and the Soviet Union; in such cases the missile homed onto the radar-reflective aerostat payload.

The K-24 programme began in 1975 as a deep upgrade of the K-23, intended to extend range and increase the effectiveness of the seeker heads, radar fuse and warhead. The SARH version—known as the K-24R—received the new RGS-24 seeker head with much-improved ECM resistance and lock-on-after-launch capability. The latter was used to avoid interference from the Sapfir-23 radar as the missile passed next to the launch aircraft's nose, but it also extended the range. The inertial phase of flight was lengthened to ten seconds, and this, combined with the larger rocket motor, gave the K-24R a range that was 30 per cent longer than its predecessors. Both the SARH and IR-variants variants of the K-24 were appropriate for use against fighter-sized targets that manoeuvred with up to 8-G. Better still, the SARH version—known after service entry as the R-24R—could even guide onto helicopters in hover, as well as onto high-speed aircraft flying in a tight formation. The missile could destroy targets flying at altitudes of between 40 and 25,000 m (131 to 82,020 feet).

Externally, the R-24 could be distinguished from the R-23 only by its forward-sweep wing trailing edge—the R-23's was straight. Internally, the new missile also featured a larger motor, a more powerful expanding-rod warhead (weighing 35 kg (77 lb), with a lethal radius of 10 m (32 feet)) and a new, more reliable radar fuse. The minimal launch distance in tailchase engagements (in rear-hemisphere attacks) was significantly reduced to 500 m (1,600 feet), compared with 1,300 m (4,160 feet) for the R-23.

The IR-variant of the R-24 was equipped with the TGS-23T4 seeker employing a liquid nitrogen-cooled detector with enhanced sensitivity compared to that used in the R-23T; however, just like its predecessor, the R-24T remained a lock-on-before-launch weapon.

The development and flight testing of both R-24 variants went smoothly, although the usual process of minor improvements and protracted testing delayed their service until 1981.

The R-60 and its improved derivative, the R-60M, were the Soviet Air Force's first true dogfight missiles, and from the mid-1970s to the late 1980s they were the principal VVS close-in weapons. Despite fleet-wide introduction of the R-73, the R-60Ms retained their significance until the early–mid 1990s. This lightweight, highly-agile missile was capable of replacing guns in close-quarters air combat.

Development work began in 1971 at Molniya design team, formerly known as OKB-4. The new missile incorporated a simple, compact and uncooled Komar IR-seeker, a radar fuse and a small expanding-rod warhead weighing 3 kg (6.4 lb), with an effective lethal radius of 2.5 m (8.2 feet). It could destroy the target only in the event of direct hit. This lock-on-before-launch weapon imposed few restrictions on the launch platform, as it could reach targets manoeuvring with a maximum of 8-G while the launch platform was restricted to 7-G during the launch. The minimum launch range—a significant parameter in a dogfight—was only 300 m (984 feet). The probability of hit of a twin-missile salvo was 0.7–0.8.

The pilot could squeeze the trigger during the pre-launch manoeuvring and the R-60 would launch automatically when the missile seeker acquired the target.

The improved R-60M that entered service in the early 1980s boasted a more sensitive Komar-M IR-seeker with a nitrogen-cooled detector, which provided a limited all-aspect acquisition/launch capability—only against targets with engines in afterburner. Better still, the R-60M had an expanded off-boresight acquisition capability of some 17° (the R-60 was limited to 12°). Its minimum launch distance was further reduced down to 200 m (656 feet), and the maximum launch was increased by 500 m (1,640 feet).

A close look at the R-24T heat-seeking air-to-air missile on the glove pylon and an R-60MK on the underfuselage pylon. (*Author's collection*)

# Beyond-Visual-Range Missiles

|  | R-23R | R-23T | R-24R | R-24T |
|---|---|---|---|---|
| Maximum launch range at low level<br>-forward quarter<br>- rear quarter | 14 km (7.5 nm)<br>4 km (2.2 nm) | 11 km (6 nm)<br>4 km (2.2 nm) | 17 km (9 nm)<br>4 km (2.2 nm) | 11 km (6 nm)<br>4 km (2.2 nm) |
| Maximum launch range at high level<br>- forward quarter<br>- rear quarter | 25 km (13.50 nm)<br>8–10 km (4.3–5.4 nm) | 11 km (6 nm)<br>8–10 km (4.3–5.4 nm) | 35 km (19 nm)<br>20 km (11 nm) | 12 km (6.5 nm)<br>20 km (10.8 nm) |
| Minimum launch range at low level<br>- forward quarter<br>- rear quarter | 4–6 km (2.2–3.3 nm)<br>1.3 km (0.7 nm) | 4 km (2.2 nm)<br>1.3 km (0.7 nm) | 2.5 km (1.4 nm)<br>0.5 km (0.3 nm) | 2.5 km (1.4 nm)<br>0.5 km (0.3 nm) |
| Maximum-g of the launch aircraft | 4 | 4 | 7 | 7 |
| Maximum-g of the target | 5 | 5 | 7 | 7 |
| Weight | 222 kg (488.4 lb) | 215 kg (473 lb) | 243 kg (535 lb) | 235 kg (517 lb) |
| Warhead weight | 25 kg (55 lb) |  | 35 kg (77 lb) |  |

# Within-Visual-Range Air-to-Air Missiles

|  | R-13M | R-3S | R-60 | R-60MK |
|---|---|---|---|---|
| Max range at low level/ rear quarter | 3.5 km (1.9 nm) | 2.5 km (1.3 nm) | 2 km (1.1nm) | 2 km (1.1 nm) |
| Max range at high level/ rear quarter | 13 km (7 nm) | 7 km (3.8 nm) | 8 km (4.3 nm) | 8 km (4.3 nm) |
| Min range/rear quarter | 0.9 km (0.5 nm) | 1 km (0.55 nm) | 0.2–0.3 km (0.1–0.13 nm) | 0.2–0.3 km (0.1–0.13 nm) |
| Maximum-g of the launch aircraft | 3.7 | 2 | 7 | 7 |
| Maximum-g of the target | 5 | 3 | 8 | 8 |
| All-aspect capability | No | No | No | Limited |
| Weight | 90 kg (198 lb) | 76.5 kg (168 lb) | 43.5 kg (96 lb) | 44 kg (97 lb) |
| Warhead weight | 11.3 kg (25 lb) | 11.3 kg (25 lb) | 3.0 kg (6.6 lb) | 3.5 kg (7.7 lb) |

## The MiG-23's Painful Induction into Service

Design problems plagued the new type's introduction and employment as an operationally-capable weapons platform for some time. In theory at least, the MiG-23M was regarded as a quantum improvement over the MiG-21PFM/SM, which was the mainstay of the Frontal Aviation arm by that time. In came as an unpleasant surprise to the MiG-23 community when the first production MiG-23Ms were pitted against the MiG-21M/SMs in practice close air combats at Lipetsk and Akhtubinsk—and lost all turning engagements against its nimble predecessor. The result was the same, if not worse, when the MiG-23M was pitted against a Northrop F-5 that was thoroughly evaluated by the NII VVS by that time (a trophy aircraft captured in South Vietnam). The MiG-23 was piloted by one of the most experienced NII VVS test pilots, Vladimir Kondaurov, but he lost all turning engagements despite his best efforts to manoeuvre at the maximum permitted AoA (and even beyond it), continuously selecting the best wing sweep for each turning speed (as angle of sweep varied somewhere between 33 and 45°) in an effort to get the maximum-possible instantaneous turn rate.

The new fighter interceptor was officially commissioned into VVS FA service on 4 January 1974. Its introduction *en masse* with the fighter regiments of the VVS's mighty 16th VA ('*Vozdushnaya Armiya*', 'Air Army') stationed in East Germany took place between 1974 and 1976. The huge fleet of MiG-23Ms available in East Germany (and also in groups of Soviet forces stationed on the territory of Czechoslovakia, Poland and Hungary) gave the VVS a temporary qualitative advantage in air superiority in the Central European theatre of war. No fewer than 450 'Floggers' equipped some thirty-three squadrons in 1976, while by 1979 their numbers had increased to at least thirty-nine squadrons with over 500 aircraft (including the two-seaters). Each VVS fighter 'Flogger' regiment had a squadron specialised in the nuclear strike role (by toss and level flight bombing) in addition to its primary air defence/air-superiority tasking.

This slight tactical advantage lasted until the McDonnell Douglas F-15A/B re-equipped the tactical fighter wings of the United States Air Force in Europe in the late 1970s. Nevertheless, the huge numbers of R-23R/T- and R-60-armed MiG-23Ms (which were complemented and gradually replaced by the refined MiG-23ML/MLA in the late 1970s and early 1980s) deployed in Central Europe—the most probable theatre of a future war between superpowers during the Cold War—ensured that the Soviet armed forces possessed sufficiently potent air-superiority and air defence assets.

The MiG-23M offered the VVS a range of combat capabilities that were unthinkable for its MiG-21 predecessor. The 'Flogger' was a high-speed energy fighter that could engage or disengage at will, and it possessed genuine head-on, side-on (on the beam) and tail-on BVR intercept capability. The R-23R semi-active radar homing (SARH) and R-23T infra-red (IR) homing missiles are believed to have revolutionised the VVS FA's air-superiority and defence tactics. The so-called 'silent' (emission-free) tail-on intercepts became possible using the combination of the TP-23 infra-red search-and-track (IRST) sensor and the R-23T AAM. The TP-23M IRST introduced on the MiG-23M had a maximum range (at high altitude, against bomber-sized targets) of up to 30 km (16 nm), and fighter-sized targets were detected by well-tuned sensors at up to 23 km (12.4 nm). Since 1974, the number of the highly-agile R-60 AAMs that could be carried was doubled thanks to the introduction of the APU-60-2 twin-rail launcher units.

At that time both Soviet pilots and those from client states were still trained mainly in the orthodox and inflexible air intercept tactics of the 1960s, which had been mastered to perfection during the MiG-21 era. In the 1970s and early 1980s the VVS and allied air arms continued to operate the MiG-23 in the same way as the MiG-21—as a high-speed point interceptor closely guided and supported by GCI. It took the VVS no less than twelve years to exploit the MiG-23's capabilities as a true air-superiority fighter, after the fleet-wide introduction of the MiG-23MLD.

The initial production MiG-23Ms suffered from numerous teething problems, the most severe of which were the limited manoeuvrability and the vicious handling at high AoA—just like the MiG-23S—as the aircraft was prone to enter an unrecoverable flat spin in such conditions. The difficult and time-consuming process of expanding the G-factor and AoA envelope began in the mid-1970s and required the extensive and often bloody development work of the Mikoyan Design Bureau and NII VVS test pilots and engineers, bidding to improve the flight control system so that adequate spin-safe handling qualities could be provided. In the event, despite the flight control system improvements and airframe strengthening measures, the improved MiG-23ML and MiG-23MLA were still subject to many manoeuvring restrictions in close air combat. They were only partially removed with the introduction of the MiG-23MLD variant, a mature tactical fighter with substantial aerodynamic and flight control system improvements.

## Notoriety in Real-World Air Combat

The lack of undisputed history of combat success by the 'Flogger' such as that enjoyed by its MiG-21 predecessor can be attributed to a combination of many adverse factors. Chief among them was use in the wrong sort of local conflicts—in most cases fighting on the side of the obvious loser—combined with the rather problematic design concept (especially during the beginning of the mass service), which required quite complex handling and maintenance-intensive mission systems that themselves demanded highly-skilled air and ground crews.

The MiG-23 was rarely employed air-to-air by the VVS during the Cold War. The first combat success of a Soviet-operated 'Flogger' was notched on 21 June 1979, when a MiG-23M of the 152th IAP from the IA PVO arm (stationed at Ak-Tepe Airfield and piloted by Capt. V. Shikinder) shot down two Imperial Iranian Air Force CH-47C Chinook helicopters violating Soviet airspace. Capt. Shikinder fired two R-60s to bring down the first helicopter, and then strafed the second one with the aircraft's GSh-23L two-barrel 23-mm gun. Some seventy-two rounds were spent in a firing pass that damaged the helicopter's starboard engine and forced its crew to attempt an emergency landing. It was the first ever successful air combat recorded by a swing-wings fighter in the history of the Soviet Air Forces.

However, the 'Flogger' performed less well in the hands of Third World client-state export operators. This is especially true for the Syrian air force MiG-23MSs/MFs over Lebanon in 1982, as well as for the Cuban and Angolan MiG-23MLs in southern Africa in the late 1980s.

Perhaps unexpectedly, this complex and dedicated air-superiority and air defence VVS FA fighter was often tasked in the ground-attack role. Used as medium and high-altitude 'bomb trucks', the MiG-23MLA/MLDs carried out many combat sorties during the second half of the Soviet invasion of Afghanistan. As many as seven 'Flogger-G/K'-equipped VVS regiments were deployed there for one year each between 1984 and 1989, based at Bagram, Shindand and Kandahar. Their aircraft were often used in the ground-attack and escort roles, as well as for quick reaction alert (QRA). The MiG-23MLD crews reported several clashes with Pakistani F-16s around the Afghanistan-Pakistani border, and during one of those engagements (on 12 September 1988) a Bagram-based MiG-23MLD from the 120th IAP (home-based at Domna, in Eastern Siberia) was badly damaged by two AIM-9 Sidewinders—but it managed to get back to base. Russian sources indicate that on 26 September 1988 a Shindand-based pair of QRA MiG-23MLDs from the same 120th IAP shot down a pair of Iranian helicopters flying in Afghanistan airspace.

As many as ten VVS MiG-23s are known to have been lost in the Afghanistan War—five downed by enemy anti-aircraft fire, and the rest written off due to hardware failures (two) and pilot error (three).

In the early–mid-1980s, the MiG-23's accident rate with the VVS averaged some 12.5 losses per 100,000 flying hours (this is equal to one loss per 8,000 flying hours), according to the VVS's official magazine *Aviatsia i Kosmonavtika* (No. 6, 1990). By that time the fighter 'Flogger' fleet operated by the VVS had built up around 1.5 million flying hours. The flight safety record in some Soviet client nations with smaller fleets was notably worse. For example, in the Hungarian Air Force service, between 1979 and 1996, their fifteen-strong MiG-23MF/UB fleet recorded a fairly high accident rate of no fewer than 24.3 major mishaps per 100,000 flying hours (equalling to one loss per 4,115 flying hours), and the attrition (overall loss) rate was 31 per cent (five aircraft lost from a fleet of fifteen). This was accompanied by a pilot fatality rate of 71 per cent—five of the seven crewmembers who had been involved in these accidents were killed. In the Bulgarian Air Force, which operated a ninety-two-strong MiG-23MF/MLA/MLD/BN/UB fleet between 1976 and 2002, the reported accident rate was eighteen losses per 100,000 flying hours (equalling to one loss per 5,500 hours), while the attrition rate was 16.3 per cent. Poland's forty-two-strong MiG-23MF/UB fleet (thirty-six MFs and six UBs), delivered between 1979 and 1982 and used until 1999, suffered five losses in 44,200 flying hours and an accident rate of 11.3 losses per 100,000 flying hours (equalling to one loss per 8,849 flying hours), while the attrition rate approached 12 per cent.

The East German air force, which operated a seventy-seven–strong 'Flogger fleet (twelve MiG-23MFs, thirty-two MiG-23MLAs, twenty-two MiG-23BNs and eleven MiG-23UBs) reported fourteen losses in 68,700 flying hours, resulting in an accident rate of 20.4 per 100,000 flying hours (equalling to one loss per 4,901 hours) and an attrition rate of 18.2 per cent.

Between 1969 and 1984, 3,630 fighter 'Floggers' rolled off the production line at Lukhovitzy, near Moscow. MiG-23's fighter derivatives saw export to at least twenty-six countries. According to official Conventional Forces in Europe Treaty data, in 1990 the Soviet Air Force had 422 MiG-23s based in the European part of the Soviet Union and Eastern Europe (including a significant number of MiG-23UB/UM conversion and continuation trainers). Additionally, the IA PVO service declared an inventory of 749 'Floggers' based in the European part of the Soviet Union. No less than 400 MiG-23s are believed to have also been on strength with the Frontal Aviation and IA PVO in the Asian part of the Soviet Union.

## MiG-25—Mikoyan's Fast and High-Flying Fighter

In the early 1970s the hectic race for speed in the Soviet Union produced the Mach 2.83 MiG-25 (NATO reporting name 'Foxbat') in its both interceptor and reconnaissance versions. Thanks to its previously unseen speed and service ceiling, combined with a sophisticated weapons system, the Soviet political and military leaders rapidly gained confidence that the air borders of the country (which occupied one sixth of the land on earth at the time) had been sufficiently secured.

The fastest combat aircraft yet identified in squadron service resulted from the hectic race for speed in the early 1960s, and it underwent an expensive and painful development that claimed the lives of four aircraft industry and VVS test pilots between 1967 and 1973—as well as the life of IA PVO CO, Lt Gen. Anatoliy Kadomtsev, who was killed in a flight in 1969.

The Mikoyan OKB (also known then as the OKB-155, OKB MiG and now dubbed 'RSK MiG's Engineering Centre'), the leading tactical aircraft design bureau in the Soviet Union at the time, embarked upon the extremely ambitious task of developing a tactical combat aircraft family capable of sustained flight at Mach 3. It was to be a high-performance yet affordable air system to be built in two principal versions—fighter-interceptor and tactical-reconnaissance aircraft—featuring a fairly high degree of airframe and powerplant commonality.

Initial design work began as early as 1961, and the general layout adopted at the Mikoyan OKB was more or less inspired by that of the North American A-5 Vigilante. Developing an all-new manned aircraft at the time was a rather uneasy undertaking as the 'missile fever' of Soviet Leader Nikita Khrushchev had considerably slowed down the country's aircraft industry, with a significant proportion of its otherwise immense design and production capability having been redirected to the missile-making sector. The new manned-aircraft development projects were drastically reduced. Nevertheless, the mass proliferation of medium-

The first of two Ye-155P prototypes made its maiden flight on 9 September 1963 in the skilled hands of Mikoyan test pilot Pyotr Ostapenko. (*Mikoyan & Gurevich OKB*)

to-high-altitude surface-to air-missile (SAM) systems meant that the PVO air defences arm still needed the support of a purposely built high-altitude/high-speed interceptor. It represented a considerably more versatile air defence weapon, endowed with a tremendous speed/rate-of-climb performance and outfitted with a powerful fire control system. It was needed to counter the soon-to-be-introduced (and expected) USAF high-speed strike and reconnaissance aircraft such as the B-70 Valkyrie strategic bomber. Later, the list of principle high-performance enemy aircraft targets included the CIA's Lockheed A-12 and its successor, the SR-71 Blackbird, operated by the USAF.

The first design work on the new-generation Mach 3 combat aircraft began in accordance with a decree of the Council of Ministers and the Central Committee of the Communist Party of the Soviet Union dated from February 1962, while the final editions of the requirements to the interceptor and reconnaissance versions were completed in June and September 1963 respectively.

The interceptor and reconnaissance derivatives of the new high-speed tactical combat aircraft were developed simultaneously; the former initially had the lead, but the latter (developed under the internal Mikoyan OKB designation Ye-155R) eventually became the first to take to the air for the VVS. The first prototype Ye-155R-1 rolled out of the assembly hall at Mikoyan's experimental plant in Moscow in December 1963, making its maiden flight on 6 March 1964. The interceptor's first prototype, designated as the Ye-155P-1, followed six months later, taking to the air on 9 September that year in the capable hands of Pyotr Ostapenko, another well-known Mikoyan OKB test pilot.

Both 'Foxbat' versions underwent somewhat-protracted, difficult and bloody development and testing programmes, mainly due to the urgency for introducing them into service as soon as possible; this was combined with a previously unseen technical design complexity that called for numerous unproven (and therefore risky) solutions implemented into the aircraft, its powerplant, its mission systems and weapons. At the same time, the MiG-25 possessed rather conventional handling characteristics, described as almost the same as that of the other Mikoyan OKB supersonic fighters of the late 1950s and early 1960s (such as the nimble, Mach 2 MiG-21). However, it featured much more inertia due to its considerably higher weight and much greater size.

The MiG-25 also had an impressive supersonic agility—while flying at Mach 2.5, the 'Foxbat' was well-capable of performing rolls and turning with up to 4-G. In the mid-1970s it became a mature design, cleared to perform aerobatic routines comprising of rolls, loops and half-loops (albeit with very big radiuses).

Between 1960 and 1985 a total of 1,186 aircraft rolled off the line at the Gorky-based GAZ-21 aviation plant (the company is now named Sokol, and the city of Gorky has since been renamed Nizhny Novgorod), though the first four prototypes were manufactured at the Mikoyan OKB's experimental plant in Moscow. Some 900 of these were MiG-25P/PD/PDS interceptors, and no fewer than seventy were MiG-25PU two-seaters for conversion and continuation training of interceptor pilots.

## The MiG-25's Novel Design Concept

The set of design requirements issued to the Mikoyan OKB called for a host of innovations to give the new fighter a previously unattained high-speed/high-altitude performance. At the same time, the fuselage layout design was to be capable of ensuring normal operating conditions for aircraft's systems, mission avionics and weapons.

The Ye-155 project was therefore a great engineering challenge, and its development was handed over to a team of forward-thinking engineers led by two chief designers; the first of them was veteran Mikhail Gurevich, who was responsible for airframe design, while Nikolay Matyuk was tasked to oversee the development and integration of the aircraft's systems and armament.

The Ye-155 was the first Mikoyan OKB fighter with a shoulder-wing airframe layout, combined with a fairly slim basic fuselage blended into two huge rectangular air intake trunks with wedge inlets similar to that used in the North American A-5 Vigilante. This was a marked change to Mikoyan's then-traditional aerodynamic layout of a circular cross-section fuselage, combined with swept or delta wings and featuring a pitot-type nose intake. The Ye-155's variable-area intakes were extremely complex assemblies, being continuously adjusted in flight by a state-of-the-art analogue electronic control unit. This was needed to ensure optimal conditions for the engine throughout the entire flight envelope.

The new aircraft also introduced for the first time a cantilever wing optimised for high speed. It incorporated sweepback on the leading edge varying from 43° 30' at the root to 41° near the wingtips, and there was 5° of anhedral on the serial production aircraft, with long anti-flutter body at each wingtip. The wing consoles were mounted high on the fuselage as this ensured a good combination with the rectangular air intake trunks and (for the sake of convenience) for missiles hanging onto the large-sized pylons. An aileron was placed at the centre of each semi-span, with a plain flap on the inboard 37 per cent of the trailing edge; no other movable surfaces were added to the wings.

Due to the short body, twin fins (canted outward and provided with inset rudders) were introduced in order to achieve sufficient directional stability. This design was preferred to the single large and tall fin. The fins were inclined outwards, as were the large ventral fins.

Designing the main undercarriage units proved to be another difficult exercise. In order to achieve an acceptable track and a compact design, the forward retracting units stowed vertically between the air intake duct and outer skin of each trunk.

Shortening of the landing roll was provided through the use of twin brake-chutes housed in a fairing above and between the nozzles.

There were fittings provided on the upper corners of the intakes of the prototype aircraft in order to allow fitting of canards on the prototypes. These were intended for improving high-speed controllability; however, in the event the canards were never flight-tested because it was discovered during the initial flight tests that the upper walls of the huge rectangular intakes could do the same job.

An affordable stainless nickel-steel alloy was selected as the main airframe structure material, accounting for 80 per cent (by weight), while titanium represented only 8 per cent (used in areas subject to extreme heating, as the maximum temperature reached 303°C) and approximately 11 per cent was of 'conventional' aluminium alloys. The tempered-steel load-bearing airframe structure was all-welded and formed a torsion box, divided by sealed and stringer-reinforced compartments, with some 70 per cent of the internal fuselage volume containing 14,570 litres (3,205 Imp. gal.) of special heat-resistant T-6 kerosene. No less than 76.5 per cent of the airframe assembly work was performed through different welding methods, while the conventional riveted joints accounted for 23.5 per cent.

In an effort to provide a normal environment for the operation of the aircraft's systems in high-speed flight—when a tremendous amount of heat was generated— the Ye-155 introduced an extremely powerful cooling system of advanced design in addition to powerful internal compartment insulation. The cooling system used bleed air taken from the compressor at a temperature of 700°C, which then passed through several cooling loops and was eventually supplied to the avionics compartment at a temperature of -20°C. This enabled the system to maintain a temperature of between 50 and 70°C in a bid to ensure an optimal working environment for the pilot and the avionics boxes. The cockpit was also provided with a thermal protection for the pilot by using cooled air supplied through a number of ducts (the so-called 'air showers' blowing between the pilot and the canopy), although the canopy heated up so much in high-speed flight that it was impossible to be touched with a naked hand.

Among the most valuable features associated with the high-speed nature of the 'Foxbat' was the considerable amount of alcohol used in the air conditioning and generator cooling systems. This amounted to a total of 240 litres of water-alcohol mixture (50/50), while an additional 95 litres of pure alcohol was provided as a cooling agent in the avionics and radar cooling system. This alcohol was completely fine to consume, and it was much-beloved by MiG-25 pilots and technicians, who used to drink it habitually. It became especially valuable in the late 1980s, when the Soviet leader Mikhail Gorbachev imposed an anti-alcoholic campaign and sales of alcoholic drinks in the Soviet Union were severely limited.

# High-Performance Engine

Selecting the powerplant presented another serious challenge for the design team. To save time and avoid having to develop a new engine from scratch, an existing turbojet design was eventually selected—the Tumanskiy 15K. It was a single-spool, high mass-flow design engine that was originally used to power the Tupolev DR-2 Yasterb reconnaissance drone. The fuel-thirsty 15K featured a compressor assembly with a fairly low compression ratio—close in its gas-dynamics performance to that of the ramjet—which was optimised to produce maximum efficiency at high altitude and higxh speed. Consequently, it had a notably increased fuel consumption in low-speed/low-level flight. The engine variant developed for the MiG-25 was designated the R-15B-300. Rated at 100.1 kN (22,509 lb st. or 10,204 kgf) with afterburner and 73.5 kN (16,505 lb st. or 7,493 kgf) dry (or at so-called 'military power'), it featured an all-new heat-resistant five-stage compressor, a modified combustion chamber (to cope with the high-altitude operating conditions) and a three-position variable-area nozzle. Turbine entry temperature was increased by 50°C and an all-new and fairly sophisticated electronic control system was introduced in an effort to meet the stringent requirements of keeping the engine in reliable operation within all conceivable flight conditions.

The R-15B-300's fuel consumption varied from 150 to 15,000 kg (333.4 to 33,340 lb) per hour, and the engine's shaft rpm control accuracy had to be kept within 0.2 per cent. In addition, the engine control system was integrated with the extremely complex intake cross-section control used to vary the area in accordance with the current flight conditions. However, the engine had a relatively long response time, accelerating from idle flight to military power in fourteen seconds. The engine had what was called 'the second afterburner stage', which activated automatically after passing Mach 1.5, providing an additional amount of thrust. This enabled a further acceleration to the maximum permitted speed of Mach 2.83, although the aircraft was well capable of exceeding Mach 3. In training flights, however, the MiG-25 was restricted to Mach 2.65 due to flight safety considerations.

In service, the R-15B-300 gained fame as a very reliable engine, able to sustain fairly serious FOD damages due to the ingestion of large birds. In high-speed flight, certain parts in the R-15B-300 heated up to 1,000°C, and this was considered to be a routine workload, the engine enduring it with ease.

The MiG-25 routinely performed take-offs at military power when carrying a 50 per cent internal fuel load, and seasoned MiG-25 pilots also recall that the aircraft was also able to take-off at military power with full internal fuel tanks; however, in this case lift-off could occur almost at the end of the runway. The runways were therefore required to be at least 2,500 m (8,200 feet) long, and ambient air temperatures were required to be moderate. In addition, the MiG-25 boasted the capability of safely continuing the take-off run in conditions where one engine was inoperative.

## The Interceptor Version Takes Shape

The first two prototypes of the interceptor version (designated Ye-155P-1 and Ye-155P-2) lacked radars and mission avionics, and were used mainly for aircraft and systems performance tests and development work. The first prototype had only two underwing pylons (outboard), each carrying a dummy K-40 missile.

An initial batch of nine development aircraft was built at the GAZ-21 in Gorky for testing the air intercept system. The first two of these were introduced in 1966, five more followed suit in 1967 and the remaining two were delivered in 1968.

The Ye-155P-5 prototype introduced the distinctive triangular endplate fins on the wingtips for improving directional stability, but these were not adopted on the production aircraft. The sixth prototype, designated as the Ye-155P-6, featuring increased-area fins (which allowed for removal of the endplate fins) and differential tailplanes, was designated as the production standard. In 1968, a preliminary conclusion on the commencement of the type's serial production was issued by the NII VVS.

On 30 October 1967 Ye-155P-1 crashed during an attempt for setting a time-to-altitude record; VVS test pilot Igor Lesnikov was killed due to an aileron reversal phenomenon that occurred after exceeding the indicated air speed limits. It is noteworthy that the flexible wing also used to twist considerably while manoeuvring with the maximum permitted 4.5-G, as the wingtips flexed some 0.7 m (2 feet 9 in) from its normal position; in fact, it was this twisting that caused the aileron reversal. After the crash, tailerons (a tailplane that is used for both pitch and roll control; for the latter task, the tailerons move differentially) were introduced. This design measure allowed the indicated air speed limit to be increased from 1,000 km/h (540 kt) to 1,200 km/h (647 kt); at a later stage the limitation was further relaxed to 1,300 km/h (701 kt). Design deficiencies of the tailplane, however, proved to be the cause for three more subsequent crashes that claimed the lives of a trio of distinguished test pilots (Maisterenko, Kuznetsov and Gudkov).

Another fatal crash during the test programme happened on 26 April 1969, when Ye-155P-11 was lost due to engine fire. The pilot, IA PVO CO Lt Gen. Anatoliy Kadomtsev, was killed during his first flight on the new fighter-interceptor at the NII VVS airfield at Akhtubinsk because his aircraft became uncontrollable a few minutes after take-off, eventually crashing to the ground. An uncontained turbine blade failure in one of the R-15B-300 engines was quoted as the cause for the crash. As a consequence, turbine blade design had to be improved, and an additional safety measure was adopted in the form of a temporary reduction of the turbine entry temperature.

The initial production at the GAZ-21 *Sergo Ordzhonikidze* factory in Gorky commenced in 1969, and a seven-aircraft pre-series production batch was offered for operational evaluation. The serial production of the new interceptor under the in-service designation MiG-25P commenced in 1971. Initially, the aircraft had only fifty hours of service life, which was gradually increased to 800, 900 and finally 1,000 hours, while the engines saw their service life being gradually increased from twenty-five to 750 hours.

The new fighter-interceptor was publicly demonstrated for the first time during the famous Domodedovo Airfield flypast on 9 July 1967. A formation took part in the air display, consisting of the third prototype of the reconnaissance version and three interceptors from the initial production batch. It is noteworthy that Western analysts observing the Soviet air power guessed that the new twin-finned Mikoyan single-seat fighter seen at Domodedovo was designated MiG-23. They also supposed that the new aircraft—officially presented at the display as a high-altitude Mach 3-capable high-altitude all-weather interceptor—may have had a multi-purpose capability.

The MiG-25P ('Foxbat-A') fighter interceptor was an integral component of the S-155 air-intercept system, and its testing and evaluation proved rather problematic due to the complexity of the aircraft and its armament, requiring a prolonged test and evaluation effort. Although the state testing effort (involving the initial development aircraft and the first three production machines) was completed in 1970, the MiG-25 did not enter IA PVO service until 17 June 1972. Designated MiG-25-40, it was a fully-fledged air intercept system comprising the MiG-25P aircraft itself equipped with the Smerch-A radar and Polyot navigation suite, and armed with the R-40 (AA-6 'Acrid') air-to-air missile. The Lasour-M

An early-production MiG-25P, with pylons for four R-40 missiles. (*Mikoyan & Gurevich OKB*)

on-board datalink system was used for remote-controlled intercept, working in conjunction with the highly-automated Vozdukh-1 ground control intercept (GCI) system. The first IA PVO fighter regiment to be reequipped with the MiG-25P was the 786th IAP, based in Pravdinsk, near Gorky, used for conducting the field testing of the 'Foxbat-A', while the 148th TsBiPLS at Savastleika was used for training an initial instructor cadre for the type, and also for developing new combat employment tactics.

## Records Set Between 1965 and 1973

In April 1965, the Soviet Union claimed that a twin-engined aircraft designated Ye-266 had set a new 1,000-km (540-nm) closed-circuit speed record of 2,320 km/h (1,251 kt), carrying a 2,000-kg (4,416-lb) payload. The attempt was made by Alexander Fedotov on 16 March, at a height of 21,000–22,000 m (69,000–72,200 feet).

This was the first news of the existence of the 'Foxbat' in the West, and also the first of the series of FAI-recognised records set using the Ye-155R-1, Ye-155R-3 and Ye-155P-1; some records were absolute and others in C1(III) class—jet-powered landplanes with an unlimited maximum take-off weight. In an effort to conceal the real designation of the record-breaking aircraft, the Ye-266 designation was used.

On 5 October 1967 Mikoyan test pilot Mikhail Komarov set an absolute 500 km (270 nm) closed-circuit speed record of 2,891.5 km/h (1,852.67 kt). On the same day, Fedotov set absolute records with 1,000 and 2,000-kg (2,200 and 4,400-lb) payloads at 27,977 m (98,350 feet). On 27 October 1967 another Mikoyan test pilot, Pyotr Ostapenko, set a new 1,000-km (540-nm) closed-circuit record with a speed of 2,920 km/h (1,575 kt).

Record-breaking activities at the Mikoyan OKB continued in 1973, as on 8 April Alexander Fedotov set a speed record of 2,605.1 km/h over a 100-km (54-nm) closed circuit. On 4 June yet another company test pilot, Boris Orlov, set a time-to-20,000 m (65,600 feet) record of 2 minutes and 49.8 seconds. On the same day, Ostapenko set new records of time-to-25,000 and 30,000 m (82,000 and 98,400 feet) of 3 minutes and 12.6 seconds and 4 minutes and 3.86 seconds respectively. On 25 July that year, Fedotov continued the successful record-breaking attempts by reaching new altitude records with 2,000-kg (4,416-lb) and 4,000-kg (8,832-lb) payloads, reaching 35,230 m (115,585 feet), as well as an absolute record (without payload) of 36,240 m (118,900 feet).

## MiG-25P's Smerch-A Radar

At this time the MiG-25P was a high-performance weapons system centred around the extremely powerful Smerch-A fire control pulse radar, developed by the Moscow-based NII-339 (now NIIR Phazotron company), and superseded by the improved and more reliable Smerch-A2 on subsequent production aircraft. A further-improved derivative designated Smerch-A3 was tested for the first time in 1975; it introduced a look-down/shoot-down (LD/SD) capability by utilising the envelope detection technique, but demonstrated a somewhat unimpressive LD/SD performance, and as a consequence it was rejected to be fielded into service.

Utilising an old-fashioned vacuum tube technology, the Smerch radar family had a large-sized parabolic-mirror antenna and boasted a fairly high output power in order to achieve a useful degree of resistance to jamming (the so-called 'burn through performance') rather than extended range. The radar's maximum detection range was reported as 100 km (54 nm), while the acquisition range was 50 km (27 nm) against a bomber-sized target in a forward hemisphere engagement (head-on attack). Due to its pulse detection method, the Smerch proved ill-suited to intercept targets flying below 500 m (1,640 feet) due to severe ground clutter problems. Its angular coverage was 60° each side and 6° up and down. There was an additional degree of ECM resistance that was provided to the radar through the introduction of a second target detection channel, which worked in the 2-cm wavelength.

For operations in the IA PVO's highly-integrated air defence network environment, the MiG-25P (just like all the other PVO interceptors of the mid–late 1960s) featured the Lasour-M automated datalink guidance equipment. This enabled the interceptor to be vectored automatically or semi-automatically onto its target, following an optimum flightpath over long ranges, and with no voice communications between the pilot and the GCI officer who manned the Vozdukh-1 GCI station.

Initially, the Ye-155P prototypes were armed with two R-40 missiles, but the production examples carried four, in two variants. The R-40R was the SARH variant and the R-40T was the infrared (IR) homing variant. The R-40R/T was a heavyweight air intercept missile (with a launch weight of 500 kg (1,115 lb)) purposely designed for use against high-flying non-manoeuvring bombers and reconnaissance aircraft. The target had a manoeuvring limitation of 2.5-G only, while the carrier aircraft itself was stressed to 4.5-G, and its angle of attack limit during missile launch was 14°.

## The 'Crash Development' of the MiG-25PD

The much-improved MiG-25PD (NATO 'reporting name Foxbat-E') with an all-new mission avionics suite was developed in a 'crash development' upgrade programme that followed the well-publicised defection of IA PVO pilot 1st Lt Viktor Belenko. He flew a MiG-25P from Tchuguevka (Sokolovka) Airfield, 200 km (108 nm) from Vladivostok in Russia's Far East (where the 531st IAP was home-based), to Hakodate, Japan, on 6 September 1976. The defector pilot provided the US and Japanese intelligence with a detailed information about the

Soviet Union's most up-to-date fighter interceptor. Belenko revealed that by the time of his defection, the IA PVO had a fleet of around 400 MiG-25Ps, and that the aircraft he had brought to Japan had been produced three years earlier.

The hijacked 'Foxbat-A' underwent a thorough examination by USAF Foreign Technology Division experts before it was returned to the Soviet Union on 12 November that year. Upon its dismantling by USAF experts, they made numerous interesting findings, including the omnipresent use of vacuum tubes instead of transistor circuitry in the aircraft's avionics. The airframe was made mainly of steel alloy, and welding was done by hand; rivet heads were well-exposed in areas not critical for creation of aerodynamic drag; the pilot had a very restricted forward visibility; the huge engines made the aircraft almost a rocket; the search and track radar set was jam-proof, though ill-suited to seeing targets below 500 m (1,640 feet) due to ground clutter; and the radar itself was so powerful (600 kW) that it could burn through electronic jamming created by the attacked bombers. The number of cockpit instruments was described as representing 50 per cent of those of the F-4EJ Phantom operated by JASDF, with the 'Foxbat' having a smaller and considerably less versatile sight. In addition, the examination revealed that the 'Foxbat-A' was a pure interceptor designed to climb at tremendous speeds, approach the selected target, fire its missiles in a single pass and then land. Of particular interest to the US specialists who examined the 'Foxbat' were the aircraft's autopilot and communications from an on-board computer to ground controllers, which were quoted as being superb.

As a consequence of Belenko's defection, the original MiG-25P design was totally compromised, particularly in regard to its sensitive fire control and IFF systems. In an effort to remedy the damage as soon as possible, a government resolution on 4 November 1976 ordered the Mikoyan OKB to launch a crash development programme. The new variant resulting from this effort was equipped with the all-new Sapfir-25 (N005) radar, developed by the NII-339 and based on the one used on the MiG-23ML/P. It was a powerful pulse radar with a twist-Cassegrain antenna, endowed with a useful LD/SD capability. This capability was achieved thanks to the use of the envelope detection technique, which was effective only for detecting air targets over flat terrain. The new radar had a bomber-sized detection range in head-on, high-altitude engagements of 110 km (60 nm), though well-tuned radars were capable of detecting high-altitude targets at up to 120 km (65 nm). Fighter-sized targets were detected at up to 70 km (37 nm) at high altitude. In LD/SD mode, the Sapfir-25 had a maximum detection range of around 25 km (13.5 nm) in tail-on engagements. The maximum target speed in head-on intercepts was 3,700 km/h (1,195 kt), while the minimum closure speed in tail-on engagements was 200 km/h (108 kt).

The radar featured an angular coverage of 60° each side, and 6° up and down, while the centre line of the sector could be manually steered (through antenna tilting) at 56° left and right, and up/down, in order to expand the searched volume.

The new BAN-75 on-board datalink hardware was installed, operating in conjunction with the Lutch-1 ground-based guidance station of the GCI centre.

The aircraft of defector Lt Viktor Belenko seen after landing at Hakodate on 6 September 1976. The hijacked MiG-25P underwent a thorough examination by USAF Foreign Technology Division experts before its return to the Soviet Union on 12 November that year. (*Author's collection*)

A drawing depicting a fold-out of the MiG-25PD cockpit, intended to be used for familiarisation purposes. (*Author's collection*)

The sensor suite of the MiG-25PD was enhanced via the integration of the Type 26Sh-1 infrared search-and-track sensor (IRST), also 'borrowed' from the MiG-23P/ML and housed in a small fairing under the nose. It was a passive sensor which proved useful mainly for high-altitude emission-free intercepts. The 26Sh-1 IRST had a maximum 'brochure' detection range at medium altitude against receding fighter-sized targets with afterburner on of 25 km (13 nm), extending to over 50 km (27 nm) at high altitude, and it was capable of cueing R-40T and R-40TD missile seekers towards the tracked target. In this mode, the radar was only required to provide range information through emitting single pulses, with a repetition frequency of one pulse per 3.5 seconds.

The MiG-25PD also introduced considerably improved weapons—the R-40RD and R-40TD BVR missiles, featuring extended range, better control system, seekers and fuses over the baseline R-40. The new version of the 'Acrid' was claimed able to be used against targets manoeuvring with up to 4-G. At low to medium level, the R-40RD had a range of some 20 km (11 nm) against fighter-sized targets when fired side-on, while in tail chase engagements the range was reduced to 3–4 km (1.6–2.15 nm). In addition to the 'mammoth' missiles, the lightweight and compact R-60 (AA-8 'Aphid') short-range IR-guided missile was integrated (later superseded by the improved R-60M), carried on twin launchers under the outer pylons instead of the R-40TD. The R-60 was useful mostly when fired at fighter-sized targets.

The MiG-25PD was adapted to carry the 5,300 litre (1,165 Imp. gal.) underfuselage drop tank 'borrowed' from the reconnaissance 'Foxbat', and this brought its maximum take-off weight (MTOW) to 36,720 kg (81,885 lb). In the event, as experienced 'Foxbat-E' pilots shared, the external tank was never used in squadron service because it imposed some prohibitive speed penalties. The supersonic range with four R-40 AAMs without the drop tank, at a cruise speed of Mach 2.35, was 1,250 km (675 nm), while the subsonic range extended to 2,400 km (1,300 nm) with the drop tank and 1,730 km (935 nm) without.

The MiG-25PD also received the improved R-15BD-300 engines with an increased service life of up to 1,000 hours. This new R-15 derivative had its afterburning thrust boosted up to 109.8 kN (24,690 lb st. or 11,193 kgf), and its last production series were further improved to develop 110.2 kN (24,780 lb st. or 11,235 kgf). With the new engines, the upgraded interceptor was able to climb out to 19,000 m (62,320 feet) in 6.6 minutes, and its practical ceiling reached 20,200 m (66,250 feet).

The MiG-25PD was easily distinguishable from its predecessor thanks to the lengthened nose housing the new radar's antenna and black boxes. The first MiG-25PD took to the air in September 1977, and this new interceptor derivative entered mass production at the Gorky-based GAZ-21 plant the following year; in excess of 150 aircraft were built there between 1978 and 1982.

The MiG-25-40D air intercept system was formally commissioned into VPVO service in 1980. Between 1979 and 1982, all the existing PVO MiG-25Ps (accounting to around 400 or so examples) were upgraded to this standard, though without the drop tank carriage capability, receiving the new designation MiG-25PDS ('S' for *Stroevoy*, i.e. aircraft upgraded in the field).

The improved MiG-25PD was commissioned into service with the Soviet Air Defence Forces in 1980. All existing IA PVO MiG-25Ps—accounting to around 400 or so examples—were then upgraded to this standard between 1979 and 1982. (*Mikoyan & Gurevich OKB*)

The MiG-25PD and PDS boasted an all-new Sapfir-25 (N005) radar (based on the one used on the MiG-23ML/P) in an effort to provide a useful LD/SD capability. (*Mikoyan & Gurevich OKB*)

## MiG-25PD Specification

| | |
|---|---|
| Dimensions:<br>Wing span<br>Length without probe<br>Height | 14.015 m<br>19.75 m<br>6.10 m |
| Wing area: | 61.40 m$^2$ |
| Weights:<br>Empty operating<br>Normal take-off with four AAMs<br>Maximum take-off | 20,600 kg<br>36,650 kg<br>41,000 kg |
| Performance:<br>Max level speed at sea level<br>Max level speed at high level<br>Max operating Mach number<br>Cruise speed<br>Take-off speed<br>Landing speed<br>Practical ceiling, clean<br>Time to 20,000 m<br>G limits<br>Rate of climb at low level<br>Take-off distance<br>Landing distance<br>Supersonic range<br>Subsonic range | 1,200 km/h<br>3,000 km/h<br>2.83<br>990 km/h<br>360 km/h<br>290 km/h<br>23,000 m<br>8.9 min<br>+4.5<br>130 m/s<br>1,250 m<br>800 m<br>1,250 km<br>1,370 km |

## Enhanced Derivatives

There were several MiG-25PDS derivatives with additional equipment, but these were only used for trials and never entered mass production. The first of these was the MiG-25PDSG, a derivative equipped with the Geran active jammer and KDS-155 flare dispensers as well as an improved Beryoza-LE radar-warning receiver (RWR). It successfully completed its trials programme in 1983, but it was eventually shelved due to a limited industrial capability to produce jamming systems.

The MiG-25PDSL was another derivative with an improved self-defence suite, comprising the Beryoza-LM RWR and pod-mounted Gardeniya-1FU jammer as well as KDS-155 flare dispensers. It saw completion of its testing effort in 1985, but, just like the MiG-25PDSG, it was never launched in production.

The MiG-25PDZ was an interceptor derivative that had an increased range thanks to the addition of in-flight refuelling equipment. Developed from 1985 to 1986, the aircraft featured a stretched nose (thanks to a newly-added plug) with an inverted, L-shaped refuelling probe in front of the windshield, offset to starboard, as well as an additional micro-control system for easier contact with the tanker.

The mid-air refuelling-capable MiG-25PDZ was successfully tested, and the equipment was recommended for mass production to retrofit the already-manufactured MiG-25PD/PDSs. However, this never happened—apparently due to a shortage of Il-78 tankers provided by the VVS in a bid to support PVO fighter operations.

In 1973 another interceptor version was tested, powered by the increased-thrust and more fuel-efficient R-15BF2-300 engines, rated at 132.5 kN (29,795 lb st. or 13,507 kgf) with afterburner and featuring an extra compressor stage. The new variant utilised a MiG-25P production-standard airframe (though it was fitted with improved avionics), and in this new guise it made its maiden flight on 30 August 1973; the aircraft actually took to the air for the first time with the old engines on 12 June 1973. The increased-speed interceptor dubbed 'MiG-25M' was designed for sustained Mach 3-3.2 operations, mainly to counter the SR-71 operations. In 1975 it received a preliminary recommendation for introduction into serial production, but the introduction never happened due to the appearance of the Soloviyov D-30F6-engined two-seat derivative, known as the Ye-155MP (MiG-25MP), which was launched in production in the early 1980s under the MiG-31 in-service designation. A MiG-25RB was also used for testing the R-15BF2-300 engines.

The MiG-25M with removed avionics was used to set a number of performance records, and it was presented to the FAI under the Ye-266M designation. On 17 May 1975, flown by Fedotov and Ostapenko, it was used to set records for time to 25,000 m (82,020 feet), 30,000 m (98,425 feet) and 35,000 m (114,830 feet)—2 minutes and 32.2 seconds, 2 minutes and 9.85 seconds and 4 minutes and 11.7 seconds respectively. On 22 July 1975 Alexander Fedotov set another altitude record, climbing up to 37,080 m (121,653 feet) with a 2,000-kg (4,416-lb) payload, while on 31 August the same pilot set an absolute and still-unbeaten world altitude record (for aircraft powered by air-breathing propulsion) of 37,650 m (123,524 feet).

In 1975 a MiG-25P powered by the D-30F-6 afterburning turbofan was tested for the first time, and a second example joined the tests soon afterwards. Rated at 93.1 kN (20,930 lb st. or 9,490 kgf) at military power and 151.9 kN (34,170 lb st. or 15,484 kgf) with afterburners, the D-30F-6 enabled the fighter's MTOW to reach 37,750 kg (83,352 lb) with 16,270 kg (36,917 lb) of internal fuel; when carrying an external fuel tank, the MTOW increased to 42,250 kg (93,288 lb). Thanks to the more fuel-efficient engines combined with the increased internal fuel, range at supersonic speed increased to 2,135 km (1,151 nm), while at subsonic speed it reached 3,310 km (1,785 nm) and the practical ceiling increased to 21,900 m (71,832 feet). By the time of testing the D-30F-6-engined MiG-25P, however, the decision was made that it was not going to be used to power a production version of the basic fighter; this was because it was intended for use on the much-improved Ye-155MP. This was an increased-weight interceptor with seats for a pilot and a dedicated weapons operator, equipped with the new Zaslon phased array radar set (originally developed at the NII-339 under the Smerch-100 designation) and armed with the R-33 long-range SARH missiles. The first Ye-155MP prototype made its maiden flight on 16 September 1975, and the new interceptor formally entered PVO service in May 1981.

There were three enhanced-performance interceptor versions of the 'Foxbat' that remained only as designs. The first of them, dubbed 'Ye-155PA', was developed in the late 1960s and was intended to be equipped with the powerful Smerch-100 radar set and the new R-100 long-range air-to-air missiles. This combination was aimed at enabling attacks against air targets flying between 100 and 30,000 m (328 and 98,425 feet) at maximum speeds of 3,500-4,000 km/h (1,888–2,157 kt). This derivative, powered by the increased-trust R-15BV-100 engines, was to be capable of flying at a maximum speed of Mach 3.5.

Another improved derivative was to be equipped with the new Vikhr radar, with a maximum detection range of between 120 and 150 km (65 and 81 nm). There was also a MiG-25PD derivative dubbed 'MiG-25PDM', which was intended to receive the R-27 (AA-10 'Alamo') BVR missile that had been purposely developed for the MiG-29 and Su-27 in the early–mid-1970s. In the event, the new missile proved to be not thermal-resistant enough, and thus would impose severe speed restrictions due to excessive heating. As a consequence, the project was shelved.

## Fighter 'Foxbats' for Export

Following 1st Lt Viktor Belenko's defection to Japan in 1976, the baseline MiG-25P equipped with the Smerch-A radar suddenly became eligible for export; before long it was offered to four friendly Arabic nations—Algeria, Iraq, Syria and Libya. By that time, all of them had introduced the swing-wing MiG-23MS 'Flogger-E', advertised as a high-performance interceptor but in fact fully stripped of any BVR intercept capability. That is why the introduction of the MiG-25P, with its impressive BVR sensors and weapons (by the standards of the late 1970s), proved to be a whole new world for these nations. The export MiG-25P was equipped with the baseline Smerch-A radar set, while the improved Smerch-A2 was used on the export derivative dubbed 'MiG-25PD' (export), enabling the use of the R-40TD and R-40RD missiles as well as the R-60 (together with a downgraded IRST derivative).

A number of export MiG-25Ps were later upgraded to the export PDS standard, which, in addition to Smerch-A2, comprised a downgraded Type-26Sh IRST and the capability of firing the improved R-40RD/TD missiles as well as the R-60. At least a proportion of these export 'Foxbats' were outfitted with downgraded-standard datalink hardware for remote-controlled intercepts. The first export deliveries were made in 1979–1980, while the last fighter 'Foxbats' sold out to export customers rolled off the production line in Gorky in 1984–1985.

The early export derivatives of the 'Foxbat' used the baseline MiG-25P equipped with the Smerch-A radar, and the type was sold in the late 1970s to four friendly Arabic nations—Algeria, Iraq, Syria and Libya (one of its aircraft seen here). (*US DoD*)

## The End of the MiG-25's PVO Service

By 1991 the PVO fighter aviation had a fleet of no less than 500 MiG-25PD/PDS/PUs, operated by no less than fifteen front-line regiments (up to seventeen, according to some sources) and one combat training/aircrew conversion centre. After the Soviet Union broke up, no less than 400 examples remained in Russia, thirteen in Byelorussia and seventy-nine in Ukraine. A small number of interceptors were also retained in Azerbaijan; these were the aircraft captured at Nasosnaya Airfield, near Baku, where the 50th IAP was based until 1992. A few examples flew until the mid-1990s. At least one MiG-25PD, also from the Nasosnaya-based 50th IAP, was hijacked to Armenia by a Russian pilot. Some twelve to fourteen aircraft remained in Semipalatinsk, Kazakhstan, and there were twenty-five more MiG-25PD/PUs kept in storage at Ak-Tepe in Turkmenistan.

The break-up of the Soviet Union saw the MiG-25PD being used in one of the flashpoints that appeared on the fringes of the former Soviet Empire. The 'Foxbat-E' was used in the armed conflict between Azerbaijan and Armenia as the former inherited a number of MiG-25PD interceptors from the VPVO regiment stationed at Nasosnaya, near the Azeri capital Baku. In fact, only one 'Foxbat-E' from this regiment was used in the ground-attack role, flown by Capt. Yury

Belichenko, a mercenary pilot of Ukrainian nationality, formerly serving with the 50th IAP (who had been hired by the Azeri military command). Capt. Belichenko flew a number of bombing sorties against Stepanakert, the capital city of the Armenian enclave of Nagorni Karabakh; for this new and rather unusual role, the pure interceptor was hastily modified with adaptor racks for two FAB-500 500-kg (1,100-lb) bombs under the wings. The bombs were suspended on the pylons originally intended for the R-40 missiles, and the MiG-25PD is said to have dropped its warload by utilising the makeshift method of navigation bombing. This is said to have been done using azimuth and range to the target, derived from the RSBN-6 tactical aid to navigation. The makeshift bomber maintained a level flight above 10,000 m (33,000 feet) in order to remain outside the reach of the Armenian Kub (SA-6) SAM systems. This improvised bombing effort undoubtedly proved very inaccurate, but it was used well for the purpose of terrorising the local Armenian population rather than destroying any targets of military significance. In the event, the MiG-25PD 'makeshift bomber' was reported as being downed by

A MiG-25PD seen while undergoing flight line maintenance at a typical IA PVO airfield. (*Author's collection – Aviatsia i Kosmonavtika*)

the Armenian air defences on 20 August 1992; the pilot who flew his last bombing sortie managed to bail out, and he was captured on the ground. Initially sentenced to death, he was later released and handed back to Ukraine.

## Fighter 'Foxbats' in the Sky of Lebanon

Syrian MiG-25Ps also saw some use in anger against Israeli fighters during the clashes over Lebanon. According to prominent Soviet air combat analyst Col. Vladimir Babich, then serving as a military advisor in Syria, the first of these clashes happened on 13 February 1981, when a lone MiG-25P was scrambled to intercept an Israeli RF-4C (other sources note it was a pair of RF-4Cs), maintaining a northern heading over Lebanon at 12,000 m (39,370 feet) and 1,000 km/h (540 kt). The MiG-25P directed by the GCI officer rushed into a head-on intercept, accelerating in level flight at an altitude of 8,000 m (26,240 feet) and then climbing to 12,000 m (39,370 feet). At a distance of 100 km (54 nm), however, the target (apparently used as a decoy) promptly executed an 180° turn and pumped chaff, which jammed both the interceptor's radar and the ground radar screens. The MiG-25P continued the pursuit but suddenly fell under attack from an Israeli F-15A, which waited, sitting in ambush, behind mountains; its approach was initially masked in the jamming that had been created by the ejected chaff. In the event, the Eagle 'popped up' from low level and rushed for a head-on intercept, promptly approaching a missile launch distance of 25 km (13 nm); it managed to shoot down the 'Foxbat' using an AIM-7F missile. The Syrian pilot was not able to detect the attacker with his own radar due to the limited coverage in elevation provided by the Smerch radar set; he was also not able to respond to the command to abort the attack, which had been issued by the GCI officer perhaps due to communication channels jamming. As Col. Babich claimed, this combat represented the first successful head-on engagement between fighters armed with BVR missiles in aviation history.

On 29 July 1981 another clash between heavy fighters armed with BVR missiles took place in the Lebanese sky; here, a pair of MiG-25Ps tried to mount a coordinated intercept against a pair of F-15As. The Syrians, as Col. Babich maintained, also sent a pair of MiG-21s to be used as decoys, while the MiG-25Ps were sitting in ambush in an area not visible to the Israeli radars. As a consequence, the F-15, which was directed to attack the MiG-21s, fell under attack from one of the two hidden MiG-25s, which attempted a head-on intercept, whereas the other MiG-25 was directed in order to carry out a side-on attack against the same target. However, the F-15 suddenly entered into a dive and swept away from the 'Foxbat' while the latter was attempting to enter in a head-on attack. The Syrian pilot reported to GCI that he had target detection at 80 km (43 nm), and acquisition followed suit at 40 km (21.6 nm); however, the radar lock was then broken due to the target's steep descent. Shortly afterwards, the Syrian pilot experienced a hit on its aircraft and successfully bailed out.

The Syrian Air Force, as Col. Babich said, also claimed that the surviving MiG-25P eventually managed to launch two R-40 missiles—the first one at a distance of 18 km (10 nm), and the second one following at 11 km (6 nm). The Syrians claimed that one of these missiles blasted out one of the F-15s, with debris falling into the sea. However, Israel still denies that they suffered any F-15 losses in air combat.

After these encounters, the Syrian air commanders decided to withdraw their surviving 'Foxbats' from the combat zone and use them for air defence of home territory. The formal reason for the MiG-25P's hastily withdrawal from the front line was that there were not enough high-altitude targets over Lebanon that would justify the employment of the heavy interceptor.

## Air-to-Air Missiles of the Fighter 'Foxbats'

The R-40R/T (NATO reporting name 'Acrid') was the MiG-25P's basic weapon. Developed under the initial designation K-40 by the OKB-4 design bureau headed by Matus Bisnovat, it had a two type of seekers—semi-active radar homing (SARH) and infrared (IR). The SARH seeker was developed by the NII-648 and was intended for use in conjunction with the Smerch-A powerful pulse radar set, which was originally developed for the Tupolev Tu-128-80 heavyweight interceptor.

The K-40 was an all-new design with a titanium body and canard aero dynamical layout, utilising large-area wings in order to ensure sufficient flying characteristics in a high-altitude flight. The rocket motor had two nozzles on the missile's sides and the two warheads were located in front of the motor and in the missile's tail section; their total weight was 36 kg (84 lb). The warheads featured directional destruction capability and were detonated upon the ignition of a combined radar/optical proximity fuse.

For the first time (not only in the Soviet Union, but in the world), the PARGS-12 SARH seeker introduced a monopulse radar information processing capability, and it had a newly added range-finding channel. This endowed the missile with a useful degree of ECM resistance (particularly against amplitude-modulated jamming). The monopulse signal receipt and processing method was claimed to be much more advanced than that of traditionally used (at the time) conical scanning. The PRGS-12 featured a twist-Cassegrain antenna with a large angle of steering—up to 70° in both azimuth and elevation.

The K-40's first ballistic launches were carried out in 1966. Initially, it was intended that the S-155 air intercept system was to be armed with two K-40s, but after testing the third prototype (Ye-155P-3), it was demonstrated that the aircraft had a relatively unchanged speed performance when carrying four missiles. During the tests, the Ye-155P-3 pre-production fighter with four missiles on board was reported to have reached a maximum speed of 2,900 km/h (1,567 kt) in level flight.

In August 1968 the second stage of the K-40's state testing was carried out, involving the fourth and fifth MiG-25P prototypes. As many as thirty-two missiles were fired; twenty of these were fitted with SARH seekers, nine with IR seekers and three lacked seekers.

The MiG-25-40 air intercept system was officially commissioned into VPVO service on 13 April 1972. The production missiles received the R-40 designation and were manufactured in two versions—R-40R with SARH seeker and R-40T with IR seeker. The production missiles were claimed to be capable of destroying targets flying at speeds of up to 3,000 km/h (1,618 kt) at altitudes between 500 and 27,000 m (1,640 and 88,580 feet), manoeuvring with up to 2.5-G. The R-40's low-altitude capability was proved for the first time in 1972 when a MiG-25P shot down a MiG-15 target drone following at 500 m (1,640 feet).

The K-40D was an improved K-40 derivative developed as a crash upgrade after the well-publicised defection of Viktor Belenko that had totally compromised the original MiG-25-40 air intercept system. The upgraded missile featured the much more modern RGS-25 SARH, a derivative of the RGS-24 originally developed in the mid-1970s for the R-24R missile carried by the MiG-23ML/MLD/P family.

The K-40D's heat-seeking derivative (designated as the R-40TD) introduced the new 35T1 seeker with a liquid-nitrogen cooled detector, which was sensible enough to enable the seeker to acquire targets in head-on attacks at medium and low altitudes (its predecessor, R-40T, was a tail-on-attack-only missile).

The MiG-25-40D air intercept system comprising the MiG-25PD and the R-40RD/TD missiles was officially commissioned into PVO service on 16 June 1980. Both the R-40RD/TD missile and the Sapfir-25 radar set significantly

A close-up view of an R-40TD air-to-air missile under the port wing of a MiG-25PD. (*Author's collection – Aviatsia i Kosmonavtika*)

enhanced the overall air intercept capabilities of the MiG-25PD compared to that of its predecessor. The R-40RD/TD AAM was capable of destroying targets flying from 50 to 30,000 m (160 to 98,400 feet) and manoeuvring with up to 4-G. The maximum launch distance in head-on intercepts reached 40 km (21.6 nm), while its tail-on range was between 1 and 20 km (0.54 to 10.7 nm).

In 1981, development of the further-improved K-40D-1 derivative was initiated, featuring a new combined radar/optical proximity fuse and a more powerful warhead that had a lethal radius of 13 m (43 feet). In addition, the K-40D-1 introduced an extended inertial phase of the flight in order to extend range; the inertial phase is said to have amounted to some 30 per cent of the missile's total flight time.

## R-40RD-1 and R-40TD-1 Missiles

|  | R-40RD-1 | R-40TD-1 |
| --- | --- | --- |
| Maximum launch range in forward quarter | 60 km (34.4 nm) | 50 km (27 nm) |
| Maximum launch range in rear quarter | 18 km (9.7 nm) | 18 km (9.7 nm) |
| Minimal and maximal altitude of target | 50 and 30,000 m (160 feet and 98,400 feet) | 50 and 30,000 m (160 feet and 98,400 feet) |
| Max g-load of target | 8 | 8 |
| Weight | 471 kg (1,036 lb) | 471 kg (1,036 lb) |
| Warhead weight | 55 kg (121 lb) | 55 kg (121 lb) |

## Two-Seat 'Foxbats'

The MiG-25PU ('Foxbat-C') was the two-seat conversion and continuation version of the MiG-25P, fitted with a redesigned nose with separate cockpits, each provided with an individual canopy. The instructor's cockpit was unconventionally placed forwards of the trainee's one, at a considerably lower level in front and below the normal cockpit, occupying the space used in the single-seater by the radar—which was absent in the two-seater. It was a design solution proven before on the trainer derivatives of the Tu-128 and Yak-28. The redesigned nose caused a reduction in the maximum speed, which was constrained to Mach 2.65 due to buffeting that occurred at high speeds. The MiG-25PU was equipped with an intercept simulation device and was able to carry R-40T/TD training missiles (captive rounds) on four underwing pylons, though former PVO pilots comment that they never used a missile-armed MiG-25PU for practice intercepts.

The MiG-25PU development formally commenced in July 1965, and the first prototype took to the air on 28 October 1969 with Alexander Fedotov at the controls. It used a MiG-25PU fuselage with a new nose section featuring the additional cockpit for the instructor. The new version was launched in production in Gorky in 1970, and no less than 180 two-seaters in both the -RU and -PU sub-variants of the two-seat 'Foxbat' rolled off the assembly line until 1985.

The MiG-25PU-SOTN was a high-profile special-mission aircraft purposely developed for the support of the Buran, the Soviet Union's space shuttle programme, which commenced development flying in April 1985. It was tasked with the development and evaluation of the flight path control algorithms, shadowing the Buran during its descent and landing approach below 20,000 m (65,600 feet), as well as training pilots destined to fly the Buran and receiving data derived from the Buran's automatic flight control system. The aircraft was extensively modified with optical and TV-surveillance cameras in the front cockpit and downlink equipment.

The TV equipment on board the MiG-25PU-SOTN comprised a Sony DXM-3P camera in the front cockpit working in conjunction with the 3800PS video recorder, DX-50 monitor and KL-108 transmitter. During the Buran landing approach, the

The two-seat MiG-25PU was designed for conversion and continuation training of interceptor pilots, but lacked the radar; this made it unsuitable for the employment of radar-guided missiles, and it was restricted to the use of heat-seeking R-40T missiles aimed visually by the pilot. (*Author's collection*)

This modified MiG-25PU–SOTN was used to support the operations of the Buran Soviet space shuttle (seen here), with the main task of shadowing it during re-entry into the Earth's atmosphere, filming its landing approach, and touching down in unmanned flight mode. (*Author's collection*)

MiG-25PU-SOTN, flown by pilots destined to fly the Buran in the future, was tasked with intercepting and lining-up with the shuttle and then shadowing it (with landing gear and airbrakes extended as well as engines throttled back) while transmitting live video until touchdown. After the Buran's first and only space flight on 15 November 1988, the MiG-25PU-SOTN was utilised for supporting other aircraft development programmes. A MiG-25RBK was also used to support the development and testing effort of the Buran's automatic flight control system.

# 4

# Fourth Generation

## MiG-29—A Highly Agile Air-Superiority Fighter

The MiG-29 (NATO reporting name 'Fulcrum') was a highly acclaimed fourth generation frontline fighter when it entered service with the VVS in 1983; over the following three decades, the type achieved a pretty good export proliferation, equal to or even slightly better than that of its predecessor, the MiG-23. Designed in the early–mid-1970s, the MiG-29 was launched in series production in early 1982, and its classic versions, using the original airframe design, have been maintained in low-rate production (albeit in a vastly improved form) until the mid-2010s. According to information released from the manufacturer, RSK MiG, the total number of classic 'Fulcrums' built is slightly above 1,600.

The Soviet military launched the very ambitious Prospective Frontal Fighter (PFI) programme in 1969. It was originally conceived in the late 1970s to replace all the second and third-generation tactical fighters and fighter-interceptors such as the MiG-21, MiG-23, MiG-25, Su-15 and Su-17, operated by both the VVS and IA-PVO air arms. The chief aim of this immense design effort was to produce a cutting-edge air-superiority fighter with a better performance than that of the McDonnell Douglas F-15, selected by the USAF in December 1969 as the winner of the FX programme and inducted into front-line service in 1976.

This new-generation multi-role fighter was intended to re-equip the VVS and IA PVO fleets, and so it also had to be able to counter the NATO's newly-developed low-level interdiction and strike jets and cruise-missile-carrying bombers, plus all other classes of front-line fixed/rotary-wing aircraft and unmanned air vehicles that might have been encountered in the air. The rather stringent PFI specification issued by the VVS called for an operating altitude of between 30 and 18,000 m (100 and 59,166 feet), while the top speed at low altitude was set at 1,500 km/h (809kt) and 2,500 km/h (1,348 kt) at high altitude. The low- and high-level combat radiuses were set at 500 km and 1,700 km (270 nm and 917 nm) respectively, while the specified rates of climb and level-flight acceleration necessitated a thrust/weight ratio of about 1.1–1.2; the turn rate/radius requirements were also very demanding. The new fighter was required to be capable of operating from so-called 'semi-prepared rough strips', but this necessitated a good short-take-off and landing performance combined with extra measures to protect the engines from foreign object damage (FOD) when taxing and taking off from unmaintained strips. It was to be also made capable of a short take-off run and landing roll, enabling the use of runways up to 1,200-m (4,000-feet) long.

The MiG, Sukhoi and Yakovlev experimental design bureaus took part in the first stage of the PFI competition by submitting their conceptual designs. The Yakovlev OKB was eliminated in the very beginning, while Mikoyan and Sukhoi remained in the game and continued further on in what had been expected to turn into a head-to-head competition.

After the first two presentations of the competing concepts, however, the Mikoyan OKB leadership suggested an idea for subdividing the PFI programme into two separate ones—for one for a heavyweight design and one for a lightweight one. This was eventually accepted by the VVS and the Soviet aviation industry leadership. The first of these programmes called for designing a large and therefore more expensive air-superiority fighter with long range and endurance, while the second one was to be dedicated to the development of a smaller and much more affordable design, better suited for mass production. The latter was conceived to be the replacement for thousands of MiG-21s, MiG-23s, MiG-27s and Su-17s soldiering on with the VVS's Frontal Aviation arm, the IA PVO's fighter-interceptor regiments and the VVS's advanced training regiments. The USAF had already embraced a similar approach at the time by electing to field into service the long-range and heavily armed McDonnell Douglas F-15 together with the lightweight and highly-agile General Dynamics (now Lockheed Martin) F-16.

In 1971 the Mikoyan OKB was eventually awarded the responsibility of designing the lightweight model (LPFI), while the Sukhoi OKB was tasked with proceeding with the heavyweight fighter (TPFI), which eventually turned into the Su-27.

The VVS specifications for the lightweight design were issued in 1972, and the following year OKB MiG submitted its preliminary design—known as *Izdeliye 9-11* ('Item 9-11'). At the same time, however, the VVS changed its range requirements, and this led to an extensive redesign of the 9-11's layout, including the addition of a larger wing. The final lightweight fighter design concept, approved by the VVS in 1974, wore the internal company designation 9-12.

The new twin fin/twin-engine fighter design featured a blended wing/body layout, better-known in Russia as 'integral aerodynamic configuration'. It comprised a mid-mounted wing with large leading-edge root extensions (LERX). An all-swept wing configuration was selected by the design team, combined with wide ogival LERXs and outward-canted tailfins installed on booms on the outer side of the widely spaced engines. The blended wing centre-section/body provided a high lift-to-drag ratio because the fuselage, together with the LERXs, acted as a lifting body to provide some 40 per cent of the total lifting force.

The airframe was made mainly from aluminium alloys, with only 7 per cent of the weight accounted for by the composite materials. Airframe life was initially set at 2,500 hours or twenty years (the initial TBO was ten years and 1,000 hours), whichever was reached first.

The MiG-29 features an all-swept wing configuration with wide ogival leading-edge extensions and outward-canted tailfins, installed on booms on the outer side of the widely-spaced engines. (*Author's collection*)

The MiG-29's airframe is made in an old-fashioned way—mainly from aluminium alloys, with only 7 per cent of the weight accounting for the lightweight composite materials. This aircraft is armed with R-73 air-to-air missiles. (*Author's collection*)

The powerplant consisted of two RD-33 afterburning turbofans designed by the Klimov engine design bureau in Leningrad (now St Petersburg), each rated at 42.44 kN (11,100 lb st. or 4,326 kgf) at military power and 81.4 kN (18,300 lb st. or 8,298 kgf) at full afterburner setting. The RD-33 was designed from the very beginning for easy servicing and repair; for instance, an engine change could be completed within forty-five minutes by a small team of technicians using only basic tools. The engine design, however, was very advanced for the late 1970s and 1980s, and as a consequence the RD-33 suffered from serviceability issues as well as from a very short time between overhauls. During the MiG-29's entry-into-service period with the VVS in the early–mid-1980s, the engine's TBO was down to fifty hours; it then gradually increased to 100 hours, and finally, in the late 1980s, RD-33 Series 2's TBO was set at 350 hours, with the total engine service life being 1,200 hours with three main overhauls. Another significant engine shortcoming (and one that has had an adverse impact on the MiG-29's overall close air combat performance) was the distinctive strong smoke trail at certain power settings; it was most evident at transient regimes, between idle and military-power settings.

In general, after overcoming its teething problems, the engine proved pretty reliable; between 1983 and 1995, as Mikoyan OKB sources reported, only six MiG-29s were lost due to airframe or powerplant-related problems, and four of them were on account of engine failures. The MiG-29 demonstrated a pretty low

The MiG-29's RD-33 engine was designed from the very beginning for easy servicing and repair; for instance, an engine change could be completed within forty-five minutes by a small team of technicians using only basic tools. (*Author's collection*)

On take-off and after touchdown the MiG-29's main intakes are blanked off by doors and the engines are fed by five louvers in top of each LERX—a measure to prevent foreign object damage to the engines when operating from dirty strips in wartime. (*Author's collection*)

accident rate for Soviet/Russian combat aircraft, as during the first ten years of service the figure was 7.8 major mishaps per 100,000 flying hours (equating to one loss per 12,820 flying hours).

The designers also introduced a fairly complex FOD protection system, using wedge-type main intakes provided with doors that close when taxiing and taking off, and engines that take air via auxiliary intakes situated on the upper LERX surface. The auxiliary intakes are also opened automatically in high AoA flight in an effort to provide additional air to the engines.

## MiG-29's High Manoeuvrability and Agility Performance

The MiG-29's mechanical hydraulically-activated flight control system is advertised as an extremely reliable and rapid-reacting one, being optimised for achieving high agility and manoeuvrability. It introduces an SOS-3M limiter to prevent the maximum angle of attack (AoA) from being exceeded, as this situation may cause a departure from controlled flight and an entry into spin (or other undesired, out-of-control effects). However, the limiter is of the so-called 'soft' type, and can be easily overridden by the pilot through pulling on the stick with increased force after reaching 26 degrees AoA (on the late production aircraft, while the early production examples were limited to 21°) at speeds below 300 km/h (162 kt). This unique feature represents an unmatched ability to venture—in a generally safe way—beyond normal AoA limits, but only when needed in turning air combat to point the nose against agile opponents or avoid incoming missiles. In addition, MiG-29 pilots can also employ the aircraft's exceptional nose-pointing capability in the yaw axis—left and right—by simply kicking the rudder; this is particularly effective at low speeds as it allows the noses to be quickly pointed at the opponent during close-in air combat, when helmet-mounted missile cueing is not being employed.

The initial production MiG-29s, however, proved prone to aileron reversal at high AoA, and this necessitated a series of aerodynamic and flight control system improvements to be introduced in an urgent manner in the early and mid-1980s, attempting to ensure safe low-speed/high-AoA handling.

The high thrust-to-weight ratio enabled the MiG-29 to continue accelerating while in a vertical climb and perform sustained turns with a 9-G-load at speeds exceeding 850 km/h (459 kt), but the aircraft's ability in this sense is said to exceed the pilot's physical ability to withstand high G-loads for prolonged periods of time.

Thanks to the combination of the high-lift aerodynamic configuration—the wing high-lift device and the thrust/weight ratio exceeding 1.1 during operations at normal take-off weight—the MiG-29's take-off run is exceptionally short—only 250 m (820 feet). However, shortening its landing roll has proved more

The MiG-29's turning ability at low level and with afterburner on is said to have had exceeded the pilot's physical ability to withstand high G-loads for prolonged periods of time. (*Lubomor Slavov*)

problematic due to the old-fashioned brakes, which are prone to overheating on hot days; this fact necessitates regular employment of the brake chute to shorten the take-off roll and alleviate the brake thermal loads. As a result, the MiG-29's landing roll is just 610 m (2,000 feet).

MiG-29 pilots are provided with greatly improved chances of survival should they have to eject in the event of deadly combat damage or catastrophic failure. The zero-zero Zvezda K-36DM Version 2 ejection seat was widely regarded as one of the best in service in the 1970s and 1980s, with a proven track record of saving the fighter jockeys in extreme conditions (when they bailed out in close proximity to the ground and at high angles of pitch and bank).

In the beginning, the Mikoyan OKB submitted a proposal to develop two different versions of its lightweight fighter design that shared the same airframe, engines and general systems, but were outfitted with different mission avionics suites and weapons. The first of them was regarded as an interim solution, and featured a Weapons Control System (WCS) and beyond-visual-range (BVR) missiles borrowed directly from the MiG-23ML 'Flogger-G' third-generation, swing-wing, single-engined fighter, flown for the first time in January 1975. Known as the MiG-29A, this interim 'Fulcrum' derivative was expected to be available for entering operational service with the VVS as soon as the late 1970s.

The second version—known simply as the MiG-29—was conceived as a much more sophisticated air-superiority lightweight fighter, boasting all-new WCS and BVR air-to-air missiles (AAMs). However, the development and testing of these advanced items were expected to be protracted and costly undertakings, and their induction into front-line service was planned to take place no earlier than in 1983. In the event, the development of the interim MiG-29A was rejected in 1976, and the VVS command authorities instead insisted that the Mikoyan OKB continue with the much more advanced 9-12 configuration, endowed with a state-of-the art WCS and AAMs.

## Flight Tests

Four prototype aircraft were built at Mikoyan's own workshop in Moscow in preparation for their participation in the extensive flight test programme. Mikoyan used many parts and assemblies manufactured at the series production plant then known as *Znamya Truda* (formerly named as the State Aircraft Plant, or GAZ-30), also located in Moscow.

It total, fourteen prototypes and pre-series aircraft were employed in the 9-12's flight test programme, which continued until October 1983; in addition, two static test airframes were made available for the comprehensive ground testing effort. The testing was set to comprise two major phases—the so-called 'factory testing' followed by the joint state testing. As it turned out, neither of these took fewer than 2,330 sorties.

The first flight test prototype of the MiG-29—aircraft No. 901 (also known as *Bort 01*)—made its maiden flight on 6 October 1977, in the capable hands of Alexander Fedotov, the Mikoyan OKB's famous chief test pilot. It was a one-off aircraft, as all the subsequent prototypes introduced serious structural changes.

The early test issues were caused by foreign objects being ingested by the engines, prompting a major redesign of the nose undercarriage leg. It was moved rearwards and shortened on all subsequent prototypes (excluding the second one, which retained the old design). In the event, aircraft No. 901 enjoyed a very long and productive life, receiving large anti-spin ventral fins, radar and the infrared search and track sensor (IRST) in the process. After amassing 182 test flights in the development programme it was upgraded with an automated stability augmentation system, performing thirty-eight more flights. It was retired on 8 August 1984, and in the following year it was handed over to the VVS Museum in Monino, near Moscow.

The second and fourth prototypes—serialed '903' and '908' respectively—were used for the testing and evaluation of the brand-new Klimov RD-33 afterburning turbofan. They were flown in June 1978 and April 1979 respectively. Both of them were lost due to engine failure, but OKB MiG test pilots Evgeniy Menitskiy and Alexander Fedotov managed to eject safely and continue their careers as aviators. No. 903 was lost on its ninth flight, on 15 June 1978, while No. 904 followed suit on 31 October 1981. The crash of the former was caused due to an uncontained compressor failure, while the latter was written off due to a combustion chamber failure that severed the tailplane control rods in a high-speed test flight at low level. Alexander Fedotov managed to bail out from No. 908 just three seconds before impact, but he sustained serious back injuries. He eventually recovered from his wounds and continued his dangerous test pilot job; however, he sadly died in an unsuccessful ejection from a MiG-31 on 4 April 1984.

The third MiG-29 prototype, serialed 'No. 902', was assembled in October 1978, originally slated for testing the all-new WCS and the new air-to-air missiles. It was also the first MiG-29 with the newly designed nose gear, shortened and moved aft, in an effort to prevent FOD ingestion in the intakes and improve manoeuvrability while taxiing, with turn radius of 8 metres (25 feet). It was also the first to introduce integral wing tanks and the new single-barrel 30-mm cannon. Aircraft No. 908 took to the air for the first time on 28 December 1978—still lacking the radar, as its development had encountered serious issues. It was equipped with an IRST only. It was the first MiG-29 to be handed over to the VVS flight-test institute in Akhtubinsk in 1980 for the commencement of the first stage of the joint state testing effort, undertaken by the VVS in cooperation with the Mikoyan OKB. Soon afterwards it was joined by No. 901 and other prototypes and pre-production aircraft. No. 902 was involved in the test programme until October 1982, amassing 182 flights within the frame of the joint state testing effort.

The prototypes and pre-production examples saw extensive use in the WCS and the protracted development and testing effort of weapons, as well as in the evaluation campaign of the MiG-29's stability and control qualities and envelope

The first MiG-29 prototype, featuring a forward-installed nose undercarriage unit, had enjoyed a productive and safe life, flying until 1984. It was then displayed at the RuAF Museum at Monino, near Moscow. (*RSK MiG*)

expansion. Some of the pre-production MiG-29s enjoyed long and useful lives, while aircraft No. 922 was retired following four flights only to be used for aerodynamic tunnel testing. In contrast, No. 920 had the longest career of the prototypes and pre-production fleet, amassing as many as 382 flights between March 1981 and November 1985. It reached the end of its life during a nuclear-survivability testing campaign at Nova Zemlya nuclear proving ground. No. 923 was another survivor, with 432 flights logged between November 1981 and March 1988, when it ended its life in combat survivability trials. No. 924 was the last pre-production aircraft to be employed in the MiG-29's comprehensive testing and evaluation campaign—it took to the air for the first time in September 1983 and saw use in various ground and flight testing campaigns, including maximum low-level speed performance, reaching a top speed of 1,520 km/h (820 kt). After amassing 369 sorties with a total of 233 flight hours, it was finally grounded in 1994, but after that it continued to be used for various ground tests, supporting the development programmes of follow-on MiG-29 derivatives. No. 925 was the last MiG-29 participating in the testing campaign, and it also became the pattern aircraft for the production-standard configuration of the 'Fulcrum'. It took to the air for the first time in December 1982, and featured the entire package of modifications introduced to remove the shortcomings that had been discovered during the extensive tests of the preceding prototypes and pre-production machines. It was used in various follow-on testing campaigns, and by December 1991 it had amassed as many as 849 sorties.

## The Two-Seat 'Fulcrum'

The MiG-29's two-seat conversion and continuation training version was developed in the late 1970s. Wearing the MiG-29UB designation, it was known

The two-seat MiG-29UB lacked a radar and was made capable of deploying heat-seeking air-to-air missiles only, cued visually by the pilot or by using the KOLS-29 IRST sensor; this machine is armed with six R-60MK close-in combat, heat-seeking air-to-air missiles. (*Author's collection*)

within the Mikoyan OKB as Item 9-51, and used the same basic airframe as that of the single-seater. The second cockpit was inserted just forward of the normal cockpit, in the place occupied by the radar on the single-seater, and it features a continuous canopy. The changed forward fuselage shape caused a slight maximum speed reduction (2,230 km/h (1,203 kt) compared to 2,450 km/h (1,321 kt) for the single-seater), a reduction in operational ceiling (17,500 m (57,400 feet) vs 18,000 m (59,040 feet)) and a reduction in low-level range (680 km (367 nm) vs 710 km (383 nm)).

The MiG-29UB lacks the radar and BVR missiles but retains the IRST and entire full close air combat capability, with an armament consisting of six heat-seeking missiles and a built-in cannon. The two-seater, however, is equipped with a simulator, allowing the instructor to generate synthetic targets on the HUD and the CRT display in the front cockpit, and thereby allowing the student to practice BVR intercept techniques.

The MiG-29UB also inherited the single-seater's internal fuel capacity unchanged, and its fuselage is only 100 mm (4 in.) longer than that of the single-seater; the single canopy sports a periscope for improving the instructor's forward visibility on take-off and landing.

The MiG-29UB's mock-up was built in 1979, while the first two-seat prototype, No. 951, was completed in 1980—taking to the air for the first time on 29 April 1981, with Aviard Fastovets behind the controls. During the flight test campaign it amassed 192 sorties, and the aircraft later saw participation in some other testing and evaluation efforts at OKB MiG; it was maintained in an airworthy condition until 1997, logging a total of 1,066 sorties.

The second two-seat prototype, No. 952, was completed in early 1982, and it joined the flight test programme in August 1982. It amassed 213 flights before retirement in April 1988.

## MiG-29 Launched in Production

The first production-standard example was aircraft No. 917, which retained the distinctive ventral fins installed for improving the anti-spin characteristics in high AoA flight. In this form, aircraft No. 917 was submitted for its joint state testing effort, which was undertaken by VVS's own flight test centre at Akhtubinsk. The MiG-29's production at the *Znamya Truda* factory was launched in 1982, and in early 1983 the first production examples were rolled out from the final assembly line at the factory's LMZ branch, situated in the town of Lukhovitzy, southeast of Moscow.

No less than seventy MiG-29s were constructed to this initial standard, but the aircraft built in subsequent production batches do not feature the huge ventral fins; however, they do have BVP-30-26M 32-round overwing chaff/flare dispensers extending forward from the fins. The chaff/flare dispenser integration was a direct result of the Soviet combat experience in Afghanistan in the mid-1980s, where the mass use of infrared flares significantly reduced combat losses caused by the man-portable heat-seeking surface-to-air missiles. This second production standard also introduced extended control surface deflection for improved control at high AoA and differential tailplane, together with extended-chord rudders, while small strakes were fitted onto each side of the nose probe, acting as vortice generators for improving the high-AoA yaw stability performance. The flight control system was also modified in a bid to use the rudders for bank control in high-AoA flight as well.

The strakes, differential tailplane and the extended-chord rudders (with the modification for use in the bank control role at high AoA) were also retrofitted to the initial-production MiG-29s. Both the initial and subsequent MiG-29 production standards of the early and mid-1980s received a common NATO reporting name—'Fulcrum-A'.

The MiG-29 single-seater was officially commissioned for service with the VVS in 1987, four years after the first deliveries to the Soviet air arm for experimental operation with the Lipetsk-based 4th TsBPiPLS (Combat Training and Aircrew Conversion Centre). The field trials were undertaken by the 234th Guards IAP at Kubinka, near Moscow, and by the 968th IAP at Ros in Byelorussia; they took their first aircraft on strength in mid-1983 and late 1983 respectively.

The MiG-29UB twin-seater was launched in production at another plant—*Sergo Ordzhonikidze* (formerly known as GAZ-21) in Gorky (in the early 1990s the city was renamed as Nizhniy Novgorod), initially using rear and centre-fuselage assemblies received from *Znamya Truda*. The twin-seater received the NATO reporting name 'Fulcrum-B'; its production commenced in 1986, but it

A scan inside the cockpit of the classic 'Fulcrum', dominated by numerous analogue instruments but described by the pilots as much better ergonomically than those of its predecessors, the MiG-21 and MiG-23. (*Author's collection*)

A pair of Russian Air Force MiG-29s pictured taking off at military-power mode (without engaging the afterburner) from Astrakhan Airfield in southern Russia, home of the 115th Fighter Aviation Branch's Combat Training Centre. (*Andrey Zinchuk*)

was only officially commissioned into VVS service in 1991, after remedying the most evident design deficiencies that had been discovered during the joint state testing and evaluation effort.

## MiG-29's Mission Avionics and Ordinance

Thanks to the major breakthroughs in avionics technology that had been made by the otherwise low-technology Soviet radio electronics industry in the second half of the 1970s and early 1980s, the MiG-29 boasted a rather sophisticated (at the time) SUO-29 multi-channel weapons control system (WCS). Additionally, it introduced digital processors for the first time on a Mikoyan front-line fighter. The WCS had three main sensor components. The first of these was the NO19 Rubin pulse-Doppler radar (known also as the RLPK-29), which used a twist-Cassegrain antenna; it was the principal WCS sensor, featuring a search range against a fighter-sized target of 38 nm (70 km) head-on (in the forward hemisphere) and 19 nm (35 km) tail-on (in the rear hemisphere). Bomber targets could be detected at up to 57 nm (105 km). The radar could track ten targets simultaneously and prioritise those that posed the greatest threat for a subsequent lock-on and missile engagement. However, the radar's development proved to be very problematic, and the reliability of the aircraft was very low at the beginning of its service with the VVS. In the late 1980s this gradually improved, with its Mean Time Between Failures (MTBF) getting to around 100 hours.

The second principal component in the MiG-29's SUO-29 WCS was the OEPrNK-29 optronic nav./attack system, which sported a high-altitude tracking range (in tail-on attacks only) of up to 18 km (10 nm). This system integrated an OEPS-29 infra-red search and track sensor (IRST) coupled with a laser rangefinder, and both sensors were slaved to the radar and the IR missile seekers. The OEPrNK-29 is restricted for employment in visual meteorological conditions only, and it is advertised as being particularly useful for emission-free tail-on intercepts; it can be also a valuable back-up sensor, suitable for situations when the radar was rendered inoperative by heavy jamming or technical failure. The IRST is also the pilot's sensor of preference in close-in air-to-air encounters, thanks to its better discrimination and higher angular tracking rate relative to the radar. In addition, the laser rangefinder is said to be a particularly useful aid during both air-to-air and air-to-ground attacks, contributing during the latter to the fairly good accuracy of unguided ordinance delivery.

The third targeting system on board the MiG-29 is represented by the Schtel'-3UM helmet-mounted sight, which is also slaved to the radar/IRST and missile seeker heads. It enables the R-73's (NATO AA-11 'Archer') tremendous off-boresight capability of 45° to be fully explored by the pilot, who can cue the seekers of its close air combat missiles by simply turning his head in the vertical and horizontal plane while visually tracking a target.

The MiG-29 retains the tradition of the second and third-generation Soviet fighters' data-link equipment, which fed intercept information derived from ground control stations to the aircraft. The E-502-20 Biryuza system enables the intercept to be performed in the so-called 'director mode', using intercept data processed by a ground station and received by the on-board datalink equipment. This method makes it possible for the guidance process to be performed during the intercept sequence without any voice commands from the ground intercept control officer.

The baseline MiG-29 lacked an internal or pod-mounted radar jammer, and the only EW equipment on board was represented by the SPO-15LM radar-warning-receiver (RWR)—an analogous device, capable of providing 360° coverage in azimuth and 30° up and down in elevation, issuing warnings in case of a lock-on from airborne, ground or sea fire-control radars.

The MiG-29's built-in-port-wing-root 30-mm GSh-301 single-barrel cannon provides with 150 rounds, and its rate of fire is 1,400–1,800 rpm. The effective range against air targets is 200–800 m (660–2,620 feet), while this extends to 1,200–1,800 m (3,940–5,900 feet) for strafing ground targets. It has a 25-round one-second burst, together with several other burst-length settings that can be selected by the pilot. The GSh-301 proved to be a remarkably precise and powerful weapon thanks to the laser rangefinder, rate of fire, projectile weight and barrel speed. It is generally considered that, in the air-to-air mode, a 20-round burst is more than enough to ensure the reliable destruction of fighter-type targets.

The Phazotron NO19 Rubin pulse-Doppler radar, installed on the classic *Fulcrum*, uses a twist-Cassegrain antenna. It has notable operating restrictions as it cannot see and track targets traveling at speeds under 110 nm (200 km/h), nor targets flying on the beam relative to the heading of the carrier aircraft. (*Author's collection*)

The 'Schtel'-3UM helmet-mounted cueing system—shown here attached to a pilot's ZSh-5 helmet—is slaved to the radar/IRST and missile seeker heads for accelerated missile seeker cueing and achieving a firing solution, mainly to facilitate cueing the highly-agile R-73 missile and utilising its great off-boresight capability. (*Author's collection*)

The beyond-visual-range (BVR) missile armament that can be deployed by the MiG-29 is represented by the R-27R1 (NATO AA-10 'Alamo') semi-active radar-homing (SARH) missile. Its maximum range in head-on attack is 50 km (27 nm), reduced to 20 km (10.8 nm) in a tail-on attack scenario at high altitude. When fired at low level, the R-27R1's head-on and tail-on ranges are reduced to 15 km (8.1 nm) and 5 km (2.7 nm) respectively. The missile is capable of engaging targets flying at altitudes from 20 m to 27,000 m (66 feet to 88,560 feet) and at a maximum speed of 3,500 km/h (1,887 kt), while the altitude separation between the launch platform and the target can be up to 10,000 m (32,800 feet).

There is also an IR-seeking version (designated R-27T1), but this could only be used by the improved 'Fulcrum' derivatives from the MiG-29S onwards. A fire-and-forget/lock-on-before-launch weapon, the R-27T1 retains the same kinetic performance as that of its SARH counterpart, but its actual launch range depends on the lock-on performance of the IR seeker, which may vary at different target aspects, altitudes and engine modes.

A close-up of two of the three air-to-air missile types of the classic 'Fulcrum'—the R-27R SARH-guided BVR missile is suspended inboard, while the agile, heat-seeking R-60MKs are present on to the other two pylons. (*Lubomir Slavov*)

The R-73 (NATO AA-11 'Archer') is the MiG-29's most capable within-visual-range (WVR) weapon, boasting a 45° off-boresight capability for easing the pre-launch cueing and achieving target lock-on, while employing a very sensitive, true all-aspect IR seeker with nitrogen cooling. It also has digital signal processing for better resistance to jamming, while the maximum range at low level is 2.2 km (1.2 nm) tail-on and 12 km (6.47 nm) head-on. At high level the tail-on and head-on ranges are 12 km and 30 km (6.5 nm and 17 nm) respectively. In order to achieve a better kill rate, the R-73 uses the 'lead bias' technique in the final guidance phase—it steers the missile ahead of the target's exhaust plume in tail-on engagements.

The MiG-29 can also use the R-60M/MK (NATO AA-8 'Aphid') lightweight AAM, optimised for dogfight situations, with a modest off-boresight capability of 17°—capable of replacing guns in close air combat. Its IR seeker has a limited all-aspect capability (as it can only acquire head-on jet aircraft with afterburner), and the maximum range tail-on is 8 km (4.3 nm), while at low altitude this is reduced to 2 km (1.1 nm).

For ground attacks, the baseline MiG-29 can carry up to 2,000 kg (4,409 lb) of unguided ordinance, including various free-fall and retarded bombs weighing up to 500 kg (1,102 lb) each, as well as 57-mm, 80-mm and 240-mm rockets. The aircraft built for the VVS and some Warsaw Pact countries (such as Bulgaria) were also wired to deploy a single RN-40 free-fall nuclear bomb.

It is interesting to note that in the late 1980s at least two VVS fighter-bomber regiments were re-equipped with the MiG-29. Their pilots mastered the ground-attack role, employing the full range of unguided ordinance cleared for the 'Fulcrum-A/B/C' derivatives, and they also received some training in the air-to-air role.

However, the basic MiG-29 had a very serious flaw—its short range. It is a well-known fact that the new fourth-generation fighter jet for the VVS's frontal aviation arm eventually failed to meet the range requirements specified in the original specification. In this respect the MiG-29 proved to be clearly inferior to its predecessor, the single-engine MiG-23. Without the external fuel tank, the short-legged twin-engine fighter has a high-level range at of only 1,430 km (771 nm), and its 'real-world' combat radius is between 400 km and 600 km (215 nm and 324 nm), depending on the operating altitude and the air combat scenario. When operating with a 1,500-litre underfuselage fuel tank, its typical air combat mission duration is between forty minutes and one hour.

When the highly-agile MiG-29 was introduced in VVS service in 1983–1985, it was utilised in the same way as its predecessors, MiG-21 and MiG-23—as a high-speed 'point air defence' fighter-interceptor, operating predominantly over the battlefield zone, closely guided and supported by the dense GCI network. The type was used only on rare occasions as a true air-superiority fighter, despite its exceptional manoeuvring performance, good sensor outfit and potent close air combat missiles; this underuse was due both to doctrine and range considerations.

An R-60 very-short-range air-to-air missile seen just after being launched from a Bulgarian Air Force MiG-29. (*Lubomir Slavov*)

The export *Fulcrum-A* was built in two subversions—the 9-12A was destined for the Warsaw Pact countries (like this Polish Air Force machine), with mission avionics almost identical to their VVS counterparts, and some aircraft even retaining their nuclear bomb capability. Meanwhile, the 9-12B was supplied to all other customer nations. (*Author's collection*)

## The 9-13 Family of Improved 'Fulcrums'

The second production variant of the single-seat MiG-29, known under the internal designation 9-13 (NATO 'Fulcrum-C'), was originally intended to remedy the range shortcoming. It introduced a bulged spine aft of the cockpit that was initially designed for increased internal fuel tankage. In the event, the additional volume provided by the reshaped spine was used to house the Gardeniya-1 active radar jammer. As a result, the internal fuel capacity was increased by just 240 litres. The new 'Fulcrum' version, however, boasted an increased air-to-ground ordinance load, reaching 3,200 kg (7,053 lb)—the heaviest configuration comprising six FAB-500M-62 500-kg (1,102-lb) high-explosive bombs and two R-73 AAMs. It was also made capable of deploying KMGU bomblet/mine dispensers. Its maximum take-off weight reached 18,480 kg (40,730 lb).

The 9-13 prototype aircraft, converted by the Mikoyan OKB from a production-standard 9-12 airframe (which amassed forty-three sorties in its original form, prior to reworking), took to the air for the first time on 4 May 1984. It was initially used in aerodynamic trials of the new bulged spine, and in 1985 it also got the Gardeniya-1 active jammer.

The new derivative entered mass production in 1986, and its formal designation, MiG-29, remained unchanged. All the examples of this version went to the VVS, while export customers continued to receive the 'flat-spined' 'Fulcrum-A' in two subversions—the 9-12A was built for the Warsaw Pact countries (with mission avionics almost identical to their VVS counterparts, with some aircraft even retaining their nuclear bomb capability), while the 9-12B was destined for all the other customer nations.

The multistage upgrade of the 9-13 subversion in the second half of the 1980s brought the more capable 9-13S derivative to life; the aircraft received the new in-service designation MiG-29S. It made its first flight in January 1989, and later remedied its predecessor's lack of range by introducing a provision for two 1,150-litre underwing tanks (later retrofitted to some 9-12 and 9-13 aircraft), making it possible to increase the total fuel capacity to 8,240 litres, giving a maximum ferry flight range of 2,900 km (1,564 nm). The MiG-29S also rectified the initial version's inability to engage more than one target via radar when firing BVR missiles. The new NO19M Topaz-M radar—boasting a maximum head-on detection range against fighter-sized targets of 100 km (54 nm)—was able to track ten targets, and offered simultaneous dual-target engagement capability as well as better protection from active radar jamming. The new radar, which used the new Ts101 digital computer, was designed to work in conjunction with the new R-77 (AA-12 'Adder') active radar-homing BVR missile in order to fully exploit the dual-target engagement capability. This enhanced 'Fulcrum-C' version was also made capable of firing the extended-range R-27RE SARH-homing and R-27TE IR-homing missiles with a maximum high-level/head-on range of 70 km (38 nm). It also boasted an improved IRST, which was able to support a more accurate gun-firing mode.

The humpbacked first-generation MiG-29 (*Product 9-13*) formed the backbone of the Soviet Air Force's 'Fulcrum' fleet. This aircraft, sporting display colours, is assigned to the aircrew combat training and conversion centre, the 4th TsBPiPLS, at Lipetsk. (*Andrey Zinchuk*)

The list of the other novelties incorporated in the MiG-29S's design included a refined flight control system, with an increased operational AoA of 28° when compared to the baseline MiG-29's limit of 26°. This provided a further gain in turn performance. The aircraft's maximum take-off weight was increased to 20,000 kg (44,084 lb), allowing the heaviest air-to-ground ordinance load to reach 4,000 kg (8,818 lb)—represented by eight FAB-500M-62 bombs carried on four tandem racks on the innermost and middle underwing pylons. It was also able to fire the GSh-301 cannon when carrying an underfuselage external fuel tank, something that is impossible on the standard 9-12 and 9-13 versions.

The MiG-29S's flight test programme was completed in September 1992, just after the Soviet Union's dissolution, and consequently only sixteen examples of this enhanced version are reported to have been taken on strength by the Russian Air Force. By 1992 the Russian Ministry of Defence decided it could no longer afford to buy more MiG-29s, leaving the manufacturer entirely reliant on the export market. In order to make the classic and yet affordable and reliable MiG-29 more attractive, a number of enhanced versions were developed over the decade. Most (if not all) of them utilised a backlog of completed 9-12 airframes left over from various failed export contracts, outfitted with new avionics and weapons. The first post-Soviet 'Fulcrums', offered as new aircraft to export customers in the mid-1990s, were designated as the MiG-29SE (9-13SE) and MiG-29SD (9-13SD). At the same time, MIG MAPO (as the parent company of OKB MiG was known at the time) offered its existing customers a package of rolling improvements, designed to bring their fleets up to the new avionics standard.

The enhanced 'Fulcrum' versions (dating from the late 1980s and early 1990s) can fire the extended-range R-27RE SARH- and R-27TE IR-homing missiles with a maximum high-level/head-on range of 70 km (38 nm). (*RSK MiG*)

The 9-14 was a multi-role prototype of the first-generation 'Fulcrum' that used the basic MiG-29 airframe without any major fuselage redesign. In the mid-1980s it was originally intended that the 9-14 would receive an all-new WCS with an external targeting pod (named Ryabina), required for the guidance of the latest generation of Soviet-made laser and TV-guided air-to-ground weapons. Another targeting pod with emitter locator system (named Progress-N) was to be integrated to enable the firing of anti-radar missiles. The heaviest air-to-ground ordinance load of this version was to reach 4,500 kg (9,920 lb), represented by nine FAB-500M-62 bombs.

The prototype aircraft for the 9-14 programme took to the air for the first time in February 1985, being tested carrying a dummy targeting pod that never materialised into a real system. However, the 9-14 programme was soon abandoned during the same year in favour of the radically-redesigned MiG-29M derivative (which first flew on 26 April 1986). The redesigned aircraft was set to be turned into the ultimate multi-role 'Fulcrum', entirely relieved from the range and avionics deficiencies of its predecessors.

## MiG-29 Specification

| Dimensions:<br>Wing span<br>Length<br>Height | 11.36 m<br>17.32 m<br>4.73 m |
|---|---|
| Wing area: | 38.1 m$^2$ |
| Weights:<br>Empty operating<br>Take-off clean<br>Take-off with 2 R-27R1 and 4 R-600 AAMs<br>Maximum take-off<br>Maximum landing | 10,900 kg<br>14,300 kg<br>15,600 kg<br>19,700 kg<br>14,200 kg |
| Performance:<br>Max level speed at sea level<br>Max level speed at high level<br>Max operating Mach number<br>Stalling speed<br>Landing speed<br>Practical ceiling, clean<br>Practical ceiling with two AAMs<br>Acceleration time from 600 to 1,000 km/h at 1,000 m<br>G limits<br>Rate of climb at low level<br>Range at high altitude on internal fuel<br>Low-level range on internal fuel<br>Ferry range with one underfuselage tank<br>Ferry range with one underfuselage and two wing tanks | 1,500 km/h<br>2,400 km/h<br>2.3<br>240 km/h<br>250 km/h<br>18,000 m<br>17,500 m<br>13.5 sec<br>+9/-3<br>330 m/s<br>1,500 km<br>710 km<br>2,100 km<br>2,900 km |

## The Radically Reworked MiG-29M

Known as the most ambitious 'Fulcrum' derivative developed in the 1990s, the MiG-29M was set to become the ultimate MiG-29, absolved from the range and avionics shortcomings of the baseline model.

The development of the much more capable MiG-29M (*Izdeliye* 9-15) was launched in 1982; it was an ambitious undertaking. It was to boast a new airframe with an increased fuel capacity, and was to be powered by increased-thrust engines and have an all-new avionics suite, enabling a full multi-role capability.

The aircraft had an all-new airframe with a better aerodynamic performance, featuring an all-new LERX design. It introduced sharp leading edges, which further improved the complex vortices field created by the airframe at high AoA. The new wing design boasted longer-span ailerons extending further outboard.

The tailplane was also vastly improved in order to be more effective at high AoA, with a greater area and a dogtooth discontinuity on the leading edge. The radar cone had an altered shape in order to provide better stability at high AoA. The end result of all the aerodynamic changes was that the MiG-29M was made unstable in the pitch axis for better agility, further improving the *Fulcrum's* formidable low-speed turning performance. This, in turn necessitated the use of an analogue fly-by-wire system, which, in its final form, had to feature three channels for roll and yaw control and four channels for pitch control.

The extensively redesigned airframe made use of use of welded aluminium-lithium alloys in order to save weight, and it also featured a greater proportion of composites in the airbrake, engine access panels, intake ducts and vertical fins.

In order to further increase the internal fuel volume, the MiG-29M dispensed with the complex FOD protection system of the original design, which made use of intake doors and auxiliary air intakes; these were now replaced by newly-added fuel tanks. Additional fuel volume was provided by using space previously occupied by the cannon ammunition box, which was of a reduced capacity (100 rounds, compared to 150 for the baseline version). In this way, the MiG-29M boasted an increased internal fuel capacity of up to 5,800 litres (1,500 litres more than the original 9-12 version), providing 30–40 per cent more range. The reshaped, flat spine also allowed some increase to the internal fuel capacity. The canopy has a greater height than that of the 'vanilla' MiG-29, improving the pilot's view forward over the nose and side-on—a welcome improvement for close-in air combat and ground attacks.

The much-improved MiG-29M was set to become the ultimate 'Fulcrum', free from the range and avionics shortcomings plaguing the baseline model. (*RSK MiG*)

The new intake FOD protection was represented by retractable meshed grills preventing ingestion of debris on take-off and landing; this much-lighter design solution was borrowed from the Su-27. The MiG-29M's spine terminated in a flattener beaver tail containing housing for twin brake chutes, which could further shorten the landing roll. A new single-piece ventral airbrake was introduced, while the fins had a modified trailing edge for improved low-speed stability and controllability. The spine also accommodated a battery of built-in chaff/flare dispensers for 120 rounds.

The new wing design retained the same span but was made capable of carrying much larger weights, with a total of eight hardpoints (four under each console). The strengthened wings enabled the MiG-29 to carry up to 4,500 kg (9,920 lb) of ordinance. It also introduced new wingtips to house antennas for the new EW systems.

The higher landing weight necessitated the use of far-improved energy-absorbing brakes compared to those on the original version, which were old-fashioned pieces of kit and proved prone to overheating on hot days. The undercarriage members were also reinforced (while remaining externally unchanged) in order to enable a maximum take-off weight of more than 22,000 kg (48,450 lb).

The more powerful RD-33K engine, originally conceived for the MiG-29K, was also installed on the M-version in order to further improve the performance of this heaver 'Fulcrum' derivative. The afterburning turbofan introduced a new low-pressure compressor in order to provide a higher compression ratio, resulting in a greater mass-flow. This, combined with the higher-temperature turbine, allowed for a sensible thrust increase. The new engine also had a hybrid digital/hydro-mechanical control system for even better responsiveness. It was rated at 86 kN (19,400 lb st. or 8,766 kgf) at full afterburner, while the dry rating was 53.96 kN (12,122 lb st. or 5,500 kgf). In order to provide a greater mass-flow on take-off, the intakes are provided with downward-hinging sections on the lower lip.

In its initial form, the MiG-29M boasted a much more modern cockpit layout, with a pair of CRT multi-function displays and HOTAS controls. It also had an all-new WCS centred on the new Phazotron-NIIR N010 Zhuk multi-functional radar, which features both air-to-air and air-to-surface operating modes. This is enabled thanks to the new digital computers used in the radar, which provide an impressive 400-per-cent improvement in the data-processing capability needed for the new modes. Employing a mechanically scanned slotted-antenna, this pulse-Doppler radar system at last introduced a true multiple-target engagement capability, which the classic 'Fulcrum' had previously lacked. It can track up to ten targets and provide guidance of active-radar-guided missiles against four of them.

In the air-to-air mode, it was claimed that the N010's detection range was up to 100 km (54 nm) and its acquisition range was up to 80 km (43 nm) against a fighter-sized target; the maximum altitude of the target in head-on intercepts was 25,000 m (82,000 feet). It offered a plethora of air-to-surface modes (such as high-resolution terrain mapping), while its maximum detection range against a large ship extended to 300 km (161 nm); a large railway bridge could be detected at up to 120 km (65 nm). However, the new technologies implemented in the N010 design initially proved to be too immature, and, during the MiG-29M's state test effort in the early 1990s, the radar was said to have demonstrated a very poor reliability performance.

The new OLS-M IRST had an enhanced performance compared to that of the OEPS-29. In addition to an IRST (with increased range) and a laser rangefinder, it also incorporated a TV targeting channel and a laser target maker for the use of laser-guided missiles against ground and sea targets.

The first MiG-29M prototype (wearing serial No. 151) was completed in 1986, and it took to the air for the first time on 26 April that year, with Valeriy Menitskiy at the controls. It was powered by the old RD-33 engines, retaining the same cockpit as the original MiG-29 but lacking the WCS. The first prototype was used for aerodynamic trials and also for trials of the new fly-by-wire system. It received a WCS later, and in 1991 it commenced trials of the new mission avionics, having amassed as many as 276 test sorties by 1992.

The first prototype was followed by as many as five pre-series aircraft. The first of these—serialed '152', powered by the new RD-33 and equipped with a full set of mission avionics—made its maiden flight on 26 September 1987. It was used for evaluation of the stability and controllability characteristics as well as trials of the new engines, fly-by-wire flight control system, fuel system, radar, navigation and the electronic flight instrumentation system. By 21 April 1992 it logged as many as 250 sorties. The third, fourth, fifth and sixth MIG-29Ms involved in the flight test effort took to the air in April 1989, July 1990, February 1990 and July 1991 respectively. The sixth MiG-29, serialed '156', was submitted to the Soviet Air Force flight test centre in August 1990 for WCS trials and evaluation of its controllability and stability performance. It was also displayed at the Farnborough Air Show in 1992, and then at the Paris Air Show in the following year.

The Soviet Air Force stopped purchasing MiG-29s in 1991, and sharply reduced the development funding allocated to the MiG-29M programme in the same year. In 1992 and 1993 the six development aircraft flew sporadically, and three were grounded; in 1993 another one followed suit. The programme was then stopped altogether, although in the late 2000s the development effort was renewed, utilising a host of new technologies.

## The MiG-29K Shipborne Derivative

The origins of the dedicated shipborne derivative built on the MiG-29M date back to the late 1970s. Detailed design work, however, began as late as in 1984, with the new MiG-29K (9-31) intended to be included in the air wing of the newly-built short take-off but arrested recovery (STOBAR) carriers of the *Riga* class—the so-called 'Project 1143.5'. The first of them was laid out in 1982 in the shipyard in Nikovlayev, on the Black Sea coast (now in Ukraine), and launched in December 1985, originally christened *Leonid Brezhnev*. In 1987 it was renamed

The MiG-29M boasted an all-new airframe with better aerodynamic performance, featuring an all-new LERX design with sharp leading edges that further improved the complex vortices field created by the airframe at high AoA. (*Author's collection*)

as *Tbilisi*, and in 1990 the ship received its latest name—*Admital Kuznetsov*. Its carrier wing was intended to comprise up to eighteen fighters and fourteen helicopters. The fighters were primarily intended for air defence of the carrier group with little or no capability for strikes against sea-surface or land targets. The first carrier, featuring conventional propulsion, was soon to be followed by another one of the same type, while the third example was to boast a nuclear powerplant. All of these ships lacked catapults, instead using sky-jump to provide the required short take-off run. In this case, the aircraft's take-off speed was to be between 180 and 200 km/h (97 and 108 kt), while the take-off run was to be between 100 to 150 m (330 and 595 feet).

The aircraft required a powerful afterburning engine, while landing was to be performed by using a desk arrestor system in conjunction with an arrestor hook. The new RD-33K engine, purposely designed for the shipborne 'Fulcrum', boasted an emergency afterburning mode, giving some 92.2 kN (9,398 kgf or 20,725 lb st.) thrust for the limited period of time needed for take-off or go-around. This mode enabled the MiG-29K to be launched off the ski-jump at a take-off weight of up to 17,700 kg (39,010 lb) from the so-called 'first start position', providing a take-off run of just 105 m (344 feet). At its maximum permissible deck take-off weight of 22,400 kg (49,379 lb), the MiG-29K was capable of being launched from the second start position, which provided a take-off run of some 195 m (640 feet). To reduce thrust losses on take-off, the intake lower lips deflected downwards. While on landing approach, the MiG-29 maintained a speed of 240

The MiG-29K with its wing folded, armed with the Kh-35 anti-ship missiles and R-73 air-to-air missiles; an UPAZ air-refuelling pod can be seen in the foreground. (*Author's collection*)

km/h (129 kt), which is 46 km/h (25 kt) slower than that required for a land-based runway, while the angle-of-attack was 14° vs 11° for the ground landing.

To become suitable for carrier operation, the MiG-29K, designed on the base of the MiG-29M's airframe, received a new wing with power folding at one-third span, as well as a new, strengthened undercarriage, body centre and nose sections in addition to an increased-area tailplane and arrestor hook replacing the MiG-29M's brake parachute. The all-new wing received broader-chord, double-slotted trailing-edge flaps and extended-span drooping ailerons (also used as flaperons at low speed), and modified wingtips with EW antennas. The wing leading edge was of reduced sweepback, and the leading-edge slats were redesigned too. The MiG-29 was also made capable of in-flight refuelling, receiving a neat, retractable probe below the forward edge of the port side of the windscreen. The fuselage received anti-corrosion treatment to withstand the aggressive saline environment during deck operations, while the avionics and equipment bays were made with much better pressurisation, again to prevent their exposure to saline environment.

The MiG-29K featured the Uzel deck-landing guidance system, enabling landing on the deck in auto mode within a circle 6 metres (20 feet) in diameter, and within very tight airspeed and rate-of-descent limits.

Due to the high degree of similarity in design and equipment with the MiG-29M (which was in extensive testing at the time), only two MiG-29K prototypes were built. The first of these, wearing serial 311, took to the air for the first time on 23 June 1988 in the hands of MiG test pilot Tokhtar Aubakirov. It lacked the WCS and was intended mainly for deck-suitability trials, which were initially undertaken at the Nitka ground deck range in Saki (on the Crimean Peninsula), equipped with a full-scale ski-jump and operative arrestor system.

The first MiG-29K was then tested on the desk of the new Soviet aircraft carrier *Tbilisi* on 1 November 1989. It bore the brunt of carrier trials, amassing as many as thirty-five deck landings. In total, No. 311 logged as many as 312 test sorties and seventy-four deck landings during the test campaign. During its last sortie in the joint state testing and evaluation effort on the carrier deck, it suffered from an unintentional retraction of the landing gear in the parking position. The fuselage was seriously damaged, but it was eventually judged to be suitable for repair. After its restoration to an airworthy condition, the first MiG-29K prototype continued flying, making eight more sorties until its final grounding in August 1992.

The second prototype, serialed '312', was rolled out in 1990, enjoying a much better fate and a much longer life. Equipped with a full-standard mission avionics outfit, it had a very restricted carrier test-and-evaluation programme. No. 312 was mainly used in the extensive mission avionics and weapons trials conducted at Mikoyan OKB's base at Zhukovskiy, with twenty-nine sorties logged until March 1991 before joining the deck testing. In the event, it amassed only six landings on the deck of the

This is the first of two MiG-29K prototypes built in the late 1980s, used as the baseline for developing the new-style shipborne 'Fulcrums' built for the Russian and Indian naval air arms. It is seen here on 1 November 1989, just after its first landing on the deck of the Soviet Navy's first 'true' aircraft carrier, then known as *Tbilisi*, and now known as *Admiral Kurznetsov*. (*RSK MiG*)

sole Soviet/Russian aircraft carrier, renamed in 1992 as *Admiral Kuznetsov*, before the termination of the type's testing programme due to lack of funding.

The dissolution of the Soviet Union in late 1991 and early 1992 (and the following sharp cuts in the defence budget) meant that the MiG-29K programme was effectively frozen in favour of the development of the Su-27K. Despite the rapid demise of the programme, both MiG-29K prototypes remained active for use in various new testing initiatives. In the event, the first-generation MiG-29Ks (especially the second prototype, No. 312) have contributed to the development of the new-generation deck-capable 'Fulcrum', the so-called MiG-29K/KUB family with an improved airframe and an all-new avionics outfit, ordered by the Indian and Russian naval aviation services in the 2000s.

There was an unbuilt two-seater training derivative of the first-generation MiG-29K, dubbed 'MiG-29KU', which featured stepped tandem cockpits. It was mainly intended to train pilots for carrier-deck landings, with an instructor in the forward cockpit and a student in the rear one; both cockpits featured an unobstructed forward view on the landing approach to the ship's deck. As could be guessed, the termination of the original MiG-29K programme in 1992 led to the cancellation of the MiG-29KU project too; only a mock-up of the forward fuselage was built for wind-tunnel testing.

## The MiG-29 in Service with the Soviet Air Force

The MiG-29s entered squadron service with the VVS in 1983, with the first deliveries made to the 4th Combat Training and Aircrew Conversion centre in February 1983. The type's field trials were undertaken by the 234th Guards IAP (guards fighter aviation regiment) based at Kubinka, near Moscow, and the 968th IAP, based at Ros in Byelorussia, which took their first aircraft on strength in June and November 1983 respectively. Meanwhile, the 176th IAP at Tskhakaya (Georgia) took its first 'Fulcrums' on strength in 1984.

A total of 1,257 single-seat 'Fulcrums' of all versions were built until the early 1990s—nearly 800 of these were the 'flat-spined' 9-12 version, followed by 450 of the more advanced 9-13 and 9-13S. In addition, about 200 MiG-29UB two-seat versions rolled out at the Sokol plant in Gorky.

During the peak period of the MiG-29's Cold War service in 1991, the Soviet Air Force and the Soviet Naval Aviation Air Arm fielded a combined fleet of no fewer than 1,100 aircraft, equipping no fewer than twenty five VVS and two Soviet Naval Aviation regiments. The MiG-29 was deployed mostly in the air-to-air role, but there were at least two VVS regiments specialised in the fighter-bomber business in the late 1980s. The type was also operated by three conversion and combat training units, which had a total of three squadrons for conversion-to-type, advanced and aggressor training.

Following the collapse of the Soviet Union, marking the effective end of the Cold War, the VVS MiG-29 inventory was redistributed to the newly independent states. The largest fleet was inherited by Russia (considered to be the legal successor to the Soviet Union), accounting for some 460 airframes. Ukraine received a fleet of 237 aircraft, while Byelorussia got eighty-two more. Other former-Soviet states who inherited the MiG-29 include Moldova (thirty-four), Turkmenistan (twenty-two), Uzbekistan (thirty-six) and Kazakhstan (twenty-two).

The first use in anger of the 'Fulcrum' happened soon after the Cold War ended—ironically, it was in the ground-attack role. This happened in mid-1993, when the 115th Guards IAP of the Uzbekistani Air Force (stationed at Kokaity, Uzbekistan) was ordered to bomb the positions of the Islamist militants in neighbouring Tajikistan. The first attacks were against the Islamist position at Ordzhenekidzebade, near the Tajik capital of Dishanbe, using FAB-250M-62 free-fall high-explosive bombs as well as RBK-250/500 cluster bombs and KMGU bomblet dispensers in the following stages of the war, attacking targets in the mountain areas. There were no losses in the campaign, while the MiG-29 demonstrated fairly good and precise attack capabilities when employed to destroy small-sized ground targets in narrow mountain valleys.

Four Warsaw Pact states received the MiG-29 in the late 1980s—Germany got twenty-four aircraft (including four two-seaters), Czechoslovakia received twenty (including two two-seaters), Bulgaria got twenty-two (including four two-seaters) and Romania and Poland each took twelve examples.

There was also a significant MiG-29 export to unaligned states in the 1980s. India was the type's first export customer, ordering its aircraft as early as 1985 and receiving the first examples in late 1986. A total of sixty-five single-seat and five two-seat 'Fulcrums' were taken on strength, followed in 1994 by ten improved MiG-29SDs. Yugoslavia, in turn, was the first European MiG-29 operator, taking its 'Fulcrum' force on strength in 1987—a total of fourteen aircraft. These were used in combat for the first time five years later, again in the ground-attack role, in operations against Croatian military targets. Iraq was the second big MiG-29 customer outside the list of the Warsaw Pact countries, with forty-one aircraft taken; the first of these were delivered in the late 1980s. Syria followed suit with about twenty-two aircraft, followed by North Korea and Cuba.

Unlike its brethren, the MiG-29 had a much shorter and not-so-successful track record in air combat. Little is known about the combat use of the Iraqi MiG-29s during the later stages of the war, and there are some indication that these early production 'Fulcrum-As' proved quite unreliable as weapons system. The Iraqi MiG-29s proved ill-fitted to mount any resistance to the coalition air assets during operation *Desert Storm*, and as many as fourteen of them fled to Iran in 1991. Likewise, the Yugoslavian MiG-29s also proved unable to mount any effective resistance to coalition air attacks during the 1999 Kosovo War—as a result, four MiG-29s fell victim to the AIM-120 launched by USAF F-15Cs, a F-16CJ and a RNlAF F-16AM. Two more losses were attributed to 'friendly fire' accidents, while another five *Fulcrums* were destroyed on the ground. It is noteworthy that the Yugoslavian MiG-29s are believed to have seen some use in the ground-attack role during the war in Croatia in 1992, without suffering any losses.

The MiG-29 was also operated against ground targets in the brief and bloody war in the Pri-Dnestrovyan region of Moldova in the spring and summer months of 1992. The Moldavian Air Force MiG-29s dropped 250-kg (550-lb) high-explosive bombs on the position of the Pri-Dnestrovyan separatists, and one aircraft was claimed as shot down by a Russian Army SAM system.

The only instance of successful air-to-air use is the shooting down of two Cessna 337s by a Cuban Air Force MiG-29UB using R-60 AAMs in February 1996. The aircraft was also used in air-to-air combat during the war between Eritrea and Ethiopia in 1999. In this bloody war, the Eritrean MiG-29s did not fare well—at least one of them was shot down, and another is reported to have been heavily damaged by Ethiopian AF Su-27s flown by Russian mercenary pilots.

## MiG-31—The Ultimate Long-Range Interceptor

The MiG-31 is a long-range interceptor based on the overall aerodynamic configuration of the MiG-25, but features an all-new structure, systems and engines. It was the world's first production fighter to be fitted with a phased array radar, optimised for intercepting a wide range of air targets—from low-flying, air-launched cruise missiles (such as the Boeing AGM-86B) traveling at subsonic speed, to Mach 3 reconnaissance aircraft in the stratosphere, such as the Lockheed SR-71 Blackbird. The formidable air intercept performance (at least in theory) was granted by the combination of a high-performance air vehicle fitted with a powerful phased-array radar and long-range SARH air-to-air missiles.

During the Cold War, the MiG-31-equipped regiments were mainly stationed on a network of so-called 'IA PVO frontier' permanent bases, in fairly inhospitable conditions offered by the Soviet Union's extreme northern territories such as Monchegorsk, Talagi and Amaderma, replacing the faithful but obsolete Tu-128.

Design work on the new prototype at the Mikoyan OKB began after the Council of Ministers decree dated 24 May 1968. The MiG-31 (NATO reporting name 'Foxhound') was initially regarded as a deep upgrade of the MiG-25P, wearing the initial designation MiG-25MP. It was set to feature a much-improved range and speed performance compared to that of its predecessor; this was to be achieved by the introduction of new powerplant (consisting of two Solovyev D-30F afterburning turbofans) and a strengthened fuselage to allow for prolonged high-speed flight at low level.

The new MiG-25 derivative was designed as a pure air-defence fighter interceptor, and just like its predecessor it was never intended for manoeuvring close air combats because of its lack of any high-angle-of-attack capability. It is noteworthy that the MiG-31 was primarily intended to counter heavy bombers and low-flying, small-sized cruise missiles, while high-altitude/high-speed interception was regarded as a secondary role. With the introduction of air refuelling on the MiG-31DZ version, the overall combat capabilities went up, thanks to extended loitering time (reaching up to five hours) in an alert position.

The first indication that the IA PVO expected to field a vastly improved MiG-25 derivative was received in the West by a defector MiG-25 pilot, Capt. Victor Belenko, after his escape to Japan in a MiG-25P in September 1976. Three years later, in 1979, the US Department of Defence released the first drawings of the new-generation Soviet fighter-interceptor, based on satellite photos and info from some other intelligence sources. Finally, the first live air-to-air encounter happened in late 1985, when a Royal Norwegian Air Force F-16A pilot managed to take pictures of a MiG-31 flying off the Norwegian coast.

A design team at the Mikoyan OKB, led by Gleb Lozino-Lozinsky, was tasked with developing the new MiG-25 derivative, using the proven aerodynamic layout but introducing an all-new structural design and materials. The essential long-range requirement called for more fuel (exceeding 20,000 litres) and more fuel-efficient engines.

The D-30F was the only available option at the time; this is a medium-bypass afterburning turbofan, developed by the Perm-based Solovyov engine design company. The engine was made capable of operating effectively at low, medium and high altitude, combining the best features of the existing Soviet-era turbojets powering high-speed aircraft with the relatively low specific fuel consumption in low-altitude cruise flight. The new engine gave the MiG-31 a supersonic mission radius of 720 km (388 nm) on internal fuel and 1,400 km (755 nm) when fitted

The MiG-31 has a very robust airframe of stainless steel and aluminium, purposely designed to withstand high aerodynamic and thermal loads resulting from low-altitude supersonic flight. (*Author's collection*)

with external tanks. The airframe structure was built from a mix of stainless steel (some 50 per cent), aluminium (33 per cent) and titanium alloys (13 per cent), while the composite materials had a share of 1 per cent. The robust airframe was designed to withstand high aerodynamic and thermal loads resulting from a low-altitude supersonic flight.

However, the D-30F6 engines required all-new and considerably enlarged intakes to provide the needed airflow at all modes of operation, especially in low-altitude supersonic flight. The fuselage also saw a significant redesign in order to accommodate the increased fuel volume. Its new shape (in terms of the combination of the front fuselage and air intakes) also provide a fraction of the lift generated by the MiG-31's airframe—believed to be about a quarter of the overall lift. The wings, featuring 4° anhedral from roots and 40° sweepback on leading edge, had a brand-new three-spar structure of much greater stiffness, and the aerodynamic scheme introduced a small leading-edge root extension—with a sweepback of 70°—for enhanced controllability at high angles-of-attack, while the twin fins we re-configured. The wings also introduced four-section slats, two-section flaps and outboard flaperons, and had a fence above in line with the stores pylon. The new engines featured exhaust nozzles extending further back from the fin trailing edge. Tails surfaces were made all-swept, with thin outward-canted fins and dihedral tailplanes. The aircraft was fitted with relatively small forward-hinged airbrakes installed under the front of each engine trunk.

The D-30F6 engines are each rated at 93.1 kN (20,930 lb st. or 9,490 kgf) dry and 151.9 kN (34,170 lb st. or 15,484 kgf) with afterburning. In addition to the internal fuel volume of about 20,250 litres, the MiG-31 featured a provision for two underwing tanks (each accommodating 2,500 litres), but this configuration was rarely used in day-to-day operations.

## Two-Seat Cockpit

The pilot and the weapons control officer (WSO) were accommodated in individual cockpits, under rearward-hinged canopies. The rear cockpit accommodated the WSO, who was responsible for operating the sophisticated navigation system, sensor suite and long-range missiles. The WSO's cockpit was also equipped with a telescopic control stick, rudders and a retractable periscope. This allowed all operational MiG-31s to be used for pilot conversion and continuation training without the need to develop a dedicated training version. The rear canopy had a limited side glazing and blended into a shallow dorsal spine fairing. The WSO's cockpit was dominated by a large cathode-ray tube (CRT) tactical display, with rectangular displays alongside it.

There was another major structural feature—the rather unusual heavy-duty main undercarriage units. The MiG-31 introduced the two-wheel tandem layout for the main undercarriage units, with tandem mainwheels on a single oleo. The front wheels were mounted inboard of the oleo assembly, and the rear wheels

A look inside the pilot's cockpit of the MiG-31 (to the right), which is roomy but crammed with instruments and switches. The navigator-operator's cockpit is dominated by a large display for tactical and intercept information and has also removable controls, enabling the production-standard 'Foxhound' to be used for pilot conversion and continuation training. (RSK MiG)

were mounted outboard. This configuration was chosen by the design team in order to enable the fighter-interceptor to operate from unpaved strips, as each wheel is provided with its own track, rendering the undercarriage unit less likely to sink into soft soil. Additionally, when taxiing on snow the rear wheels were prevented from sleeping or skidding on ice compressed by the front wheels.

The powerful N007 Zaslon radar, designed by the Zhukvskiy-based Tikhomirov NIIP Company, was, in fact, the first Soviet airborne electronically-scanned radar set in front-line service. It was made capable of scanning an area out to 70° on each side of the centreline, and out to 70° above/60° below the nose. It could track ten targets and could simultaneously engage four of them with R-33 long-range SARH missiles. The MiG-31 could also be used as a min-AEW&C platform, providing guidance to other types of fighters with less-capable radars, in non-emitting mode, against multiple targets. The Zaslon radar had a reported detection range of 180 to 200 km (97 to 108 nm) against fighter-sized targets at medium and high altitude, and low-flying targets at 120 km (65 nm) in the forward hemisphere (head-on intercepts). During tail-on intercepts, the maximum detection range was 60 to 80 km (32 to 43 nm) against targets at medium and high altitude. The detection range of cruise missiles at ultra-low altitude in

During the Cold War, most of the MiG-31-equipped regiments were mainly stationed on a chain of frontier permanent bases in the Soviet Union's extreme northern and far-eastern territories. (*Andrey Zinchuk*)

head-on intercepts was quoted as about 60 km (32 nm). The radar's reliability performance—represented by the mean time between failures (MTBF)—was 55 hours. The N007 Zaslon was advertised as the first true Soviet look-down/shoot-down pulse-Doppler radar featuring digital data processing techniques. The mission computer was able to prioritise the tracked targets, select the four most dangerous ones, and then generate targeting data for a simultaneous attack on them (or any other four selected by the WSO), firing R-33 AAMs. The MiG-31 was also the first fighter to boast the highly-capable phased-array radar. No other aircraft, either in the Soviet Union or abroad, featured such technology in the mid–late 1970s. This new technology enabled the 'Foxhound' to track and fire at up to four targets at the same time; it was also able to look up at some of the tracked targets while looking down on others, and there were no restrictions to the missile launch region, so it could fire at widely-spaced targets.

The N007 Zaslon radar was provided with extensive resistance to jamming in order for the MiG-31 to be able to operate effectively in an environment of dense electronic countermeasures; it featured a pretty good electronic counter-countermeasures capability (ECCM). This was enhanced by the use of targeting options provided by the digital datalink equipment, which passes information on targets seen by the radars of other MiG-31s in the group as well as by airborne or ground-based early warning and control systems. In case of encountering heavy jamming, the radar's processing circuits could use special algorithms to recover missing target information by employing a set of kinetic and triangulation methods. As MiG-31 pilots shared, passive jamming with chaff has no effect at all on the radar's target detection and discrimination capability.

The radar was complemented by the 8TP retractable infrared and search (IRST) sensor under the nose, integrated with the radar through the mission computer (as it is also implemented on the MiG-29) in order to provide an additional degree of ECCM capability. It can detect air targets at up to 50 km (27 nm) at high altitude, scanning through 60° left and right, and 6° up and 15° down relative to the aircraft's centerline. In addition to target detection, the 8TP can cue the seekers of the R-40TD and R-60 heat-seeking air-to-air missiles.

The MiG-31 was also made capable of performing so-called 'semi-autonomous group missions' with occasional hand-offs from ground-controlled intercept (GCI) stations. This mode of operation was particularly useful in huge areas without dense ground radar coverage, where four-ship MiG-31 formations were routinely used to cover the gaps in the radar cover. This situation was a common occurrence in the extreme northern territories in the Soviet Union. A group of four 'Foxhounds', performing this semi-autonomous patrol missions with their radars in co-ordinated search mode pattern, was able to cover a strip 600 to 800 km

The last MiG-31Bs were rolled out in Gorky (renamed as 'Nizhny Novgorod') in 1994, with the total 'Foxhound' production numbering about 500 aircraft. (*RSK MiG—Sergey Kuznetsov*)

(324 to 431 nm) wide. This method of operation is especially useful to counter mass attacks without relying on ground radars for target detection. A group commander could perform target distribution among the aircraft in his group and could coordinate the operation with several other groups in the same area, covering a vast airspace, performing target hand-off from one aircraft to another in a better attack position, or launching missiles at the most threatening target.

## Weapons

The MiG-31's primary weapon was the all-new R-33 SARH missile, using inertial guidance in the initial stage of flight to extend range (with mid-course correction provided by the launch platform). Four R-33s were carried, semi-recessed, on AKU-410 ejector racks under the belly. A lock-on-after-launch weapon, the R-33 initially flew towards the assigned target by following a lofting trajectory in a bid to extend range (climbing out to 30,000 m [98,400 feet] and then diving towards the target on a ballistic curve). After launch it utilised inertial guidance (10 to 20 per cent of the total range to target) and then switched to the semi-active homing mode. When fired head-on against a high-altitude target, the R-33's maximum range was 120–130 km (65–70 nm). This guidance method enabled the missile to be re-targeted while in flight (before activation of the SARH seeker), in case more

The large R-33 missile pictured here is ready to be loaded onto a MiG-31. It had a launch weight of 491 kg (223 lb), and the expanding-rod warhead weighed 55 kg (121 lb); its maximum range in head-on attack against high-altitude targets is 130 km (70 nm). (*Andrey Zinchuk*)

dangerous targets popped out. There was also an option for the R-33 to be fired from one MiG-31 and terminal guidance to be provided by another in a more favourable position. The probability of a hit when employed to shoot down manoeuvring targets, turning with up to 4-G, was advertised to be between 0.6 and 0.8. It was capable of destroying targets flying between 50 and 28,000 m (164 and 91,840 feet) at a maximum speed of 3,700 km/h (1,996 kt). The R-33's launch weight was 491 kg (1,083 lb), and the expanding-rod warhead weighed 55 kg (121 lb).

The R-33 was complemented by the R-40TD (AA-6 'Acrid') carried on underwing pylons, designed for use in situations when SARHs are rendered ineffective. When carrying the R-40TD, the MiG-31 can be armed with only three R-33s; this is because the place that would be occupied by the fourth is instead used to accommodate a pod containing equipment to enable the use of the R-40TD. The underwing pylons could be also fitted with twin-round launch rails for the short-range, IR-homing R-60 or R-60M missiles (AA-8 'Aphid').

The MiG-31 also boasts an internal cannon, the 23-mm GSh-23-6; a six-barrel Gatling-gun-type with a rate of fire of 8,000 rpm and 260 rounds, it was mounted in a fairing scabbed on to the side of the starboard engine nacelle, just above the main wheel well.

The mission avionics suite also incorporated the APD-518 secure digital datalink and the BAN-75 command datalink. The autonomous long-range operating capabilities became possible thanks to the integration of the sophisticated NK-25 navigation system, including a duplicated IS-1-72A INS, an A-331 short-range aid to navigation, an A-723 long-range aid to navigation and the Tropik long-range aid to navigation.

The other avionics suite components included the SPO-15SL Beryoza RWR, SRO-2P IFF transponder and SRZ-2P IFF interrogator as well as an R-862 UHF radio, an R-864 HF radio and a BAN-75 secure digital link.

## A Protracted and Painful Testing Effort

Two prototypes, designated as the Ye-155MP, were built at Mikoyan OKB's own workshops in Moscow. The first of these, designated 83/1 and wearing the appropriate serial '831', took to the air for its first flight on 16 September 1975, in the capable hands of Mikoyan OKB's chief pilot Alexander Fedotov. The second, No. '832', flown by Pyotr Ostapenko, featured the full mission avionics set and built-in cannon, and made its first flight in May 1976. The two prototypes were later joined by several pre-production examples. In the event, the very complex MiG-31 had a protracted and problematic test and evaluation programme, and as a result its in-service introduction was delayed in comparison to the original plans.

By mid-1977, Sokol built the first two pre-series interceptors for participation in the flight test effort. These had many differences compared to the design of the prototypes, such as increased-span flaps and a reduced-area tailplane, which had altered deflection angles. The airbrake shape and area were also altered.

Two MiG-31 prototypes (designated as the Ye-155MP) were built at Mikoyan OKB's own workshops in Moscow; the first of these was serialled '831', and made its maiden flight on 16 September 1975 with the Mikoyan OKB's chief pilot, Alexander Fedotov, behind the controls. (*RSK MiG*)

Production of the MiG-31 was launched at the GAZ-21 at Gorky in 1977, with the type wearing the internal designation I-01. (*RSK MiG*)

The Ye-155MP was submitted for its joint state testing effort in May 1977, which also saw the use of several testbeds to evaluate the mission suite components—including two Tu-104s and one MiG-21, MiG-25, MiG-25PU and MiG-25RB.

The most complex evaluation during the effort was the flight experiment made on 15 February 1978, proving the aircraft's capability to detect, acquire and track as many as ten targets. The aerial targets used were represented by the M-16 (the remotely-piloted Tu-16 bomber) and M-28 (the remotely-controlled Il-28), flying in a widely-spaced formation towards the interceptor (the distance between the outermost targets was about 150 km (81 km)) and in a wide altitude range. On 28 August 1977, a 'Foxhound' demonstrated a simultaneous engagement of four aerial targets, with R-33 missiles destroying all of them.

Phase A of the type's joint state testing effort was officially completed in December 1978, and it resulted in issuing the so-called 'preliminary conclusion' for launching the new fighter in full-scale production at GAZ-21 in Gorky.

Compared to the pre-series examples, the production-standard aircraft sported a number of design changes—such as four-section slats, the strengthening of the wings structure by adding a third spar, and the relocation of the air brakes.

## Launch into Production

The flight testing and evaluation effort was fully completed in December 1980, while on 6 May 1981 the new air intercept system was commissioned by the IA PVO. Production of the MiG-31 was launched at the GAZ-21 at Gorky in 1977, wearing the internal designation I-01. The production-standard aircraft differed from the prototypes in some minor details, such as altered undercarriage

The first production-standard MiG-31s were rolled out in 1977, and the initial deliveries to the IA PVO took place in 1980. (*RSK MiG*)

doors and airbrakes, overwing fences and LEREXes. The production-standard 'Foxhounds' received improved radars and D-30F-6s engines. The first production examples were delivered to the IA PVO in 1980.

The MiG-31DZ (I-01DZ) was an improved 'Foxhound' derivative featuring a retractable air-to-air refuelling probe in an effort to gain more range and endurance. The need for a longer-legged air interceptor became evident when the MiG-31 saw use for escorting maritime reconnaissance and anti-submarine aircraft off the Kola Peninsula, alongside the Norwegian coast.

In the early 1980s the Soviet air arms initiated the mass introduction of air refuelling systems, and the MiG-31 was among the several new fighter and bomber types earmarked to receive a refuelling probe. The MiG-31's probe assembly was made semi-retractable, installed in front of the cockpit and offset to port. The flight control system was also modified in order to provide the enhanced stabilisation mode needed for fine control inputs during refuelling contacts. The first MiG-31 equipped with an air refuelling probe also received long-range navigation equipment, and was involved in a number of long-range test and research flights. In total, forty-five MiG-31DZs were originally built between 1990 and 1991.

The probe-equipped MiG-31 became the first Soviet fighter to fly over the North Pole on 30 June 1987. Flown by Mikoyan OKB test pilot Roman Taskayev and WSO Leonid Popov, its route stretched from Monchegorsk, on the Kola Peninsula, via the North Pole to Anadir, on the Chukotka Peninsula, situated deep in the Soviet far eastern territories; the flight necessitated two air refuellings. On its route back, the MiG-31 flew non-stop to Moscow on a route stretching along the entire northern coast of the Arctic Ocean; this took nine hours. This particular flight was used to test the MiG-31's sophisticated navigation suite in different conditions, including in the presence of magnetic anomalies in extreme northern latitudes.

The MiG-31B (I-01B) was a further-refined version with an air refuelling probe and an improved N007 Zaslon-A radar system, endowed with better processing and ECCM capabilities in addition to the upgraded R-33S long-range AAMs and an A-723 long-range navigation system. This last derivative was launched in production in 1990. Additionally, a number of early-production MiG-31s were brought to this standard during their overhauls in Gorky, receiving the new designation MiG-31BS. The last examples of fifty newly-built MiG-31Bs were rolled out in 1994, and the total 'Foxhound' production numbered about 500 aircraft.

There was a dedicated export version of the 'Foxhound' developed in the early 1990s, designated as the MiG-31E. Conceived as a slightly downgraded version of the MiG-31B, it featured sanitised ECCM features, a less-capable radar and R-33 missiles. A prototype (serialed '904') was tested and used for marketing purposes, being displayed at several air shows—the first of which was in Paris in June 1991. China, Syria and Iran were hinted to be the most likely customers for the MiG-31, but in the event no contracts were signed. The multi-role MiG-31F was also

The MiG-31DZ (I-01DZ) boasts a retractable air-to-air refuelling probe in an effort to gain more range and endurance. (*RSK MiG*)

The export version of the 'Foxhound' was designated as the MiG-31E; it was, in fact, a slightly downgraded version of the MiG-31B, with a less-capable radar, downgraded ECCM resistance and the old R-33 missiles. In the event, it has never found export customers. (*RSK MiG*)

The MiG-31B was a further-refined version featuring an air refuelling probe and an improved N007 radar system; it was also endowed with better processing and ECCM capabilities in addition to the upgraded R-33S long-range AAMs and an A-723 long-range navigation system. (*RSK MiG*)

offered for export, featuring the ability to use air-to-ground guided weapons such as anti-radar missiles (represented by the Kh-31P) as well as bombs and missiles with TV/laser guidance—such as the Kh-29T or Kh-29L missiles. Its maximum take-off weight was increased to 50,000 kg (110,200 lb), allowing the weapons load to reach 9,000 kg (19,840 lb), carried on six hardpoints.

## MiG-31B Specification

| Dimensions:<br>Wing span<br>Maximum length<br>Height | 13.46 m<br>22.69 m<br>6.15 m |
| --- | --- |
| Wing area: | 61.6 m$^2$ |
| Weights:<br>Empty operating<br>Maximum take-off | 21,820 kg<br>46,200 kg |
| Performance:<br>Max level speed at sea level<br>Max level speed at high level<br>Max operating Mach number<br>Supersonic cruise speed<br>Subsonic cruise Mach number<br>Landing speed<br>Practical ceiling, clean<br>G-limit<br>Climb time to 10,000 m<br>Combat radius at Mach 2.35<br>Ferry range with external tanks<br>Flight endurance with external tanks<br>Landing distance<br>Take-off distance | 1,500 km/h<br>3,000 km/h<br>2.83<br>2,500 km/h<br>0.85<br>280 km/h<br>20,600 m<br>+5<br>7.9 minutes<br>720 km<br>3,330 km<br>3 hrs 36 min.<br>800 m<br>1,200 m |

## The Anti-Satellite 'Foxhound'

The MiG-31D (also known as *Item 07*) was a derivative modified in 1987 to be used as a launch platform for an anti-satellite missile. The development of the system was initiated by a Soviet Council of Ministers decree dated 6 January 1983. The first of the two prototypes was built in Gorky in late 1986, and it took to the air for the first time on 17 January 1987 in the hands of Mikoyan OKB test pilot Aviard Fastovets and test navigator Leonid Popov. The second prototype followed suit on 28 April 1988, flown by Anatoly Kvochur and Leonid

The MiG-31D (known also as *Item 07*) was a derivative modified in 1987 to be used as a launch platform for an anti-satellite missile, which still remains a top-secret project. (*Author's collection*)

Popov. The factory testing effort of the new MiG-31 derivative was completed in the early 1990s, and they were relocated to the Sari-Shagan range in Kazakhstan in readiness to commence anti-satellite missile trials; however, these trials never happened as the missile was not ready for test-firing before the programme was terminated.

The standard weapons system of the two MiG-31Ds involved in the programme was removed, with the radar replaced by a 200-kg (441-lb) balance weight and the radome replaced by a metallic cone; the missile recesses were faired over. Both aircraft received modifications to carry a single advanced anti-satellite missile—something like the USAF's F-15/ASM-135A ASAT system. Suspended under the centerline, it was to be launched at high altitude and speed; there are reports that the launch speed was to be 3,000 km/h (1,618 kt) at 17,000 m (55.760 feet). In order to improve the high-speed yaw stability performance, the anti-satellite derivative received new wingtip fairings with triangular endplate fins. The anti-satellite missile, developed by the Vympel design bureau, was designated as the 79M6 and wore the name 'Kontakt'. It was designed to destroy the target with a direct hit, using only the kinetic effect of its warhead.

## The MiG-31M—A Mega-Interceptor

The MiG-31M (internal Mikoyan OKB designation I-255) had the distinction of being the most advanced 'Foxhound' derivative, with a reworked airframe, upgraded D-30F-6M engines and an all-new mission avionics suite for longer-range intercepts and missile firings. It was designed around the Zaslon-M enhanced radar and the K-37 long-range AAM, with a claimed maximum range of 300 km (162 nm). In addition, it was made able to carry up to four new-generation R-77 AAMs fitted with active radar-homing seekers.

Externally, the MiG-31M can be easily distinguished from the baseline 'Foxhound' thanks to the one-piece rounded windscreen, the all-metal rear canopy with small side windows, rounded wingtips, taller fins with larger root extensions and the enlarged dorsal spine (accommodating more fuel). The nose section contained a new shape in order to provide more lift in cruise flight, while the nose was dropped by 7° for an improved pilot view forward. The inflight-refuelling probe was moved to starboard and the new 42P IRST was made non-retractable. The gun was deleted. The seventh MiG-31M prototype was fitted with fixed wingtip pods of unknown purpose, featuring triangular upper and lower finlets. The engines were more spaced out than those of the original, and also canted outwards.

The new wing layout incorporated enlarged LERXes with curved leading edges, while the rudders featured increased chord. The new equipment, heavier missiles and the additional fuel increased the maximum take-off weight to 52,000 kg (114,640 lb), but it retained the speed and altitude performance of the original 'Foxhound' almost unchanged.

A total of six MiG-31M prototypes were built at Gorky. The first of them, serialed '051', was the first flying example, which lacked radar and other mission systems. Intended for testing the new aerodynamic features, '051' was built in 1984 as an initiative project by Gorky plant and it took to the air for the first time on 21 December 1985 in the capable hands of Mikoyan OKB test pilot Boris Orlov and WSO Leonid Popov. This aircraft, serialed '051', had a short life, being lost during a test flight on 9 August. Another example was lost shortly afterwards. Both of these crashed during flight tests conducted by the Russian Air Force's Flight Test Institute in Akhtubinsk.

The six K-37 ultra-long range AAMs were accommodated in three side-by-side recesses, each housing a pair of missiles. The rear cockpit lacked the control stick, rudders, engine throttles and forward-looking periscope; it therefore could not be used by an instructor pilot during conversion or continuation training.

The aircraft's first flight tests showed that the extra 1,500 litres of fuel accommodated in the redesigned airframe changed the position of its centre of gravity, worsening stability and controllability. The MiG-31M completed its flight-testing effort in April 1994. The final exam in this effort was the launch of an K-37 AAM, which hit an aerial target drone 300 km (162 nm) away. Despite this, the type was not launched into serial production because Russia was suffering from a financial crisis at the time, with all large-scale military procurement programmes being terminated.

The most advanced 'Foxhound' version, dubbed 'MiG-31M', had a reworked airframe with larger internal fuel capacity, upgraded D-30F-6M engines and an all-new mission avionics suite for longer-range intercepts and missile firings; however, it never progressed into production. This is the second prototype. (*RSK MiG*)

The MiG-31M introduced a single-piece rounded windscreen, the all-metal rear canopy with small-sized side windows, rounded wingtips, taller fins with larger root extensions and an enlarged dorsal spine accommodating more fuel. The new forward fuselage shape generated additional lift in cruise flight and the nose was dropped by 7° for an improved pilot view forward. (*Author's collection*)

## The Su-27—Sukhoi's Masterpiece

A heavy fighter with origins dating back to the early 1970s, the Su-27 and Su-30 family (NATO codename 'Flanker') are widely known as capable heavyweight fighters that achieved remarkable export success in the 1990s and 2000s. At least 180 examples have been sold to China (plus local assembly and production), 272 to India, forty-four to Algeria and twenty-eight to Vietnam, while four other countries—Malaysia, Uganda, Venezuela and Indonesia—also procured either newly-built two-seaters or a combination of single-seaters and two-seaters (as was the case with Indonesia), totalling no fewer than fifty-eight examples.

Just like the MiG-29, the much larger and heavier Su-27 traces its origins back to 1969, when the Soviet Air Force outlined its initial set of technical and tactical requirements for developing a new-generation air-superiority fighter, viewed as a counter to the US Air Force F-X programme that eventually resulted in the development of the McDonnell Douglas (now Boeing) F-15 Eagle. The main objective of the Soviet new-generation fighter programme was to develop a capable heavyweight fighter that was well-suited to tight manoeuvring, with a huge internal volume and the ability to carry a large number of long and short-range air-to-air missiles. Its overall air-superiority performance was required to be at least 10 per cent better than that of the F-15.

The first prototype, designated as the T10-1, made its maiden flight on 20 May 1977, powered by interim AL-21F-3 turbojets, in the capable hands of Vladimir Ilyshin, Sukhoi's legendary chief test pilot. It was followed by three more examples. These prototypes featured curved wingtips and tailfins mounted above engine bays, while the engine nacelles were widely separated, ending in a flat beaver tail. This configuration promised low drag and high lift and had sharp leading-edge extensions running forward from the wingroot. The main undercarriage doors, opening forward and downward, were also used as airbrakes. The aircraft was designed from the outset to be unstable, provided with a fly-by-wire control system in the pitch axis for improved manoeuvrability.

On 7 July 1978 the second prototype used in the flight tests, T10-2, crashed, with the loss of the pilot, Evgeniy Solovyov; the aircraft disintegrated in the air due to pilot-induced oscillation and resultant excessive G-forces.

The new AL-31F engine, purposely designed for the T10, was installed on the third prototype, T10-3, which took to the air for the first time on 23 August 1979.

In a bid to accelerate the T10 test programme, five more pre-series T10 aircraft were built at the Komsomolsk-on-Amur plant (GAZ-126). However, early on in the flight test programme it became clear that the original T10 was a flawed design with a notably inferior aerodynamic performance when pitted against its US rival and the designer's benchmark—the F-15.

## Urgent Redesign Effort

As a consequence of the aircraft's poor performance, the leadership of the Sukhoi OKB undertook the bold step of radically redesigning the underperforming original T10 in an effort to cure its most serious aerodynamic shortcomings. The end result of this enormous effort was the virtually all-new T10S production configuration, the first prototype of which took to the air for the first time on 20 April 1981—again in the capable hands of Vladimir Ilyshin.

Amid a compressed, stressful and rather troublesome flight test and evaluation programme, the T10S was cleared to enter series production at the Komsomolsk-on-Amur's GAZ-126 (named after Yury Gagarin) in 1982, under the in-service designation Su-27 (NATO 'Flanker-B'). The development was not without major setbacks, as the T10S-1 prototype was lost on 3 September 1981, with Sukhoi OKB chief test pilot Vladimir Ilyshin being able to eject safely; on 23 December the same year another prototype, T10S-2, crashed, killing Sukhoi OKB pilot Alexander Komarov.

The 'Flanker-B' entered front-line regimental service with the IA PVO in late 1984, lagging behind its US F-15A and F-16A rivals by eight and five years respectively. However, its formal acceptance in Soviet Air Force (VVS) and Soviet Air Defence Force (PVO) service as a fully-fledged combat-capable weapons system did not take place until August 1990, following completion of the type's

The first Su-27 prototype, designated as the T10-1, made its maiden flight on 20 May 1977, with Vladimir Ilyshin, Sukhoi's legendary chief test pilot, at the controls. (*Sukhoi OKB*)

Early on in the flight test programme it was discovered that the original T10 was underachieving due to flawed aerodynamic performance, making it vastly inferior to the McDonnell Douglas F-15 Eagle. (*Boris Lilov*)

exhaustive testing and evaluation programme. The first Soviet unit to take the new fighter on strength was the 22nd IAP of the IA PVO fighter force, based at Dzemgi Airfield, just next to the Komsomolsk-on-Amur factory.

From mid-1989 IA PVO fighter regiments began taking the Su-27P (T10P) on strength, a 'sanitised' derivative that was stripped of its capability to employ air-to-ground weapons. This measure was deliberately undertaken by the Soviet military in a bid for the PVO 'Flankers' to be excluded from the number of ground-attack aircraft falling under the limits of the Conventional Forces in Europe (CFE) Treaty; a proportion of the Su-27s built before 1989 were similarly modified during their major overhauls.

## Sensors and Weapons

The basic Su-27/UBs and their Su-27SK/UBK export derivatives were equipped with the Tikhomirov-NIIP N001 and N001E Myech radar respectively. It uses a twist-Cassegrain antenna and can detect large and small-sized fighters in head-on, high-altitude engagements at 110–120 km (60–65 nm) and 80–100 km (43–54 nm) for the Russian Air Force and export versions respectively, while tracking is conducted at 80–90 km (43–48.5 nm) and 65–85 km (35–46 nm) respectively.

The second on-board targeting system is the OEPS-27, integrating an infra-red search and track (IRST) sensor and a laser rangefinder slaved to the radar. The OEPS-27 has a claimed high-altitude detection range of 50 km (27 nm) against a receding target (in tail-on attack) with engine at military power; the head-on detection range against a high-altitude target with afterburner on is between 90–100 km (48–54 nm), while the system's tracking range is around 70 per cent of the maximum detection range. The OEPS-27 is advertised as being particularly useful for emission-free (stealthy) head-on and tail-on intercepts, enabling the employment of both the R-73 or R-27T/ET infra-red homing missiles. However, the system is restricted to employment in visual meteorological conditions (VMC) only.

The third targeting system is represented by the Shchel-3UM helmet-mounted sight, slaved to the radar/IRST and R-73 missile seeker heads for accelerated cueing and to achieve a faster firing solution. Its angular coverage is 60° left and right, 60° up and 14° down.

The Su-27's self-protection suite includes the SPO-15LM radar-warning receiver (RWR), the L005 Sorbtsiya (or the L203/L204 Gardeniya on the export 'Flanker-B/C') two-pod electronic countermeasures (ECM) system and APP-50 chaff/flare dispensers. The RWR, utilising sensor antennas on the sides of the air intakes and the tail boom, features 360° horizontal coverage and 30° up and down in elevation. Its accuracy in providing information about the direction of enemy radars 'painting' the aircraft is claimed to be within 10° in the forward hemisphere and 45° in the rear hemisphere. A 1970s-vintage device, the RWR has often been described by pilots as non-flexible and somewhat oversensitive in a dense emitting environment, and incapable of full operation in certain complex

Fourth Generation

The extensively-redesigned T-10S-1 prototype took to the air for the first time on 20 April 1981, again flown by Vladimir Ilyshin. (*Sukhoi OKB*)

During the Cold War, the Soviet forces fielded no less than seventeen Su-27-equipped air defence regiments in addition to four regiments assigned to the frontal aviation force. Furthermore, the 'Flanker' was also operated by two combat training and aircrew conversion centres and one air display squadron. (*Andrey Zinchuk*)

A Russian Air Force pilot wearing the ZSh-7 helmet, siting in the cockpit of his well-decorated 'Flanker'. (*Andrey Zinchuk*)

situations. For instance, the RWR cannot operate properly when the radar and the on-board jammer are employed at the same time. The SPO-15LM is further characterised as being ill-equipped to issue warnings of a lock-on by enemy fighter radars operating in the track-while-scan mode.

The basic Su-27 was provided with a total of ten hardpoints for missile carriage, while the Su-27SK built for export has twelve. Two of the hardpoints, located on the wingtips, are typically occupied by the two-pod ECM system, or alternatively they can carry the R-73 missile.

The remaining eight on the Su-27/P/UB and ten on the Su-27SK can be used in various combinations, but most often accommodate four R-73 WVR combat missiles and up to four R-27R/ER or R-27T/ET BVR combat missiles.

The basic BVR weapons in the 1980s were the SARH R-27R and IR-homing R-27T (R-27R1 and R-27T1 derivatives, while in 1987 they were complemented by the extended-range R-27ER and R-27ET (R-27ER1 and R-27ET1 derivatives cleared for used by export 'Flankers'). The baseline R-27R, using inertial guidance with datalink correction after launch and then switching to SARH, was often described as being a short-legged BVR weapon that did not allow the full use of the Su-27's radar detection/acquisition range, especially in high-level, head-on engagements. Soviet air combat manuals describe its high-level range as being limited to 42.5 km (23 nm) when fired against fighter aircraft in head-on encounters. The R-27R weighs 253 kg (556 lb) and is described as being capable of destroying targets travelling at a maximum speed of 3,500 km/h (1,891 kt), flying at altitudes from 20 to 20,000 m (66 to 88,560 feet), while the maximum altitude separation between the launch platform and the target is 10,000 m (32,800 feet). The warhead—used in all 'Alamo' versions—is of the expanding rod type, weighs 39 kg (72 lb) and is detonated using either radar or contact fuse.

The R-27T is a lock-on-before-launch weapon with an IR seeker, described as having a shorter maximum range than the R-27R. The R-27ER/ET derivatives introduced in 1987 (export versions were sold to China in the mid-1990s) feature the same SARH and IR seekers as the baseline versions, but they are powered by a larger rocket motor that increases the range of the missiles and (more importantly) renders them notably faster in the end-game phase. The R-27ER's maximum range when fired against fighter-type targets at high altitude is 66 km (36 nm), while that of the R-27ET is 52 km (28 nm). It is noteworthy that the availability of the R-27T and its boosted R-27ET derivative provided the 'Flanker' pilot with a useful advantage in BVR scenarios during the pre-AMRAAM era, and when attacking other SARH-armed opponents armed with the AIM-7 Sparrow or the MATRA R530. It was a genuine 'fire and forget' weapon (albeit limited to VMC use), enabling the Su-27 to initiate missile-evading manoeuvring immediately after launch.

In contrast, following the R-27R/ER launch the 'Flanker' pilot is permitted to change course by up to 60° (with an optimum turn angle of 40°) by executing the so-called 'tactical turn', since the target is required to be kept within the radar's gimbal limits and lock-on maintained until impact. Russian air combat analysts assert that in duel situations the 'tactical turn' would reduce the enemy's BVR missile range by 30–40 per cent when both fighters fired at each other simultaneously, but its usefulness against AMRAAM-equipped opponents is doubtful.

The R-73 is an all-aspect WVR missile employing a compact IR seeker that makes use of digital signal processing for better ECM resistance, and it has a detector cooled by liquid nitrogen. Its off-boresight capability, up to 45° in all directions, is considerably better than that of the previous generation of Soviet WVR missiles, and it boasts an impressive 60°-per-second line-of-sight tracking rate. The missile's combined aerodynamic/thrust vector control makes it remarkably agile; the maximum G-force of the launch aircraft can reach nine units as it can engage targets manoeuvring at up to 12-G. The weapon weighs 105 kg (231 lb) and combines a radar proximity fuse with an expanding-rod warhead weighing 7.4 kg (16.3 lb) and providing a lethal radius of 3.5 m (22 feet). The R-73's maximum range in tail-on engagements at low level is 2.2 km (1.2 nm), while at high level this increases to 12 km (6.5 nm); in head-on encounters at high altitude, maximum range can reach 30 km (16.1 nm).

The Su-27's GSh-301 30-mm cannon is built into the starboard side of the forward fuselage, with the end of the barrel next to the pilot's cockpit. The gun is provided with 150 rounds. It provides five to six seconds of continuous firing of highly destructive 390-g projectiles at a rate of fire of 25–30 rounds per second. It is recommended that in order to achieve a sufficiently high probability of a hit, the gun should be fired at the shortest minimum distance possible—said to be between 50–200 m (160–600 feet)—while the maximum useful distance is 600 m (1,900 feet).

## Su-27 and Su-27SK Specification

|  | Su-27 | Su-27SK |
| --- | --- | --- |
| Dimensions: | | |
| Wing span | 14.70 m | 14.70 m |
| Wing span with wingtip R-73 AAMs | 14.95 m | 14,95 m |
| Length without probe | 21.935 m | 21.935 m |
| Height | 5.93 m | 5.93 m |
| Wing area: | 62.037 m$^2$ | 62.037 m$^2$ |
| Weights: | | |
| Empty operating | 16,380 kg | 16,380 kg |
| Normal take-off | 23,140 kg | 23,140 kg |
| Maximum take-off | 28,300 kg | 33,000 kg |
| Performance: | | |
| Max level speed at sea level | 1,400 km/h | 1,400 km/h |
| Max level speed at high level | 2,300 km/h | 2,500 km/h |
| Max operating Mach number | 2.17 | 2.35 |
| Landing speed | 225 km/h | 225 km/h |
| Practical ceiling, clean | 18,500 m | 18,500 m |
| G limits | +9/-3 | +9/-3 |
| Rate of climb at low level | 330 m/s | 330 m/s |
| Take-off distance | 650-700 m | 650-700 m |
| Landing distance | 620-700 m | 620-700 m |
| Range at high altitude clean | 3,720 km | 3,680 km |
| Range with 10 AAMs | 2,800 km | 2,800 km |
| Operational radius at high altitude | 1,090 km | 1,560 km |
| Operational radius at low altitude | 420 km | 420 km |

## The Two-Seater

The Su-27UB (NATO 'Flanker-C') fully combat-capable two-seater, also built in prototype form at Komsomolsk-on-Amur, took to the air for the first time on 7 March 1985 in the capable hands of Sukhoi OKB test pilot Nikolay Sadovnikov. It was followed by a small batch of pre-series aircraft for testing and evaluation, with the type entering serial production at the aircraft factory in Irkutsk (now known as the Irkutsk Aviation Plant, part of the Irkut Corporation) the year after, and the first production example taking to the air in September 1986. The 'Flanker-C' retained most of the single-seater's design and systems unchanged, with the insertion of a second cockpit only slightly reducing fuel capacity.

The Su-27's mass production for the Soviet/Russian Air Force ended in 1992; the Komsomolsk-on-Amur aviation plant continued to manufacture single-seat 'Flankers' for export customers until 2004. (*Andrey Zinchuk*)

## Su-27UB Specification

| | |
|---|---|
| Dimensions: | |
| Wing span | 14.70 m |
| Wing span with wingtip R-73 AAMs | 14.95 m |
| Length without probe | 21.935 m |
| Height | 6.357 m |
| Wing area: | 62.037 m$^2$ |
| Weights: | |
| Empty operating | 17,900 kg |
| Normal take-off | 24,110 kg |
| Maximum take-off | 30,450 kg |
| Maximum take-off for last production series | 33,500 kg |
| Performance: | |
| Max level speed at sea level | 1,300 km/h |
| Max level speed at high level | 2,150 km/h |
| Landing speed | 230 km/h |
| Practical ceiling, clean | 17,500 m |
| G limits | +8.5/-3 |
| Rate of climb at low level | 330 m/s |
| Take-off distance | 750-800 m |
| Landing distance | 650-700 m |
| Range at high altitude clean | 3,000 km |

## The 'Flanker' in Service

The agile, fast-climbing, well-armed and long-legged heavyweight fighter was initially taken on strength with IA PVO regiments, and the VVS (Frontal Aviation) arm followed suit several years later. By the end of the Cold War, and just before the Soviet Union broke up in late 1991, the combined 'Flanker-B/C' inventory in Soviet service (both PVO and VVS arms) numbered just over 400 examples, including some 100 two-seaters. These equipped no fewer than seventeen IA PVO fighter regiments, plus four VVS front-line fighter regiments, two combat training and aircrew conversion centres, and one air display squadron.

The type's production for domestic use ended in 1992 (with the exception of a batch of eight newly-built single-seaters, which were handed over to the Russian Air Force in 1998).

By 2001 the Russian air arm had in excess of 300 airframes on strength, while in early 2013 some 180 of these remained in active service, with no fewer than ten front-line and two training squadrons, one display team and a small test and evaluation unit. The days of the vast majority of non-upgraded 'Flanker-Bs' in Russian Air Force front-line service seem to be numbered, however, as the type is set to be gradually superseded by both the Su-30SM and Su-35S between 2014 and 2020.

After the break-up of the Soviet Union in 1991, the 'Flanker-B/C' was also taken on strength by the newly-created Ukrainian Air Force, which inherited sixty-seven examples, while twenty-three more Su-27P/UBs were inherited by Belarus (the last survivors of which were withdrawn from use in December 2012), and thirty-one more were taken by Uzbekistan. Meanwhile, Kazakhstan received twenty-six ex-Russian 'Flankers' between 1996 and 2001, exchanged for Tu-95MS strategic bombers.

## First-Generation Exports

The Su-27SK is the baseline export derivative of the 'Flanker-B', provided with enhanced air-to-ground capabilities and developed in 1991–1992 for China's People's Liberation Army Air Force (PLAAF). It features a strengthened fuselage and undercarriage to allow a maximum take-off weight (MTOW) of 33,000 kg (72,750 lb), an increase of some 5,000 kg (11,020 lb). The Su-27SK was therefore made capable of operating with a full fuel load and maximum weapons load. The export 'Flanker-B' derivative was provided with twelve rather than ten hardpoints for up to 8,000 kg (17,537 lb) of weapons, including free-fall bombs, rockets and gun pods, while the wiring and panels enabling the use of nuclear bombs were stripped out. The aircraft also had a downgraded radar (N001E), communication suite, datalink, electronic countermeasures system (Gardeniya instead of Sorbtsiya jamming pods) and a modified IFF system.

The air-to-air weapons sold with the aircraft initially included the export-standard R-27R1 and R-27T1 (AA-10 'Alamo') beyond-visual-range (BVR) missiles—using semi-active radar and infra-red (IR) homing respectively—as well

The Su-27UB prototype is seen here with a variety of air-to-air and air-to-ground ordinance. (*Author's collection*)

The Su-27UB two-seat conversion and continuation training version inherited the entire spectrum of single-seater's combat capabilities unchanged. (*Andrey Zinchuk*)

as the R-73E (AA-11 'Archer') within-visual-range IR-homing missiles. Later, the Chinese 'Flanker-B/C' fleet received the extended-range, export-standard R-27ER1 and R-27ET1 BVR missiles.

There were two export contracts for delivery of Su-27SK/UBKs to the PLAAF—the first batch (comprising twenty Su-27SKs and six UBKs) was taken on strength from June to November 1992, while the second (comprising eighteen single-seaters and six two-seaters) followed in 1996. In December 1998 another contract was signed—this time covering twenty-eight Su-27UBKs—and all of these export-standard two-seaters were delivered between 2000 and 2002. In total, therefore, as many as seventy-eight Russian-built Su-27SK/UBKs were delivered to China between 1992 and 2002, plus a reported pair of Su-27SK attrition replacements. In addition, it was originally agreed that the Shenyang Aircraft Industry Corporation (SAC) would build 200 more single-seat 'Flankers' under license (designated as J-11). The respective contract was signed in February 1996, with aircraft parts, engines and avionics to be delivered from Russia.

The first Chinese-assembled 'Flanker-B' assembled from a Russian-delivered knock-down kit took to the air in December 1998, though series production did not commence until 2000. In the event, ninety-five knock-down Su-27SK kits (produced at KnAAPO) were delivered to China by November 2004, instead of the originally planned 200; this was because the Chinese military rejected the delivery of the remaining 105.

As a result, a number of already manufactured but non-delivered airframes and assemblies were left unused at KnAAPO in the early 1990s. The parts were

The Su-27 entered front-line regimental service with the Soviet Air Defence Forces arm in late 1984, but the type was not officially commissioned until August 1990. (*Andrey Zinchuk*)

At the end of the Cold War and just before the Soviet Union broke up in late 1991, the combined 'Flanker-B/C' inventory in Soviet service numbered just over 400 examples, about 100 of which were two-seaters. (*Andrey Zinchuk*)

This ex-Soviet Air Defence Forces Su-27—the early-production, single-seater 'Flanker'—has been inherited by the newly-created Ukrainian Air Force in 1992; this once powerful air arm took as many as sixty-seven 'Flankers' on strength. (*Author's collection*)

eventually utilised in the assembly of fifteen single-seat enhanced 'Flankers' destined for both export customers and the Russian Air Force.

Vietnam was the second customer for the type, ordering a first batch of six 'Flankers' (including one two-seater), priced at $150 million and delivered in 1995. The second batch of six—comprising two Su-27SKs and four Su-27UBKs and priced at $120 million—was delivered in 1998. Also in 1998, Ethiopia purchased ten second-hand ex-Russian 'Flanker-B/Cs', upgraded to Su-27SK/UBK export standard, while in 2003–05 another batch of six ex-Russian Air Force aircraft followed suit. The Indonesian Air Force, which acquired two Su-27SKs in 2003, became the first and only customer for the improved Su-27SKM single-seater, taking three of these enhanced-capability 'Flanker-Bs' on strength in September 2010.

'Flanker-B/C' exports also included four ex-Ukrainian aircraft sold to Eritrea in 2002 and three more to Ethiopia in the mid-2000s, while Angola is known to have received two 'Flankers' in 1999 from a still-undisclosed source. Companies from Ukraine, Belarus and Uzbekistan were touted as the most likely sellers or re-exporters of these 'Flankers'. In addition, one Belarusian Su-27 was exported to the UK in 2000, and two demilitarised ex-Ukrainian Su-27UBs were sold to a civilian customer in the US in 2009.

## The Carrier-Borne Su-33

The Su-33 (Su-27K and T10K, NATO 'Flanker-D') is a carrier-borne air-superiority and air defence fighter. Its development started in the early 1980s, and the first prototype, T10K-1, made its maiden flight on 17 August 1987 with Sukhoi OKB test pilot Viktor Pugachev at the controls. The flight test and evaluation programme involved two prototypes and seven pre-series aircraft, and the type's state acceptance trials were completed in October 1994. However, commissioning of the 'Flanker-D' in Russian Navy service did not take place until 1998.

The Su-33 features many design alterations, such as an arrester hook under the tailboom (no brake parachute); all-moving canards (with symmetrical deflection only); a folding tail 'sting', considerably shorter than that of the Su-27; folding wings and tailplane; twin nosewheels; a modified flight control system (with fly-by-wire introduced for the flaperons); double-slotted trailing-edge flaps and drooping ailerons; an increased-area fin with reduced angle on the tips; a retractable refuelling probe on the port side of the nose; re-located chaff/flare dispensers; and extensive corrosion protection.

Furthermore, the 'Flanker-D' was equipped with a purpose-developed carrier deck landing system and was made capable of carrying the UPAZ-A buddy refuelling pod under the fuselage. In order to improve the deck take-off and landing safety (deemed useful in cases of forced go-around or a missed approach), the Su-33's AL-31F Series 3 engines introduced an emergency afterburning mode, developing 125.57 kN (28,219 lb st. or 12,800 kgf) of thrust; they also featured corrosion protection for prolonged operation in a salty environment.

The basic Su-27 was provided with a total of ten hardpoints for missile carriage, while the Su-27SK/UBKs built for export to China (seen here) and Vietnam have twelve. (*Author's collection*)

There were two export contracts for the delivery of Su-27SK/UBKs to the PLAAF—the first batch covered twenty-six Su-27SKs and six UBKs, while the second comprised eighteen single-seaters and six two-seaters. (*Author's collection*)

The contract for China's licenced production of 200 Su-27SKs was signed in February 1996, with aircraft parts, engines and avionics to be delivered from Russia. In the event, only ninety-five kits were delivered until November 2004. (*Author's collection*)

The weapons control system is similar to that of the baseline 'Flanker-B', built around the N001K radar and OEPS-27K IRST (installed offset to starboard). The maximum weapons load is 7,045 kg (15,531 lb), and, in addition to the baseline R-27R/T BVR missiles, the Su-33's arsenal also includes the R-27EM semi-active radar-homing (SARH) missile, featuring a seeker optimised for use over the sea against air targets at low and ultra-low altitude (such as cruise missiles).

The Su-33's close-in weapons include the R-73 missile and the GSh-301 30-mm single-barrel cannon. At least in theory, the fighter was made capable of employing the entire range of unguided rockets and bombs of its land-based predecessor, but in fact no air-to-ground ordnance has been cleared for deck operations on the 'Flanker-D'.

Series production at KnAAPO commenced in the early 1990s, and in 1993 the first batch of four Su-33s joined the 279th Independent Carrier-Borne Fighter Aviation Regiment (279th OKIAP), based at Severomorsk-3 Airfield, not far from the city of Murmansk on the Barents Sea. As many as twenty-four 'Flanker-Ds' were received by the Russian naval aviation service until 1998, and four of these have been lost in accidents.

Both the small carrier-based fighter unit and the solitary Russian aircraft carrier *Admiral Kuznetsov*—officially known in Russia as a 'heavy aircraft-carrying cruiser'—are assigned to the Russian Navy's Northern Fleet and are considered to have more 'flag-waving' and training roles than real-world operational value. The primary mission of the regiment's 'Flanker-Ds', which lack any surface attack capabilities when operating from the ship, is to provide the long-range air defence of the carrier group. This capability, according to the Russian Navy's

The Su-27K prototype, T10K-1, took to the air for the first time on 17 August 1987, with Sukhoi OKB test pilot Viktor Pugachev at the controls. (*Sukhoi OKB*)

current concept of operations, is essential for naval strike groups operating in a blue-water environment, well outside the umbrella of shore-based long-range surface-to-air missile systems. The Su-33 is also intended for airspace control over the designated patrol areas of Russian ballistic missile-armed submarines, which could otherwise be exposed to the threat posed by enemy long-range anti-submarine aircraft.

The Su-27KUB is a two-seat, side-by-side carrier-borne fighter. Its development started in the late 1980s. The sole prototype (using the single-seat T10K-4 prototype airframe) was built in 1999, fitted with lighter, new-generation avionics; its take-off and landing weight remained the same as that of the single-seat Su-33.

The variant made its maiden flight on 29 April 1999, and the first deck operations were reported in October that year. In the early 2000s it was envisaged that the Su-27KUB would be developed as a ship-borne training aircraft, as well as a multi-role platform for strike and reconnaissance missions. In the event, it remained in prototype form only, failing to attract interest and the requisite funding to complete development and enter series production.

# The Su-30 Two-Seat Long-Range Interceptor

The Su-30 interceptor for the Soviet and then Russian Air Defence Forces was developed from the two-seat Su-27UB combat trainer in the late 1980s, under the initial Su-27PU designation. The original idea was to use the Su-30 as a long-range interceptor in the far northern territories of the Soviet Union, where a two-man crew was preferred for prolonged combat air patrol missions over

A production-standard Su-33 operated by the Russian Naval Aviation Service. (*Andrey Zinchuk*)

the sea or inhospitable terrain; it was a well-established tradition to employ the two-seat Tupolev Tu-128 and Mikoyan MiG-31 long-range interceptors in such operating environments.

An Su-27UB was equipped with a flight refuelling system in 1987, and it was also used as a buddy tanker when equipped with the UPAZ-A refuelling pod. It was used to test the long-range capability originally conceived for the dedicated two-seat combat version, performing a flight from Moscow to Komsomolsk-on-Amur and back, amassing fifteen hours and thirty-one minutes in the air and making four air-to-air refuelings. The total distance travelled was 13,404 km (7,230 nm).

The Su-30's main differences compared to the 'vanilla' Su-27UB two-seater included an in-flight refuelling probe and improved life-support equipment for further extending the range and time on station, as well as a modified SDU-10U flight control system, an improved navigation suite (with a newly-added RSDN long-range aid to navigation) and dedicated communications and datalink equipment in order for the type to be used as the commander's aircraft during group operations, with the tactical commander sitting in the rear cockpit.

The Su-30 prototype made its maiden flight in autumn 1988, and the new derivative was launched into production at the Irkutsk Aircraft Plant (now part of the Irkut Corporation) in 1991, just in time for the break-up of the Soviet Union. In the event, the Russian Air Defence Forces only took five examples on strength between 1994 and 1996, inducted into service with the 148th TsBPiPLS at Savastleika, north of Moscow.

The Su-27KUB is a two-seat, side-by-side, carrier-borne fighter built in one copy only. (*Sukhoi OKB*)

## The Enhanced Su-27M Single-Seater

The T10M programme was initiated by a Soviet Council of Ministers decree dating from 29 December 1983. It obliged the Sukhoi OKB to develop a multi-role derivative of the Su-27, dubbed 'Su-27M', boasting a much-improved avionics suite, including a track-while-scan radar capable of simultaneously tacking fifteen to twenty-four air targets. The new 'Flanker' derivative was also required to boast an improved manoeuvrability due to the combination of a refined aerodynamic layout, newly-added engine thrust-vectoring and flight control system improvements.

In order to achieve an even better dogfighting capability, the design team introduced canard foreplanes to explore the advantage of the so-called 'tandem triplane configuration', with instability some 3.5 times greater than that of the Su-27; it was combined with the new SDU-10M fly-by-wire flight control system, providing control and stabilisation in the three axes. A further increase in manoeuvrability and agility was planned to be achieved at a later stage through the use of thrust-vectoring engines. The new 'Flanker' derivative was also provided with more fuel, using tailfin tanks. The total internal fuel volume was set to reach 10,400 kg (22,921 lb), and there was an option for fitting two underwing fuel tanks, each holding 1,540 kg (3,394 lb) of kerosene. The aircraft was also equipped with a retractable air refuelling probe on the port side of the front fuselage.

The new RLSU-27 weapons control system was built around the NIIP N011 radar, with a flat slotted-array antenna covering 90° left and right (in azimuth) and 90° up and down (in elevation). The new antenna required reshaping the forward fuselage and attaching an all-new radome. The advertised maximum search range for a fighter-type target was between 80 and 100 km (43 and 54 nm) in head-on encounters, while its tail-on range was up to 40 km (22 nm). The radar's track-while-scan mode allowed tracking of up to fifteen air targets simultaneously, and engagement of four to six targets with radar-guided missiles—either SARH R-27 derivatives or the ARH R-77. It also had a newly-added air-to-surface mode, with a detection capability of up to 200 km (108 nm) against large radar-contrast land and sea targets; it was also endowed with ground-mapping, terrain-following and terrain-avoidance functions. The radar, however, suffered from developmental problems, and the real detection and tacking capabilities demonstrated during the testing and evaluation phase differed from the brochure specification.

The optic-electronic search and track systems were represented by an improved OLS-27K system incorporating an IRST, a TV camera and a laser rangefinder/designator.

The redesigned cockpit sported four multi-function displays—with configuration varying from aircraft to aircraft—and an improved heads-up display.

The Su-27M's self-protection suite incorporated the new-generation SPO-150 Pastel RHWS active radar jammer and a Mak-UFM missile warning sensor on the spine.

The powerplant consisted of two AL-31M afterburning turbofans rated at 75.2 kN dry (16,895 lb st. or 7,666 kgf) and 125.5 kN (21,196 lb st. or 12,793 kgf) at full afterburner mode. The last pre-series aircraft—T10M-11, appropriately

The Su-30 is provided with an in-flight refuelling probe for extended range and endurance, needed for operations in remote Arctic regions. (*Sukhoi OKB*)

The prototype of the Su-30 two-seater took to the air for the first time on 7 March 1985. This long-range/long-endurance heavyweight interceptor for the Soviet and then Russian Air Defence Forces was developed from the two-seat Su-27UB combat trainer in the late 1980s, under the initial designation Su-27PU. (*Andrey Zinchuk*)

serialed '711'—received AL-31FP engines endowed with thrust vectoring capability. These engines featured 2-D axis-symmetrical nozzles deflecting 15° in each plane, actuated hydraulically, with an emergency pneumatic system used for returning the nozzle to the neutral position in case of failure of the main actuation system. The moving nozzle design proved to be 110 kg (242 lb) heavier and 400 mm longer than the AL-31F's fixed nozzle.

The first Su-27M prototype (T10M-1) took to the air for the first time on 28 June 1988 at Zhukovskiy, near Moscow, with Sukhoi OKB test pilot Oleg Tsoi at the controls. The T10M-11, powered by the AL-31FM thrust-vectoring engines, made its first flight with the new powerplant on 2 April 1996.

The public unveiling of the new Su-27 version was made in February 1992, during the big new aircraft display in front of the CIS leaders at Machulishche, Byelorussia. The first pre-production example—T10M-3, wearing serial '703'—was shown at the Farnborough Air Show in September 1992 under the new designation Su-35.

In total, the Su-27M's flight test programme saw the use of two prototypes built at Sukhoi's test plant in Moscow (T10M-1 and -2), as well as three more converted from production-standard Su-27s (T10M-5, M-6 and M-7) and six pre-series aircraft (T10M-3, M-8, M-9, M-10, M-11 and M-12) built at Komsomolsk-on-Amur, while in 1996 three production Su-27Ms were handed over to the Russian Air Force. However, due to the lack of funding in Russia's defence budget, the Su-27M programme was shelved shortly afterwards.

The first Su-27M prototype—dubbed 'T10M-1' and pictured here on display at the Russian Air Force Museum—took to the air for the first time on 28 June 1988, with Sukhoi test pilot Oleg Tsoi at the controls. It introduced the so-called 'tandem triplane configuration', with instability some 3.5 times greater than that of the Su-27 in order to achieve much better manoeuvrability. (Boris Lilov)

The Su-27M's extensive flight test programme saw the use of two prototypes built at Sukhoi's experimental plant in Moscow, as well as three more converted from production-standard Su-27s and six pre-series examples. Three more production-standard Su-27Ms were handed over to the Russian Air Force. Due to the lack of funding in Russia's defence budget, the ambitious Su-27M programme was shelved in the second half of the 1990s. (*Sukhoi OKB*)

The T10M-11 prototype, powered by AL-31FM thrust-vectoring engines, made its first flight with the new powerplant on 2 April 1996; it was lost in a non-fatal crash on 19 December 2002, caused by a hardware failure. (*Sukhoi OKB*)